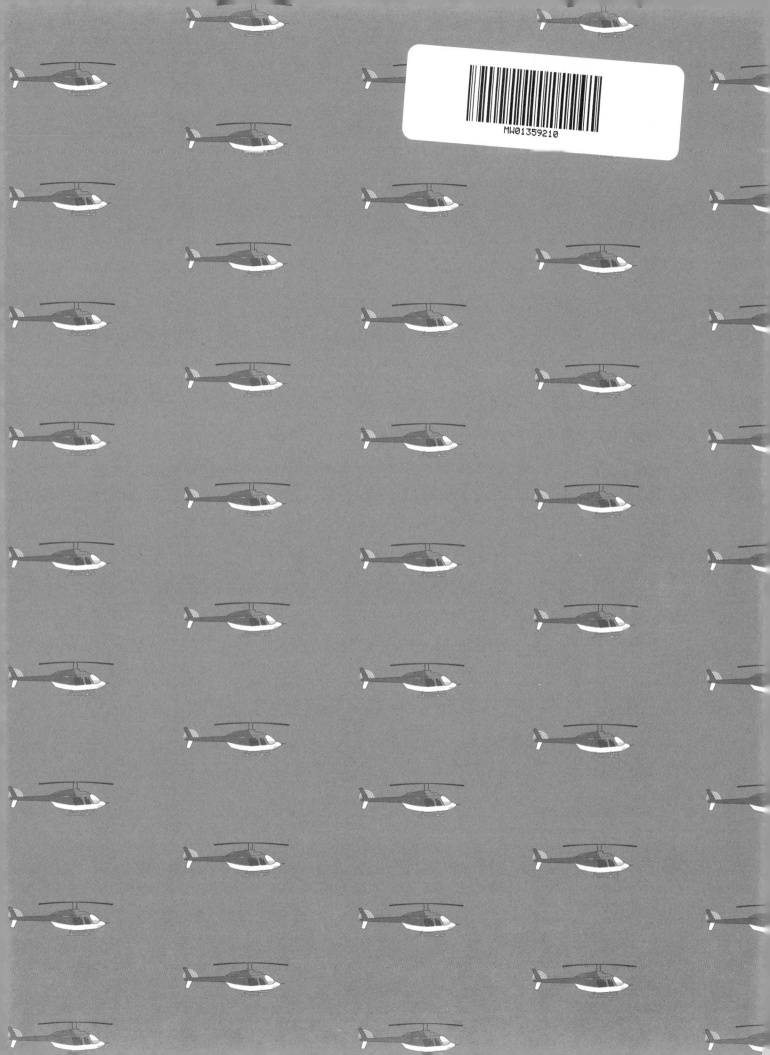

VERTICAL HORIZONS

Vertical Horizons

THE HISTORY OF OKANAGAN HELICOPTERS

Douglas M. Grant

HARBOUR
PUBLISHING

COPYRIGHT © 2017 DOUGLAS M. GRANT
1 2 3 4 5 — 21 20 19 18 17

All rights reserved. No part of this publication may be reproduced, stored in a retrieval system or transmitted, in any form or by any means, without prior permission of the publisher or, in the case of photocopying or other reprographic copying, a licence from Access Copyright, www.accesscopyright.ca, 1-800-893-5777, info@accesscopyright.ca.

HARBOUR PUBLISHING CO. LTD.
P.O. Box 219, Madeira Park, BC, VON 2H0
www.harbourpublishing.com

EDITED by Betty Keller
INDEXED by Kyla Shauer
TEXT AND DUST JACKET DESIGN by Shed Simas / Onça Design
PRINTED AND BOUND in Canada
PHOTOS on p. 2 and 126 courtesy of Okanagan Helicopters; photo on p. 6 courtesy of Tellef Vaasjo; photo on p. 8 courtesy of Sikorsky Historical Archives

Harbour Publishing acknowledges the support of the Canada Council for the Arts, which last year invested $153 million to bring the arts to Canadians throughout the country. We also gratefully acknowledge financial support from the Government of Canada and from the Province of British Columbia through the BC Arts Council and the Book Publishing Tax Credit.

LIBRARY AND ARCHIVES CANADA CATALOGUING IN PUBLICATION
Grant, Douglas M. (Douglas McGregor), author
Vertical horizons : the history of Okanagan Helicopters / Douglas M. Grant.

Includes bibliographical references and index.
Issued in print and electronic formats.
ISBN 978-1-55017-813-5 (hardcover).--ISBN 978-1-55017-814-2 (HTML)
1. Okanagan Helicopters Ltd--History. 2. Helicopter transportation--British Columbia--History. I. Title.

HE9793.C22B7 2017   387.7'335209711   C2017-903641-6
C2017-903642-4

This book is dedicated to all the pilots and engineers who lost their lives during their service with the helicopter industry.

Table of Contents

Introduction	9
PART ONE	
Chapter 1—The Early Years: 1945–50	13
Chapter 2—The Second Decade: 1950–60	33
Chapter 3—The 1960s	73
Chapter 4—The Early 1970s	101
PART TWO	
Chapter 5—The Late 1970s	129
Chapter 6—The 1980s	165
Epilogue—1988 and Beyond	219
Appendices	223
Endnotes	238
Glossary	242
Bibliography	247
Acknowledgements	250
Index	252

Introduction

I was employed by Okanagan Helicopters from the mid-1970s until the mid-1980s, but it wasn't until 2006, when I was working on an aircraft restoration project in Vancouver, that a friend, after listening to one of my stories, asked if a history of the company had ever been written. I was certain that someone had already done it but was surprised to discover the only information on the company was in *Helicopters: The British Columbia Story* and *Helicopters in the High Country* by Peter Corley-Smith and David N. Parker. While excellent, these books only cover the company's early days and touch briefly on the Kemano project of the 1950s. I realized how much more there was to be told and that, if nothing was written down, an important part of Canadian aviation history would disappear.

Okanagan Helicopters went from humble beginnings in August 1947, when Carl Agar and Alf Stringer landed their first machine, a new Bell 47B-3, in Penticton, BC, to become the third-largest helicopter company in the world 40 years later, with 600 employees and over 125 machines in 33 countries. During my research I came to understand the extent of their accomplishments. In the early years Carl had faced the challenge of flying high-mountain terrain and started the first training school in Penticton to teach others how to do it. As the company grew, it began providing support to geological and topographic surveys, the forest, fisheries and mining industries, hydroelectric construction projects, petroleum exploration and operations as well as firefighting, heli-skiing, air ambulance and taxi services. The company's helicopters seeded large areas of forest, trained military and civilian pilots in mountain flying, carried out polar bear counts in the High Arctic in all weather conditions and supported hydro tower installation. Two of their more dramatic operations involved relocating a 2,750-pound (1,250-kilogram) orca from a swimming pool to an aquarium and installing a rod to measure wind speed and air temperature on the top of the CN Tower in Toronto. The introduction of instrument flight rules (IFR) made it possible for Okanagan's helicopters to fly to oil rigs 150 miles (240 kilometres) offshore and operate in the High Arctic in winter; one of their biggest challenges was flying IFR with under-slung loads in those long, dark Arctic days.

In 1965 they flew the first unescorted commercial helicopter ferry flight from the USA to the UK. A few years later an Okanagan S-61, again unescorted, flew from Sydney, Nova Scotia, to Songkhla, Thailand, a distance of 12,659 miles (20,322 kilometres). Some of the countries that saw the bright orange helicopters with Okanagan's hummingbird logo were Pakistan, India, Zaire, Egypt, Ireland, Thailand, the Philippines, Singapore, Myanmar, Cambodia, China, Australia, New Zealand, Papua New Guinea, the USA, Puerto Rico, Nicaragua, Guyana, Haiti, Suriname, Peru, Venezuela and Greenland.

On the engineering side, in the early days Alf Stringer always found ways to keep the machines flying with a minimum of support when even the Department of Transport knew little about helicopter maintenance or operation. Often it was the crews in the field who came up with solutions to operational problems, which, once proven successful, were recorded in the company's safety and operational standards manual and then adopted by other operators. Some of the more impressive engineering feats included the development of a monsoon bucket for forest fire control, a power-line stringer installed on an s-58 and a special bucket for moving salmon to spawning grounds. Other notable innovations included tree clippers for forestry operations, spraying equipment and drip torches, and Bambi Buckets for firefighting.

This book is an attempt to provide a record of Okanagan Helicopters' entire 40 years of operation, the developments the company pioneered and the stories of the crews that made its success possible.

Douglas M. Grant,
West Kelowna, BC

Part One

In 1947 when the fledgling company that would become Okanagan Helicopters was beginning to take shape in BC's Okanagan Valley, I was just taking my first tottering baby steps in the little town of Nairn on the northeast coast of Scotland. My father, who was stationed at RAF Dalcross nearby, subsequently took his small family to more exotic places—Ceylon (Sri Lanka), Singapore, Yemen—and at sixteen I followed him into the RAF where I trained as an air radar mechanic. It would be two more decades before my own history and that of Okanagan Helicopters ran in parallel. Thus, the story of the company's early development that I have recounted in Part One of Vertical Horizons *is taken, not from first-hand experience, but from both published and unpublished documents and from personal interviews with the people who were there at the time and who made it all happen.*

Chapter One

THE EARLY YEARS: 1945–50

In June 1945 Carl Agar, recently demobbed from the Royal Canadian Air Force (RCAF), walked into the Rienterer-Bent car dealership in Penticton, BC, where he met Barney Bent. Like Carl, Barney was wearing his old air force officer's jacket, and the two men began talking about ways to make flying a career. That chance meeting would ultimately lead to the founding of one of the world's largest helicopter companies.

Carlyle Clare (Carl) Agar was born on November 28, 1901, in Lion's Head, Bruce County, Ontario, but the family moved to Edmonton four years later. Carl was the second child, six years younger than his brother Egan, who became his hero in 1917 when Egan and his friend Wilfrid Reid "Wop" May enlisted in the Edmonton battalion. On arrival in England both young men transferred to the Royal Flying Corps, and teenaged Carl was thrilled when his brother sent pictures of himself standing beside a fighter plane that was capable of travelling over 70 mph (112 km/h). But early in 1918 Egan was shot down and killed during a low level attack over German lines. He had survived a full 50 hours of combat, which suggests that he had been very good at his job as ground-attack pilots normally did not last that long. His friend Wop May survived the war and returned to Edmonton where he became one of the most legendary of the bush pilots who opened Canada's North.

Even with his brother's death, Carl's enthusiasm for flying did not subside, although his parents, having lost one son to aviation, did not support his career choice. When the family moved to a farm southwest of Edmonton, Carl left school to work with his parents. In 1928 he married Ann Short and the following year their first child, Dorothy, was born; a year later a second child, Egan, arrived. With a family to support, Carl took on extra work with other farmers in the area in order to accumulate the $250 he needed to enrol in the Edmonton Flying Club. His first instructor there was Maurice "Moss" Burbridge, who was also teaching another young man named Grant McConachie. The two would meet again years later when McConachie was president of Canadian Pacific (CP) Air and Carl was vice-president of Okanagan Helicopters.

By 1929 Carl had obtained his licence, and Wop May promised him a job if he acquired a commercial licence. Unfortunately, the crippling effects of the Great Depression were beginning to hit Canada's Prairie provinces, and Carl's parents were getting older and needed more help on the farm; he could not turn his back on them. Knowing that farming could not support his flying, he reluctantly put away his logbook and licence. For a brief period between 1932 and 1934 he worked for the Department of Indian Affairs in agriculture then returned to farming full-time until World War II broke out in September 1939.

◂ Alf Stringer (left), the first employee of Okanagan Air Services, and Carl Agar (right), OAS co-founder, just back from the bush in 1948. PHOTO COURTESY OF EVELYN AND PAMELA STRINGER

He tried to enlist with the RCAF, but at age 39 he was considered too old for active service and was only offered general duties. Devastated, he picked up his logbook and walked out. However, a chance meeting with his old flying instructor, Moss Burbridge, rekindled his hopes. Burbridge told him about the British Commonwealth Air Training Plan (BCATP), which trained pilots, navigators, air gunners and wireless operators at various sites across Canada. They used the de Havilland Tiger Moth and Fairchild Cornell for elementary training and the Harvard and Anson for advanced training. Initially, instructors needed 250 hours in the air, but Burbridge was certain that this was about to change as more instructors were needed, and not long afterward he showed Carl a telegram stating that civilians with 30 hours total air time would be considered for positions as training instructors. Carl returned to the recruiting office in Edmonton, this time with a slightly amended logbook showing 39 hours and 25 minutes of air time.

He was sworn in as an aircraftman second class and sent to Moose Jaw, Saskatchewan, for basic training. The course was very demanding with a high number of washouts at the start, and while all the candidates were under considerable physical and mental pressure, at 39 Carl realized he would have to keep up with them as he would never get another chance. Twice he was grounded and twice he survived the washout check; after his second grounding, he had to wait three weeks for his check ride, spending his time pushing aircraft in and out of hangars and mopping up. When the day of the check ride finally came, his confidence was at its lowest, but somehow he managed to pass even though he had not touched the controls for over three weeks.

After earning his wings, Carl went on to Trenton, Ontario, where he obtained his instructor's rating before returning to Edmonton. He still hoped to be posted to an operational squadron overseas, but his age prevented that. Instead, he was sent to No. 5 Elementary Flying Training School (EFTS) at High River, Alberta, followed by a posting to No. 3 EFTS Calgary, Alberta, and to No. 24 EFTS, Abbotsford, BC. He soon became known as an excellent instructor as he had empathy for his trainees and brought out the best in them. He also developed new methods of flight-testing that were eventually adopted by all the flying training schools across Canada. For his wartime services, in 1944 he was awarded the Air Force Cross, which was given for an act or acts of valour, courage and devotion to duty while flying, though not in active operations against the enemy.[1] (It was finally presented to him in 1954 at a special ceremony in Victoria, BC.) After his honourable discharge in 1945, he tried farming in Abbotsford but after six months moved his family to Penticton.

Arnold H. (Barney) Bent was born on November 9, 1914, in Revelstoke, BC, and moved with his family to Penticton in 1919. His father, Percy, had been a coppersmith during World War I and later started a welding business in Vancouver with his brother. However, since Percy suffered from severe asthma, his doctor advised him to move to the Okanagan, and there he opened another welding shop and developed a low-pressure irrigation system for use in the local orchards. Eventually he branched out into heating and sheet metal jobs. Barney learned to weld in his father's shop and worked in the family business from an early age, but when orchard business declined in the 1930s, he went to Vancouver to work with his uncle. An industrial accident at a local refinery damaged his leg, but he underwent therapy and eventually made a full recovery. On returning to Penticton he married Aurelia (Rilla) and they had three children.

In 1943 Barney, now aged 29, was inducted into the RCAF as a trainee pilot and within three months had gained his wings. After basic training, he was sent to No. 6 EFTS, Prince Albert, Saskatchewan, where he was selected as a candidate for flying instructor. He taught at many of the BCATP elementary flying schools in western Canada, but after the war he returned to Penticton and the family business. Carl Agar's chance visit to the Penticton garage reignited his love of flying.

With their air force experience behind them, both men wanted to find a way to make flying a career, so they decided to start a flying club, a relatively simple process in those days. By associating with the Royal Canadian Flying Club, they were able to purchase two Tiger Moths, including spares, for the sum of $200; both aircraft were in excellent condition and had low airframe time.

With two aircraft to maintain, they needed to hire a licensed air-maintenance engineer. The lack of suitable candidates in the Okanagan sent Carl to Vancouver, but he found that none of the engineers at the Vancouver Airport were willing to give up secure airline jobs to work for a small flying school in the Interior. However, he did hear of a man with an aircraft engineer's licence who had recently been discharged from the RCAF and who was working in a garage in downtown Vancouver.

That man was Alfred (Alf) Stringer, who was born in Lancer, Saskatchewan, on July 26, 1921. His father, a Yorkshireman, had come to Canada in 1912 but returned to England with the Canadian Army to fight in World War I. While convalescing from wounds in England, he met his wife who was a nurse at the hospital. The couple settled in Lancer, a very small town started by the Canadian Pacific Railway, and that is where their three children were born. Alf, the second child, began helping with the tractors and farm equipment at an early age.

Alf's mother, however, did not like small-town Prairie life, and following one particularly violent hail storm, she moved with the children to Vancouver to stay with her sister; Alf's father joined them after he sold the farm. Alf attended Vancouver Technical School, in those days an all-boys trade school, where he learned the automotive trade. In 1943 with his apprenticeship complete, he joined the RCAF as an air-maintenance mechanic. During his service he was stationed at a number of air-training stations in western Canada and eventually was commissioned as an engineering officer. On discharge he had returned to Vancouver looking for aircraft-maintenance work, but finding no vacancies with the airlines had returned to automotive work in a garage in downtown Vancouver. In an interview from the 1990s he recalled that he had been down in the grease pit when Carl tracked him down in 1946:

> Carl Agar came down to Vancouver; he spent some time talking to me and decided, I guess, when he went back to the people who were going to form this club, that I would be a likely subject to tighten the nuts and bolts for them, so they hired me and I headed up to the Okanagan Valley. In fact, this deal in Penticton didn't sound too awe-inspiring, but there wasn't much going on in aviation at the time anyway, so I thought I'd give it a whirl.[2]

Carl must have been very persuasive because he was only offering a small salary; in fact, for the first few months until the business got going, Alf got no money at all. Carl did, however, provide food and lodging and gave him a chance to work in aviation. Alf fit in; he was a good engineer with a very cheerful disposition regardless of the circumstances. He had a great knack for keeping everyone on the ground in good spirits while Carl was flying.

*

From the start, the South Okanagan Flying Club was in trouble because the expected deluge of potential customers did not materialize, and their association with the Royal Canadian Flying Club, which had made it so easy to get started, became a burden by virtue of its charter, which only allowed them to offer training. Then just as they were managing to break even, another operator set up at the airport with more modern equipment, and

▸ Penticton mayor Robert Lyon hands parcels to Carl Agar, who sits in the South Okanagan Flying Club's de Havilland Tiger Moth. In 1946, Agar started an air parcel service between Penticton and Kelowna. PHOTO COURTESY OF THE OKANAGAN ARCHIVES TRUST SOCIETY

it became obvious that they were not going to survive. Reluctantly they sold their assets. However, the failure of the South Okanagan Flying Club did not discourage them as they were convinced that a commercial flying venture in the Okanagan was feasible.

When Andy Duncan, another ex-RCAF pilot, joined them and contributed $1,500 in war bonds, they formed a new partnership called Okanagan Air Services (OAS). The Department of Transport granted them a charter for not only Penticton but also Kelowna, which unfortunately did not have an airport. However, the residents of nearby Rutland, then a small village to the northeast of the city, changed that by turning out in force with graders and rollers to produce a landing strip that was perfectly adequate for small aircraft.

OAS's new charter gave them the right to continue training and to carry out contract work. Barney travelled to Wichita, Kansas, to pick up their first new aircraft, a Cessna 140, registration CF-EHE. The business started off so well that they soon acquired a second Cessna 140 and became the Cessna agents for the Okanagan. When instructing took a downturn during the winter months, they decided to concentrate on charter work to provide a more reliable source of income.

Since the economy of the Okanagan at that time was almost entirely dependent on orcharding, they came up with the idea of establishing a spraying operation and contacted Dr. James Marshall, the entomologist in charge of the nearby Summerland Research Station. Okanagan orchards were experiencing serious pest control problems, and Marshall agreed that using aircraft could improve spraying efficiency as it would use only five to six gallons (23–27 litres) to the acre (0.4 hectare) rather than the 500–1,000 gallons (1,890–3,790 litres) required in ground applications. Carl and Barney decided to investigate a similar operation in Yakima, Washington, about 280 miles (450 kilometres) south of Penticton. That was when they learned about the high mortality rate for spray pilots and concluded that the risk of becoming a "cropper chopper" was far too great to spray using fixed-wing aircraft. It was shortly after making that decision that Carl read a story in an aviation magazine about helicopter spraying. Alf Stringer recalled that:

A company called Central Aircraft out of Yakima in Washington . . . who had been in the aerial spraying business for years, were going to go into helicopters because they looked like the answer for spraying.[3]

The magazine article described a new machine, the Bell 47 helicopter, which was capable of flying forward at around 90 mph (150 km/h) as well as backwards and sideways and hovering. Its advantages included slow speed and remarkable manoeuvrability, and when spraying crops, the downwash from the rotor blades tended to drive the insecticide down into the foliage of the plants below. This machine was easy on gas and did not require a large landing area, but the thing that really raised their interest was that it was fitted with an agricultural spray boom.

The two-seat Bell 47, which had been designed by the talented inventor Arthur Middleton Young, had been the first commercial helicopter in the world to receive a certificate of airworthiness. The Bell Helicopter Corporation, founded in July 1935 by Lawrence Dale Bell in Buffalo, New York, had initially built fixed-wing aircraft for the military and only began experimenting with helicopters in 1941. By 1947 they had Civil Aviation Authority (CAA) certification for the NC-1H Model 47. At first their market was mainly with the military, but they had also opened an agricultural division, which sold the Bell 47B-3; a 1946 advertisement offered a Bell "Roadster" Model 47B-3 for $35,000. Capable of carrying a 400-pound (180-kilogram) disposable load, this machine had an open cockpit with a rear-view mirror, a belt-driven blower and dust agitator as well as a spray-valve indicator mounted in the cockpit, and it came with accessories for crop-dusting and spraying.

In Canada the first commercial helicopter, a Bell 47D with registration CF-FJA, was bought by Photographic Survey Corporation of Toronto and registered in March 1947. Later that same year Skyways Services of Winnipeg bought CF-FQR and CF-FQS, but both Skyways machines crashed, one in June and the other in July; to replace the two that had crashed, Skyways purchased another machine, CF-FZN.

Carl and Alf went to Yakima to meet with Herman Poulin of Central Aircraft, the agent for Bell Helicopters. He took them for a ride, flying low and slow, sideways and

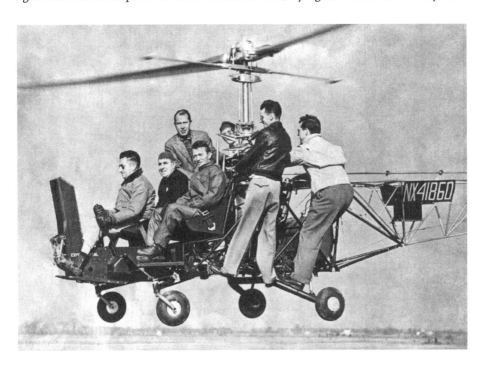

◂ Arthur Young (far left) and friends demonstrating the power and handling of the Bell Model 30. Young, an American helicopter pioneer, designed the Model 30 while working for Bell Aircraft of Buffalo, New York. This was the precursor of the famous Bell 47, which would appear on the television series M*A*S*H. Bell, with its Model 47, was the first company to get type certification for a commercial helicopter. PHOTO COURTESY OF BELL TEXTRON

backwards as well as hovering, ascending and descending. Given his fixed-wing experience, Carl was immediately sold on the machine and could see potential far beyond the manufacturer's vision. Returning to Penticton full of enthusiasm, the two men realized that it was the answer to the problems of aerial spraying. All they needed was the $35,000 for the machine and another $1,500 for insurance, spares and training.

It happened that a consortium, formed by Douglas Dewar, CBE, a retired financier who had been deputy chairman of the Foreign Exchange Control Board during World War II and now spent his summers in Penticton, and Ernie Buckerfield, a Vancouver businessman, had applied to the Department of Transport in early 1947 to start an airline service between Vancouver and a number of towns in the BC Interior. Carl and Alf knew Dewar through his association with the flying club, and when his consortium's application for an airline service was rejected in favour of Canadian Pacific Airlines (CPA), Carl, Barney and Alf approached them about financing their OAS proposal. However, after they had demonstrated the feasibility of their operation, Dewar suggested they approach the local fruit growers for financing, as they were the ones who would benefit from a spraying program, and he offered to arrange an introduction to Pat Aitken, the president of a local investment company. Dewar explained that if OAS could come up with a convincing argument to support their proposal, Aitken would assist in working out the details.

It fell to Carl to sell the plan, and he arranged for a group of fruit growers to go to Yakima for a demonstration. Also included on this trip were Pat Aitken and a Vancouver *Province* newspaper reporter named W. Beaver-Jones, whose story about that trip, "Helicopter to Spray Okanagan Orchards," appeared in the *Province* in March 1947. Carl followed this trip with numerous meetings to convince the growers that helicopter spraying would be effective on their orchards. Not long afterwards, Okanagan Investments Ltd., the newly formed company that had taken over the assets of the OAS partnership, including the two Cessna 140s, all the parts and equipment plus the operating certificate, put a public issue of 50,000 one-dollar common shares on sale. The four partners—Carl, Barney, Alf and Andy—received a number of shares to pay for helicopter training for Carl and Alf.

At the end of May, Carl and Alf returned to Yakima to start training, but Carl was only partway through the course when he received an urgent phone call from Penticton. The sale of shares was going badly and he was needed back at base to head a promotion campaign. It seems that the fruit growers, being generally very conservative, were not completely convinced that a helicopter was the answer to their spraying problems. Now the directors began promoting the shares by tapping everyone they knew: friends, relatives and business acquaintances—no one was spared. In spite of the hard work, sales remained slow, and when the target date arrived, they were still short. After a meeting of the directors, Dewar picked up 10,000 shares, and a Penticton bank manager agreed to loan Carl, Barney and Alf funds for shares, making it possible to reach their goal.

Okanagan Air Services was incorporated on April 18, 1947, with the following registered directors:

Carl Agar, Penticton	Gordon Butler, Kelowna
O.St.P. (Pat) Aitken, Kelowna	Douglas Dewar, Penticton
Arnold Bent, Penticton	James Kidston, Vernon
Ernest Buckerfield, Vancouver	P.D. O'Brien, Penticton (secretary)

The new company continued operating the two Cessnas out of the Rutland field, which was overseen by Andy Duncan, and built its first hangar in Penticton for the sum of $275.

*

Although he was already 45 years old, Carl Agar quickly adapted to helicopter flying. After just 7 hours and 50 minutes he made his first solo flight; his instructor, Carl Brady, aged 26, had a total time of 35 hours in his logbook. Alf was trained by Joe Beebe, the chief mechanic for Central Aircraft; Beebe had been one of the first men to assemble a helicopter in North America. On August 9, 1947, Carl Brady and Joe Beebe watched Carl and Alf take off in their new Bell B-3, CF-FZX, en route to Penticton, Carl with his 27 hours of helicopter time and Alf with his maintenance certificate. Carl Brady's parting words to them were: "Keep it low and keep it slow," but the flight was uneventful as they followed the valley north. However, flying in an open cockpit was not pleasant, even on a sunny August day, and by the time they reached their destination, they were so cold that they downed several cups of coffee before they realized that they had forgotten to fill out the import forms—as a result the first helicopter to enter British Columbia did so illegally.

They put CF-FZX right to work with the Summerland Research Station where they participated in a series of experimental spraying projects on orchard plots chosen by Dr. Marshall. He thought that dusting the orchards would probably not work but decided to try it anyway. The day of the first test was sunny and bright. Carl took to the air and as he released the dust over the orchard, it billowed out to form a huge cloud behind the helicopter. To the observers on the ground it was a spectacular sight, but when they examined the plot they found that very little of the insecticide had adhered to the foliage. Most had fallen to the ground or just drifted away. The test confirmed

◄ Logbook entry of Carl Agar and Alf Stringer's landing in Penticton on August 9, 1947. PHOTO COURTESY OF EVELYN STRINGER

Carl Agar (left) and Alf Stringer land in Penticton on August 9, 1947. PHOTO COURTESY OF THE OKANAGAN ARCHIVES TRUST SOCIETY

that, as a means of controlling insects and disease, dusting from a helicopter was not effective.

The next experiment, involving a liquid spray, was not without problems either. Dr. Marshall and his staff had calculated that the optimal application was five gallons per acre (20 litres per half hectare) at a speed of 35 mph (55 km/h). While more successful than dusting, this method left the mobile ground crew struggling to keep up with the helicopter as it sprayed about one acre (a half hectare) per minute. Another problem was that some areas within the patchwork of plots contained a variety of trees, each requiring different applications. As well, there were mechanical problems because the liquid spray, which was in a concentrated form in tanks on either side of the machine, plugged the spray apertures and caused load imbalance, leading to the instability of the machine. As a result, on a few occasions disaster was only narrowly avoided. In addition, the spray was corrosive and the helicopter had to be meticulously cleaned after each operation. Carl, sitting in the open cockpit, was thoroughly soaked by the end of each flight; the hazards of pesticide exposure were unknown at the time so there was no understanding what it was doing to his health on a long-term basis.

On September 1, 1947, OAS very nearly ceased operations at a demonstration at the 2.5-acre (one-hectare) apple orchard owned by Andy Duncan's father. The orchard was triangular in shape with fir trees, some as high as 70 feet (21 metres), on one side and a road and power and telephone lines running along another. On the evening before the demonstration, Carl had looked over the orchard and come to the conclusion that, given the prevailing winds, he would have to drop over the telephone and power lines, spray the designated rows of apple trees, and then make a sharp turn to avoid colliding with the fir trees. The next day he circled around the plot a few times before dropping over the power lines. At a speed of 30 mph (50 km/h), he sprayed the first row, cleared the fir trees, and circled around for his second run, again nicely clearing the trees, before coming in for the third run. This time he found that the fir trees formed a barrier between him and

◂ Carl Agar at the controls of Okanagan Air Services' first helicopter Bell 47 CF-FZX flying over Okanagan Lake in 1947.
OKANAGAN HELICOPTERS PHOTO

◂ Carl Agar crashed Bell 47 CF-FZX into power lines during a spraying demonstration on September 1, 1947.
PHOTO COURTESY OF THE OKANAGAN ARCHIVES TRUST SOCIETY

the row he was about to spray. Concentrating on his approach, which took him very close to the trees, he lost sight of the telephone and power lines that were in his path and eased off on the pitch of the main blades, allowing the helicopter to sink. Suddenly in front of him were four power lines. He made a desperate effort to recover by pulling back on the cyclic while pushing up on the collective. The helicopter climbed very steeply, missing the high voltage power lines by a few feet, but it was too much and too fast for the machine, over-pitching the main rotor, causing loss of lift and dropping the ground speed to zero. Seconds later the helicopter was straddling the top two power lines. Then it fell through the lines with a sharp crack like a pistol shot, followed by blue flashes and flames. As it crashed through the power lines, the main blades chewed through the fir trees, and the helicopter fell with a resounding thud onto the road, spilling the contents of the spray tanks in all directions and leaving tangled power cables all over the ground.

Alf Stringer dismantles Bell 47 CF-FZX for shipment to Yakima, Washington. PHOTO COURTESY OF THE KELOWNA PUBLIC ARCHIVES

Bell 47 CF-FZX on a truck on Penticton's Main Street. PHOTO COURTESY OF THE OKANAGAN ARCHIVES TRUST SOCIETY

As the bystanders watched open-mouthed, Carl stepped out of the helicopter and began surveying the chaos around him. As luck would have it, he had been sitting on a thick rubber cushion and wearing heavy rubber boots, and the handles of the controls were either rubber or Bakelite, an early plastic. The electrical cables had shorted out through the helicopter airframe. He walked away with minor injuries to his shoulder and a few bruises, but the same could not be said about CF-FZX.

The directors of OAS had a meeting, but in the end they agreed to let Carl make the decision on how to proceed. Although he was anxious to get right back to work, OAS did not have a helicopter and it would take all winter to rebuild CF-FZX. Fortunately, the Winnipeg company Skyways had brought CF-FZN to BC but had not found sufficient work for it, and when Carl approached them about a possible lease, they were more than happy to oblige. Using the leased machine, he soon completed OAS's spraying contracts and returned it to Skyways.

In the meantime Alf had loaded a truck with all the bits and pieces of CF-FZX and headed down to Yakima where he spent the winter rebuilding the machine. During that period Carl and Andy Duncan continued to train pilots on the two Cessnas at the Rutland airstrip, but winter brought the operation to a close and with it went their remaining source of revenue. Due to the accident, their first year of operation, from July 15 to December 31, had resulted in a loss of $13,650. To obtain financing to cover the deficit and the next year's operation, they approached the Royal Bank of Canada for a loan, backing it with the personal guarantees of all the directors.

1948

In the spring of 1948 Alf returned to Penticton with the rebuilt CF-FZX, and it was put straight to work on new spray tests for the Summerland Research Station. However, in a very discouraging start to the season, problems again arose with corrosion and clogging, resulting in frequent changes of the hose nozzles. April, May and half of June passed while they struggled to complete all the sprays that had to be applied before and during blossom time. At one point they decided to abandon sprays and try dusting again, but when the winds increased to 10 mph (15 km/h), the operation had to stop due to excessive drift. The dust got into their eyes and mouths and covered their clothes. Thorough cleaning of the helicopter at the end of each day was difficult because the dust stuck to the machine and the process left their hands raw. The growers were not impressed, and Carl and Alf had to admit that, with the equipment that was available and the nature of the area, neither spraying nor dusting could be done effectively with a helicopter. The

◂ In the spring of 1948, the Fraser River flooded, leaving large parts of the valley under water. This photo shows the area of Chadley and Sumas roads, Chilliwack. The water level peaked on June 10, leaving 16,000 people evacuated and 200 homes destroyed. Okanagan Air Services was hired by the provincial government to spray for mosquitoes. It was their first big break. CHILLIWACK MUSEUM ARCHIVES

company directors, remembering the crash scene, were also uneasy about spraying, and so the hunt for other work began.

It was the disastrous flood of May 1948 in the Fraser Valley that gave OAS a fresh opportunity. On the weekend of May 24 the mighty Fraser River broke its banks, flooding the area around Chilliwack and Mission to a depth of about 25 feet (7.5 metres), leaving over 50,000 acres (20,000 hectares) of farmland under water and providing ideal breeding grounds for mosquitoes. That was when the BC government contacted Pat Aitken in Kelowna to see if the helicopter could be sent to Chilliwack to be used in a mosquito control program.

On June 17 Carl and Alf left Penticton for Chilliwack, a distance of 177 miles (285 kilometres) through rugged mountain terrain. Keeping to the river valleys and following the route that would become Highway 3 from Princeton to Hope, they heeded Carl Brady's words and flew low and slow. Their arrival in Chilliwack attracted a lot of attention. This spraying was a much simpler operation than in the Okanagan orchards because the terrain was wide and flat, leaving the helicopter plenty of room to manoeuvre, and the spray, which was a mixture of a small amount of DDT and light diesel, was less corrosive, easier to clean up, and did not plug up the spray nozzles.

The free publicity gained with this job drew the attention of provincial Department of Lands and Forests officials who offered OAS a contract to spray an infestation of the false hemlock looper insect that was damaging a crop of commercially grown Christmas trees near the BC-Alberta border. Carl and Alf left Chilliwack heading east for the Windermere area on a long flight path that took them across almost every mountain range in southern BC and gave Carl more experience in the art of mountain flying. It also made them realize how vast and remote the BC Interior was. When they arrived at Invermere in the Windermere Valley, Carl met with the Forestry people while Alf serviced the helicopter. The area to be sprayed was 11,000 acres (4,450 hectares) at altitudes varying from 2,500–4,000 feet (760–1,220 metres) and required the application of one gallon per acre (four litres per half hectare) to be sprayed in 60-foot-wide (18-metre-wide) strips. Carl devised a marker system using helium balloons attached to fishing line. The ground crew placed one of these markers at the end of a strip and, once that row had been sprayed,

▲ Carl Agar learns the techniques of mountain flying in the Windermere area, where he would attain altitudes of between 2,500 feet (760 metres) to 4,500 feet (1,370 metres). PHOTO COURTESY OF THE ROYAL BC MUSEUM AND ARCHIVES, FONDS PR-1842

▶ Okanagan Air Services' Bell 47 CF-FZX being refuelled while on a contract to spray for a false hemlock looper infestation near Windermere in the Kootenays. PHOTO COURTESY OF THE ROYAL BC MUSEUM AND ARCHIVES, FONDS PR-1842

moved the marker to the next strip. When Carl stopped for refuelling, the markers showed him where he had left off. Spraying started on July 1 and was completed by July 24 with a total of 466 flights. The operation achieved a 100 percent kill rate of the insect and more good publicity for OAS.

Carl had now flown at higher altitudes and had learned the idiosyncrasies of handling the helicopter in a wide range of terrains, and with two very successful operations to their credit the company had the confidence to tackle fresh challenges. Before they could take on any more work, however, the helicopter had to return to Penticton for routine maintenance. The early Bell 47 was underpowered with a Franklin 178-horsepower engine mounted horizontally rather than vertically as in fixed-wing aircraft. Since grease boots had not yet been invented, it was necessary to take the helicopter apart after every 25 hours flying time for lubrication. In addition, the transmission bearings had to be replaced every 25 hours, and the high-tension cables on the engine ignition were prone to failure. This left Alf with responsibility for a great deal of maintenance plus assembling and cleaning the spraying equipment as well as organizing the refuelling, but because of his training under Joe Beebe at Central Aircraft and rebuilding CF-FZX, he had already become an experienced field engineer.

In Chilliwack on August 2, 1948, Carl met with provincial surveyors Norman Stewart and Gerry Emerson who explained that only 2 percent of the province had been adequately surveyed and that better topographical information was required. These two surveyors could see the efficiency of flying in men and equipment compared to long, exhausting treks on horseback and/or foot, and they quizzed Carl on the possibility of delivering them and their equipment safely to high altitudes and remote valleys via helicopter. Carl and Alf were confident that the machine was more than capable as long as they did not overstep its limitations. As a test project, the topographical survey department offered OAS a contract to transport men and equipment from a base in Chilliwack at $85 per hour plus living expenses for the pilot, an engineer and a helper. On the first day Carl took Stewart and Emerson on a familiarization flight into the rugged and forbidding Mount Cheam area of the Skagit Range. The actual spot had been selected by aerial photography and maps and was at the 5,300-foot (1,615-metre) level. Both surveyors were very impressed with the helicopter and became enthusiastic about its possible uses, but as Carl was rather quiet during the flight, deep in concentration, neither of them fully appreciated the machine's limitations at such a high altitude. They looked over the area carefully from the air, paying special attention to the proposed landing site, but Carl explained that for safety reasons he would have to make the first landing by himself. They returned to Chilliwack and signed a handwritten agreement on BC government letterhead:

> I, Carl Agar representing Okanagan Air Services Ltd of Kelowna, BC, agree to provide a helicopter for transporting men on a topographical survey under G.C. Emerson, BCLS, from an air base at Chilliwack to their work on mountains south and east of Chilliwack insofar as it is practicable, at an hourly rate of eight-five dollars ($85) plus living expenses for pilot, engineer and helper and 8 cents per mile for jeep transportation for the ground crew.[4]

That night Carl did some serious thinking about the next day's work. Under the best conditions, the Bell 47 B-3 had a normal operating ceiling of 3,000 feet (915 metres); the clearing he was to land on was a full 2,300 feet (700 metres) higher than that. He knew that above 3,000 feet he would encounter problems with air density, winds and downdrafts, as well as temperature changes, especially since it was August and the temperature was above normal, but he still hoped that he could develop a technique that would enable him to get the men into the places they wanted to go. When he left on his own the next morning, he had no clear picture of what he intended to do, but to monitor the temperature, he stuck an ordinary household thermometer in the cockpit; the rest would be based on his judgement and skill.

Barney Bent, writing many years later, recalled how that day had gone for Carl:

> This type of helicopter flying had never been tackled before, and the slight distortion of Carl's facial muscles was the only sign of stress. To his dismay he discovered that, when he flew at slow speed alongside the cliff face, he was gripped with acrophobia, a fear of heights, which he had never experienced when flying fixed-wing in the Royal Canadian Air Force (RCAF). When he touched down on a tiny ledge at high elevation, he felt his palms sweating and had to prevent himself from closing his eyes and freezing at the moment that required all his attention and co-ordination. He managed to conquer his fear and went on to complete even more difficult landings in places no one had ever reached on foot. He explored the helicopter's potential and discovered its characteristics in the unpredictable air currents and extremes in temperature and humidity.[5]

Later Carl told Barney that the tiny clearing on Mount Cheam had been his "mountain-flying schoolroom."[6]

The following day Norman Stewart became Carl's first passenger, and he deposited him at the landing spot he had selected about a half-mile below the mountain's summit then returned to pick up Emerson and Ernie McMinn of the Surveyor General's office. The landing site was not ideal as it was at the foot of a glacial cirque—a ridge of gravel in front of a little lake with a wall of ice behind it—and cold air poured off the ice like a waterfall. The three surveyors hiked to the top of the mountain and on the way discovered the remains of an air force Lockheed Lodestar that had crashed and burned there in 1942. Carl returned for them just as fog was rolling in.

For Ernie McMinn this was the first of many helicopter survey operations with Carl Agar, and he would later remember the thrill of "sailing over the ground at 60 mph (95 km/h)." He also remembered that:

> The helicopter had four little wheels . . . and if you landed on a slope, the machine would start to roll. There were no brakes. I remember once they tried to take off from the top of a snow slide and couldn't quite make it so they had to land again on the slope and rolled all the way down the snowbank—about three or four hundred yards [274–366 metres]. Eventually they reached a flat space and stopped. After a good deal of soul searching, they took off again.
>
> But still, apart from the wheels, the biggest problem was getting off with a load when you were high up about five or six thousand feet (1,500 or 1,800 metres). You had to carry a theodolite and tripod, which weighed about 35 pounds (16 kilograms), and a camera, which in those days weighed about 30 pounds (15 kilograms). So Carl came up with the idea of landing on the edge of a drop-off. He'd take some extra revs. I can remember some of those takeoffs: the rpms were dropping back from 3,600 to about 2,800, and the thing was falling, but it was falling clear and gradually we'd pick up the revs again.[7]

To address the challenge of landing on a slope without brakes—and while they waited for Bell to develop hydraulic brakes—Alf came up with a temporary fix using strips cut from old car tires and wedges between the axles and the tires. He also told Bell that they needed a fixed skid-type undercarriage—which duly arrived a year later.

Once, when asked to land on the top of another mountain, Carl went off by himself to look at the location. On his return he informed the survey boss that he had found the spot but had to chase a black bear off the clearing before he could land. On completion of the three-week trial survey, the surveyors assured Carl and Alf that their helicopter would be fully utilized the following season.

Landing survey crews at high altitude was a turning point for OAS in the exploration of the rugged areas of British Columbia. Surveys that would have taken weeks or even months on foot or horseback could now be completed in a matter of hours. To the surveyors, prospectors and explorers that he carried, the helicopter was even more valuable than a float plane because of its ability to hover when it could not land. During later topographic work, Carl was able to make safe landings up to 8,200 feet (2,500 metres), and he could see that once Bell Helicopters developed a more powerful engine, the ceiling would be even higher. With his background as an instructor, he also realized that he would need to train other pilots, and once he was confident with mountain flying, he began to make notes about what he had learned. His edited notes formed the basis of a flight manual that would eventually be used by Canadian, US and other armed forces military pilots.

*

Carl Agar was not the only pilot on a survey project in 1948. Al Soutar of Kenting Aviation flew CF-FJA, a Bell 47D, in the Watson Lake–Teslin area of the Yukon for the Dominion Geodetic Survey that summer.[8] He reported 210 flying hours hampered by bad weather, and F.P. Seers of the Federal Geodetic Survey reported that the operation was not a success due to unfavourable weather and limited payloads of the helicopter above 4,000 feet (1,220 metres).[9]

Later that year OAS was offered a contract with a logging company to conduct a survey to estimate the amount of timber contained in an inaccessible area in Knight Inlet, about 155 miles (250 kilometres) north of Vancouver. Carl was advised that a successful operation would result in additional contracts, giving them a fresh source of revenue, so he and Alf flew the helicopter up the coast and landed at a small floating base camp near the site. The logging engineer provided aerial photographs to help identify the area and a detailed list of the company's expectations. The helicopter proved to be perfect for this type of work, able to cover a vast area in a few weeks. From the aerial survey, the logging company was able to read growth patterns and species, assess the general condition of the timber and plan logging roads and service areas sites. This was the start of an operation that years later would lead to Okanagan's dedicated heli-logging division.

In early September 1948 Carl and Alf were back in Vancouver but, not finding any work opportunities, returned CF-FZX to Penticton where they reluctantly took on another spraying job. Fortunately, the spray, which was to prevent apples falling off the trees prior to harvest, was in diluted form and did not clog the equipment. This time, the fruit growers were happy with the results.

By the end of 1948 the working relationship between Carl and Alf had strengthened and become indispensable to the business. Initially Barney Bent had intended to take a more active part in the operations, but as long as it had been only a fixed-wing operation, there had been insufficient work and revenue to support an additional full-time flying position, and he had only flown on weekends. Once the fixed-wing operation was placed in the hands of Andy Duncan, Barney had been gradually drawn back into his family's business, and eventually he stopped flying even on weekends. He stayed on as a director of the company and was associated with the company's activities into the 1980s. He remained one of Carl's staunchest allies.

During their flights around the province over that summer, Carl and Alf realized the enormous potential for helicopter work in forestry and mining surveys and wildlife and forest control. They discussed moving the operation to Vancouver in order to be closer to potential resource industry customers, but in the end they decided to remain in the Okanagan. Coincidentally, about this time the city of Kelowna decided to build a new airport with a 3,000-foot (915-metre) runway, just north of the existing Rutland field, hoping to get full licensing for hangars and shop facilities as well. When they agreed to rent space to OAS, the OAS board of directors decided to move the fixed-wing operation to the new airport. About this time Andy Duncan stepped down as chief pilot for OAS to return to the more lucrative business of fruit growing. Under his direction the flight school and charter operations business had considerable success during the summer months but had declined over the winter. His replacement was Doug Anderson, another ex-RCAF flying instructor, who was highly regarded as a pilot, and he led the transition to the new airport. The company took on A.L. Johnson, a retired RCAF air commodore, as vice-president.

Although 1948 had been a better year, the improvement in finances was not enough to pull the company out of the red. Prospects looked bright overall, however, especially if OAS could capitalize on Carl's hard-won expertise. Based on the year's activities and the potential he identified in transportation, agriculture and construction, he argued for the purchase of a second helicopter, although the company had not yet made money with their first machine. Knowing the publicity they had received would bring in competition, Douglas Dewar began negotiating to buy Skyways Ltd., which had continued to operate its sole helicopter out of Vancouver, but he discovered that Skyways' financial situation was weak and they had no work for their machine, CF-FZN, which OAS had leased the previous year. Dewar also discovered that the company had a number of outstanding insurance claims and that, apart from CF-FZN, their assets consisted of the helicopter parts from the two machines wrecked in the summer of 1947, which had been salvaged but not re-certified. At that point, negotiations were dropped. However, when Skyways went into receivership, Okanagan re-opened negotiations, this time with the insurance company that held the assets. It agreed to sell CF-FZN plus spares for $20,000 with a down payment of $1,000, subject to an engineer's airworthiness report.

1949

Unfortunately, the winter of 1948–49 featured severe weather with heavy snow in the mountains, delaying the start of mining, forestry and survey work in the spring. For a young company bursting with ideas and know-how and desperately short of cash to cover overheads, the wait seemed endless and frustrating.

Finally in April 1949 OAS received a letter from an Idaho mining engineer inquiring about the use of a helicopter to move a diamond drill rig to a height of 3,500 feet (1,065 metres) from an operating base at Moyeha Bay in Clayoquot Sound on the west coast of Vancouver Island. On a reconnaissance flight later that month, Carl took one of the prospectors up to the site, and while the helicopter hovered above the snow pack, the prospector jumped out and promptly sank up to his waist. Fortunately, with Carl in a low hover he was able to climb back on board, but it was a clear indication that this operation would require careful planning. The following day when the snow was frozen, they flew back to the site and placed two by eight–foot (.6 by 2.4–metre) plywood sheets down to act as a landing platform for the helicopter's front and rear wheels. Then, since the blast from the rotor blades tended to move this makeshift landing pad, they covered the plywood sheets with a heavy duty tarpaulin weighed down with pieces of mining equipment. Base camp for the operation was an offshore log float covered with cedar shakes to form a landing pad and service area.

The helicopter was fitted with litter carriers on each side for transporting the diamond drill, the crew, their personal effects, tents, cookhouse, supplies and tools. Each load had to be broken down so that no item weighed more than 250 pounds (115 kilograms) then tied down in the carriers to ensure that the weight remained evenly distributed. Usually one of the crew flew in the passenger's seat to balance the load. It took 80 trips to move over 28,000 pounds (12,700 kilograms) to the drilling site including 16 passenger trips. Each lift covered eight and a half miles (13.5 kilometres) and took about 17 minutes.

As spring advanced and the snow melted, there was insufficient space on the mountain landing site for the helicopter, so they used the plywood to build a six-by-ten-foot (two-by-three-metre) landing platform higher on the side of the mountain. A toboggan was brought in to move the cargo from the new landing site down the incline to the drill site. The weather that summer was unpredictable with low cloud, considerable rain and headwinds, and as a result, the helicopter had to be tied down on the log float every night so that Alf could carry out servicing and checks on it. It was a crude arrangement but provided convincing proof that the helicopter could take real punishment.

The mining crews occupied the site from June until October. Mining company officials who visited the project were impressed with the operation, especially when they factored in their savings in time and money compared to putting trails into that heavily wooded and rocky terrain.

With all this fresh interest in OAS's services, the arrival of ex-Skyways CF-FZN that summer was a cause for celebration as they now had backup for the contracts that they had signed, and Carl and Alf began looking for another pilot and more maintenance staff. When CF-FZX returned to Vancouver from Clayoquot Sound, it was immediately contracted for another timber surveying job by the same company that had hired OAS for the Knight Inlet job. This time the operation was on the Elaho River, north of Squamish, BC. Using the helicopter, they were able to complete the job in two weeks.

Their next contract involved taking two mining engineers, W.J. (Bill) MacKenzie and George Warren from Kelowna, to prospect in the Gott Peak area near Lytton, BC, about 160 miles (260 kilometres) northeast of Vancouver. The morning after Alf completed the maintenance, Carl set off, following the Fraser River north through the narrow canyon to Lytton at the confluence of the Fraser and Thompson rivers. During the flight he encountered severe turbulence, including violent downdrafts and updrafts that threw the helicopter about. He recorded these problems and his observations for future reference.

Lytton is set among deep gorges and high mountains, and in summer the terrain, coupled with high temperatures, creates intense thermal activity so that the helicopter's descent to the valley floor was impossible. Even though Carl tried to dive it down in short steps, he could not lose altitude and, concerned that the machine would sustain damage, he was forced to climb out of the area and land elsewhere. He realized he still had much to learn about mountain flying. He picked up Warren and MacKenzie and in two trips had them and all their gear on the 9,700-foot (2,955-metre) summit of Gott Peak where there were plenty of landing sites, including snow patches, alpine meadows and the ridges between peaks.

These two engineers would use OAS again. In the April 1950 issue of *Western Miner* they wrote about their experiences with high-elevation landings and pointed out that the helicopter would greatly accelerate mineral exploration, assist in the development of mines and facilitate topographical and geological surveys. The helicopter, they said, had replaced fixed-wing aircraft and jeeps as the main means of transportation into remote sites. This article certainly reinforced what Carl had been saying about the value of helicopters to primary industries.

Bill MacKenzie was appointed to the OAS board of directors the following year. With 25 years of experience in mining in Canada and Africa, his knowledge was invaluable to the company.

*

On completion of the Gott Mountain contract, Carl returned CF-FZX to Vancouver where he found a message that Professor Wilfred Heslop of the Civil Engineering faculty at the University of British Columbia had requested a meeting to discuss using a helicopter to conduct a survey for power-line routes in the northern part of the province. In the course of the meeting Carl sensed that this survey job was the beginning of a very big project and decided to give the professor a demonstration of what CF-FZX could do. He flew him over Vancouver's North Shore, up the mountain slopes, along the ridges and peaks, landing in alpine meadows and deep canyons. The demonstration also included flying slowly over the treetops to the inaccessible site of the Palisade dam project on the Capilano River. Afterwards Heslop made a commitment to meet Carl in Terrace, BC on August 31 to begin a two- to three-week preliminary survey in that remote area for the Aluminum Company of Canada (Alcan).

For some years Alcan had searched for the ideal site for a large aluminum smelter with access to an abundant supply of low-cost electrical power. By 1949 the company had selected the Kitimat Mission area, a First Nations village on the Kitimat Arm of deep-sea Douglas Channel. Extensive studies of maps, topographical surveys and aerial photography indicated that a huge network of rivers and lakes in the Coast Mountains could be diverted to a powerhouse at Kemano. The purpose of Heslop's survey was to determine the best route for the 70 miles (112 kilometres) of power transmission lines from Kemano over Kildala Pass to Kitimat, and the OAS contract involved checking 16 possible routes. Most of the year the area was plagued by heavy precipitation and dense fog, while in winter the deep snow brought a high risk of avalanches; thus, the choice of route was one of the most critical aspects of the project because any disruption of power would be disastrous for the smelter.

When Carl met him in Terrace on August 31, Heslop directed him to fly to the village of Kitimat, where he had secured temporary accommodation for him as well as access to supplies at the local store. The helicopter had to be refuelled on the beach, so a fuel cache was brought in by boat to the Kitimat dock and, with Heslop's assistance, the drums were rolled down the main street to the beach where Heslop had designed an ingenious landing platform. The slope of the shoreline and presence of debris at the high-water mark dictated that, while the helicopter hovered, Heslop had to dig two holes in the sand for the front wheels so that when the helicopter was lowered its axle was level. To raise the rear wheels, he built a frame of logs covered with cedar shakes held down with large rocks to prevent movement by the tide or rotor blast. This novel landing pad worked throughout the operation but had to be repaired after each high tide, which filled the holes with sand. Each day Heslop had to guide Carl into a hover while he re-excavated the holes.

With refuelling completed, they flew to Kemano where they refuelled again and then flew a different route on the return to base, eliminating the need for a second base at Kemano. Fortunately, during the survey period, they had CAVU (ceiling and visibility unlimited), enabling close scrutiny of the terrain. Heslop could note contours, heights, rock formations, water speed, soil composition, high-water marks and timber stands. He was also able to identity areas at risk for rock slides and flooding and determine possible locations for roads.

Once all of the 16 routes had been examined, Heslop eliminated some as impossible, others as inadvisable, and two or three as possibilities. At the end of 20 hours flying time with an additional eight hours for ferrying from Terrace, Heslop had his data and was able to make his final decision. A ground party would have needed three to five seasons to complete the same work. Heslop was impressed with the helicopter and assured OAS that if the contract did go ahead the company would be involved. Carl had already realized the magnitude of the project and was convinced they should start planning immediately to expand the OAS fleet. In fact, Alcan's Kitimat-Kemano project would become the turning point for OAS as well as the entire civilian helicopter industry.

*

In the spring of 1949 A.L. Johnson, OAS's new vice-president, began final negotiations with the BC Electric Company and the Vancouver Water Board on the Palisade dam and reservoir project. The dam, built to increase Vancouver's water storage capacity, was located at the 3,000-foot (915-metre) level at the headwaters of the Capilano River. Base camp, which was on a jeep trail that started at Britannia Beach, was about five miles (eight kilometres) from the dam. The contract provided for a monthly patrol of the power lines as well as lifting 500,000 pounds (225,800 kilograms) of equipment—everything from a two-storey bunkhouse, 13 men and their gear, construction materials and a concrete mixer pump to rock drills and boats.

Within days of the contract signing, Okanagan hired pilot Paul Ostrander, who had flown CF-FZN for Skyways, and Carl checked him out on airlift work. The Palisades job involved as many as 40 trips in a day, each of them 12 to 15 minutes in duration. Most of the materials went into the lightweight carriers installed on the helicopter's outer airframe, with no component exceeding 200 pounds (90 kilograms). The mixer barrel, which weighed over 400 pounds (180 kilograms), was transported by a hook attached to the four wheels and positioned to maintain the machine's centre of gravity. As work on the dam progressed, Ostrander also picked up company directors from downtown Vancouver and flew them to the site for the occasional inspection.

In July Douglas Dewar announced that the company had concluded a contract for a topographical survey in the Hazelton, BC, area. With Carl on that survey with CF-FZX and Paul on the Palisade project with CF-FZN, Alf had to commute between Hazelton and Vancouver to do the maintenance. When he was in Hazelton, he usually worked through the night to have the machine ready for next day. Fortunately, CF-FZX was equipped with a 300-hour transmission bearing that required very little attention other than 25-hour checks. Cracking in the engine's high-tension cables did not cause any serious downtime, and the blades, which were made of wood, were easily repaired with household glue. The Palisade machine, CF-FZN, had two incidents of tail-rotor damage from rocks and experienced fairing on the leading edge of the rotor blade due to water freezing. While looking after CF-FZN in Vancouver, Alf also analyzed the progress on the Palisade dam and acted as the company's expeditor.

Carl's report on the dam project, which was based on Alf and Paul's detailed notes, became part of the OAS flight-operations manual.

*

The fall and winter of 1949 were quiet. Snow had brought an end to the Palisade dam project for the season and the departure of Paul Ostrander from the company. Meanwhile, a well-known mining entrepreneur approached OAS about a helicopter operation and, confident they would get the contract, OAS provided comprehensive details. A few weeks later, however, management discovered that the individual who had approached them was actually setting up a rival company.

By the end of the decade OAS had successfully made the transition from a local flying school to a crop-spraying operation and then to a province-wide service. Most importantly, in their move from fixed-wing to helicopters, they had gained experience in high-altitude flying on topographic surveys and airlifting construction material.

Chapter Two

THE SECOND DECADE: 1950–60

1950

With more work on the Palisade dam project, a second Alcan survey and construction of a test transmission line, the company's outlook for 1950 was positive. However, the first job of the year was a small one in the Bridge River–Lillooet area, delivering supplies to the Bralorne Mine and carrying out a power-line patrol after a heavy snowfall blocked the railroads and roads leading to the mine.

Although the company's helicopters had been busy moving from one job to the next in 1949, OAS had still not broken even, and as most financial institutions felt helicopter ventures were far too risky, it was difficult to obtain further financing. The situation was eased somewhat when a bank extended a line of credit and Douglas Dewar contributed a modest personal loan.

Over the course of the summer of 1950, the financial situation improved as funds from the various contracts came in, though it continued to be a hand-to-mouth existence. There was simply no money to hire additional staff or buy another helicopter. Cash flow for the fixed-wing side of the company was barely covering expenses, and after a devastating accident that killed a student pilot and destroyed one of the company's Cessnas, the directors agreed to sell that part of the operation for any reasonable offer.

At one of the directors' meetings Carl and Alf's optimism clashed head-on with the financial team led by Douglas Dewar. Carl pointed out that the company needed financing for more equipment or the competition would move in and take the work. While Dewar respected Carl's skills as a pilot, he felt that he did not have business sense. In the end they reached a compromise: even though Carl did not get his expanded fleet, he did get funding to hire more operational staff, with a priority on engineers to assist Alf who had been stretched to his limits the previous year. As a result, by the end of the year, CF-FZX and CF-FZN each had a dedicated aircraft engineer.

The company had no problem attracting aircraft engineers as they all wanted to work on the "egg beater." The first to be hired was John "Jock" Fraser Graham who had trained with the British Royal Air Force (RAF) and worked on flying boats for Coastal Command. He'd had a colourful career as a flight engineer, including time spent as a prisoner of war just outside Casablanca. Two Canadian pilots had encouraged him to emigrate to Canada, and on arrival he had joined Queen Charlotte Airlines (QCA), which had a diverse fleet of Norsemen, Stranraers, Cansos, Ansons and DC3s. He had hoped to become a commercial pilot and was trying to build up his hours in anticipation of a position flying float planes, but in the summer of 1949 he had encountered his first helicopter (CF-FZN) after OAS rented space in a corner of the QCA hangar at Vancouver Airport. He was impressed with Alf and Carl's ability to handle problems without getting excited: the first time they met, Carl was running the machine after a transmission change when a swarm of bees settled on the tail boom. As the bees were not bothering the run-up, Carl continued until he had finished the checks, then shut the machine down and went to find a beekeeper. Toward the end of that year Carl and Alf told him they would hire him effective January 1, 1950. His training was on the job, rebuilding CF-FZN, but he was happy to give up his secure airline job to become a field engineer. He told an interviewer:

> You felt like you were really pioneering because [the helicopters] were open cockpit Bell 47B-3s. You felt you were right back with Wilbur and Orville Wright and you had a sense of flying. You had to be dressed for it. In the winter you had to wear everything you had.[10]

OAS also needed a pilot to replace Paul Ostrander. Carl had developed a very demanding training plan that incorporated his own experiences and observations, but he looked for pilots who already had a well-developed air sense, experience in mountain flying and the ability to anticipate trouble and take appropriate action. OAS pilots were expected to fly in rugged mountains, land on isolated peaks or tiny platforms and tolerate primitive living conditions. They also needed to command respect and appreciate the customer's point of view.

Carl met Bill McLeod, an ex-RCAF flying instructor, in a Vancouver airport coffee shop. During the war Bill had applied for aircrew, but when he was initially turned down, he had spent some time as an engineer before being finally accepted for pilot training. Later he had become an elementary flying instructor, and when he was posted to Abbotsford, Carl had been his commanding officer. After the war Bill got a job flying QCA's Stranraer flying boats and Norseman float planes in difficult weather through the maze of inlets and islands along the West Coast of BC. When Carl asked him if he would like to fly helicopters, he replied that he had never even seen a helicopter, so Carl invited him to join him on a little job hanging a hook attached to a long rope on a smokestack at one of the lumber mills on the Fraser River. This set-up would allow steeplejacks to climb the stack then pull up the equipment they needed to work on it. McLeod recalled:

> So I climbed into this stupid machine—at that time I figured it was a stupid machine—it was the open-cockpit Bell 47B-3 with the four wheels. They had had a hook manufactured—a homemade thing with a sort of a loop on the bottom and a long arm welded to it so I could reach out and clip it over the edge of the steel chimney. The rope went through the loop and I had the rest of it, a big coil of heavy rope, in my lap.
>
> So we took off and chugged off along the Fraser. There was a nice brisk wind blowing from the west about 25 miles an hour [40 km/h], which gave us a bit of added lift. Carl steamed up alongside this smokestack, and I found I couldn't handle the pole sitting down. I had to put the rope on the floor, undo my seat belt, climb half out of the machine and put one foot on the wheel leg to hold the pole properly. Anyway, I got the hook on, picked up the rope and threw it down and got back into my seat. Then I realized the long handle of the hook was against my stomach, and if Carl started to move forward I was going to end up with a bad stomach ache. So I got back out again, held onto the door frame, put my foot against the smokestack and gave a good shove. The machine moved away and the handle dropped out. I sat down again and

gave Carl the thumbs up and away we went. By the time we got back to the airport, I was thinking: "Anything you can do that with, I've got to learn to fly."[11]

Carl trained Bill McLeod over the winter, and by the time he took on his first job with OAS in the spring, he had put in a total of 60 hours. Bill recalled the encouragement he received at the start of his first helicopter operation:

> When the machine was loaded up and I was ready to leave for Kispiox, [BC], Carl came out and shook hands with me, and he said, "Well, Bill, remember one thing—if you get through the season without breaking a helicopter, you'll be the first man who's ever managed to do so." With those happy words ringing in my ear, I climbed in the machine and took off. As it turned out, I did manage to get through the first season without breaking a helicopter, but I sure scared the hell out of myself a few times.
>
> You see, the truth was you had to learn a whole new ball game. Remember that in an airplane you're trained right from day one to approach a landing and to take off into wind. If you persist in this in a helicopter in mountain terrain, you're dead—you're going to kill yourself; it's just that simple. Because it means that if you're approaching a mountain and you're into the wind, you're also in the down draft. If you do that, pretty soon you'll find yourself looking up at the place you were going to land, instead of down at it . . . An awful lot of what I learned that first season wound up in the mountain training manual Okanagan produced, because I wrote a lot of it—but only after I'd discussed my experiences with Carl Agar. That was Carl's great talent: he had a very special ability to talk to a pilot after the pilot had had some shaky experience and reduce it to its elements. He seemed to be able to see through what you were saying to the essence of what had happened. I guess this came from his long experience as an instructor. I think it was this ability to sort out the meat of an experience and then analyze it that made Okanagan Helicopters what it became . . .
>
> I'll give you one example. I had landed on a ledge at about 6,500 feet [2,000 metres] . . . jutting out from the mountain. There was a short cliff on one side and a sheer drop on the other, and the ledge would be about, oh perhaps 150 feet [46 metres] wide. I landed about 60 feet [18 metres] in from the edge on a nice flat spot . . . facing the cliff. What I learned then was that you never land unless you have figured out how you are going to take off again . . . But this time I did my jump takeoff too far from the ledge. The body of the machine was going to go over the edge all right, but I knew the tail wasn't. I was already losing revs by the time I realized this. I shoved hard forward on the stick and then kicked on full rudder. I cartwheeled over the edge—cartwheeled so far that I was inverted at one stage and then I pulled out and got clean away with it . . . But after that I always landed very close to the edge of the drop-off, and I always jumped sideways off a ledge.[12]

In 1950 the provincial topographical survey, again headed by Gerry Emerson, carried on from the point where the previous year's crew had left off, covering the area northwest of Kispiox, up the Nass River to Brown Bear Lake and into the valley of the Bell-Irving River. It began on June 1 with a flight from base camp to a site at the headwaters of the Kispiox River. The valley there is approximately 30 miles (50 kilometres) wide and broken up by a series of ridges and low hills with hundreds of small lakes. The Nass River flows through the western side of the valley, the Kispiox the eastern side and the Cranberry River forms the southern boundary. To cope with the difficult terrain, Emerson divided the area into five-mile (eight-kilometre) circles and positioned a survey crew in the centre of each circle to cover it on foot, taking barometric readings on all the lakes and meadows.

While fixed-wing aircraft brought in the equipment and supplies, the helicopter moved the five survey crews from one site to the next. As this meant the machine was flying every daylight hour of those long northern days and on numerous occasions the pilot also had to act as recorder for the surveyor, Carl and Bill split the flying duties. Sig Hubenig, who had been a pilot in the RCAF and worked for QCA as an engineer before joining OAS, carried out maintenance. To maintain the helicopter in serviceable condition, he carried out periodic checks each day, with Alf coming up from Vancouver to assist him with the hundred-hour check because this involved removal of the main rotors.

As the work progressed and the terrain gradually emerged from under the snow, it became possible to set up station cairns to assist with the work. Once each section was covered, crews re-occupied the control points that had been set up in the valley and the main triangulation stations in the mountains. During the Swan Lake base camp phase, the helicopter moved 18 fly camps over a period of 120 hours. On July 3 a QCA Norseman arrived to move the base camp to Meziadin Lake, and the pattern of work changed. Here the valley was narrower with ridge country behind it, making it easier for a single crew to handle the survey work while the other crews worked in the mountains. More food and gas stoves were needed as these camps were above the timberline, most at altitudes of 5,000–6,000 feet (1,525–1,830 metres), but the helicopter pilots had no difficulty finding good landing spots. Three weeks later the crews were repositioned partway between Meziadin Lake and the final camp at Bowser Lake where an additional 22 fly camps were set up in 90 flight hours. As the operation for the year moved into its final phase at Bowser, the mountain landings again became difficult due to more rugged terrain, and some of the 14 fly camps were exposed to high winds, which on one occasion destroyed a camp, leaving the crew to walk to the next camp for help. On August 3 visitors from the Forestry Service's public relations department arrived to film the operation; their film was called *The Flying Surveyors*.

The skills and ingenuity of the pilots were often put to the test on this job. Few of the lakes in the initial area had suitable landing spots due to the heavy underbrush around them, although in the spring the nearby meadows made excellent landing sites. However, by mid-summer the grass had grown significantly, creating problems for the tail rotor-blade tips. This problem was overcome by having the helicopter hover over the grass while a surveyor used a machete to cut a 10-foot (three-metre) circle to allow the helicopter to land with the tail rotor in the centre of the circle. On one occasion Carl had to land on a tiny, isolated patch of ground just west of the Nass River. Unfortunately, the ground sloped away from it at a 45-degree angle, so the full weight of the helicopter could not rest on its wheels. Always resourceful, he had his passengers move to the front of the helicopter, then while it was in a hover, he guided it another foot forward to take the rear wheels off the slope. Afterwards, the front wheels had to be blocked to prevent the machine from rolling backwards.

The biggest challenge was the weather. At first widespread morning cloud and fog at high levels made it impossible to operate in the early hours of the day. But by mid-June the temperature rose to 100°F (38°C) each day, creating problems for the helicopter at high altitudes, and flights had to be restricted to early morning or evening. In July and early August they were plagued by winds and extreme turbulence, especially from late afternoon until dark, and at one point, all flights had to be suspended because landings were usually in tight spaces, often on the edge of a precipice. Fortunately, by mid-August the winds had dropped and flights could be resumed, but over the course of the project, they had lost 21 days on the job due to weather.

The season ended with the helicopter carrying out work on former survey stations and making reconnaissance flights to assist with planning for the following year. On August 17 the last crews were moved into base camp, and the following day the helicopter left for Prince Rupert. The machine had racked up 294 flight hours including ferry flights. Some days it had made as many as 25 mountain landings with 950 of the total at 4,000 feet (1,220 metres) or higher; the highest was at 6,700 feet (2,042 metres).

From Prince Rupert, Bill moved the machine to the Palisade project where he kept the "elevator service" to the dam site moving ahead of schedule and also managed to free up time to take on additional assignments. The dam contract was a resounding success, and the water board began considering a similar project at Burwell Lake north of Vancouver.

*

As Carl was nearing 50 and knew his flying days were coming to an end, he began looking for a pilot to replace him. His choice was D.K. "Deke" Orr, an experienced fixed-wing pilot who had flown charters on the BC coast. After Deke was checked out as a helicopter pilot on May 31, his first job was on a mining contract near Hope, BC, about 90 miles (150 kilometres) east of Vancouver. This is where the Reco Copper Mining Company was developing some claims on a mountain ridge above sheer rock cliffs that dropped 1,000 feet (300 metres) to the valley floor. Jock Graham, who went with Deke to carry out the maintenance, recalled:

> When this mining promoter asked us for a quote and we said $100 an hour, he thought it was absolutely crazy. We pointed out to him that we were going to take 300 pounds [135 kilograms] in every 20 minutes, 900 pounds [410 kilograms] in one hour, which worked out at 11 cents a pound. That didn't sound too bad.[13]

The scenery was beautiful, but the mine site lay between the jagged, snow-covered peaks of mounts Cheam and Foley on one side while Wahleach Lake and wooded hills separated it from the Fraser Valley to the southwest. As a result, everything the mining company needed had to be airlifted in, including a bunkhouse, its furnishings and supplies, mining equipment and crews. Deke, at the time still a novice helicopter pilot, had to deal with downdrafts and updrafts along the ridge as well as the fickle nature of the local weather conditions. Until almost the end of the year he shuttled back and forth every day the weather permitted, and in that six-month period, he flew approximately 80 hours, made about 200 landings and moved 35 tons (31.7 metric tonnes) of supplies, all of it to and from a helicopter platform located at the 6,500-foot (1,980-metre) level.

Two years later the project was still ongoing with a new pilot, Leo Lannon, who as a charter pilot had experience in the North and on Vancouver Island and was used to dealing with weather changes. As the mine had become fully functioning by that time, there were some changes in the type and volume of freight, though the procedures remained much the same. In 1952 Lannon submitted the following report describing his day's work:

> Off to an early start, the helicopter is loaded with 6 cases of dynamite, a 400-pound [180-kilogram] load for the first trip. The pilot hovers for a moment to check the load balance and then is away, climbing close in to a hillside

searching for an assist from any updrafts. The air is unstable and turbulent. Up on the peaks, clouds seem to be moving in towards the landing spot. The weather is not very promising. Carburetor ice has been a problem in this area, and the pilot must be constantly on the watch for it. The helicopter, climbing steadily, is now in close to the glacial ice and snowfields with the cloud-ringed peaks towering above. The pilot is heading for the tiny landing spot on the top of the ridge at 6,500 feet [1,980 metres] where it joins Mount Foley in a sheer cliff. At 6,000 feet [1,830 metres] he passes below the landing spot and, glancing up, sees a man standing with his arms extended and his back to the wind. It is a reassuring sight. The pilot runs past a short way, makes a short 180-degree turn, still climbing. When getting close to the 6,500-foot mark and the final approach is made, the pilot gets set, ready for split-second action, slowing speed and gradually decreasing height. The helicopter arrives over the landing spot with inches to spare . . . All that is visible is the tall slim pole of the radio telephone antenna. The house that shelters the miners is more than 30 feet [nine metres] high but has long been buried in snows of another winter.

The landing spot has to be shovelled level by the men after each snowstorm and is only a shade bigger than the skid gear of the helicopter, the four corners of it being marked with something dark—10-gallon [38-litre] drums or anything handy. The snow has been so heavy this past year that the helicopter is now landing 20 feet [six metres] higher than the roof ridge-line of the house . . . The tail rotor of the helicopter is suspended out over 4,000 feet [1,220 metres] of space as the snow and mountainside drop away at a 60-degree angle. Two or three feet ahead of the helicopter, the snow and mountain also drop [a]way 3,000 feet [915 metres] at a 40-degree angle.

When unloaded, the helicopter lifts an inch or two and once more slips out into space for a downhill run for another load. The round trip from base to the mine site is 20 minutes. The cost runs 8.33 to 10 [cents] per pound to move freight into an area which is inaccessible to anything but a helicopter.[14]

Because the landing site was next to the Trans-Canada Highway, many people stopped to watch. For most of them, it was the first time they had seen a helicopter.

*

In July 1950 Carl received a phone call from W.G. Huber, president of BC International Engineering Company, to announce that the aluminum smelter project at Kitimat had been approved and to discuss a contract with OAS to provide helicopter support for the engineering staff who were to complete the previous year's survey and install test towers for the power line. Carl was also assured that, once the main phase of construction began, OAS's services would be required to support construction. At last he had a contract to take to the board to back his argument for more resources, especially more helicopters.

The Alcan project was made up of five massive construction sites, stretching across 5,400 square miles (13,985 square kilometres) of watershed from the Nechako River south of Vanderhoof to the Coast Mountains. It would link several large and many small lakes and rivers to create a series of dams and a giant reservoir. From there the water would be channelled into a 10-mile-long (16-kilometre), 25-foot-diameter (7.5-metre) tunnel through the mountains, dropping nearly 3,000 feet (915 metres) to a powerhouse blasted out of a mountain. The entire project depended on the successful construction of the transmission line linking that powerhouse at Kemano to the smelter at tidewater. While the data from the previous summer's survey had pointed to a promising route, engineers were still concerned that the towers and cables would not be able to withstand winter conditions in the area, and they planned to construct a test line, which had to be in place by winter, only months away. The project involved erecting two sets of towers connected by cables. One set was to be built at 5,498 feet (1,676 metres), the highest point on the route, but when the rocky terrain at that level proved unsuitable, the towers were erected on a granite ledge 200 feet (61 metres) lower. The engineers were particularly interested in the degree of ice accretion that might cause the towers to twist and break, and measuring equipment also had to be in place to monitor this and other aspects of weather before men could be stationed on site during the winter.

With the topographical survey in the North over for the year, Carl left Vancouver in early September in CF-FZX and flew via Squamish, Lillooet, Williams Lake and Prince George to the Alcan base camp in a total flying time of 10 hours and 20 minutes. He went to work immediately, flying the surveyors over the proposed route and transporting the seven passengers and 19,300 pounds (8,754 kilograms) of freight required to set up the work camps at the base of Kildala Pass. After 40 hours flying time spread over 13 days, he returned to Vancouver for a major overhaul of the helicopter.

He was back in the Kildala Pass area by October 12. During his absence, construction crews had started to build a cabin at the lower test site to house the recording crews, and they had cut a trail between it and base camp for emergency maintenance during winter. Over the next eight days, Carl hauled the crew and all the freight needed to complete the tower construction and brought in the recording equipment. The towers, which had been prefabricated in Vancouver so they could be transported by helicopter, were delivered by ship to a large float at the mouth of the Kildala River where Carl had set up a base. One by one, the tower sections were strapped onto the carriers on each side of the helicopter and lifted to the construction sites. At the upper test site this required the helicopter to carry each load from sea level to 5,300 feet (1,615 metres). As the snow line was creeping steadily down the mountains, Carl was under a lot of pressure, but he completed the job by October 20.

Meanwhile, in addition to more pilots and engineers, the company needed more space, and they built a hangar and offices at Vancouver's south terminal at a cost of $120,000. They also needed someone to run the office, a job that both Carl and Alf hated, and they were happy when the wife of a friend jumped at the opportunity. Ada Carlson stayed with the company as the executive secretary until her retirement in 1963. "It wasn't much of a job to begin with," she recalled, "just a corner of the old Queen Charlotte Airlines hangar. They didn't even have a ladies' washroom; I had to go across to the airport terminal."[15]

Unfortunately, the vice-president of OAS, A.L. Johnson, died suddenly about this time. Although he had only been with them a few years, he had taken charge of operations, releasing Carl from the administrative duties. Now as well as resuming those duties, Carl continued his efforts to consolidate the company, lobby the directors for more equipment, prepare the operations manual and develop a syllabus for a flight-training program. He also contacted Bell about the shortcomings of the Bell 47 for mountain and northern operations—shortcomings that included the machine's open cockpit, its under-powered 175-horsepower Franklin engine and wheels rather than skids. Because he had become recognized as an expert in mountain flying and OAS was one of the few commercial operators in North America, Bell listened to his advice. At the same time, a young helicopter designer named Stanley Hiller, whose Hiller 360 had been the first helicopter to fly across the United States back in 1948, had been working on a new machine that was similar in size to the Bell 47 and already included some of the features that Carl had recommended. However, after his initial investigation of the Hiller machine, Carl decided it needed more testing in the field and instead chose to continue pressing Bell for further improvements.

The early 1950s also saw the start of the company's unique Mountain Flying School in Penticton. As soon as Carl had started flying in the mountains, he had realized how many of the parameters such as winds, air pressure, altitude, temperature and airflow impacted the helicopter's performance, and he had begun taking detailed notes. Those notes and his experience as an instructor led to the development of a training manual and eventually to the establishment of a training school. In addition to 75 hours in the air and large doses of ground-school training, to graduate each pilot had to put in time in the maintenance shop working on the helicopters to become familiar with the mechanical aspects of the machine.

1951

With more work pending, in 1951 OAS acquired Bell 47 CF-FJA from Kenting Aviation, an eastern Canadian company, for the sum of $15,000; CF-FJA had been the first licensed helicopter in Canada. Carl also contacted Igor Sikorsky about acquiring two S-55s, which Alcan wanted to purchase because of their increased payloads. Sikorsky, one of the world's great innovators in fixed-wing aircraft design, had built one of the first successful helicopters in the world, the Vought-Sikorsky VS-300, its single main rotor and small anti-torque rotor establishing the classic configuration for helicopter design. By 1942 a military version of the VS-300 was in production as the R4, but the machine really came into its own during the Korean War (1950–53) as the S-55. In 1951, when Carl approached Sikorsky, the S-55 did not have commercial certification and, with the military still absorbing all of Sikorsky's output, none were available. However, he was confident that situation would soon change.

▲ Igor Sikorsky and Orville Wright in 1943 at Wright Field for the handover of the first VS-300 to the US Army. PHOTO COURTESY OF SIKORSKY HISTORICAL ARCHIVES

▶ Igor Sikorsky wearing his famous fedora while flying the VS-300, which was first flown on September 14, 1939. PHOTO COURTESY OF SIKORSKY HISTORICAL ARCHIVES

The new round of OAS recruits at this time included pilot Fred Snell, a former RAF wing commander who had flown just about every type of aircraft used for transport and combat. He had come to Canada after the war and held a number of jobs in the lumber industry and agriculture, ending up in Penticton where he met Carl, who hired him on the spot. Next came Pete Cornwall, a young fixed-wing bush pilot from Kamloops who had become enthralled with helicopters. Another highly qualified applicant, Don Poole, joined on May 18; an RCAF-trained pilot who had served with Bomber Command, Don later became the chief pilot of the Penticton Mountain Flight Training School, where he trained many military pilots.

On the engineering side, the company hired Bill Smith in April 1951; Bill went on to become chief inspector for Okanagan's Vancouver base. The next hired was Gordon Askin, who had also trained in the RCAF and worked for QCA. In time Gordon would become the general manager of Canadian Helicopters Overhaul, the subsidiary company that specialized in component overhaul. Both men were highly qualified airline engineers who gave up secure jobs to become part of this new industry, one that challenged them with technology and terrain and required exceptional improvisational skills.

*

On February 11, 1951, Bill McLeod and Jock Graham set off from Vancouver for Kitimat in the open-cockpit CF-FZN for the 405-mile (652-kilometre), seven-hour trip to Kemano. En route they landed at the dock at Butedale (now deserted) on Princess Royal Island for fuel. While Bill went off to see someone, Jock waited on the dock. A local man came down to look at the helicopter, moved the cyclic and wandered around to where Jock was sitting.

> Jock addressed him in the Hollywood version of an Indian lingua franca. "How!" he said. "Heap big machine, eh?"
> The Indian studied the small Bell for a few seconds. "Mmm," he agreed gravely, "but not nearly as big as the Sikorsky S-51."[16]

It seems that an S-51 had landed on Princess Royal on its way to look for the 12-man crew of a United States Air Force B-36, en route from Alaska to Fort Worth, Texas, who had bailed out after their plane had lost two of its engines to icing.

Once at their destination, Bill and Jock were put right to work positioning the survey crews before the arrival of the construction crews who were building a 10-mile (16-kilometre) road from the powerhouse on the Kemano River to the Gardner Canal. Bill also flew the engineers in to check the test towers. Their base for all this work was a barge anchored in Kemano Bay, which, in addition to acting as a landing platform, provided very cramped living quarters and storage for the engineers and their equipment. OAS's base was later moved to Base Camp Two, which was five miles (8 kilometres) farther up the river. Construction of the road from the bay to the powerhouse site, surveyed with the assistance of the photos taken by Professor Heslop the previous year, forged on rapidly while CF-FZN carried about 100 passengers and two tons (1.8 metric tonnes) of freight over 12 flying days.

March brought winds ranging from 50–100 mph (80–160 km/h), and temperatures dropped into the minus range. Deke Orr arrived to relieve Bill, and Alf came up to help Jock with a 100-hour inspection. Deke started work on the triangulation survey for the tunnel, which involved setting up 20 stations at elevations ranging from 3,000 (915 metres) to 7,200 feet (2,195 metres), and he completed the operation in 90 flight hours spread over 28 days. During this time the helicopter usually positioned survey teams in the morning and hauled freight and passengers between camps for the rest of the day; in one period of 76 flight hours they carried 126 passengers and four tons (3.6 metric tonnes) of freight.

Spring brought improved weather, allowing construction on the tunnel to start in June. The diamond drilling crew began testing the rock for the location of the powerhouse with the helicopters—a second OAS helicopter, CF-GZJ, piloted by Fred Ellis had now arrived—positioning men and equipment on wooden platforms at 800-foot (243-metre) intervals. Survey work on the road to Horetzky Creek was completed in 100 hours, a significantly shorter time than it would have taken the surveyors on foot.

The main camp, situated at the confluence of two streams and the Kemano River, was made up of rows of wooden-walled tents erected the previous year. Although it was set among magnificent snow-capped mountains, the view from the camp was composed of the muddy river and the low cloud banks hugging the slopes. This newly created settlement was a highly structured society where supervisors and workmen did not mix socially—with the exception of one place: Joan McLeod, the wife of pilot Bill and the only woman in camp, was an excellent cook and their tent provided a rare opportunity for everyone to socialize. Joan, who enjoyed being surrounded by interesting people, had been educated in Toronto but had grown bored with city life and taken a job with QCA in Prince Rupert. It was there she met Bill. After they went south to Vancouver so that Bill could train as a helicopter pilot, she was unable to find a job and, when he was assigned to the Kemano project, she joined him. Some of their recollections of that time on the Alcan project are contained in *Helicopters: The British Columbia Story* by Peter Corley-Smith and David N. Parker.

▲ An early campsite in Kildala Pass during power line construction. PHOTO COURTESY OF GORDON ASKIN

> In the fall of 1951 [Bill McLeod] ... was flying construction crews into the newly installed helicopter pads on the sidehills of the mountains. Work had begun on the tunnel from the west end of Tahtsa Lake and on the main excavation for the power house. The two helicopters, one flown by Bill, the other by Fred Snell, were constantly in demand ...
>
> Joan McLeod ... heard a commotion outside her tent. She stuck her head out of the fly to see what was going on and saw the engineering supervisor spring towards her along the lane between the rows of tents.
>
> "Where's Bill?" he demanded as he reached her. "Fred Snell's killed himself."
>
> "Fred's not flying today—Bill is."
>
> "Then where's Fred? Bill's killed himself."
>
> Not surprisingly, Joan abandoned her cake[-making] and followed the supervisor in his search for Fred Snell. Failing to find him, they returned to the river where the accident had occurred. Standing on the far shore, looking depressed but obviously not dead, was Joan's husband. After shaking his head, he turned and disappeared into the trees again.

Later Bill explained to the authors of *Helicopters: The British Columbia Story* that it had been raining so hard that day neither he nor Fred had flown:

> Horetzky Creek, which flowed down into the Kemano River, was rising at a rate of about a foot an hour and a log jam had developed. They were afraid the camp would be flooded. A bulldozer went out to try to clear the jam and it dropped into a hole. There were three people on the "cat." One fell off and managed to swim ashore; the other two were up on the canopy, ankle-deep in the water. The water was still rising and two of the supervisors came to me and said those guys are going to drown; you'll have to get them off. So I said

okay, but here's where I made my mistake: I didn't go over and tell those guys on the "cat" what to do myself—I told the others to tell them while I ran for the helicopter.

The story in *Helicopters: The British Columbia Story* continues:

> The instructions Bill wanted relayed to the men on the bulldozer canopy were to wait until [he] had put one skid on the canopy then, and only after [he] had given them the nod, they were to climb into the helicopter, one at a time. Bill had taken the doors off, and when he got within two or three feet of balancing one skid on the canopy, one of the catskinners made a wild leap and grabbed the front of the skid. The helicopter dropped violently and the nose of the skids actually went into the water. The only thing Bill could do now was to pull up hard on the collective and twist on as much throttle as he could. But the weight of the man on the front of the right skid pulled the helicopter down and to the right. There was . . . "nothing on the right but trees," and he went barrelling right into them.
>
> "When the noise finally died down," Bill recalls, "I was still 30 feet [nine metres] above the ground in the trees, inverted, swaying gently up and down and listening to the pitter-patter of the rain drops. The fellow who was riding the skid was still there; he was half in the machine and half out; he was sort of pinned. Of course, the bubble was gone and I noticed the battery was smoking . . ."
>
> The over-eager passenger was unconscious. Bill's first attempts to get him out of the machine failed. So he climbed to the ground and found a branch to use as a pry . . . He managed to work the passenger free of the helicopter, ease him onto his shoulder and climb down to safety. The passenger recovered consciousness a few minutes later, but they were on the wrong side of the river, and Bill emerged from the trees to see what was going on . . .

◂ Bell 47B-3 CF-FJA crashed into the trees while trying to rescue men from a flash flood at Horetzky Creek, Kemano, in 1951. Pilot Bill McLeod was not seriously injured. PHOTO COURTESY OF GORDON ASKIN

There were some 400 people on the far bank and they were in the grip of a remarkable panic. One man was rushing into the water with a first-aid kit. He would rush in until the water reached his thighs, realized that he couldn't go any further, retreat to the shore, only to rush back into the water again, sobbing with frustration. A little further along, someone had backed a bulldozer with a logging boom on it up to the water. A man was standing on the logging boom with a coil of rope, hurling it towards the far bank. It never reached more than halfway across the river, but doggedly he retrieved it, coiled it and tried again. An hour later he was still doing exactly the same thing. "It was unbelievable," Bill recalls. "All that crowd of people—it was mass hysteria."

Joan McLeod, surrounded by irrational panic, finally did the one thing that is effective for hysteria. She ran up to the engineering supervisor and booted him as hard as she could in the backside.

Shocked, he turned to look at her. "What did you do that for?" he demanded.
"To make you start thinking."

It worked. The engineer sent for a mobile crane. They strapped a large log to the boom, lowered it across the river and succeeded in rigging up a sort of boson's chair that got Bill and his passenger back across the river safely, as well as the man still stranded on the bulldozer. Kemano at that time boasted a hospital of sorts and they were taken there to be treated. It turned out that Bill was more seriously damaged than his passenger. He had broken off the instrument pedestal in the helicopter with his shin, and he was in considerable pain and some shock. Fortunately, Bill's injuries were not serious and he was very quickly back flying again.[17]

Joan continued to live in the camp, first in a tent and then a Quonset hut, through 1951 and into 1952. Life became much more complicated with the arrival of the couple's first child in 1952. After the arrival of the second in 1953, Joan left the project for good.

Gordy Askin, a helicopter engineer, arrived in Kemano to replace engineer Bill Smith an hour after that accident.

▸ The Okanagan Air Services crew at dinner in the Kemano camp's main cookhouse in 1952. The two men on the far left are Jock Graham (left) and J. Radovich (right). From left to right, the three men in the foreground on the right are Locky Madill, George Chamberlain and Bill Brooks. PHOTO COURTESY OF GORDON ASKIN

"Bill told me that the machine was stuck 30 feet [nine metres] up a tree and the pilot was okay," Askin said. "With the help of a construction crew, we managed to get it down using a block and tackle."[10]

Two more accidents occurred that summer on the Kemano project. In the first a construction worker was seriously injured when he walked into the tail rotor of CF-GZJ. In the second, Fred Snell's machine was badly damaged after it suffered an engine failure, and he autorotated into some rocks. He was unharmed, but the machine was badly damaged. Less than a year later Bill McLeod was involved in an accident that he was extraordinarily fortunate to survive. He told the authors of *Helicopters: The British Columbia Story*:

> I was just heading back out of the [Kildala] pass when the machine started to develop a very heavy bounce; it was bouncing up and down about a foot, and it kept getting worse. I was about 1,500 feet [460 metres] above the ground when it started, and I set down as fast as I could. Then the bubble broke; finally, the engine quit and the tail rotor let go—it was bouncing so badly the tail rotor driveshaft tore right out of the transmission—and I had to dump collective. Even then, I was spinning. All the controls went; the whole bottom end of the engine fell out. I had cartons tied on the racks and they all flew off.
>
> I was lucky, though, I hit on the only patch of snow in the whole area. It was about 80 feet [24 metres] wide and 100 feet [30.5 metres] long on a steep slope. I hit right in the middle of it. I slid down and hung up on boulders. Eighty feet farther on, there was a drop-off of some 500 feet [150 metres] down onto a glacier. When I stopped, I looked up and I could see the sun shining. I said, "Boy, that was a nice looking landing field!" Because I really didn't expect to [get] out of that one.

Later it was discovered that Bill had cracked a vertebra, but his passenger had only cuts and bruises. Jock Graham, who was by this time Okanagan's Kemano base engineer, was determined to find the cause of the machine's failure:

> It was a broken yoke [the hub on top of the rotor mast to which the main rotor blades are attached]. Bell had come out with aluminum yokes to save weight, and they sent out a directive that, if you ever had a blade strike, you had to throw away the aluminum yoke. We had bought the machine, JAA, from another company, and I went back through the logbook. Sure enough, I found an instance where they changed the blades. The obvious question was why had they changed them? It took me some time, but I managed to get in touch with the engineer working on the machine when they had changed the blades, and he admitted they had done so because the tip had hit an oil drum. They were a small outfit. They didn't want to spend the money on a new yoke, so they didn't throw it away.[19]

By this time, however, the helicopter crews on the Kemano job had more to worry them than accidents:

> Their dissatisfaction was brought into focus by a recent immigrant who spoke little English and whose job was to clean up around the camp... The labourer had heard that the pilots were only earning $350 a month while he was earning over $500. Every time he saw the helicopter crews, he would shake his head and begin to laugh. And now that some of the initial glamour was beginning to

▲ Gordon Askin, a young Okanagan Air Services engineer, outside the OAS hut at the main Kemano camp in April 1950. PHOTO COURTESY OF GORDON ASKIN

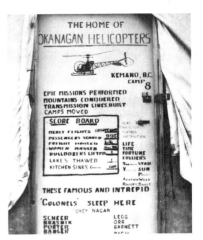

▲ The home of the OAS's crew, in the Kemano camp. PHOTO COURTESY OF GORDON ASKIN

wear off and the danger becoming more apparent, the helicopter crews grew increasingly resentful. They had played a vital part in the accelerated progress of the whole [Kemano] project and at the same time were the lowest paid employees. This, too, led to some lively exchanges between Carl Agar and his fellow directors down in Vancouver—particularly since profits, which stood at $10,000 in June, had risen to $58,000 by the end of August 1951.[20]

The problem was not limited to Kemano where at least they were fed and housed while on the job. On projects such as mining exploration and survey work in the bush there was another problem: although customers realized that helicopters were able to cover ten times the area and accomplish in one season what would have taken five, they were shocked with the $100-per-hour rate so they cut back on food, accommodation and supplies. Crews found themselves living in worn-out tents with little or no food. Fixed-wing re-supplies were kept to a minimum, which also meant lack of news and mail. Helicopter engineer Ian Duncan recalled: "No bread, no vegetables, no meat. I didn't have scurvy, but I was awfully close to it. My gums were all sore and I lost 30 pounds [14 kilograms]."[21]

But there was good news for the company that year, too. At a dinner given in his honour on October 30 Carl was awarded the McKee Trophy, for outstanding service to Canadian aviation, which had also been awarded to his friend Wop May in 1929. Carl was also dubbed, in 1954, "Mr. Helicopter" by the Canadian Aeronautics and Space Institute. These events resulted in invitations to speak at the International Air Transport Association's annual convention and the Helicopter Association of America in Washington, DC, where he met Igor Sikorsky for the first time.

1952

The company underwent another name change in 1952; it now became Okanagan Helicopters Ltd., a name that would last for the next 35 years.

During the year Alf began fitting skid gear and installing Plexiglas bubbles on the first Bell 47s. He also removed the covering on the tail boom, replaced the tail rotor skid and raised the fuel tank behind the rotor mast, converting these machines into 47D-1s, which were altogether more practical machines. Although the Kemano project remained the company's major contract throughout this period, interest was coming from a number of other sectors, including several levels of government. Federal contracts called for a Bell 47D-1 to support marine research at Cape Harrison off the coast of Labrador and train coast guard and military pilots in mountain flying as well as provide support for a number of federal ministries. On the provincial level the company received inquiries for more topographic surveys and mining exploration contracts. As a result, tension between Carl and some of the directors resurfaced over the financing of additional helicopters.

Meanwhile, the company had grown so much that management needed more staff. Ada Carson was joined in the Vancouver south terminal office by bookkeeper Frances Heron, and, to relieve Carl of administration and operations duties, Glenn McPherson, whose background was in law, politics and business, was hired as vice-president and treasurer. On his first day he was the butt of a typical Okanagan prank: on leaving the office at 6 PM, he found his car stuffed with an inflated life raft. His struggle to open the door and insert the valve remover took quite a while and was observed by all the staff. But after he removed the life raft and returned it to the hangar, he announced that he had found a bottle of whiskey and invited everyone to have a drink. Then he was accepted.

Carl, free now to concentrate on training, produced the first manual outlining operational policy and maintenance and personnel procedures, and he began advising the militaries of both Canada and the United States.

*

At Kemano the three Bell 47s now stationed there clearly did not have the capacity to meet the project's needs. While they had lived up to expectations, by 1952 the pressure was on for additional machines and staff. Alcan purchased two new Bell 47-Ds (CF-GZK and GZJ) and two Sikorsky S-55s (CF-GHV and CF-FBW) and gave Okanagan first option to purchase them. Unfortunately, the Korean War was still having an impact on the availability of additional machines and spares.

This expansion required the hiring of more pilots and engineers. The 1952 intake included pilots John Porter, Tommy Gurr, Bill Brooks and Fred "Tweedy" Eilertson and engineers Stu Smeeth, Keith Rutledge, Hank Ellwin, Ivor Barnett, Rod Fraser and Eric Cowden. Eric, who was another ex-QCA engineer trained in the RCAF, had managed QCA's component overhaul shop. He had to get a Bell 47 licence before he went out with a machine, but the Ministry of Transport (MOT) did not have a licence program at that time. He recalled:

> Alf Stringer said to me: "Take this manual home with you and study it." The following week I went to the MOT inspectors [who were] also learning the mysteries of the helicopters as well.[22]

In the spring of 1952 Jock Graham became the first Okanagan employee to attend the S-55 course at the Sikorsky plant in Connecticut. As it was nearing completion, Carl joined him to do a conversion course. About this time the first commercially certified S-55 went to Los Angeles Airways, but a tail rotor failure during a demonstration there resulted in

▲ Carl Agar looks up at pilot Bill McLeod sitting in S-55 CF-GHV in 1952. PHOTO COURTESY OF THE KITIMAT MUSEUM

◂ Sikorsky's "Mountain Men." PHOTO COURTESY OF SIKORSKY HISTORICAL ARCHIVES

an accident that caused several casualties and the grounding of the machine until Sikorsky could locate the problem and incorporate modifications. This accident delayed Carl and Jock in the east for another three weeks, but when they finally headed home with their first S-55, CF-GHV, they stopped in Cleveland to pick up Bill McLeod who had been in Toronto, and he completed his conversion training on the way to Vancouver.

When CF-GHV arrived in Vancouver on Saturday, April 24, 1952, the press was on hand, and the *Vancouver Sun* ran the following story:

> Largest helicopter ever seen at Vancouver Airport landed today. A Sikorsky S-55 helicopter was flown from Bridgeport, Connecticut, by Carl Agar of Okanagan Air Services. The aircraft was for the Alcan Kitimat project.
>
> The biggest "egg beater" ever seen at Vancouver whirled in at 100 mph [160 km/h] and dropped like a leaf on the runway. It took 35 hours from Bridgeport ... to Vancouver ... Carl Agar ... himself was in high praise of the $190,000 aircraft.[23]

▲ Kemano base pilot D.K. "Deke" Orr (left) and engineers Jack Rich (centre) and Gordon Askin (right) with S-55 CF-FBW in 1953. PHOTO COURTESY OF GORDON ASKIN

▸ A Bell 47 piloted by Tommy Scheer in Kildala Pass during the Kemano project.
PHOTO COURTESY OF GORDON ASKIN

By early May S-55 CF-GHV was working in Kemano, lifting men and material up to the Kildala Pass. Because of the loads it could carry, crews found it invaluable; it had only been in service a few days when it was called on to ferry drums of oil to a bulldozer that had broken an oil line while clearing snow at Tahtsa. CF-GHV was followed within a few months by the second S-55, CF-FBW, which on one occasion hauled over 123 tons (111.5 metric tonnes) of lumber up to the summit camps in 116 hours over 18 flying days. (When the load included 1,000 pounds (455 kilograms) of dynamite, the slings were set down as gently as possible.)

The first of the new Bells to arrive was CF-GZJ, which was to be used ferrying workers from Kemano to Tahtsa to work on the Dala River section of the power line. Due to weather conditions, the machine was unable to fly into the worksite and had to be hoisted by crane aboard the *Nitnat*, the Alcan workboat, for the journey upriver with pilot Don Poole and engineer Gordon Askin along for the ride. Once on location they operated it from a barge moored to the workboat. Soon after the machine arrived, alternate pilot

Fred Eilertson was flying it to Tahtsa when he spotted a snow scooter upside down on the lake. Dropping down to investigate, he found a couple of badly injured men. He loaded the first on board and took him to East Tahtsa before returning for the second man whose condition was more serious. As the pass to Kemano was closed by the weather, he flew him to the Burns Lake hospital 100 miles (160 kilometres) away.

In June, Fred Snell and Carl arrived with the second new Bell, GZK, closely followed by engineer Gordon Askin. Next to arrive were pilot Leo Lannon and engineer Bill Smith to take over CF-GZJ, while Deke Orr and Gordon Askin returned CF-FZN to Vancouver to work on the Palisade project.

Heavy spring rain made it impossible to keep the Kemano road open. As a result, Okanagan was called on to move over 11 tons (10 metric tonnes) of freight and 390 passengers by helicopter, even flying out striking miners from the Horetzky Creek project. By May camps had been established along the transmission line with a fly camp at the summit of the pass, but with snow still on the ground, the pilots had to choose their landing sites very carefully. In some cases, the helicopter would hover above the chosen site while a man on snowshoes packed down a landing area and then set up a red wind flag. The first load always consisted of precut lumber, and this was followed by a carpenter and labourers to build a 20-by-20-foot (six-by-six-metre) landing platform. Only then could the machine begin to bring in the riggers to work on the transmission lines.

The work crews came to appreciate the helicopter's assistance as they were able to complete their tasks quickly compared to past bush construction jobs. The story of "Smoke" Kole, the rigging foreman for Morrison-Knudsen, the company that built the transmission line, was a good example. When he first came to Kemano, he was afraid to ride in a helicopter and spent most of his time climbing up and down mountains and accomplishing very little. Finally, with many misgivings, he consented to ride in the helicopter, and as the summer wore on, he became a convert and was soon flying up and down the mountains several times a day. He told one of the Okanagan pilots that a helicopter was the answer to a rigger's prayer as it was a lot easier to rig downhill than uphill. Instead of 75 percent of pay being spent on travel time, only about eight percent was charged by using a helicopter.[24]

During the summer, Art Fornoff, the Bell Helicopter representative from Los Angeles, visited the project and was so impressed that he phoned Bell's head office (recently moved to Fort Worth, Texas) to arrange for Jim Fuller, Bell's publicity agent, and photographer Tom Free to come to the Kemano project. When Free came back from taking pictures of the pass section, he shook his head and said in his Texas drawl: "Man, we have fellows back in Texas who think they can fly helicopters. Man, they ain't seen nothing."[25]

By the autumn of 1952 the road over the pass section was complete, and the passenger rate and amount of freight carried by Okanagan's helicopters declined. On October 8 the diversion tunnel at Nechako was sealed off so that the reservoir could begin its four-year filling phase. A spillway system for returning spawning salmon had been installed at Cheslatta Lake, and Okanagan pilots Pete Cornwall and Lock Madill spend ten days taking officials around to check on the fish; Alcan was hoping that the fish population would increase due to changing the water's direction of flow. By December a weather station had been established on the summit, staffed by three men and supplied by helicopter; they had a long-range radio and managed to keep current on local and world news throughout the winter.

1952 ANNUAL REPORT

Since starting the Kemano operation the previous year, Okanagan Helicopters had carried out a number of medevac flights taking injured men to hospital and, as a result, the project had only one fatality. The period 1951–2 had seen flying time increase by 196 percent, flight hours by 204 percent, passengers by 212 percent and freight by 375 percent. At year-end the company's annual report announced profits above $68,000, and the directors approved an order for a Sikorsky twin engine s-56. The civilian version of this machine, which had been designed for the US Marine Corps, was said to be capable of carrying 26 passengers. Unfortunately, the machine never materialized.

1953

▲ Camp security at Beatton River, BC (northeast of Fort St. John), in 1953.
PHOTO COURTESY OF GORDON ASKIN

▲ Hotel Kotcho, Kotcho Lake, BC (east of Fort Nelson). PHOTO COURTESY OF GORDON ASKIN

By the early 1950s the value of the helicopter had become widely recog-nized, and the industry expanded quickly. In the United States the 1,000th machine came off the Bell Aircraft assembly line, the new Hiller UH-12A was gaining in popularity, and Sikorsky Helicopters announced the construction of a new plant in Stratford, Connecticut, while on November 16, 1953, Igor Sikorsky was featured on the cover of *Time* magazine. In England, Westland Aircraft UK Ltd. signed a contract to build the Sikorsky s-51 under licence, and it went into commercial service with British European Airways (BEA) as the "Dragonfly." The British company Autair Helicopters was formed, while Sabena Airlines of Belgium inaugurated a helicopter service from Liege to Brussels and began operating helicopters in the Belgian Congo. Within a few years the helicopter had become a fixture in the aviation world and the "eggbeater" nickname began slowly disappearing.

Although Okanagan's involvement with the Kemano project continued throughout 1953, the company signed other contracts that year, including one supporting gravitational surveys for Imperial Oil in the Fort Nelson area, another that used Bell 47 CF-FZN with a Canadian Armed Forces survey team in Norman Wells, Northwest Territories, and yet another exploring for uranium using a specially adapted scintillometer, a device for detecting and measuring radioactivity. Farther south, Okanagan transported personnel and equipment during the construction of the 712-mile-long (1,145-kilometre) Trans Mountain pipeline running from Edmonton to Vancouver, and after it was completed in the fall of 1953, Okanagan was awarded the contract for routine inspections and other flight services. The inspections, carried out three times a month at 200 feet (60 metres), checked for rock slides, a common occurrence in that terrain. Later a new four-passenger Bell 47-J model provided an improved visual inspection platform for this work. In July Trans Mountain employed Okanagan Helicopters to install a special telephone line along the pipeline and place high frequency transmitters at Hope and Kamloops in BC and at Brookmere, Blue River, Edson, Jasper and Black Pool in Alberta.

On Vancouver Island pilot Pete Cornwall and engineer Sig Hubenig were assigned to a MacMillan Bloedel contract, at that time one of BC's largest forestry companies, for the control of gophers and squirrels in the area of the Harmac pulp mill. The contract called for a helicopter, flying at 45 mph (72 km/h) at a height of 100 feet (30.5 metres), to seed bait over a logged-out 120-acre (48.5-hectare) section of rolling hills at Copper Canyon. The company borrowed Bell 47D CF-FSR, which was fitted with seeding equipment, from a pest control company in Yakima, Washington. When it arrived in Vancouver, it had to have floats installed before it could cross the Strait of Georgia, a 35-minute trip, and then on landing it was immediately changed back to skid gear. On MacMillan Bloedel's recommendation, the provincial forestry department requested that additional seeding be done from September to the end of October.

Meanwhile, pilot Don Poole and engineer Eric Cowden were sent north with the brand new Bell 47D-1, CF-ETQ, for a job that was supposed to last ten days, but it was five

▸ Engineer Frank Ranger with Bell 47 CF-FJA in a "maintenance hangar" in Kotcho Lake, BC, in 1953. PHOTO COURTESY OF GORDON ASKIN

and a half months before they returned to Vancouver. In an interview in May 2009 Eric described that season—his first—in the field:

> In the spring of '53, Don Poole and I set off for Stewart, right on the tip of northern BC about 900 miles [1,450 kilometres] from Vancouver ... On the way ... we had a terrific head [outflow] wind; we were so heavily loaded and on floats that I remember us chugging along at about 20 mph [30 km/h] into a stiff northwesterly wind when I saw two ducks fly past us doing quite nicely. We landed on the American side of the border, which we weren't supposed to do, but we had to gas up somewhere. After refuelling, we set off up the Portland Canal. We were going nowhere, and it was one of those low overcast days, which means we could not climb out of the Canal and land. There wasn't even a boat around—nothing.
>   Finally, Don said, "What do you think?"
>   I said, "Well, Don, my watch says we're not going to make it."
>   "You know what?" he replied. "So does mine."
>   There was no place to land, so we just kept chugging along up the Canal, doing a little praying. Finally we turned a corner and got some shelter from the wind. When we landed at Stewart, I drained the fuel tank and we had two gallons [7.5 litres] left, enough for about six or seven minutes of flying.[26]

Their first job with CF-ETQ involved flying between Stewart, BC and the Granduc Glacier, the site of a copper mine that operated sporadically over the years due to the fluctuating copper market. On completion of that job, they moved on to other mining exploration projects and, as Eric recalled, that's when things started to go downhill:

> From Stewart we went [north] to Bobquin Lake with two geologists—MacKenzie and Warren were their names—who believed in living on bacon, bannock and beans with a little tea and sugar. That's about all they had in

▸ Jock Graham during maintenance on S-55 CF-GHV, Okanagan Air Services' first S-55, in 1953. PHOTO COURTESY OF THE KELOWNA PUBLIC ARCHIVES

their so-called camp. For several weeks we worked out of a little island in the middle of Bobquin. We stayed there for five weeks, and I'll never laugh again when people make jokes about beans.

From there we moved to Hottah Lake and then on to Chukachida, more or less in the middle of the province. We were with some hotshot mining promoter now—I remember he was worth lots of money and behaved accordingly. The first day we were there he came into the camp in a beat-up old [Beechcraft] Travel Air... and the next morning the weather was socked right in, right down to the deck. I heard him say to the party chief, George Radisics, "What's the weather like, George?"

And George said: "It's socked in tight, but I think it'll clear by noon."

The promoter said, "That's not good enough. I want it to clear now!" I guess he thought he could buy the weather, too.[27]

Eric had other problems. The fixed-wing aircraft used on that operation, the hotshot promoter's venerable Travel Air, was in sad shape, and the company operating it had not provided a licensed engineer. Instead, Eric was expected to inspect it and sign the logbook when it was due for its 100-hour maintenance check. However, every time the Travel Air, which of course was on floats, was pulled up onto the beach to be loaded or unloaded, he had heard what he described as "a funny noise." When the time came for the inspection and his signature in the logbook, he got someone to grab the tail section and rock the machine up and down. Sure enough, one of the mounts on the struts that connected the floats to the fuselage was about ready to fall off. Eric refused to sign the log until the aircraft had been repaired—something that could not be done in the bush—and he was exposed to ferocious recriminations from the mining promoter. In the end the promoter and his crew took off in the Travel Air for Prince George, leaving Don and Eric sitting alone in camp for three days.

The next move for Don Poole, Eric Cowden and CF-ETQ was to Yehinika Lake, a little to the southwest of Telegraph Creek, BC. This was still Eric's first season in the bush, and even though CF-ETQ was brand new, it was giving trouble:

We'd been having the usual snags with those Franklin engines . . . We were constantly having to change plugs and dig the lead out of the electrodes, and the fan belts kept letting go. When they did, they'd smack into the back of the firewall, scaring the hell out of the pilot . . . and then he'd have to get [the helicopter] down on the ground within a couple of minutes and shut down or the engine would over-heat.

Those were routine problems, but this engine began to give me much more [grief] than that . . . I thought the timing of the magnetos was out. Trouble was I didn't have a manual with me on the trip, and this was a 200-horsepower engine. I'd been working on a 170-horsepower one, so I didn't really know what the timing should be. I thought I remembered Sig [Hubenig] say it was 36 degrees—so I retimed the whole thing. It didn't do a damned bit of good. Yehinika Lake was well up in the mountains, and we still had a very rough engine. I checked the plugs and points—re-set the gap—and everything was as it should be. Had me baffled there for a while. Then, when I was shutting down—I shut down with the mixture control—and just before the engine quit, it suddenly smoothed out.

So I fired up again and played with the mixture—we had a manual mixture control in those days. It would run fine just before it quit. I came to the conclusion it just had to be the carburetor. Trouble was I had never taken one apart before. I pulled the carb off the intake and split it, and out fell a little ball check-valve. It was a bad scene because I hadn't the faintest idea where it had come from. I thought, Oh my God! Here we are, way out in the tul[i]es [bush] and our only way to get out is in that damned helicopter!

Anyway, I found the float level was way out, way beyond limits, so I set that all up. Now I really had to decide where this little ball had to go. In the end the only place that looked likely was the accelerator pump, so I popped it in there, clamped the carburetor together and bolted it back onto the manifold. When I fired up the engine, it ran like a charm. I didn't bother telling Don about the worry-session with the check-valve. When he got back from a quick test flight and thanked me because the engine was running good, I just shrugged and said, "That's what I'm here for."[28]

Engineer Ian Duncan and pilot Mike McDonagh had a similar experience when they worked for the Canadian Army doing barometer surveys out of Puntzi Lake, about 50 miles (80 kilometres) west of Williams Lake. Ian Duncan recalled:

About a week after we'd arrived here, Mike took off with this lieutenant and his barometer and all his instruments and away they went. Be gone four hours, Duncan, he said . . . So four hours went by and then five hours, and I started to get up off my cot in the tent; I started to walk around the tent. By the time it got dark, I had worn a trench about two feet deep around the tent—just walking around . . . Finally, just after breakfast next morning, in comes [Mike] back to camp. He'd walked all night and you could see the blisters on his feet; his feet were bleeding.

It seems that Mike had been taking off from a little sand beach and tried to pull up too sharply and lost his revs. The helicopter had ended up in the lake. The Army lent Ian a four-wheel-drive Dodge Power Wagon, and "making use of the winch on the front of it, [he] hauled the vehicle through several swamps and forded rivers to get to the damaged helicopter. Then [he] used the winch to pull [the helicopter] up onto the beach." Okanagan sent a new engine, and they proceeded to rebuild the helicopter right there.

> About a month later they moved from Puntzi Lake right up to Satigi Lake, just south of Aklavik [on] the estuary of the Mackenzie River. A week after that, Ian recalls, the helicopter disappeared again:
> "Mike went off on another of these barometer trips. He said he'd be back by four o'clock, but he wasn't, and I wore another trench around my tent. It took us four or five hours to get through to Aklavik [on the radio], where we could get some help to go and look for him."
> Eventually a Beaver belonging to BC Yukon Air Services and flown by company owner Bill Dalzell was sent from Aklavik to Satigi Lake to start a search. The Beaver's condition shocked Ian Duncan: "He had the most beat-up old Beaver you ever saw in your life. The rudder cables on the floats were so loose he'd tied knots in them to bring them up to proper tension. You couldn't see the front of the engine for the bugs and oil and stuff. You've never seen such a shambles in your life."

From the Beaver Ian spotted smoke and saw the undersides of two helicopter floats sticking up out of the water. This time Mike had been the victim of glassy water, and the machine's floats had dug into the lake bed. He and his passenger escaped just before the machine turned over and sank.

> Everyone was flown back to camp in the Beaver. Another Okanagan pilot, Eddy Amman, brought a replacement machine up from Vancouver. Meanwhile, Ian returned to the accident site in the Beaver, and after a struggle with come-alongs [manually operated ratchet winches], they managed to get the submerged helicopter ashore where they dismantled it, loaded the pieces into the Beaver and flew them back to camp to start the rebuild. Mike McDonagh was "given a rest" after this second accident, but it was merely a temporary setback for Mike; he went on to a distinguished career as a helicopter pilot.[29]

The living conditions in the camps continued to be appalling. Eric Cowden remembers that after Yehinika and Chukachida lakes, he and Don Poole were sent to Paddy Lake, about 30 miles (50 kilometres) south of Atlin, to work with a topographic survey crew:

> Well, when you were at this camp at Chukachida, you were lucky to get a can of sardines thrown at you. And when we were ferrying from there up to Paddy Lake near Atlin—incidentally, by now the old girl was perking along fine, no plugs missed or twitches or anything—Don suddenly made like he was going to land. And I thought, I wonder what that old bugger heard that I didn't hear.
> Anyway, we landed in a moose patch, and I said to Don, "What the hell did we land here for?"
> "Well," he replied, "you and I have been out a long time. We're going to take ourselves a couple of days off. We're going up to Atlin."
> So we poured in our spare gas, and when we took off again, Don flew much higher than I'd ever seen him fly before, and we went right over Paddy Lake. Of course, there's a brand new crew down there, all excited, all ready to go to work. They were waving frantically. We pretended we didn't even see them.

> Old Don was a good 5,000 feet [1,525 metres] [up] and we just chugga-chugged right up into Atlin.
> The first thing we did in Atlin was to go to the café and order lunch, and the first thing I ordered was a salad.
> "Aren't you going to have a steak?" Don asked.
> "Yes, later, but I need to start with this. I think I'm getting scurvy. My gums are all sore."
> "Me, too," said Don. "That's why we're here!"
> We lived like peasants out there in those days. It was expected of you, part of the job, so you accepted it. Changed days now; nobody'll do it anymore.[30]

Eric Cowden also remembered the mixture of anxiety and boredom on the job. He spent most evenings doing maintenance under constant attack by mosquitoes and blackflies, but during the day when the machine was out flying he had nothing to do:

> You could usually fish and walk around the shore of the lake, learning something about the vegetation and the animals, but most of the time it was sheer boredom. You had nobody to talk to during the day but the cook, and he was nearly always a cranky old bastard. I tell you, I've read thousands—and I mean thousands—of pocket books. In fact, I can pick one up even today and probably go through the first paragraph and say, "Dammit, I've read that one!"[31]

Later that year, Eric was sent on the s-55 course, the only civilian in the class:

> I had the instructors at Sikorsky breaking down the engine, gearbox and transmission and anything I felt that I would have to repair in the field. The military guys were not happy campers as it added a lot more time on the course and took up the instructors' time. The military guys were just used to changing parts, which they had many on hand. I was going to Kemano and would need all the information on the s-55 that I could get. I tried hard to beat Sig Hubenig's course marks but he beat me by one mark. That's why I guess he was my mentor.[32]

Eric Cowden became the base engineer of the Kemano project, in charge of the s-55s as well as the Bell 47s. By that time Bell CF-JJB had been involved in various accidents and rebuilt a number of times, whereas JJC was accident-free, and pilots noticed that JJB's performance always lagged behind JJC's. This really bothered Eric, so he changed all JJB's components including the engine, swash plate and transmission. However, he could never get that machine to perform as well as JJC.

Okanagan's first s-55s were leased from the RCAF and, though they had the Okanagan name on the machine, they still retained the RCAF logo on the tail boom, which shows up in photographs. Eric recalled:

> Bill Brooks used to say to me, "Eric, the 55 is a great machine. Throw in the grease, the oil and fuel, kick the tires, and she will never let you down." He just loved that machine. I remember one incident, though, in Kemano. To get the machine in the hangar, you folded the blades, and it was the line engineer's job to ensure the locking pins were in when the machine was doing a trip. I guess [Bill] must have missed one [on his pre-flight inspection] because, when he started up the machine, he chopped off the tail boom. The engineer sure got heck for that and sure felt bad about it.[33]

1954

For Okanagan Helicopters the year 1954 was very eventful. The company introduced a newsletter and established the Penticton Mountain Flying School, which is still in existence. The company's machines carried out several medical emergency flights while working with Newfoundland's Department of Fisheries, flew the Duke of Edinburgh from Kemano to Kitimat and Governor General Vincent Massey around Vancouver Island. Carl undertook a promotional tour to the USA, UK, Europe and New Guinea. In addition, the company began work on a new Vancouver airport facility at 4391 Agar Drive in Richmond with 10,000 square feet (930 square metres) of hangar space and 5,000 square feet (465 square metres) for offices. It would remain the company's head office until 1987.

As work on the Kemano project wound down, Alcan cut its operating fleet to one S-55 and two Bell 47Ds, releasing the remaining S-55 and two Bell 47s for purchase by Okanagan, the S-55 going for $115,000. Fortunately, offsetting the loss of revenue from Alcan, the company received numerous inquiries from all over Canada and the US, including one for a geological survey in the Harrison Lake area of BC for the Dominion Exploration Ltd., a scintillometer survey of the North Thompson River for Warmac Exploration, and a freight lift operation in the Anyox area, 37 miles (60 kilometres) southwest of Stewart, BC. As a result of all this interest, management decided to set up two new subsidiaries to handle the workload. Agar Helicopters Consultants Ltd. would deal with both the Canadian and US military, and Scintillopter Ltd. would provide airborne Geiger and scintillometer surveys for geological exploration.

About that time all the S-55s in North America were grounded because of a manufacturing mistake. Jock Graham, who had left Okanagan to become a technical representative for Pratt and Whitney, discovered the mistake. He had been called to a mining camp in the Yukon to solve a problem with an S-55:

When the Kemano project was winding down, Carl released the following operational facts:

Flying	2,203 days
Helicopters in service	4,551 days
Number of trips	21,722
Platform landings	18,561
Number of landings	42,021
Passengers	20,433
Freight	2,008,405 pounds [91,0997 kilograms]
Air miles	6,214.25 [10,000 kilometres]

▸ Despite some success in the early 1950s, Okanagan still faced financial problems. Alf Stringer looks to Carl Agar for more money for spares; Agar, in turn, questions company president Glenn McPherson, who shows them his empty pockets. IMAGE COURTESY OF THE ROYAL BC MUSEUM AND ARCHIVES, FONDS PR-1842

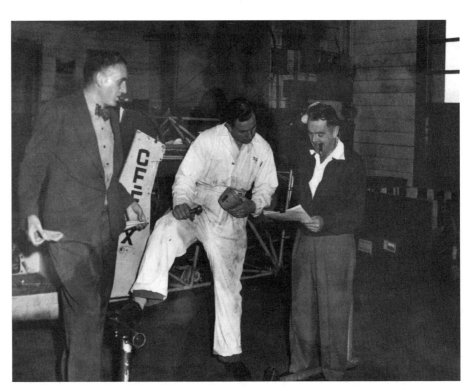

The pilot, Russ Lennox, kept having the engine almost fail. It looked like fuel starvation. He would land, shut down and then start the engine again, and everything would be good. He'd come back to camp, and the other engineer and I would just about tear the whole fuel system apart, and we couldn't find anything. I was baffled. Then one day we were sitting around with all the screens [filters] out of the fuel system. One of them was a finger screen—a hollow tube with a fine mesh screen like a thimble on top of it. The mechanic from the Otter we were using picked it up and tried to poke a piece of grass up through the bottom hole. The grass wouldn't go. When I had a good look, I found there was another very fine screen in the hole, where it certainly shouldn't have been. The people who had made the filters for Pratt and Whitney had misread the drawings and this extra screen was causing the fuel starvation. So we had to ground every S-55 in North America until the second screen had been punched out.[34]

Another first for Okanagan was a contract at Fort Good Hope, 90 miles (145 kilometres) northwest of Norman Wells, where local game warden O. Eliason wanted to carry out a survey of the beaver population in the Hume River watershed, which was reported to have the richest beaver stock in the Northwest Territories. The survey had to take place in late August or early September due to the beavers' habits. The project, undertaken using a Bell 47 flown by J.P. Smith, required about 30 hours flight time to cover approximately 2,500 miles (4,025 kilometres), flying tracks a mile apart over 50 square miles (80 square kilometres). This was the first beaver survey in the area and certainly the first anywhere using a helicopter. With the success of the survey, similar studies were proposed for other areas.

Rumour had it that Shell Oil was doing exploration work in the Mackenzie area and needed something larger than a Bell 47. Jock Graham arranged a meeting with the executive assistant to Shell's president and their chief pilot and suggested they call Okanagan. That call resulted in a three-month contract for the S-55 with pilot Bill McLeod at the controls. It was, Bill reported, the most enjoyable job of his career:

That was the first year that Shell had used a helicopter. They got a 55 and a Bell and I flew the 55. We did a preliminary geological survey of the Mackenzie Mountains, starting at Fort Liard and working our way not quite to the Arctic coast. We were back in the Richardson Range by the time we finished up.

They were surveying a swathe of country approximately 40 to 60 miles [65–100 kilometres] west of the river, depending on where the pre-Cambrian rock occurred; in other words, it was soft rock geology. That was extremely interesting because we stayed only ten days to two weeks in any one location; then we moved on.

They had three geologist, three helpers, my engineer George Chamberlain, myself and a cook on our part of the operation. In the morning I would load all six of the geology crew and put two crews out to measure sections and take samples. Then I would travel with the third crew until it was time to pick up the others in the evening. Dr. Matthews from UBC was the geologist, and I became a one-man classroom for him for the season. By the end of it, he would pick up a fossil, hand it to me and say, "Well, what is it Bill?" and I'd reply, "Oh, that's Middle Devonian; it's a brachiopod." I could reel it all off, and it made the job much more interesting.

But that was one of those good years. Even the cook was good, and we were on the move all the time. We got to the point where the engineer and I, we slept in the helicopter. We didn't bother setting up the tent; we just rolled out our sleeping bags on the floor of the helicopter and went to bed at night—what there was of it.

I had one engine failure and they had to come looking for me... The radio didn't work—usual I think in those days... I had a magneto pack up on me. I tried to fly back to camp, but the engine got rougher and rougher. Then she started missing on one cylinder, so I thought I'd better put her down because I still had some 60 miles [100 kilometres] of muskeg to go over. We were working out of Fort Norman at the time... I put down on a river called the Redstone on a sandbar which was composed of red and cream sandstone. [But] the helicopter was painted cream and red [so] I had the best camouflaged helicopter you every saw. And when I landed, there was thunderstorm activity and there were fires burning—little plumes of smoke all over the country.

I did the usual thing: I laid out a square on the sandbar with a W in it, meaning "I need an engineer." Then I gathered a big pile of brush to make smoke to compete with all the other smokes. Airplanes flew right over the top of me and never saw me. The fellow who finally found me was flying over a ridge 10 miles (16 kilometres) away, and he saw the sun glint on the Plexiglas. Even then, he had trouble seeing exactly where I was.

It wasn't a big deal. I was only out one night. The engineer came in and changed the mag—the drive had sheered—and we flew back to camp.[35]

1955

In April 1955 Okanagan Helicopters underwent a major expansion by purchasing two eastern companies, Canadian Helicopters Ltd. and Smart Aviation of Toronto, although they continued to operate separately. However, these purchases complicated the company's structure because the previous year Okanagan had acquired United Helicopters, another eastern company, and appointed Jack Charleson as president; back in 1945 Jack had been the first licensed helicopter pilot in Canada. Originally, United had been a Newfoundland-based company with contracts for one S-55 and two Bell 47s on a sealing operation contract with the Fisheries Department. However, United had merged with Kenting Aviation and Smart Aviation, and as the latter was the product of a merger between Ambank Airlift Ltd. and Abitibi Power and Paper Company, when Okanagan Helicopters purchased Smart, Abitibi acquired a substantial share in Okanagan Helicopters. Charleson now became the managing director of the newly merged company, with Leo Lannon and Sig Hubenig transferred in from Okanagan as chief pilot and chief engineer respectively.

With the purchase of Canadian Helicopters, Okanagan added six Bell machines and a Sikorsky S-55 to the fleet as well as bases at Toronto Island Airport, Fort William (Thunder Bay), and Gander, Newfoundland, along with a branch office in Calgary. Okanagan Helicopters' fleet now totalled 22 Bell 47s and 8 Sikorsky S-55s, making it the largest commercial helicopter operator in North America. Alf Stringer was appointed general manager and moved to Toronto to run the operation.

*

Meanwhile, in the field the year had begun with a setback for the Alcan project when power lines were knocked down by snow slides. Two Bell 47s were required to perform emergency repairs, which took two months—from January 26 to March 28—and about 160 flight hours to complete.

About the same time Okanagan was awarded a new federal government contract for two S-55s to support a survey of the Arctic Islands from June through September. Pilot Fred Snell and engineer George Chamberlain were in charge for the company while the government team was headed by Dr. Y.O. Fortier, chief of operations, with Dr. E.F. Roots, deputy chief responsible for air movements. This survey was to cover the Queen Elizabeth, Somerset and Prince of Wales islands and the northwest part of Baffin Island with the objectives of completing the mapping of the area and carrying out geological and wildlife surveys of the coastal inlets. A challenging project of this size and in this area required careful planning for the number and placement of base camps and fuel caches. Base Camp One was established at Resolute Bay on Cornwallis Island with a fuel cache 110 miles (177 kilometres) to the northeast on Devon Island. Base Camp Two was at Oksey Bay on Ellesmere Island with a sub-station at the Eureka weather station and a fuel cache on Cornwallis Island. Base Camp Three was on Ellef Ringnes Island with fuel caches on Axel Heiberg and Lougheed islands, and Number Four was on Melville Island with a fuel cache on Bathurst Island.

On June 7 the two S-55s, CF-HHU and CF-HVR, were loaded onto an RCAF C-119 freighter at Toronto's Malton Airport and flown to Resolute Bay where they were re-assembled and test flown. It was arranged that the RCAF would fly in spares as needed. Fred Snell, who arrived on an Arctic Air DC-3, checked the fuel caches and carried out a general reconnaissance of the terrain they would be flying over, and by the following week the operation was underway with flights to Somerset and Devon islands. Each field party consisted of a geologist and an assistant who embarked with enough food and equipment for 14 days; the combined weight was about 700 pounds (317.5 kilograms). Each flight, with the geologists acting as navigators, required careful pre-flight planning and absolutely no deviation from the flight plan. The helicopters cruised about 70 mph (112 km/h) and carried one hour's reserve fuel.

The base radio in Resolute was in continuous contact, providing up-to-date weather conditions, and the helicopters were equipped with new high frequency (HF) radios for long-range communication, directional gyro compasses and automatic direction finding equipment. George Chamberlain modified the HF antennas to increase their range to 200 miles (322 kilometres) for voice transmit and receive functions. CW (Morse code) keys were also installed to provide an additional range of up to 300 miles (483 kilometres). Although the G-2 compasses were not much use in the area, the pilots used them as directional gyros; navigation over the pack ice was often by dead reckoning and directional gyro, and whenever the weather deteriorated, the patterns created by blowing snow and ice packs plotted on maps helped the flight crew. Emergency equipment on board consisted of sleeping bags, one tent per person, ten days food supply, gasoline for cooking, a shotgun plus shells and blade and hub covers. On a number of occasions, the crews had to spend three or four days in the helicopter waiting for the weather to improve. When one of the pilots was taken ill, an RCAF Lancaster was dispatched from Resolute to fly him to Churchill for treatment.

With work at Base Camp One completed by mid-July, the crews moved on to Base Camp Two on Ellesmere Island, which has peaks up to 8,500 feet (2,590 metres) high and numerous snowfields and glaciers. During their stay at Eureka, just 250 miles (400 kilometres) from the geographic North Pole, American and Canadian military personnel stationed there provided the crews with food and accommodation. Most of the scheduled work in that area was completed by July 24 but continued on Axel Heiberg and Amund Ringnes islands.

During August the weather deteriorated with snow, drizzle, fog and low stratus clouds, grounding the helicopters for days at a time. Although the ice in the area was still solid, it was breaking up along the shoreline, and as a result, Dr. Fortier decided to abandon Base Camp Four. On August 26 the crews and equipment on Axel Heiberg Island were flown back to Base Camp Three to consolidate operations and reduce the number of flights. In spite of the weather, surveys continued at Lougheed, Cameron and Bathurst islands, which are relatively flat; as Bathurst's highest point is approximately 2,000 feet (610 metres), it proved ideal for helicopter operations.

In September, with the inclement weather and ice fog persisting for days on end, the last crews were flown back to Resolute Bay from Bathurst Island. On September 15 CF-HVR flew a circuit around Cornwallis Island to clean up expedition sites from previous years, while CF-HHU flew around the Resolute area taking local people for short flights to thank them for all their help during the summer. Two days later an RCAF North Star transported most of the personnel out of Resolute to Ottawa, but as the C-119 was not available to airlift the S-55s until 10 days later, George Chamberlain and another engineer remained behind to fly home with the machines.

The operation was declared a success in spite of weather delays caused by the worst summer on record. By the end of the project CF-HHU had flown 292.45 hours and CF-HVR 263.40 hours. In its final review, the company decided that the Arctic was a suitable place to operate helicopters, but the crews recommended the addition of directional gyros with less precision because of the distortion caused by the magnetic field, an attitude direction indicator (ADI) and emergency flotation gear, essential over open water. This equipment would become standard in all future offshore and IFR operations. Later the pilots agreed that the geologists had been excellent navigators.

During the summer the geologists had made a count of wildlife, identifying approximately 600 musk oxen ranging from the Grinnell Peninsula on Ellesmere, over Axel Heiberg, Graham, Bathurst and Cornwallis islands. Caribou were plentiful on these same islands as were arctic wolves, polar bears, walrus and seals. The bird life included large numbers of snow geese, brant geese and ptarmigan. A few bumblebees were seen on Ellesmere even though the vegetation was very sparse with only inch-high pussy willows, Arctic poppies, some coarse grasses and lichens.

Okanagan Helicopters' other contracts during 1955 included a forestry inventory of the area between Kitimat and Prince Rupert, a distance of 134 miles (215 kilometres), and geological surveys in the Pelly Lake area, 230 miles (368 kilometres) north of Prince George, and in the Fort Simpson and the Mackenzie delta area for Shell Oil. Another operation that summer was a contract for CF-GZJ with Northwest Exploration ferrying prospectors in the Watson Lake area. Operations like these raised the company's profile because they demonstrated how much more work could be achieved during the summer months by using a helicopter.

In another major development, Okanagan's management began negotiating with the federal government for a construction and maintenance services contract on the Mid-Canada Line, part of the radar system set up to defend North America against nuclear attacks. The government, however, gave the contract for construction and maintenance to other operators who flew the RCAF's Vertol 42s and 44s. Okanagan's consolation prize was a contract to train 24 RCAF pilots to fly the S-55, which became a story covered by reporter Mac Reynolds of the *Vancouver Sun* in November 1955. It appeared under the headline: "Air Force Fliers Learn How to Manoeuvre Flying Whales."

Like a frisky whale, the helicopter manoeuvred a few feet above a soggy Ladner field. Two men in air force coveralls ran beneath the landing gear, the wind from the whirling rotor blades knifing at their faces, and attached a cargo sling to the dangling clamp.

In the cockpit of the helicopter Flying Officer Carl Bond of Edmonton turned to a man wearing an Indian sweater and asked, "How was that?"

"Good enough for a beginner," grinned Bill McLeod... McLeod is an instructor with the remarkable company that's running the schoolroom, Vancouver's Okanagan Helicopters, the world's largest commercial operator of helicopters.

The course began in September and ends in mid-April. At Ladner, using four plastic bubbled Bells and the odd Sikorsky, the air force flyers practice [sic] hovering, sideways flight [and] dike landing. At Penticton they learn to drop their large Sikorskys on mountain peaks the size of a double bed... The RCAF-Okanagan training contract is officially recognized as one of flying's most whirlwind success stories... Today the company that [Carl] Agar launched in the Okanagan on a frayed shoestring... has flown more than 15,000 hours, carried more than 20,000 passengers [and] moved more than 2 million pounds of freight...

"I believe a man has to gamble security," said Agar in a recent interview. "If his dream is big enough, then security is what he makes it. This country, Canada... and all that sky that's up above... why, a man's future is unlimited."

Bolstered today by some of the continent's shrewdest financial brains, Agar says of helicopters: "They have brought in an era of their own. With helicopters, every square foot of the earth's land or sea surface is now conveniently approachable."[36]

The Mountain Flying School alternated between civilian and Canadian military intakes at that time, although that year they also trained 22 pilots from US Army Transportation Helicopter Battalion and received a visit from a French armed forces colonel. However, the school was not popular with people living nearby who complained that they had to have bedroom and bathroom blinds because the helicopters cruised too low and too slowly.

The year 1955 ended with Okanagan placing an order for an S-58, making it the first commercial operator outside the United States to purchase the 12-passenger aircraft. Glenn McPherson, Okanagan's president, told *Sikorsky News*:

The purchase of this type of aircraft is the beginning of a new expansion program at Okanagan... More of the big Sikorskys will soon be on order, but first we have to train our crews and maintenance personnel in the operation of this particular aircraft... The increased carrying capacity of the S-58—more than twice that of the S-55—is expected to substantially reduce the cost per ton mile for Okanagan's freighting operations.[37]

1956

The new year began with a Pacific Western Airlines (PWA) contract to recover a de Havilland Beaver that had crashed on Sovereign Lakes, east of Quesnel, BC. Okanagan sent S-55 CF-GHV with a crew consisting of pilots Bill McLeod and Fred

Eilertson and engineers Alf Stringer and Frank Ranger. When they arrived at the site, the crew found the area unsafe to land due to thawing caused by warmer than normal temperatures, but the Beaver was eventually slung out after a temporary site was set up and PWA engineers had prepared the aircraft for the lift.

Contracts in the summer of 1956 included a stratographic survey in the Jasper-Banff area for Imperial Oil and a geological survey at Dease Lake, BC, for the Department of Mines and Surveys. The company also transported crews to the BC-Yukon border for North West Power and carried equipment and supplies for Canadian Nickel in Manitoba. Okanagan's helicopters also returned to the Kitimat area for a steel line construction contract. In the meantime a number of contracts, such as that for the Trans Mountain Pipeline patrol, were ongoing; by 1956 Okanagan had flown 355 patrols over 1,200 hours in 380 days.

In September, Boyles Brothers Drilling contacted Okanagan about moving a complete diamond drilling camp to a site on Takomkane Mountain (known as Timothy Mountain by the locals) in the Forest Grove area near 100 Mile House in central BC. Pilot Bud Tillotson and engineer Ian Duncan flew the Bell 47 CF-HDP to a rancher's field east of Forest Grove, but during a flight over the site, Bud realized that the mine was located in a very steep ravine, which, due to prevailing westerly winds, caused a formidable downdraft. After talking it over with Art Hall, the geologist in charge, it was agreed that the helicopters would airlift the freight to a meadow with clear approaches at the 6,800-foot (2,072-metre) level, and a pack train would move the equipment from there to the site.

Their mountain flying training helped the crew face the greatest challenge at the site—taking off in circular winds. By flying at a 23-degree climb and holding to a speed of 50 mph (80 km/h), they were able to reach the base of the mountain and then, with a healthy updraft, the machine could reach the 7,000-foot (2,135-metre) level without difficulty. Within a week they had made 41 trips and moved 7.5 tons (6.8 metric tonnes) of equipment, averaging about 45 minutes per trip.

*

On October 22 Bell 47 CF-FJA, pilot Bill Calder and engineer Mark Adams were called on to join the search for Harvey Garrison, an 18-year-old high school student from Princeton, BC, who had become lost while hunting with a friend near Granite Creek, about 18 miles (30 kilometres) from Princeton. The boy's father had gone into the area with a search party and located his son's tracks but lost them again in the dark. The next day a party of over 300 searched the area in adverse weather conditions. They picked up his tracks but realized that he was walking in large circles. Fires were lit in the area and a searchlight installed.

Okanagan was called on when the RCAF's Piasecki was unable to join the search as it was undergoing maintenance. CF-FJA left Vancouver but bad weather prevented it from continuing beyond Hope. The next day they loaded the helicopter onto a flatbed truck and drove up to Sunday Summit where they were able to take off. Arriving in Princeton at 4:30 PM, they made a low sweep over the area, but in the gathering darkness they could only make out the fires below. The aerial search continued until the following Monday, but the boy was never found.

On the East Coast, Okanagan's new acquisition, Canadian Helicopters, had secured a contract for an S-55 to take personnel to various Newfoundland fish processing plants. The province also chartered a helicopter to operate as an air ambulance, providing emergency services for people living in the isolated and scattered coves around the 900-mile (1,450-kilometre) coastline. When the formation of ice stopped water transportation

◂ In 1956, Okanagan Helicopters' subsidiary, Canadian Helicopters Ltd. won a five-year contract with the Newfoundland Fisheries Department for two S-55s. Pictured here is one of the S-55s. PHOTO COURTESY OF THE ROYAL BC MUSEUM AND ARCHIVES, FONDS PR-1842

between Belle Isle and the Newfoundland mainland, the helicopter was also used to lift passengers and freight across the straits. These contracts would last for the next five years.

In Labrador, the company's first S-58, CF-JIB, started work on the eastern end of the Mid-Canada Line, and on October 16 *Sikorsky News* announced that:

> An S-58 helicopter delivered to Okanagan Helicopters Ltd. of Canada was put into operation last month carrying freight to radar installations in the Mid-Canada Line.
> The aircraft was one of the first delivered when CAA approval was granted for its use in commercial service. Its receipt by Okanagan brings to 33 the total number of helicopters operated by the firm.
> Flight delivery from Sikorsky Aircraft was made by Okanagan's chief pilot, Fred Snell. Fitted out as a cargo transport, the helicopter will carry the majority of its loads externally by slinging beneath the cabin.[38]

During the autumn of 1956 pilot John McNulty and engineer Peter Berendt went missing for 11 days in the Great Slave Lake area of the Northwest Territories after their Bell 47 ran low on fuel and they were forced to land. The search for them covered a large area and involved many of their bush pilot friends from Yellowknife. As hope began to fade, the searchers decided they had been looking in the wrong area and headed out again in a Norseman to look at the second of two very similar bays. John's son, Mike McNulty, recalled the rescue:

> Before my dad left Vancouver, my mother bought him a battery razor. It was in a little case that also had a mirror. My dad spotted the Norseman when it was miles away. He used the mirror to catch the sun. He taught me later how he ran the reflection up a tree until it was abreast of the aircraft then flashed it back and forth. They were spotted immediately. The part of the story I remember so well was the pilots on board all took out their cigarettes and put various brands in one Players Plain package and, after writing . . . humorous notes, dropped

it to my dad and Peter. For years my dad kept the package on a shelf in our rec room to be brought out at parties when he would tell the story. Around the time I was 15 he did it again only to find the package empty. For some reason I was called onto the carpet as the most likely culprit. I remember the tobacco was so old that I had to smoke the cigarettes vertically or the tobacco would pour out ... Because he and Peter had spent the entire time around a campfire ... just to stay warm, dad was very tanned from the neck up, and no one believed that he had not been on a beach somewhere.

It was years later when I was flying the S-61 on a sling job in the Arctic [that] I had Peter Berendt as our engineer. My dad thought this was wonderful and knew I was in good hands. Peter was very shy when I asked him for his side of the story. He was certainly one of the best Sikorsky engineers and loadmasters and I was very lucky to work with him ...

The final note: not only was my dad found after 11 days with a tan, but he was also clean shaved, and that's why mother got me a battery razor the year I started flying in NWT.[39]

Although Okanagan Helicopters was growing year by the year, they were beginning to face competition, especially in the West where Vancouver Island Helicopters (VIH) had signed contracts with forestry companies, and Pacific Western Airlines (PWA), where Bill McLeod, now manager, was using helicopters to work on the Bennett Dam in the Peace River area. Later PWA, which also had a large fleet of fixed-wing aircraft moving crews and materials around the DEW Line (Distant Early Warning) sites, opted to stick with fixed-wing and sold off its bush operation, including its helicopters.

1956 ANNUAL REPORT

In spite of the competition, by the end of 1956 Okanagan Helicopters had become the world's largest commercial helicopter operator with a fleet of 36 machines: one S-58, 13 S-55s (10 RCAF and 3 Okanagan) and 22 Bell 47s, most of them converted to G-2 models with the more powerful Lycoming engine. The company's four-passenger Bell 47 Ranger was in use on the Trans Mountain pipeline to provide a better inspection platform, while four of the S-55s and four of the Bell 47s were at work on the Mid-Canada line. That year,

Trans Mountain Pipe Line from Edmonton to Vancouver, a distance of 712 miles (1,145.8 kilometres):

Number of patrols	355
Hours flown	1,234.5
Days down	380
Take offs and landings	1,415
Miles of pipeline patrolled	805.1

▶ Igor Sikorsky says farewell to Okanagan Helicopters chief pilot Fred Snell in 1956 at the Sikorsky plant in Stratford, Connecticut. PHOTO COURTESY OF JACK MILBURN

working in seven of Canada's ten provinces, Okanagan machines had flown 16,000 hours, for a grand total of 48,000 to date. The company had increased staff to 108 with 12 new pilots in training in Penticton.

In a sign of recognition, that fall Igor Sikorsky paid a surprise visit to the board of directors at the company's annual general meeting in Vancouver, and at the annual convention of the Helicopter Association of America (HAA) held in San Francisco, Carl Agar was elected as its first non-American president.

▲ Igor Sikorsky visits Okanagan Helicopters in Vancouver. PHOTO COURTESY OF GORDON ASKIN

1957

As the new year began, Okanagan Helicopters joined other operators in filing a complaint with the Conservative government's Minister of Transport, George Hees, about a new commercial aviation policy that allowed start-up companies to bid on government contracts before they had bought any aircraft or hired any crews. The established operators were concerned that this would compromise safety by allowing small, one-man operations with no backup and limited staff to cut corners on maintenance and use unqualified crews when under the pressure of deadlines.

The Okanagan name began appearing in advertisements for aviation products in magazines such as *Canadian Aviation* where an ad for a hose-line replacement showed a Bell 47 on floats with the name "Okanagan" written on it. The caption read: "We use Aeroquip exclusively on our helicopter fleet" and quoted Alf Stringer, as vice-president in charge of operations.

Nine Okanagan helicopters continued work on the Mid-Canada Line, an S-55 was still involved in mineral development with Canadian Nickel in northern Manitoba, and a new venture, fire lookouts, would eventually become a regular contract with the BC Forest Service. The company fleet was also busy with aerial surveys for forestry companies, geological surveys for oil and gas exploration and mining companies, an electro-magnetic survey, several hydroelectric surveys and railroad construction. Another new project was taking soundings on the St. Lawrence River at Lachine Rapids to measure the water depth to update navigation charts. The S-58 was the only machine that could take the strain in this operation, which involved carrying a four-man crew plus equipment consisting of a 600-pound (272-kilogram) winch, two 100-pound (45-kilogram) batteries and spare cable while hovering for approximately an hour and 15 minutes at an altitude of 300–1,300 feet (90–400 metres). The technique involved dropping a weighted wire into the water every 1,500 feet (456 metres). A red marker was attached 150 feet (45 metres) above the weight, and when the weight touched bottom, the slip clutch on the winch was turned on and the helicopter lifted up until the clutch indicated it was slipping. The radio operator in the cabin then gave the pilot a signal to stop and notified the land station, which in turn, signalled the three other stations to transmit readings on the marker and calculate the depth at that point.

1957 ANNUAL REPORT

By 1957 the hourly cost of hiring a helicopter had increased to $105 for the Bell 47D, $230 for an S-55 and $480 for the S-58. Monthly charges ranged from $5,000 plus $17 per hour for a Bell up to $15,000 plus $40 per hour for the S-55 and $30,000 per month plus $95 per hour for the S-58. The year-end report showed that both revenue and profit had increased, and annual total flying hours had reached 22,000. During the year the company had trained 14 new pilots in Penticton and increased its fleet to 48, now made up of one S-58, 21 S-55s and 26 Bell 47s.

1958

In mid-July 1958 at the annual Farnborough Airshow—it would not become biennial until 1962—Fairey Aviation demonstrated the world's first vertical takeoff transporter. The VTOL (vertical takeoff and landing) Rotodyne was powered by two Napier Eland turboprop engines, which together delivered 7,000 horsepower, allowing it to carry 48 passengers or five tons (4.5 metric tonnes) of freight. The pilot demonstrated its horizontal and vertical manoeuvrability turning at high speed and coming in for a vertical landing with the gear up until it was just inches from the ground. Impressed, Okanagan's management placed an order for three with the expectation of taking delivery within two to three years, although the purchase was dependent on its performance in a number of tests still to be undertaken by Fairey Aviation. However, a feasibility study carried out in Vancouver later in the year indicated that the Rotodyne would be ideal for a scheduled service between Vancouver, Victoria and Seattle.

*

On July 4, Bell 47 CF-HNW with pilot M. Hern and engineer Ron Sturges aboard left Kamloops to fly to Tuktoyaktuk on the shores of the Arctic Ocean about 200 miles (320 kilometres) east of the Alaska border. The purpose of the 1,864-mile (3,000-kilometre) flight was to support DEW Line supply ships. Hern and Sturges documented their trip in an internal report entitled "Diary of the Sea Lift to DEW Line: Summer 1958." In it they described how, while en route to the Arctic, they stopped in Fort St. John to have floats installed before carrying on to Fort Good Hope. They arrived in Tuktoyaktuk on July 9:

> July 10: Took Captain Thomas onto LST [Landing Ship, Tank] 692, also R. Sturges and gear, following inspection of landing area amidships.
> July 12: Did first reconn flight, spotted numerous floes, some rotten ice, some arctic blue. Saw numerous seals about 20 NE of ship. Sea temp. reported at 32°F.
> July 13: Took 1st Mate on ice reconn early AM. Ships obscured by a fog patch about 4 miles square. Using 423 for ADF [automatic direction finder], which worked well. Took 3rd Mate on trip, good vis but too much ice for ship to make much headway. Radio (on ship) failed to reach A/C [aircraft], but relayed through other ship.
> July 15: Numerous ice floes laying around the ship, present position NE point Bathurst. Right mag. went U/S [unserviceable]. Ron working most of night.
> July 16: Fog off and on all day. ADF proved invaluable. Ship stopped by heavy ice in evening.
> July 23: Reached Pin A, caught up [US Coast Guard cutter] *Storis*, LST 1072 and *Chastity*. Went up to Site to clear deck for unloading.
> July 24: Anchored. Visited 1072; seems in good shape by our standard.
> July 27: Reached Pin C. Took Capt. on harbour flight. Many Eskimos reported to have died here some years ago. Skeleton remains lying about. Re-erected one of the radar beacons on site but couldn't be seen from ship. Lately skyline refraction makes things appear larger on horizon, also creates impression of solid ice where none exists. Temp. here today 69°F, quite a heat wave.

August 3: Ship arrived Tuk. Windy and warm.
August 8: Left Tuk.
August 12: J. model from US Coast Guard cutter *Storis* visited flight deck. Now 3 ships in convoy.
August 14: Large puddled ice field with *Storis* pushing a path through. No definite leads in ice field. Our charts in error Etah Island area. Simpson Strait observed open. Storis plotting new shoal area NE of Hat Island.[40]

Meanwhile, Okanagan's Mid-Canada Line contract had been extended for another year, and the RCAF provided four S-55s for the job to replace the company machines that were required for other contracts.

In western Canada 1958 was one of the worst forest fire years on record, with 4,000 fires burning over 2 million acres. The year also saw a helicopter water tanker used for aerial firefighting for the first time after Okanagan's engineering group fitted a 225-gallon (850-litre) tank into the cabin of an S-58; the tank was given specially designed plumbing and a discharge nozzle fitted underneath the belly. Later, to give the machine more flexibility, they developed an aluminum tank and slung it under the machine's fuselage; it was first used on fires near the headwaters of Ashlu Creek and Squamish River, north of Vancouver. Now besides being able to land crews close to fires quickly, the S-58 was able to fight the fire with water dumps, scoring direct hits almost every time. Donald Owen, a forest protection officer, described the S-58 as a great addition to firefighting.[41]

1958 ANNUAL REPORT
In the course of the year, Okanagan had acquired four more Bell 47G-2s, making a total of 52 machines operating across Canada, and they flew 24,000 hours, an increase of 2,000 over the previous year.

At year-end Douglas Dewar retired as chairman of the board.

◂ Four new Bell 47s leave Bell's plant in Fort Worth, Texas, for Vancouver in 1958. Pilots: C. Weir, Jack Godsey, Bill Pinner, Jack Milburn; engineer: Ed Brown. PHOTO COURTESY OF JACK MILBURN

1959

The late 1950s had seen a number of important technical developments in the helicopter industry and many of them went on display in 1959. On January 6, Hiller Helicopters was awarded its first FAA (Federal Aviation Agency—now the Federal Aviation Administration) certificate for its three-seater 12E, a more powerful version of the US Army's "Raven" helicopter. It had a 305 horsepower Lycoming engine, and at 2,700 pounds gross weight, it carried a payload of 1,000 pounds (453.6 kilograms), had a ceiling of 16,200 feet (4,937.7 metres), and a hover ceiling of 9,500 feet (2,896 metres). In the UK, Fairey Aviation announced that the Rotodyne had established a world speed record when it flew a 60-mile (100-kilometre) circuit at an average speed of 190.9 mph (307.2 km/h).

The 1959 Farnborough Airshow saw the first public appearance of Saunders-Roe's P531, a five-seater gas turbine helicopter powered by the 425 horsepower Blackburn Turbomeca Turmo engine. Cessna also entered the commercial helicopter market with the YH-41, a four-seater that had been designed for military use and powered by a 270 horsepower Continental piston engine. Two years previously, the YH-41 had established world altitude records of 29,777 feet (9,076 metres) and 28,090 feet (8,561.8 metres) in various weight categories.

In February 1959 it was apparent that Carl Agar was looking to the future when he was interviewed by a reporter for the *American Helicopter Society Newsletter*:

> The equipment situation keeps changing so rapidly that it's hard to tell exactly what will be needed in the future. [Carl] believes, however, that there will always be a place for the small helicopter such as the Bell and the larger craft such as the S-58 which, he says, "is the first helicopter ever to give us a surplus of power needed for operation in high and rough terrain."
>
> [He] foresees a need for a flying crane . . . that maybe . . . ought to look like a crane and not necessarily like a helicopter. "There's nothing beautiful about an oil rig . . . It's built for strength. So there's no need to build something that looks like Marilyn Monroe to carry it around."[42]

In 1959 Okanagan carried out "Operation Skyhook" for the Southern California Edison Company, to discover whether using helicopters to build a power line was economically viable in difficult terrain. The experiment involved the construction of a 12,000-volt power line in Soledad Canyon, northeast of Los Angeles, up to the US Navy's radar station on top of Pleasants Peak. Two large buckets, each capable of lifting a ton of concrete, were modified for the Sikorsky S-58, and the helicopter's job was to pour 106 concrete bases and then insert the 40-foot-long (12-metre-long) wooden poles complete with cross arms and insulators into them. As each pole site required a perfectly level platform, a hopper or vertical chute was placed over the hole prepared for the pole, while in the helicopter the engineer lay on the cabin floor and, peering out through the open door, gave instructions to the pilot over the aircraft's intercom system. On completion of the pour, the machine returned to the base camp where the bucket was dropped and the pole picked up, using a hook designed for the US Marine Corps and lent to Edison for this trial. The entire operation was carried out without the machine landing except for refuelling.

The next part of the operation involved the steel rigging. The helicopter placed bundles of steel, each weighing 3,000 pounds (1,360 kilograms), at marked intervals along with the required hardware. The riggers, who were transported to the site by the S-58, set the line in place on the ground using a gin pole (a rigid pole with a pulley attachment used for lifting) while the hovering helicopter manoeuvred the pole upright. Once the tower was in place, the gin pole was dropped to the ground and the helicopter picked up the long lead and moved to the next site. The operation, which initially took about 25 minutes, was eventually reduced to 10 to 15 minutes, proving helicopters to be cost effective for a project in difficult terrain.

At home BC Telephone chartered a Bell 47 to put technicians onto the top of Lost Mountain near Salmo after a snowstorm damaged its tower there and disrupted service in the West Kootenay area. The technicians were transported by helicopter from Trail to the site in 40 minutes, a journey that would have taken 18 hours if they had relied on snowplows and snowshoes.

Over the summer, Okanagan again had a contract for Northern Transportation's "Sealift" operation in the Arctic, this time using two Bell 47G models. CF-HNV was crewed by pilot Bill Marsh and engineer Al Hambleton and CF-HUD by pilot Bob Roberts and engineer Roy Robson. Dispatched from Toronto to Tuktoyaktuk, a distance of 3,960 miles (6,373 kilometres), the helicopters left within two days of each other in mid-June, flying via Fort Nelson, Norman Wells and Inuvik and arriving at Tuktoyaktuk on July 10 and 12 respectively. CF-HNV was assigned to supply the vessel LST-1072 under Captain Allen and CF-HUD to LST-692 under Captain Thomas. The operation encountered the usual Arctic conditions—poor weather, fog, ice floes, poor radio reception and wide temperature variations—but there was little evidence of the musk ox, seals, polar bears and whales seen the previous year. However, radio reception in the Arctic conditions was improved with a new Sunair HF transceiver that worked exceptionally well to provide long-range communications, and the helicopter crews found the best solution to corrosion problems that had plagued their machines the previous year was to periodically wash them down with warm fresh water.

Meanwhile, S-58 CF-JIB and Bell 47G-2 CF-LRE had been contracted to move a diamond drilling camp from Mile 397 to Mile 442 on the Alaska Highway, north of Fort Nelson. Problems arose at one of the sites when the S-58 was unable to land due to the 45-degree slope of the landing strip. Even the smaller Bell had only two feet of blade clearance on the uphill side of this strip. The solution involved using the Bell 47 to move cargo from the S-58's landing site up to the 3,000-foot (915-metre) level. In this way the operation moved 21,800 pounds (9,890 kilograms) of equipment and 12 passengers in just two hours 22 minutes. On completion of that job, the S-58 moved to the Drayton Valley, 70 miles (112 kilometres) southwest of Edmonton, for an Imperial Oil contract carrying the microbar mud used to seal gas pockets during drilling operations. Flying 17 trips in 10 hours 35 minutes over a period of two days, the helicopter carried 61,200 pounds (27,760 kilograms) of mud and three passengers in 40-mile (64-kilometre) round trips.

In May pilot Ray McGowan and engineer Bill Foote were assigned to take Bell 47 CF-LCL on a five-month bush contract with an oil company's crew into the Northwest Territories. The report Ray prepared after this assignment was published as "The Way it Was" in *RotorTales* Volume 2 in 1981. He and Bill set off from Vancouver on May 23, 1959, and on the way to their initial destination, Cli Lake, Northwest Territories, they encountered strong headwinds in central BC's Cariboo and heavy snow in the Prince George area, leading inevitably to delays. In Cli Lake they met the oil company team, which consisted of geologists, a student, a cook and a camp helper as well as the pilot of the Beaver floatplane that would work with them. Work began on May 29 with the helicopter transporting the crew and their emergency gear out to the field in the morning and picking them up in the late afternoon. The treeline on the mountains that surround Cli Lake is around the 3,000-foot (915-metre) level so there were plenty of landing sites, but while some of the countryside was ideal for operating helicopters, other areas were much tougher with muskeg, heavily treed mountainsides and steep slopes above narrow, winding creek beds.

Ray's report describes the day-to-day routine of the camp, moving the crew to new camps and establishing fuel caches, and he comments on the welcome visits of people passing through and the arrival of new crew members as well as the importance of mail day to those in the isolation of the bush. The weather was a constant challenge. He describes an unexpected delay on June 5:

> While waiting [for the crew] out in the bush, the weather started to deteriorate very fast, and by the time they arrived, I could not take off, so we sat on the ground for about six hours waiting for the storm to pass. When we got airborne, the temperature had dropped to 25°F [-3.9°C] and the airspeed was up to 70 mph [112 km/h]. There was also driving snow, which froze to the helicopter upon contact. I would like to mention that the emergency stove proved invaluable in keeping us warm during our wait and also after when we had to melt the snow that was completely blocking the pilot's pitot tube [the pressure measurement device that provides the pilot with air speed]. I always make sure that I have it with me on all my flights ... It was touch and go whether the machine would start after six hours in freezing weather; luckily it did.

By early July temperatures were hitting 90°F (32°C), creating problems for helicopter performance at elevations of 3,000 feet (915 metres) and above and resulting in reduced loads. They also began to see forest fires in the distance, and Ray writes that after one flight:

> When I arrived at the base camp, I had picked up a load of bugs on the main rotor. It really aggravates the poor performance characteristics, so I must keep a closer watch for things like that from now on, as I could easily have gotten into trouble.

Rain finally arrived a week or so later, bringing cooler temperatures, putting out the fires. However, in addition to the plagues of mosquitoes and black flies, they had ongoing encounters with larger wildlife, including a big stag caribou on June 26:

> He was determined I wasn't going to land on his mountaintop, and every spot I picked to land he charged into the machine. Needless to say, the caribou won out as I could just picture the helicopter if he ran into the main rotor.

A few days later three grizzly bears came into the camp, and Ray had to chase them off with the helicopter. But this was not his last encounter with bears:

> I left CF-LCL at Iverson [base at Iverson Lake] ... riding back and forth in the Beaver to save time on the helicopter ... Have been weathered in for the past two days, and we went to get the helicopter and bad news: we found CF-LCL badly damaged by bears. The doors were ripped off, the bubble smashed and hoses and wires ripped out of the engine. I will be flying to Smith River in the Beaver tomorrow to call Vancouver. Bill Foote and one geologist will camp near the machine to prevent any further damage.

The bear was eventually tracked down and shot when it was found to have a bad gash on its front leg where it had gone through the bubble.

Routine helicopter maintenance was a challenge in the bush as parts had to be flown in on the supply runs, potentially grounding the helicopter while they waited. Engineer Bill Foote had already coped with the replacement of the rotor tachometer, which indicates the rotor RPMs, as well as the routine replacement of the tail-rotor pitch bearings. The repairs to the bear-damaged helicopter, however, were a much bigger problem, though he managed to repair it sufficiently for Ray to ferry it to Fort Simpson for major repairs, including replacement of the bubble. Ray describes the flight:

> It was quite an experience but all worked out well. Forty miles per hour [64 km/h] proved to be the most comfortable speed and also the fastest cruising speed we could get using normal cruise power.

The regularly scheduled airline flight arrived in Fort Simpson two days later with replacement parts, minus the bubble, which arrived a week later, and by noon the following day the helicopter was back in business. On the morning of August 13 the helicopter began moving the camp to Wrigley Lake, north of Fort Simpson, for the last campsite of the year. Ray describes the area as:

> ...good helicopter country with the highest mountains being around 7,000 feet [2,135 m] [and the] campsite . . . on hard rock, which is a nice change from muskeg. It's quite cold these days, and the mosquito season seems to be over.

A few days later the office tent burned down. Nothing of value was lost although the tent normally contained all the records of the summer's work. By late August snow and strong north winds had returned, and the shortening days made Bill's routine maintenance more difficult. By the end of the month there had been two days of snow, effectively ending the geologists' work. On September 8, Ray flew the head geologist to Norman Wells, a 175-mile (282-kilometre) trip that required visiting a fuel cache at the halfway point. They returned to Wrigley Lake the next day in time for the crew to catch the oil company's Boeing back to Edmonton.

With the contract completed, Ray and Bill began their ferrying flight south, but upon arriving in Fort Simpson, they received instructions to proceed to Nahanni Butte, about 140 miles (87 kilometres) to the southwest. There they were told they were to fly on to Fort Providence for three days' work with another company. The accommodations were an improvement over their last job, the only challenge here being the constant strong westerly winds. Ray noted that, "the flight from Fort Providence to Great Slave Lake took 1:50 while the return flight was 40 minutes."[43]

By September 16, with that job complete, they began the ferry flight south again but ran into strong headwinds all the way to Dawson Creek, where they received instructions to proceed to Fort St. John where Ray was to fill in as base pilot while Bill proceeded to the Clear Hill area to relieve the engineer. Finally, on September 26 CF-LCL re-started the ferry flight home. At Prince George, they met an Okanagan machine piloted by Egan Agar, and the two machines flew south together, arriving in Vancouver on September 27.

After working for Okanagan Helicopters as a pilot from 1958 to 1961, Ray McGowan went on to become an inspector with Transport Canada, and one of his duties was to conduct annual proficiency checks on Okanagan Helicopters' pilots in the Pacific region.

*

That summer Okanagan crews also participated in a number of rescue flights in western Canada. Dexter Dimick and Dave Waterhouse rescued five people whose aircraft had crashed 60 miles (100 kilometres) south of Fort McMurray. Pilot Jim Grady rescued a lost hunter west of 100 Mile House, and Ken Carlson brought an injured person through a fierce snowstorm to the hospital at Hinton, Alberta. North of Vancouver, Bud Tillotson spent a day searching Mount Seymour for a missing hiker without success.

1959 ANNUAL REPORT
This final year of the decade saw Okanagan Helicopters acquire the assets and equipment of Pacific Helicopters, but at the same time the company sold United Helicopters to Eastern Provincial Airways. Okanagan also began providing third party maintenance for small operators with limited maintenance facilities, beginning with a Canadian Aero Service s-55 that arrived from Alaska for a 1,000-hour inspection. At the Penticton Mountain Flying School pilot Bud Tillotson took over as the chief instructor after incumbent Don Poole took a job flying on Baffin Island. And Okanagan continued its move into the logging industry when, on November 4, pilot Doug Callin and engineer Ev Cameron demonstrated Bell 47 CF-FJA to attest to the potential and adaptability of helicopters to an ever-wider range of operations.

The decade had seen a dramatic increase in the size of the company's fleet and, with the introduction of the s-58, in its lift capacity as well. Although the Alcan contract had concluded, the company had signed on to a wider range of projects from construction of the Mid-Canada Line and the Trans Mountain pipeline to forestry, geological and wildlife surveys. It had gone from a small provincial company to one capable of operating right across the country as it expanded into the eastern Canadian market and operated from Newfoundland to the High Arctic.

By the end of 1959 Okanagan had a fleet of 54 machines flying just under 25,000 hours annually.

Okanagan Helicopter profits as presented in the company's annual reports:

1951	$58,000
1953	$93,000
1955	$127,000
1957	$312,568
1958	$254,412
1959	$282,659

Chapter Three

THE 1960s

1960

The 1960s saw a continuation of the technical improvements to helicopters that had occurred in the previous decade. In January 1960 Glenn McPherson and Fred Snell attended the 12th annual convention of the Helicopter Association of America in Anaheim, California, to investigate the new equipment promoted by manufacturers such as Sikorsky, Bell, Hiller, Cessna, Hughes and Brantly. Sikorsky presented a cargo hook for the S-58 and a power line–laying dispenser that could hold around 8,000 feet (2,440 metres) of cable, ideal for the transmission line installation projects on the horizon for Okanagan Helicopters in Canada. Hughes demonstrated its 269A, a two-seater machine and announced the development of a four-seater machine with the new Lycoming 540-horsepower turbo-charged engine; it was expected to be on the market by the end of the year along with a supercharger kit that would be available for current Hiller UH-12E operators. Hiller showed off its latest UH-12E agricultural model with a 50-gallon tank and spray booms as well as an executive model with a plush interior and soundproofing. Glenn and Fred also visited the Hiller plant in Palo Alto, and although they didn't commit to purchasing a UH-12E, they enrolled Jack Rich, one of Okanagan's engineers, in a three-week course on the machine.

In Edmonton, Don Poole and new pilot Don MacKenzie evaluated the "Jaycopter" simulator to determine if it could be used to train students; it was capable of copying the helicopter in many aspects except airspeed, rate of climb and descent. In addition, pilot Bud Tillotson and engineer Howie Gatin visited the Cessna factory in Wichita, Kansas, to evaluate their latest helicopter, the Skyhook, a four-seat rotary-wing aircraft powered by a 270-horsepower supercharged Lycoming, which gave it full power at 8,000 feet (2,440 metres). In his report to Okanagan, Bud gave it high marks for its roomy cockpit with its excellent visibility, well-laid-out instrumentation and its flight controls, which had a mechanical gyro connected to the lateral hydraulics for stabilization. The utility model provided removable seats and a collapsible internal cargo deck. He found it was relatively stable in minor turbulence and there was little difference in its centre of gravity whether occupied or empty. On the negative side, however, the machine had problems in rough terrain with poor visibility on landing, poor ground clearance on rough surfaces, and rotor blades that drooped to shoulder level when slowing down. He felt that the Skyhook had potential for operations such as magnetometer surveys and patrol work and that its performance was on par with the Hiller UH-12E up to 4,000 feet (1,220 metres); above that altitude, however, the Skyhook was superior to the UH-12E, taking into account the former's heavier gross weight. Cessna agreed to test the machine in the mountains and made plans to bring a Skyhook to Vancouver the following April.

Meanwhile, in June a Hiller UH-12E set an altitude record during the rescue of two injured climbers from the 18,000-foot (5,485 metre) level of Mount McKinley (now Denali) in Alaska. The pilot, Link Luckett, who operated a charter service out of Anchorage, flew to the base camp at 10,200 feet (3,110 metres). Then to prepare the helicopter for the next leg, he reduced the fuel supply to 10 gallons (38 litres), giving him just 20 to 30 minutes flying time, removed the 28-pound (13-kilogram) battery and took off one door so that he could throw out smoke bombs to determine wind direction. In spite of wind turbulence, he was able to airlift the first climber, who had a broken leg, then return for the second. The trip from the 10,200- to 18,000-foot (3,110- to 5,485-metre) level and back took 30 minutes. Luckett was awarded the silver Carnegie Medal for heroism.

*

Early in the year, due to increased demand for communication in the North, Okanagan opened its first radio shop. The first radio tech, Dick Browne, was nicknamed "Smokey" because of the number of high frequency (HF) transmitters that went up in smoke when installed in helicopters. His assistant was George Annesty. At that time radio equipment was bulky and heavy due to the use of vacuum tubes. Reliable equipment for helicopters would not be available for another ten years, and by then the radio/electrical man would be known as the avionics (aviation electronics) technician.

The company continued to increase the number of aircraft and scope of its operations in 1960, building on existing contracts in the North and elsewhere for geological surveys and exploration. BC Telephone (now Telus) was using Okanagan's Bell 47G-2 by this time to take servicing personnel to the thirteen remote microwave towers across the province that carried its long-distance telephone traffic and network television programs.

Meanwhile, Okanagan's order for the Fairey Rotodyne they had planned to use for a Vancouver-to-Victoria commuter flight was cancelled after the British government cut two aviation industry defence contracts; this cutback precipitated the merger of Fairey Aviation, the Bristol Aeroplane Company, Saunders-Roe and Westland Aircraft. At the same time a decline in orders for Fairey's Rotodyne resulted in it being scrapped. The only piece of that machine still in existence is the cabin section that is on display at the Helicopter Museum in Weston-super-Mare, Somerset.

In spite of this setback, however, Okanagan's interest in setting up a commuter service between Victoria and Vancouver continued, and in the spring of 1960 it became known that the company was negotiating a merger with the Canadian division of the Bristol Aeroplane Company in Winnipeg in order to get the $3 to $4 million necessary to finance it. This time the plan was to use helicopters for the service, and in April a Sikorsky S-62 crewed by pilot Bryce Firmingham and engineer John Martin arrived in Vancouver to give a demonstration as a possible contender for the job. The machine was accompanied by the Sikorsky sales team as well as representatives from General Electric, which supplied the S-62's engines (T58-GE-8B). Over the S-62's six-day visit, it carried out 39 flights to demonstrate its performance to 305 passengers from Victoria, Duncan, Vancouver and New Westminster, most of them civic officials and representatives of local businesses. They assembled in the lobby of the Empress Hotel in Victoria to be taken aboard the S-62, where they experienced a smooth, quiet takeoff and cruised at an average speed of 100 knots (185 km/h). Arriving at the downtown Vancouver landing site near the meeting of Pender and Georgia streets, they disembarked and walked across the street to the lobby of a nearby hotel. The total time from Victoria to Vancouver was just under 40 minutes.

For employees of Okanagan Helicopters who had not been present during the visit by the Sikorsky, Jock Graham, who was now with Pratt & Whitney, wrote an article that appeared in the company's newsletter the following month:

> The recent successful demonstration of the Sikorsky S-62 turbine-powered helicopter in the Vancouver area was the first link in a chain which will eventually connect downtown Vancouver with downtown Victoria... The S-62 is the little brother of the S-61 helicopter, the latter being a twin-turbine, 28-passenger model, which should be available for commercial service in mid '61.[44]

On the operations front, 1960 began with an emergency search when on January 17 an Okanagan S-58 flying from Hopedale to Goose Bay, Labrador, was forced to land due to freezing rain. Pilot Harvey Easton and his eight passengers spent three days and two nights in the bush before they were able to continue. During that time they tried out the machine's new emergency kit, which proved itself—although the flares were a problem. When debriefed after the adventure, they recommended the addition of a tent to the kit, as they felt it would have been much warmer than sleeping in the helicopter cabin.

On March 15, at approximately 3:00 pm, a US Air Force Lockheed U-2 crashed somewhere in mid- to southern Manitoba. It had lost power in the High Arctic, and the pilot tried to make the USAF base in Grand Forks, North Dakota, but due to headwinds its glide path was cut short, and it was forced to land on a frozen lake. As Cranberry Portage, the RCAF's Mid-Canada Line sector control station, was close to the most likely crash site, Lake Athapapuskow, Okanagan's Sikorsky S-55 CF-JTE, the resident helicopter, was scrambled at 4:25 pm. Pilot J.P. Smith, engineer Dayton Reid and spotter E. McNair were instructed to proceed to the area where the pilot was thought to have ejected and parachuted, after which they were to contact a USAF C-54 for further search orders. However, while proceeding toward La Ronge for refuelling, the helicopter crew noticed an unidentified object on the ground just west of Lake Wapawekka and altered course to port to get a better look. As they closed in, they saw the U-2's tail fin and the waving pilot and contacted the search aircraft. They landed at 6:05 pm, just 2 hours and 35 minutes after the U-2 touched down, and flew the pilot to Cranberry Portage, landing there at 8:45 pm. Crews from the USAF were brought in to make repairs to the U-2 on site, and they flew it out under its own power.

In another rescue the Okanagan crew of Bill Brooks and Greg Temperley were called out on May 6. When it was over, W.R. MacBrien of North American Air Defense Command, sent the following letter:

> I wish to express my appreciation for the way Mr. W. Brooks, a helicopter pilot with Okanagan Helicopters, contributed to the rescue of Mr. J. Hambrook, a forest fire casualty. Mr. Brooks undertook this flight at night, landed in a small clearing in the forest fire area and lifted Mr. Hambrook to safety and back to Dawson Creek. His speedy and forthright action doubtlessly contributed to Mr. Hambrook's survival.
>
> Such demonstration of personal initiative and concern for the welfare of others brings a feeling of satisfaction to all . . . Mr. Brooks will be made aware of my appreciation through the Commanding Officer of RCAF Station, Dawson Creek.
>
> (Signed) W.R. MacBrien, Air Officer Commanding, Air Defense Command

Sadly, by 1960 Carl Agar's health had begun to deteriorate. He was diagnosed with emphysema, raising questions about the impact of his days of spraying from an open cockpit.

Hiller 12-E pilot Bill Janicke (left) and engineer Mark Valpy. PHOTO COURTESY OF JACK MILBURN

1960 ANNUAL REPORT
Over the year the fleet had grown from 54 to 63. It now consisted of three s-58s, 21 s-55s, 36 Bell 47s and three Hiller UH-12Es. Then in December, management announced the purchase of an s-62 to operate out of Goose Bay, Labrador. Flight hours increased to 26,000 in 1960, giving the company in excess of 150,000 hours of total operating time. Okanagan opened a new base at Fort St. John, BC, while in Montreal, Canadian Helicopters inaugurated the first aerial traffic report in the country.

1961

In January 1961 Okanagan Helicopter's commuter service between Vancouver and Victoria moved a step closer toward reality when the company filed an application to the Air Transport Board. *Sikorsky News*, announcing Okanagan's recent acquisition of an s-62 for this service, advised its readers that:

> Okanagan, one of the world's largest helicopter operators, has made an application to the Air Transport Board of Canada for a license to operate a passenger service between the two [BC] cities. However, action on the application has been delayed in order that satisfactory equipment with complete instrumentation may be selected and downtown heliports established. Acquisition of the S-62 is described by Okanagan as a progressive step in the inauguration of the service while equipment, operating and economic studies are made of larger twin-turbine helicopters. The Sikorsky S-61L is under active consideration by Okanagan in this connection.[45]

Unfortunately, shortly after that announcement the proposed merger of Okanagan Helicopters with Bristol fell through. Okanagan was forced to abandon the commuter project because of cost, Department of Transport regulations and concern about single-engine performance over water. The company did not look at the idea of a regular service between Vancouver and Victoria again until 1985, basing the project this time on using an s-61 (twin-engine), but after a feasibility study decided against it. Helijet did start the service a year later using a Bell 412 and later a Sikorsky s-76.

Meanwhile, CF-OKA, the s-62 that had been sent to work in the Goose Bay area on contract to the Newfoundland Telephone Company and on the Pinetree Line at Hopedale, Labrador, was found unsuitable because, given the fuel it required, the distances were too great to allow it to carry a reasonable payload. It seemed that the "Finger Ferrets," as Alf Stringer referred to the company's accountants, had miscalculated. As a result, CF-OKA was returned to Sikorsky and a new s-58, CF-LWC, replaced it on the Pinetree contract, which was extended to six years.

Tragically, on July 3 Okanagan s-58 CF-LWC went missing on a flight between Cartwright and Goose Bay, Labrador, with pilot Bud Pearson and six passengers on board. The official search was called off on August 1 but continued on a limited basis, and some months later a local hunter spotted the wreckage of the bright orange machine below the water of a remote lake. The subsequent investigation determined that it had suffered an engine failure. There were no survivors.

More routinely, in June the three Hiller UH-12E helicopters added to the fleet the previous year were assigned to install an air raid warning siren in West Vancouver. That same month the company went back to the Arctic with an s-62 and two s-55s to carry out an aerial survey based in Resolute Bay. These helicopters were expected to reach close to the North Pole. In the meantime, in Resolute, pilot Dave Alder and engineer Bill Foote, flying Bell 47 CF-JYQ, developed engine problems due to a broken impulse drive unit, and although the pilot carried out a successful auto rotation, on landing, the main blades and tail rotor were damaged. Fortunately, the replacement parts were flown north by Wardair's Bristol Freighter, and the machine was back in service after only eight days.

On November 30, 1961, Carl Agar submitted his letter of resignation to the board of directors. In it, he praised the morale of the staff over the years but said that it had recently declined because, in his view, the company was now run by a small dictatorship. He felt management was putting the blame for financial problems on the engineering department and targeting Alf Stringer in particular. Because of his illness, Carl felt he was no longer strong enough to put up a fight and had decided to resign. At a special meeting called by the board of directors, Alf presented an analysis of the negative impact caused by a number of management decisions that both he and Carl had opposed. Glenn McPherson offered to resign, but a compromise was reached: Carl agreed to a three-month leave of absence, Alf and Glenn would remain on the board, and a management consultant would conduct a study and come up with recommendations. In the end Carl remained on the board to act as a consultant while Fred Snell became vice-president in charge of operations.

1961 ANNUAL REPORT
During the year, the company had continued to operate 64 helicopters, which flew 27,000 hours, while revenue and profits had continued to rise. Bases were opened in Nelson, Kamloops and Prince George, while the Canadian Helicopters facility at the Toronto Island Airport was closed and that operation moved to Dorval, Quebec. A number of new opportunities had arisen for the company, including a service contract with Shell Oil Company for the offshore exploration of 13 million acres (5.3 million hectares) of British Columbia's continental shelf.

1962

Okanagan's contract for work on the Mid-Canada Line, which the company had held since 1956, was not renewed in 1962 and instead went to an eastern competitor. This resulted in the removal of 14 government-owned s-55s from the company's equipment roster, leaving a fleet of 52 helicopters, including five new Hiller UH-12Bs for a total of eight, three Bell 47G-3Bs, and Canadian Helicopters' new Bell 47J model. Loss of the contract also resulted in a 30 percent reduction in staff and closure of the Ottawa office, but management predicted that these two moves would increase net profits for 1962/63; instead, at year-end 1962 the company reported a loss. Out of this situation arose the concept of regional self-sustaining bases, suggested by the employees themselves.

Don MacKenzie, who later became the company's chief pilot, remembered:

> That was a tough year, 1962. We had our very first lay-offs. And the first guys in from the bush at the end of the summer got laid off. We all tried to jockey for position. I think it was the only year in memory when people actually tried to stay in the bush... A number of us decided that, instead of sitting at home licking our wounds, we should bloody well do something. So we said to the company, "Give us a machine and we'll go out and try to get some work for it." Glenn McPherson, the president, was apprehensive at first but eventually agreed, and I took a machine and went up to Squamish and worked out of a resort called Paradise Valley, flying skiers to Diamond Head and Whistler, doing a bit of hydro work, an occasional trip for Highways and BC Rail—that sort of thing. It tided us over the winter months.[46]

Ground maintenance personnel also came up with a number of innovations, including a hydro-line stringer underslung on an S-58. They pioneered the technique in the Peace River and Columbia River areas then moved it to a power-line project near Rocky Mountain House, Alberta, which entailed erecting aluminum towers, each one of them 90 feet (27.5 metres) tall and weighing 3,000 pounds (1,360 kilograms). Okanagan was also involved in the construction of transmission lines through Banff National Park; using an S-58, crews erected a 34-kilovolt line and eight miles (13 kilometres) of H-frame structures between Banff and Lake Louise in two or three weeks. In the Ashcroft area of BC they erected 119 power poles, each weighing about 3,400 pounds (1,540 kilograms), 33 of them in very difficult terrain. Similar projects were carried out in Cranbrook and Prince Rupert. The crews also experimented with airlifting prefab housing units, weighing about 1,100 pounds (500 kilograms) and measuring 10 by 10 feet (three by three metres); these buildings were suitable for ski cabins, bunkhouses and line camps and could be moved onto other sites.

In early 1962 the BC Forest Service awarded Okanagan a five-month contract to supply 12 helicopters for forest fire protection and suppression. Firefighting had already been greatly assisted by an invention originating at the company's new base in Nelson, BC, where pilot Jim Grady and local machine shop owner Henry Stevenson had come up with the "Monzoon Bucket." Initially it was just a 45-gallon (170-litre) drum with a basketball plugging a hole in the bottom. While hovering over a fire, the pilot would pull a line attached to the ball, releasing the water, but pilots complained about having to lean out to pull the cord, thereby risking falling out of the helicopter and into the fire below. The next version of the bucket had a circular cast aluminum plate with a hole in the centre corresponding to the hole in the bottom of the drum; a lid was hinged onto this plate to cover the hole. After several experiments with seals, they found that machining a 45-degree-angled groove on the plate and installing a neoprene ring worked best. The release mechanism was a strong latch operated by an electric solenoid connected to a button on the cyclic control. A counterweight attached to one side of the upper rim of the bucket made it tip, sink or fill, and a block of wood attached to the lower side of the lid pushed it up or closed it. Forestry officials who received a demonstration on Kootenay Lake were very impressed. Jim Grady and Henry Stevenson were granted a patent in 1965.

Not all of the company's innovations were as successful. In April a new venture named Copter Cabs was introduced to provide a taxi service between downtown Vancouver, Vancouver International Airport, North and West Vancouver, Burnaby, New Westminster and Nanaimo. The helicopter chosen as the taxi was the Bell 47J-2, which offered fantastic views for the passengers. However, airport authorities were reluctant to handle Copter Cabs' passengers and landing and takeoffs from the airport apron, and it soon became apparent that sightseeing offered more promise. They switched to operating from the Bayshore Inn near Stanley Park and charging $20 for two persons with a third person free. On May 14 a television crew from the Canadian Broadcasting Corporation (CBC) aired a half-hour show filmed from a Copter Cabs' machine while flying from a downtown hotel to the airport. The high-speed photos, which captured the construction in downtown Vancouver, made the 47J-2's rotors look like a lazy windmill.

In another innovation that year radio station CKLG began broadcasting morning and evening traffic reports from one of Okanagan's 47J models with pilots Jim Foster and Jim Murphy at the controls. But Okanagan soon had competition as another station began broadcasting from a Bell 47 owned by Thunderbird Helicopters, and a third station jumped into the act with a Brantly B-2. Meanwhile, to improve performance on three Bell 47G models operating out of Vancouver, Fort St. John and Kamloops, Okanagan installed new turbo supercharged Carson Helicopters engine kits, and Franklin Carson came to Vancouver to advise on the tuning; once properly rigged, they improved both performance and handling.

That summer the company set up an accident investigation committee, headed by Carl, for the entire Okanagan group, and it was not long before a pilot was fined $500 for making an unnecessary practice autorotation that resulted in heavy damage to a Hiller UH-12E. Autorotation is a technique utilized in the event of engine failure because it exploits the airflow through the rotors in order to make a controlled descent. The pilot adjusts the pitch angle of the main blade to create enough drag to keep the blades turning. At about 100 feet (30.5 metres) off the ground, he uses the cyclic to pull the nose up to stop the forward air speed. At 10 feet (3 metres) from the ground, he pulls up the collective to flatten the rotor disc, which cushions the landing.

During August, Okanagan crews participated in two rescues in BC. On August 27 pilots Tommy Scheer and Tom Lanceley airlifted an injured logger from Knight Inlet to the hospital in Campbell River. In Prince George a helicopter spray crew spotted a house fire. Their early warning allowed time for the family with nine children to escape; the fire was subsequently extinguished, saving the house and the surrounding buildings.

1962 ANNUAL REPORT

By the end of this challenging year Okanagan had laid off 81 people. Flying hours had decreased to 19,000, down 8,000 from the previous year, largely due to the loss of the Mid-Canada Line contract, although the company had also been hobbled by poor flying weather. Five Bell 47G-2s, an S-55 and the S-62 had been sold or returned to their manufacturers. On the positive side, the company had acquired a Bell 47J-2, three 47G-3Bs, and eight additional Hiller UH-12Es, set up new bases at Cranbrook, Campbell River,

Revelstoke and Terrace, and continued to operate on contracts in Labrador, Baffin Island and Kemano as well as carry out inspections every three months on the 712-mile-long (1,146-kilometre) Edmonton to Vancouver oil pipeline.

1963

Early in the year, management consultants Peat Marwick Mitchell & Company released their recommendations on the disagreement between Carl Agar, Alf Stringer and the board members. Unfortunately, this report did not resolve the dispute, and Alf submitted his resignation to the board, stating that he was not prepared to continue under the current president after the February 1, 1963, AGM. Instead he took over the management of Vancouver Island Helicopters, while Carl opted to retire. It was the end of an era.

During this first year without the founding partners Okanagan renewed a number of contracts such as that with the BC Forest Service's firefighting division to provide 12 helicopters and another for two Sikorsky S-55s to service the Distant Early Warning Line sites on Baffin Island. The company also returned to the Mid-Canada Line to operate 14 S-55s for the RCAF. And the year saw the company's first international contract when late in the year a Bell 47 and its crew were shipped to Pakistan for a nine-month land survey project funded by the Colombo Plan.

In March, pilot Grant Soutar, who had become known as "The Arctic Fox," flew an S-55 on a search and rescue mission from Cape Dyer on Baffin Island and submitted the following report:

> On the 22nd of January, four men, three teams of dogs with three loaded komatiks [dog sleds] left Foxe 5 [DEW line station] for Kivitoo, 55 miles [88.5 kilometres] direct distance, and about five days later a dog team showed up at Foxe 5 with its traces chewed apart. A search was started by dog team, and the RCMP Otter with Staff/Sgt. Jack Austin [as] pilot, Cpl. Calvin Alexander and Spec. Const. John Dailla... along with Wheeler's [Air Service] Aztec began searching as soon as the weather broke and they were able to get up from Frobisher [now Iqaluit].
>
> Austin found a trace of them on the 31st—one man who was living and many dogs in a snow-filled gully, about 50 feet [15 metres] across, which ran up from the shore, 25–30 miles [40–50 kilometres] north of Foxe 5... He could not land anywhere near this man as the sea-ice was badly broken and piled up. I was flying about 70 miles [112 kilometres] south... so I was sent to help out.
>
> I stopped at Foxe 5 for gas, picked up Alexander and Dailla and went to the spot. [The man] was sitting with the sleeping bag wrapped around him, his hands and feet were bare. He was able to wave to us. With him were 13 dogs and a partially consumed body. We were able to land close to him... and load him into the aircraft, wrap him in a sleeping bag, and be air-borne within ten minutes. His hands and feet were badly frozen.
>
> Wheeler's Aztec had left for Frobisher, but we were able to have him return. He returned, loaded the man aboard and was off for Frobisher within 20 minutes of our landing. He arrived two hours later. The doctor looked at [the man] and he was shipped off to Montreal where he was operated upon that night. I am sure he could not have lasted much longer.

> His story was that the ice they had been travelling on had broken beneath them. They managed to cut the dogs loose after driving them into and across open water, hung on themselves or jumped or swam, or in some fashion managed to get onto the shore ice. They had lost the komatiks and all the gear except one sleeping bag.
>
> Joahanesee and the old man Mowyakbik had stayed in the sleeping bag. The two younger men, Peterose and Poisey, left for Kivitoo, 30 odd miles [50 kilometres] to the north. Joahanesee had been unable to move about for 4–5 days, but about this time Mowyakbik had died and the dogs had taken him from the bag that the two were using.

Grant Soutar and the RCMP went back to the site and shot all the dogs, loaded the remains of Mowyakbik into a tarp and left him for a later pickup. They then started tracking the other two men. To continue Grant's story:

> The weather had been snow, high winds (during this time we had winds of over 100 mph [170 km/h] at Cape Dyer) and a few days of clear weather, so their trail was far from distinct. By moving along the tracks that [Dailla] had found, a continuation of them could sometimes be found by getting the sun in the proper relationship, and the line of faint shadows could be seen. These tracks went across three mountain saddles of 2,000 to 2,500 feet [610 to 760 metres] onto two inlets and then onto the third.
>
> They had come down the steep slope of the last mountain and walked out onto the inlet for about one-half mile towards Kivitoo where the tracks showed quite a bit of thrashing about, and the frozen body of Poisey. The single tracks then went back towards the head of the inlet in a disjointed manner for two miles [three kilometres], wandered in all directions until he had stopped, sorted himself out, and headed straight for Kivitoo. A half-mile [800 metres] farther on he had gone to his knees, eventually leaned over backwards, died and froze. He was close to seven to eight miles [11 to 13 kilometres] from his destination.
>
> We had to chop the men loose from the ice and melted snow, load them into the aircraft and took [sic] them both to Kivitoo, return for the body of Mowyakbik, and took it back to Foxe 5 where the RCMP Otter would take it to Kivitoo the next day and arrange for burial.
>
> It was amazing that these men had been able to cover so much ground of a particularly difficult type. The only satisfactory part of the search was that all men were accounted for, and that the survivor had been taken care of so quickly. This is an unforgiving country.[47]

In another type of rescue mission, Copter Cab CF-JYQ flew to the assistance of a barge carrying a cargo of lumber, which had run aground about 200 yards (183 metres) off the beach below the University of British Columbia in Vancouver. Pilot Jim Murphy and assistant Jim Foster were called out around 3:30 pm. The operation involved attaching a 500-foot (150-metre) line from a tug to the barge. The pilot put Foster and two others aboard the barge then picked up Foster as they started to pay out the line to the tug. The first attempt failed when the line snagged. By the second attempt the tug had been grounded twice in the heavy swells and had moved out beyond the reach of the line. Jim flew back to the barge, picked up the two men and placed them on the beach. The next attempt was made without the use of a helicopter, and the machine flew back to the Bayshore Inn to continue its Copter Cab service.

On April 26 and 27 Okanagan put on a helicopter industry forum at its Nelson base in BC's West Kootenays. The brainchild of base manager Jim Grady, the event was open to invited guests from the logging, power, forestry, mining and telephone industries. It included demonstrations of the features of Bells and the S-58 and the equipment they used for tasks such as sling work, spraying, drilling pickups, firehose drops and water bombing, including the soon-to-be patented Monzoon Bucket.

During 1963 Okanagan experienced a number of incidents that damaged equipment. The first occurred on Baffin Island on January 5 after a ground crew left one blade of S-55 improperly locked. Later that month, Bell 47 JBC suffered structural failure while in a hover, causing it to roll and burn. A Hiller UH-12E had a clutch failure, and a Bell 47G-3 was damaged in an emergency landing. None of these events helped the company's bottom line.

1964

In 1964 an estimated 30 to 40 percent of the company's business involved supporting geological surveys, mostly flying in equipment, supplies and crews for oil and mining interests; one project in northern BC required both an S-58 and a Hiller UH-12E to assist a large mining venture. A new S-58D model, registered as CF-OKB, was added to the fleet to work on a seismic survey contract; the "D" indicated that the American Federal Aviation Agency had designated it for air freight only. The company obtained the right to use a newly invented automatic stabilization system called the Hoversight and modified two Hillers in order to install it. Fitted with it was a Tellurometer, the first successful microwave electronic distance-measuring device, which could provide accurate surveys over 20 to 30 miles (30 to 50 kilometres).

At the same time, the potential for the company's helicopters to work in the forest industry remained significant with the signing of a two-year contract with the BC Forest Service for patrol work and firefighting. The company also signed a contract for the installation of a microwave tower, requiring the airlifting of over 700 tons (635 metric tonnes) of construction material to the 3,600-foot (1,100-metre) level of Mount McLean, 40 miles (64 kilometres) west of Terrace, BC; the job used two machines flying 800 trips. The new helicopter power-line stringer developed by Okanagan engineers was used for the first time to string lines across Seton Lake, west of Lillooet, BC.

In June two French Air Force Dassault Sud Nord transport aircraft arrived at Vancouver International Airport with two Aérospatiale Alouette turbine helicopters on board. The Alouette III was able to carry a pilot and six passengers while the Alouette II carried a pilot and four passengers. During two days of demonstrations, Okanagan managers, pilots and engineers were given test flights and maintenance overviews of both machines, leaving them impressed, especially with the simplified maintenance programs.

Okanagan pilots continued to pull off dramatic rescues. Pilot Mark Adams was flying out of Campbell River in Bell 47 CF-JSK while on contract to a major oil company when he received an urgent rescue call. High seas had prevented surface craft from accessing the site in the Bella Bella area where a fisherman had been shipwrecked. Although facing high winds and minimal visibility, Mark managed to pluck the fisherman off a tide-swept reef; just an hour after the rescue the high seas and rising tide covered the reef. In early August pilot Mike McDonagh carried out a rescue in Glacier National Park by airlifting a mountain rescue team up to the 8,400-foot (2,560-metre) level. The team then climbed a steep ridge in cloud to reach a climber who had a broken back and legs. After they got him back to the helicopter, Mike flew him to the nearest hospital and then returned to pick up the rescue team.

Up to this time, the 58-plus helicopters owned by Okanagan and its subsidiaries had been operating almost exclusively from Goose Bay in Labrador west to Vancouver Island and north into the Arctic, but during 1964—with the nine-month-long Pakistan land survey contract already in hand—the company began to look with more interest at the international market. The first move was to form a subsidiary called International Helicopters in order to enter the bidding competition with other major operators to provide an s-61 to support Shell UK's North Sea rigs. This search for oil and gas was considered the most important maritime venture since the Normandy invasion and was estimated to cost what was then a staggering $250,000,000.

1964 ANNUAL REPORT
By year-end the company's profits and flying hours were up over the previous year but still well down from 1960–61 levels.

1965

In Okanagan's first international venture, pilot Jack Milburn, the Prince George base manager, and engineer Ev Cameron flew to East Pakistan (now Bangladesh) in December 1964 to meet up with Bell 47 CF-IVE, which had left Vancouver by ship in October. After delays caused by Pakistani officialdom, they re-assembled the helicopter to be ready to begin work in January 1965 for Forestall, the Vancouver contractor that had obtained a contract under the Colombo Plan to gather data in order to suggest better land use. Okanagan Helicopters' job was to provide transportation for Forestall's agriculture experts.

From January to July, Milburn and Cameron sent back letters containing detailed descriptions of the people and notes on the operation, which were reprinted in the *Okanagan Reporter*. The following, written by Jack Milburn, is taken from those letters:

> The Chittagong Hill Tracts Division is a remote and sparsely populated area in the SE of East Pakistan with India on the N & NE borders and Burma on the SE & S borders. The Hill Tracts are an irregular mass of steep hills and ridges covered with dense jungle. The area is approximately 120 miles [193 kilometres] long (less than [from] Prince George to Williams Lake) and 30–40 miles [48–64 kilometres] wide. In 1961 a dam was completed on the Karnaphuli River at Kaptai (Project headquarters) forming a large lake, which flooded most of the paddy land and displaced more people into the already populated hills, thus making a shortage of land and food. Some 100,000 people were displaced of a total Hill Tracts population estimated at 300,000 people.
>
> The Hill Tracts people make up some twenty tribes and are Burmese in appearance and mainly Buddhists. They are simple, happy, family people who live in a communal primitive existence practicing *"jhuming"* or shifting cultivation. This means they burn the jungle and plant. Cotton, vegetables, etc., are all planted together in small holes. The second and third year on the same *jhum* brings successively poorer crops so the people move their garden to a new piece of jungle. An eight-year cycle or more before cropping the original *jhum* is satisfactory for soil recovery. Because of the displaced people from the

lake area and the land shortage, the *jhuming* cycle has been shortened so crops are not adequate and the people are facing hardships. Many of the villages are borrowing money to purchase food to supplement their poor crops. This means going into debt to the Bengali (Plainsmen) merchants who operate the bazaars and control the money ... Villages are numerous, sometimes less than a mile apart and vary greatly in size. A large village will have 20–30 bamboo houses raised several feet off the ground on poles. Roofs are thatched sun grass and fireplaces are clay with no chimney ...

The nature of the topography and lack of roads make the helicopter ideally suited as a transport vehicle in the Hill Tracts area. Most landings are made in *jhum* gardens. Typical helicopter hazards of the area are sun grass and elephant grass up to 10 feet [three metres] high on old *jhumed* areas and sharp bamboo cuttings which pierce the floats.

A helicopter landing at a village goes something like this. The pilot circles the landing spot sizing up its suitability—it is usually a *jhum* garden adjacent to a village. People, pigs, cattle, chickens and dogs look up in wonderment. On the helicopter's approach for landing all village inhabitants run in great confusion under and in bamboo houses. After the helicopter has landed, the headman or a very old man who has got nothing to lose cautiously comes forth to see what kind of supernatural thing is visiting the village. The helicopter occupants greet the headman with hands held peaked in front of the forehead and say "*numb-a-ska*" in the traditional greeting. The headman responds with a relieved grin, and soon the whole village is chatting and laughing around the helicopter. The people gently run their hands over the smooth metal, push the floats and form a ring in front of the Perspex bubble looking in the cabin or admiring their reflection in the glass. The odd village is Christian and by the time we finish shaking everyone's hand, including babies, we feel like LBJ after his election campaign. Many villages have never seen white people so we get the "once over" after the helicopter. Our gift before departing may be one egg, a piece of papaya or bananas or a ten-foot length of sugar cane. The primitive people are generous, kind and scrupulously honest. Their only vices seem to be heavy smoking of the bamboo "hookah" (five years old and up) and taking the occasional snort of "jungle juice"—100-proof rice liquor.

It would take a book to tell everything about this contract, however, I trust this brief report will partly describe Okanagan's work on this side of the world.[48]

On January 31, Ev Cameron wrote to Gordy Askin:

Still in jungle operation but plan to be back to Kaptai first week in February. One week's rest and back to south area.

Engine has 584:00 hours and is running good. Changing oil at 25 hours. Oil temp running 100[°F (38°C)] at hottest with three people (pass) on board, prolonged flight, outside 80[°F (27°C)]. Found must clean oil cooler fins daily as fine species of grass and some "*jhuming*" ash clog air spaces. Blow out from outside with float pump. This seems to be prime heat factor and oil temp can be lowered all of 10 [degrees] by this means. (Head temps very normal). Found spares to be short elevator cable for which I have cabled. Pre-monsoon storms are reported to contain hail stones as large as a man's fist so preparing bamboo covers for blades and bubble. Machine operating well and Jack doing good job with it.

100 hr. inspection, 25 hr. and 50 hr. carried out. Replaced M.R. pitch link rod ends, replaced T.R. pitch change links. Replaced floats and repairing old ones. Having good luck with new set. Outside air down to 38[°F (3°C)] in AM but to 85[°F (29°C)] midday. 100W oil heavy for starts and must have long warm-up period. However working OK. Fuel good and no plug trouble.

Ev Cameron wrote again on February 28, this time from Chittagong:

The following is a supplement to my Feb. monthly report, intended to give more detailed account of operation of this period.

Feb. 1–15 found us based in the Khagrachari area, finishing the northern portion of the hill tracts soil survey. Apart from the odd case of dysentery among the boys, things went quite smoothly. The weather stayed clear and wind generally light, although a few isolated gusts around the hills . . . caused some turbulence.

Temperature at night down to 35[°F (2°C)], almost causing a need for pre-heating the 100 wt. oil, however daytime rising to 85[°F (29°C)], making it necessary to go light on clothes, only BVDs desirable. The helicopter performed well with only normal mtce [maintenance] and checks required.

Feb. 15–21: Operating in Bandarban jungle base in the southern area of the survey, conditions similar to northern part, although temperatures now rising a few degrees (45 night, 87 day). Still no problem with engine temperature.

600-hr inspection carried out this week. Replaced fan belts (found to be checking badly). Slight oil seepage coming from #6 cyl [cylinder] push rod housing seals, inboard exhaust. Replaced seals of this cyl. Replaced two spark plug leads due to cracked insulation and mis-firing. Removed leads from standby engine #6 and rear.

IVE away as usual morning of 22nd but did not return as planned in evening. Due to inaccessibility of the region, action was taken this evening to acquire transportation to cover Jack's intended flight route . . . Pakistan Air Force promptly dispatched an S-55 to leave Dacca at 5:00 AM of the 23rd.

I boarded the Air Force machine at Chittagong along with tools, medical supplies, water and Adolph Geottal (soil survey lad familiar with area). We proceeded along intended flight path of CF-IVE and located it on a river sand bar, one mile from Ali Kadam bazaar at 10:00 AM.

Upon landing found machine to be in one piece but very oily. Jack and his three passengers, we learned, had acquired a country boat and proceeded down the river, leaving about 1:00 PM of the 22nd, destined for the nearest main road (40 miles [64 kilometres] distant by river). A Pakistan police officer had been left to guard the machine, but he spoke no English so didn't get much information as to the exact cause of what had happened.

Washed CF-IVE and engine down, checked oil level, which was three qts [2.8 litres] lacking and pulled screen (found OK). Ran up engine and located oil leak at inboard exhaust push rod seal of #4 cyl. I deduced that Jack had landed, spotted the oil and wisely decided to finish trip by river boat.

I checked my box and found I was in possession of three seals. In view of this and to save some time, I remained behind to repair leak and sent the S-55 back to inform Jack and for him to return at his earliest convenience. By 12 noon of same day, I had replaced both seals in exhaust push rod of #6 cyl. Upon removing old ones, found inboard to be deteriorated and cracked, fully across its width. Ran up engine and found oil leak stopped. I wondered about the remaining seals, but as I brought a gal of oil and had topped tank, I figured if one or more seals went, we would still have no sweat in reaching the road and fuel cache, which was twenty minutes by air.

I remained at the machine until Jack arrived by PIA E4. The delay was due to the fact that the country boat trip down river took 2 days and to return upstream would have taken three. Therefore Jack decided to wait for the availability of the civil E4 which was undergoing some mtce work, the Air Force being indisposed in its own capacity, [there] being no longer a state of emergency.

Saturday of the 25th saw us depart from Ali Kadam for the ferry trip back to Kaptai. On board was Jack, myself and the chief engineer of Civil Aviation for East Pakistan, who had come along to investigate the incident.

Upon landing at the first fuel cache, twenty minutes later, found more oil beginning to show. Coming from exhaust of #3 cyl. push rod. Removed seals and replaced remaining two I had. As we had lost very little oil and the next part of the flight was over paddy land (open areas), we pressed on and arrived Kaptai without further incident.

We were obliged upon arrival to complete various forms and write reports of what had happened for the Govt. of Pakistan Civil Aviation Authority. These were the routine type and similar to DOT [Department of Transport] procedures. The Pakistani representative proved to be an interesting fellow who was quite familiar with Sikorsky types and very co-operative. He suggested I replace the remaining seals, which we both considered mandatory under the previous circumstances. He mentioned that this type of seal has a short life in this area, due to heat, humidity and some vague other unexplainable reason. I was a bit skeptical as to this being the cause but didn't comment and took it for what it was worth, there being no other explanation I could think of. He took one of the seals back to Dacca with him to analyse but I haven't heard further from him.

PIA [Pakistan International Airlines] is operating three S-61s on a scheduled short haul passenger service. Having many problems gearbox.

Upon changing the seals in CF-IVE, we returned to Bandarban and caught up the four lost days and concluded the major part of the soil survey the following week. The above situation, mechanical-wise turned out to be of relatively minor nature, which was rectified. However, the complications which arose from it proved to cause considerable inconvenience and some anxiety. Operation now normal again and flying daily. Air Temp increasing now and humidity is rising so we'll be starting to get uncomfortable from now on.

I've been looking over the air-conditioners closely as of late. Spare parts for them have been depleted and have been in use eight years. We are comparing these little machines here to furnaces in Canada and come second only to your gin supply.

I hear Jack hovering in over the lakeway and our bearer is shouting, "Sahib! Sahib! Coming Helicopter!" so will finish here.

See you all this summer!

The *Okanagan Reporter* of July 1965 reported:

JACK MILBURN and EV CAMERON pukka sahibs both are back at Prince George from the land of softly chiming temple bells, with no No. 1 boys to stir their coffee and fan their fevered brows with tender, even anxious concern. However, both the lads are glad to be back, they claim. Altogether they flew over 400 hours in the Chittagong Hill Tracts and did a wonderful job for us in Bell 47J CF-IVE. Each has many good stories to tell, including a stock of original elephant stories, which we hope to relate here from time to time. The girls there? Jack and Ev look at you blandly—and smile enigmatically. Sly dogs, both of them.[49]

Okanagan's second international venture—its first under the umbrella of International Helicopters—was a contract with Shell Oil Company to provide offshore support in the North Sea. The full story of this adventure was finally told in the *Okanagan Reporter* after it was all over:

> When Shell Oil called for tenders for the offshore drilling work in the North Sea, [Okanagan was] specifically asked to tender. A very detailed proposal was submitted to Shell Oil and [Okanagan] won the contract. Prior to making the proposal, discussions [had taken] place with the [British] government representatives concerning the problems of a Canadian company going to Britain and the possible difficulties obtaining operating certificates and the licences required for pilots and engineers. Okanagan was assured at the time that no road blocks would be put in the way and that the [British] authorities would accept Canadian licences for both pilots and engineers, subject to some minor examinations with reference to radio aids and communications. It also suggested that, if Okanagan Helicopters won the contract, they should be willing to train British crews as quickly as possible rather than [use] a continuation of rotating Canadian crews.[50]

However, when Okanagan Helicopters was advised by Shell Oil Company that they had won the contract, they were also advised that the UK Ministry of Aviation expected them to take a partner in order to obtain the appropriate licences. That partner, they were told, had to be the government crown corporation, British European Airways Helicopters (BEA Helicopters). Negotiations would take place for BEA Helicopters to receive 50 percent of International Helicopters and in return BEA Helicopters would assist in getting the appropriate licences. (In effect, the British government would be the 50 percent shareholder.) BEA Helicopters would pay nothing for its 50 percent but as a contract shareholder would put up one Sikorsky S-61 helicopter with Okanagan putting up the other. International Helicopters Ltd. did obtain the appropriate licences from the Air Registration Board but had many problems dealing with the Ministry of Aviation, and the handwriting was on the wall when the ministry refused to accept copies of the BEA Helicopters Operations Manual for the S-61, which was, in fact, the International Helicopters Ltd. manual. The Ministry of Aviation stated that BEA Helicopters could operate under it but not International Helicopters.

Okanagan then became aware that BEA Helicopters had never made a profit and was being subsidized to the tune of £100,000 annually to cover its losses. BEA Helicopters had 75 employees for four helicopters and in the previous year had flown fewer than 1,500 hours with all four helicopters. The management proposed by Okanagan Helicopters and the profits anticipated would, in fact, make BEA Helicopters look good, and if BEA Helicopters could get full control of the Shell Oil Company contract, they could absorb those profits into their overhead and administrative expenses to make the company look much better. Then Okanagan Helicopters would have served its purpose and the company's personnel could go back home to Canada.

It was a very frustrating time for Okanagan management who had worked so hard to get the Shell Oil Company contract, and they certainly did not receive the cooperation they expected from either BEA Helicopters management or British government officials. The company was finally forced to sell out. However, they still had a commitment to the Shell Oil Company contract, which required them to provide a helicopter, and after much consideration, management decided to fly their S-61, CF-OKY, to England via a North Atlantic route. Igor Sikorsky supported the plan because it would be the first unescorted civilian helicopter to complete this run. A military flight had taken place in 1952 when a US Air Force Sikorsky H-19 flew from Massachusetts to Prestwick, Scotland, in a flight time of 42.5 hours; the H-19's final destination was Germany for a journey of 3,410 miles (5,488 kilometres).

The highly experienced crew of CF-OKY was made up of Ross Lennox, the test pilot for Pratt & Whitney (P&W), Tom Harrison, their technical representative, Okanagan pilot Tommy Scheer, who had been with the company since 1952, and engineer Keith Rutledge, who joined in 1951. After CF-OKY was modified at the Sikorsky plant to take additional fuel tanks, increasing its capacity to 2,500 pounds (1,134 kilograms) and flying time to seven and a half hours, the crew flew it to the P&W plant near Montreal.

The flight began in May with the first leg taking them from Montreal to Baie-Comeau, northeast of Quebec City. From there, they flew to Schefferville, Quebec, and then to Fort Chimo before going on to Frobisher Bay (now Iqaluit) where they were delayed for two days due to fog. They then flew to Cape Dyer on the southern tip of Baffin Island. After refuelling, they were ready for the trip across Davis Strait to the west coast of Greenland. CF-OKY was flying at an altitude of 5,000 feet (1,524 metres), which was clear of the cloud layers, and once they reached Greenland, the weather was CAVU (ceiling and visibility unlimited) to 10,000 feet (3,048 metres) for 10 miles (16 kilometres), giving them a clear run down Kangerlussuaq into Sondrestrom where the aircraft was refuelled and checked.

On the next section they encountered a glacier, which started at sea level, rose to 11,000 feet (3,353 metres), ultimately reaching 14,000 feet (4,267 metres), but flying over the ice rather than along the coast would cut 900 to 1,000 miles (1,500-1,600 kilometres) off the journey. Besides, the weather was perfect and they set off over the ice for the east coast of Greenland where they landed in the fishing village of Kulusuk. The next stop was Reykjavík, Iceland, which necessitated crossing about 100 miles (160 kilometres) of pack ice before they reached open water. An American-operated radar station monitored aircraft flying this gap between Iceland and Greenland 24 hours a day.

The crew stayed in Reykjavík for three days, taking in the sites including the volcanic activity, before embarking for the fishing village of Höfn in southeast Iceland for refuelling. During a two-day weather delay there, they visited the volcanic island of Surtsey. When the weather finally cleared, they flew on to Vágar on the Faroe Islands; Vágar airport had been built by the Royal Engineers in 1942 for RAF Coastal Command's search for German U-boats and surface ships. From there, they flew southeast to the Outer Hebrides, a distance of 218 miles (351 kilometres), then on to Prestwick, Scotland, where they cleared customs. In their bright red flight suits they were easy to spot in the crowds there, and they were approached by an American air force pilot who informed them that he had been onboard the USAF picket aircraft monitoring their flight between Greenland and Iceland. He said he thought they were crazy flying a helicopter across that stretch.

The weather was good for the final leg, and the trip ended in front of the BEA hangar at Gatwick Airport without incident. The total distance from the Sikorsky factory in Connecticut to Gatwick via Greenland was 3,551 miles (5,715 kilometres) in a flight time of 34 hours and 14 minutes. The crew were met by Fred Snell, who was in charge of the

Okanagan Helicopters North Sea operation, and they received congratulatory telegrams from BC Premier W.A.C. Bennett and Okanagan management and staff in Vancouver. While Ross Lennox, Tom Harrison and Tommy Scheer soon headed home on commercial flights, Keith Rutledge stayed to visit London while waiting for completion of the British certifications and modification for the Air Registration Board.

After six months in the UK, Okanagan's flight and ground crews returned to Canada. By this time the company's management had realized that it would be difficult to work with a crown company and make any money. As Keith Rutledge wrote in *Aviation News*, "You just absorb half the loss. The partnership had to cease . . . so the taxpayers in Britain now own our share of the operation."[51]

The first rescue operation of 1965 by an Okanagan machine turned out to be the most challenging of the year. The previous year the Granby Consolidated Mining, Smelting and Power Company had begun driving an 11-mile-long (18-kilometre-long) tunnel through a mountain in order to connect the company's new Granduc copper mine, 30 miles (50 kilometres) north of Stewart near the Alaska-BC border, with the company's concentrator that was under construction at Tide Lake. The company had also built a camp for 160 workers along with an airstrip on the nearby Leduc Glacier. At 10:16 AM on February 18 a massive avalanche buried half of the camp and 68 men, leaving only the office, four bunkhouses and the first aid shack intact. Fortunately, the camp radio operator used auxiliary power to transmit a mayday, which was picked up by both BC and Alaska rescue services.

Okanagan crews joined the rescue operation along with Klondike Helicopters from Whitehorse, TEMSCO Helicopters out of Alaska and the US Coast Guard, and the next morning in atrocious weather with wind gusting up to 70 mph (112 km/h), the aircraft were guided to the site by ground fires. Okanagan's Terrace base had sent a Hiller UH-12E flown by Ed Phillips and the Smithers base an S-55 with pilot Ed Dunn and engineer Konrad Busch. They were joined by S-58 CF-OKS with pilot Don Jacques, co-pilot Don Crowe and engineer Barry Stone. On its first trip CF-OKS picked up five seriously injured men, along with two doctors and a nurse, and flew them to Ketchikan, Alaska. That day they made three more trips in the extreme weather conditions. During the initial phase of the rescue, which continued until February 24, the operation took out 120 survivors including 17 who were badly injured; 28 men died.

Another rescue took place in October when Okanagan became involved in the search for two hunters reported missing in the Prince George area after their boat capsized in the McGregor River and they were swept downstream. A 12-man search party and a helicopter were called out soon after the alarm was raised. The helicopter located survivor Davey West, an ex-professional football player, in a canyon a few miles downstream from where the boat had capsized. He had managed to clamber ashore and spent 46 hours wandering in the bush clad only in his underwear. The search for the other man continued without success.

A third rescue took place on the Tulsequah River, a tributary of the Taku River in northern BC. Pilot John Watson and engineer Doug Lieb were working with Bell 47D-1 CF-GGC out of a camp on the Taku River when word came that two American tourists were missing on the Alaska side of the border. John started the helicopter search in the late afternoon in poor weather conditions. The gas can belonging to the tourists' boat had been found on the bank of the glacier-fed river, which was about 150 feet (45.5 metres) wide and in full flood, and about six miles (10 kilometres) from their campsite John spotted the two men clinging to the remains of an old bridge. The two had already been there for over 54 hours after their boat had capsized when they had tried to navigate through the woodpile that had been the bridge.

John realized the men probably would not survive another night. Unfortunately, the machine had room for only one passenger, so he slung a strong rope between the skids and then moved into a hover over the men, lifting them one at a time as they hung onto the rope and depositing them on the riverbank. John, who himself had been rescued not too far from there in February 1957, commented afterwards that: "For me, it was a case of the once-rescued doing the rescue." The rescued men showed their appreciation by sending him a unique pipe, which he used constantly.

In an incident at the Sikorsky plant, Okanagan pilot Fred Eilertson, who was there for s-61 training, suffered minor injuries when a tail rotor failed during a hover about 25 feet (eight metres) off the ground. The Sikorsky pilot escaped with cuts and bruises, but the machine was badly damaged. Meanwhile, Okanagan got the job of training test pilot John Anderson on both the Bell and the Hiller machines; his job was to ensure that every Bell and Hiller that came out of a major component overhaul had between two and five hours flight time before being returned to service.

1965 ANNUAL REPORT

The record-breaking journey of CF-OKY contributed to an increase in the company's annual flying time and, despite some setbacks, an improved financial position. Meanwhile, the merger with Pacific Helicopters and the end of the Mid-Canada Line contract had added more equipment to the roster, including three s-55s along with s-62A CF-ELO. The company also acquired two Bell 204B single-turbine helicopters that year, and they became essential when a mining company chartered s-58 CF-OKS for five months in 1966.

On the horizon was a second contract with Shell Oil Company, but this time it was to provide support for a proposed drilling operation off Tofino on the West Coast of

▸ A float-equipped Bell 204B services Shell Oil's semi-submersible off Vancouver Island in 1965. This was the first helicopter to use instrument flight rules (IFR). Pilots: Grant Soutar and Roy Webster. PHOTO COURTESY OF JACK MILBURN

Vancouver Island. The contract called for one of the new Bell 204B models flying in VFR (visual flight rules) conditions. However, due to the unpredictable weather in the area, for safety the crews were also instrument-rated.

By the end of the year sales of the company's aerial line stringer for power-line construction looked promising after it was demonstrated at the Paris air show and a number of European sales were concluded.

The end of the year was marked by the passing of Douglas Dewar, the honorary chairman of Okanagan Helicopters board of directors, on November 8. He was 82 and had been involved in the management of the company since 1947. With Dewar's passing, Carl re-joined the board and continued as a consultant.

1966

In January 1966 one of the worst winter storms in years caused slides in BC's Fraser Canyon, cutting rail lines between the Coast and all points east. One of the slides stranded the eastbound Panorama, a Canadian National (CN) transcontinental passenger train, about 20 miles (32 kilometres) north of Hope, and an Okanagan crew in a Bell 204B landed on a make-shift pad near the train to deliver food for the passengers and crew. A second helicopter, a two-seat Hiller UH-12E, brought in a CN team to assist in extracting the train. Two days later the train was still stranded and, with fuel to power its heaters running low, CN decided to remove the passengers. The Rescue Coordination Centre arranged for an RCAF Piasecki Vertol H-21 helicopter to work alongside Okanagan's Bell 204B, and between them they evacuated 209 people.

On February 2 Okanagan Helicopters celebrated the launch of the Grouse Mountain Skyride, the gondola service that lifts passengers from North Vancouver to the top of the mountain. The company had been involved in the erection of the pylons on the 3,500-foot (1,067-metre) run, using both medium- and heavy-lift helicopters.

Later that year the Department of Fisheries contacted Okanagan after a large rock slide occurred on the Tahltan River, a short distance upstream from its confluence with the Stikine River, preventing salmon from reaching their spawning grounds. The crew of the Okanagan S-55 used an underslung 45-gallon (170-litre) drum filled with water to transport the salmon upstream; each trip took about a minute and a half, and the mortality rate was only about one fish in every three or four loads.

After a few thousand salmon had been moved, the Department of Fisheries checked the lake about 40 miles (64 kilometres) upstream but found that no fish had arrived; the problem this time was a number of beaver dams that had been built in a canyon above the slide, creating low water levels. The S-55 was then used to take Department of Fisheries personnel and equipment into that area to net the fish and place them in a pool above the canyon. Although a fish ladder was installed, the fish refused to use it, so the netting process had to continue. Over a 20-day period a number of other methods were tried before an experiment was set up to determine if adult salmon could be carried over the entire distance from below the slide using a 100-gallon (378.5-litre) tank slung below the S-55. To overcome problems with aeration, Roy Edwards and Tommy Gurr, who formed the crew of the S-55, suggested using the helicopter's undercarriage compressor and a hose. The carrier, loaded with 50 salmon and water to about two-thirds of its capacity, was able to make the journey in 20 minutes with a survival rate of 38 out of the 50. A light tranquillizer added to the water reduced the loss. Fortunately the slide was eventually cleared and the river reverted to its normal condition.[52]

In 1966 Okanagan officially opened a new hangar and landing pad in Prince George with a reception for 150 people. The new facility, which had capacity for 12 small helicopters, also provided maintenance and fuelling services, including jet fuel for the anticipated turbine helicopters. This base had begun only six years earlier as a one-man operation with pilot Jack Milburn operating from an unheated hangar at the airport. The majority of the contract work in the area came from the forestry, oil and gas industries and BC Hydro. However, Prince George's location made it a natural transportation centre for the company to extend its operations north to the Yukon and Northwest Territories and south and east as required.

Summer ended with a demonstration at Vancouver's Pacific National Exhibition (PNE) for a delegation from the Canadian Forestry Association's fire-protection course. Using a Hiller UH-12E, pilot Art Bates from the company's Terrace base laid 3,000 feet (915 metres) of fire hose at a speed of 50 mph (80.5 km/h).

In October the flying school in Penticton got a boost when *Vertical World Magazine* published "Okanagan Helicopters' Copter College" by freelance writer and photographer H.E. McLean, who billed himself as "the first magazine writer ever permitted to 'take the dose' in the school's 15-year-history." McLean described the Penticton operation as "the world's toughest school of 'higher learning' ":

> Canada's "Copter College" lists blue ribbon graduates from half a dozen foreign countries (US included), plus Canada's military services. [But] this is a civilian operation, conceived and run by Okanagan Helicopters Ltd. of Vancouver, whose 58 helicopters and some 70 pilots make it by far the largest bush copter outfit in the world. The school is primarily run for those 70 pilots, who take a gruelling five-week course, followed by annual refresher "check-ups" in the high country. Some 30 students tackle the session each year, spending up to 35 hours in some of the toughest terrain that the teachers can find.

When McLean arrived at Penticton Airport, he was expecting to find actual school buildings and a campus; instead he found "just a couple of copters on a dirt field off to the side."

> "Our school's really out in those mountains," explained red-capped Bud Tillotson, chief instructor. He rotated his arm in a 360-degree circle. "Within 30 miles [50 kilometres] any way you want to go is every flying condition we'd ever encounter. That's our classroom. And there's our maintenance hangar." He pointed to a toolbox in a car trunk.
>
> Tillotson commands a four-man cadre of instructors whose aggregate total of 18,000 copter hours and 33 years of rotor experience go far towards calming the mountain-frayed nerves of green "*ab initios*" (fixed-wing pilots in first-year helicopter work) and more advanced second-year men.

McLean was taken aloft to follow student pilots, and he watched in fascination as "they threaded the breezes upward, danced through approaches to a precarious mountain-top" and "made those detestable—but necessary—ledge-side landings." He concluded with:

> No textbook has yet been written about the sophisticated, finer points of this kind of flying. At Okanagan's mountain school, a penciled note-book kept by Tillotson over 5,500 hours of mountain copter flying holds some of the knowledge. Fellow instructors Fred LeGrice, Mike McDonagh and Dick Biggs— who average better than 4,000 hours of copter time, add their experience as

seasoned Okanagan experts. And from bush flying experience over the nearly two million square miles and four Canadian provinces served by Okanagan comes further acumen from pilots back for refresher courses. The gruelling course is so effective, so complete that Okanagan's red-capped graduates are certified without flight checks on graduation by Canada's Department of Air Transport (equivalent to the US Federal Aviation Agency).

What about the men who wear the coveted red caps of Okanagan—the graduates of [the] mountain school? It seems strange at first that to a man, they're neither "hot shots" nor show-offs in any sense. They're family men as a rule, about 35 years old. And they are just as stable on the ground as they are in the mountains.

Okanagan finds it difficult to find such people, rejects 14 of 15 applicants, then washes out at least a quarter of the remaining copter students in basic company training at Vancouver. A few more can't make the grade in mountain school.

"They do fine to the last 10 hours of high-altitude work. Then they just can't make it," explains Tillotson. "But they can still go back with a 'flatland' copter outfit and make excellent pilots."

During the year Okanagan also made some changes to its equipment roster by leasing a Fairchild Hiller FH-1100 to test the new turbine utility engine, and by December the company had placed an order for 10 of them with the option of 20 more within two years. Designed in 1961, the FH-1100 had taken its maiden flight in January 1963, but when the US Army chose the Hughes OH-6 over the FH-1100 for light helicopter observation work, Hiller decided to introduce its new machine to the civilian market instead and equipped it with the new Allison Model 250-C18 engine, the same as Bell's JetRanger. In Quebec, Okanagan's subsidiary Hélicoptères Canadiens, which was on contract to a radio station to provide news and highway reports, switched to the new small, turbine-engined Bell JetRanger to replace their Bell 47 then negotiated with a Toronto radio station to provide a similar report service. Meanwhile, Okanagan's engineering management had entered into discussions with Sikorsky and United Aircraft of Canada about replacing the S-55's R-1340 Pratt & Whitney piston engine with the PT6 turbine.

1967

The modernization of Okanagan's fleet, which had begun the previous year with the purchase agreement for the FH-1100s, continued when early in the year the Department of Transport issued a certificate of airworthiness to the company for an S-61A model. Since this helicopter's military designation prevented it from carrying civilian passengers, it was first contracted out on the construction of a power line in the Peace River area of northern BC.

In January the ten new FH-1100s were flown from the factory in Maryland to Vancouver. Each helicopter had been given a different colour scheme to give Okanagan a choice, prompting an air traffic controller to comment: "Wow, I have never seen a flock of parrots landing here before."[53] They were put to work soon after their arrival, seven of them joining the S-61A on the Peace River power-line contract. Another was involved in the construction of a power line from the Portage Mountain dam, 300 miles (483 kilometres) north of Prince George, to Vancouver, a total of 765 miles (1,231 kilometres). The ninth was sent into the Fraser Canyon to work for Catre Hi-Line Ltd., and the last was put to work covering a variety of smaller tasks from shuttling crews to hanging insulators on the cross arms of hydro towers and stringing power lines. It achieved a new record by stringing 54,000 feet (16.5 kilometres) of line in less than five hours.

With the arrival of these light turbine helicopters, the older piston machines became less popular. A 1967 issue of *Shell Aviation News* carried a report by Okanagan pilot Roy Webster on the FH-1100 in which he stated that it was ideal in the bush because the high skids were an asset when landing in the middle of nowhere and it was able to lift more than piston helicopters. It was almost twice as fast and carried nearly twice the load of the older UH-12E. In addition, the FH-1100 carried the helicopter underslung spray system (HUSS) developed by Okanagan; it was the first successful liquid spray system.

In early 1967 Okanagan also awaited delivery of its first Bell YOH-4As, which had first flown in December 1962 as a military machine. However, in May 1965, like the Hiller, it had lost out to the Hughes OH-6 in the US Army's contract competition for a light observation helicopter, and Bell had subsequently redesigned it for civilian operators and re-designated it as the Bell 206A model JetRanger. In April and May JetRangers CF-OKN and CF-OKS were put into service on the West Coast and CF-OKU went to Montreal.

By late spring Okanagan's management had negotiated a contract with the new federally organized and funded company Panarctic Oils to provide support services on Melville Island in the Northwest Territories. Then, anticipating the further expansion of exploration in the north that would require increased helicopter services, especially medium to heavy machines, the company ordered an FH-1100 to be modified for the specific use of the oil and gas industry. The next step was the establishment of a full-time sales manager in Calgary to liaise with the oil and gas industry and support the headquarters of service companies.

On the West Coast, although the Shell Oil Company contract in BC had been delayed by problems with the construction of the semi-submersible drilling platform that was to drill there, Okanagan had arranged to occupy a portion of the old RCAF hangar in Tofino for an office, radio room and maintenance facilities, while the helicopter crews and their families were housed in the Department of Transport buildings at the airport.

▸ Okanagan Helicopters office staff assists with the unloading of a new Fairchild Hiller FH-1100 in 1967; from left to right: unknown, Linda Hoban, Diane Jeffries, Leslie Rourke (née Birch). PHOTO COURTESY OF LESLIE BIRCH

In power-line construction, the company set a record when a Bell 204B set 68 aluminum transmission towers in a single day in the Alice Arm area near the tip of the Alaska Panhandle. A similar construction project in the Pine Pass–Peace River area of BC used a Sikorsky S-58T to set 24 steel towers, after which a Bell 204B strung the line and attached the conductors. Later that year, a consultant released a study on power-line construction safety, which showed that the fatality rate of one person for every 100 miles of power line built by standard methods had been reduced to nearly zero over the hundreds of miles built using helicopters.

Okanagan further diversified that year with the purchase of a 50 percent interest in Aeriel Engineering Ltd. Then in association with Canadian Air Borne Surveys Ltd., they continued to develop innovative helicopter mapping techniques, especially in the measurement of distance and angles, which resulted in a giant step forward in survey accuracy. Another innovation from Okanagan's engineering staff was an underslung, circular, multi-hook cargo system for medium and heavy helicopters that allowed crews to take on a combination of loads; this became especially useful when moving mining camps and their diverse equipment inventories.

In August Russia's export trade agency, Avia Export, arranged for representatives from Okanagan Helicopters and Aeriel Engineering to visit the USSR and tour the Mil Helicopter plant in Rostov-on-Don, near the Black Sea. The Canadians' primary purpose was to assess the Mil Mi-10 sky crane, a huge helicopter capable of lifting 15 tons (13.6 metric tonnes), for its feasibility for work in the western Canadian oil, gas and forest industries. Don Jacques, Okanagan's chief pilot, and Lionel Cook, president of Aeriel, who were permitted to fly this machine, were impressed with its handling. Don also had the opportunity to fly the Mi-6 and Mi-8. They estimated it would cost about $2 million to position a Mi-10 in Vancouver, and it would require an hourly lease rate of $1,700 to $2,000, but due to differences in aviation standards, Okanagan did not place an order for Mil helicopters.

Penticton's Helicopter Mountain Flying School became newsworthy when it celebrated its 16th anniversary. Over the years it had expanded to provide year-round basic, advanced and refresher courses for both commercial and military pilots from many different countries. The course had increased to 75 hours with the first 25 hours spent on conversion to type with an endorsement. The training during this part of the course was over relatively flat terrain and included autorotation, emergency procedures, ground school, and a Department of Transport exam. The second part, an advanced low-level course, combined basic mountain work with flying in confined areas and included some sling work and a check-out on floats. The final 25 hours focussed on flying in rough country, mostly at altitudes above 6,000 feet (1,830 metres), while the last ten hours were spent at 7,000 to 8,300 feet (2,135 to 2,530 metres).

▲ An Okanagan delegation at the Mil Helicopter plant in the USSR in 1967 looking over the Mil Mi-10, which was capable of lifting 15 tons (13.6 metric tonnes). Chief pilot Don Jacques had a chance to fly the machine. OKANAGAN HELICOPTERS PHOTO

1967 ANNUAL REPORT

By the end of 1967, which was Okanagan Helicopters' 19th year in operation, the company owned seven subsidiaries across Canada and had 18 bases, mainly in British Columbia. Having now flown in Pakistan and over the North Sea, the company was confident of its ability to operate abroad and that fall sent two Hiller UH-12ES, CF-MLW and CF-OKG, to work in New Zealand with Alexander Helicopters. Although the fleet had been reduced by six machines after selling off a number of its older piston-engine machines, revenue hours had increased over 1966 from over 27,000 to just under 32,000, due in part to the serious forest fire situation. However, in early July the company lost the contract with the USAF in Goose Bay to a Newfoundland company, Eastern Provincial Airways (EPA). The two S-55s in use there were flown out, one to Montreal and the other one farther north.

1968

On January 29, 1968, Carl Agar passed away after a long illness. He was 67. His obituary, which appeared in the *Penticton Herald*, described him as a good friend of the Okanagan Valley and a "pioneer who never stopped pioneering." He was well known in the aviation world for that spirit and for his knowledge of rotary-wing aircraft, a knowledge that was sought after by such helicopter designers as Igor Sikorsky and Bell Helicopters. He had nurtured a vision of a nationwide helicopter fleet in Canada at a time when few people had ever seen such a machine.

In addition to the McKee Trophy, he was awarded the Captain William J. Kossler Award for his work on rotary-wing aircraft, the first non-US citizen to be so honoured. At the time of his death, he was honorary board chairman of Okanagan Helicopters. In spite of the ill health that had forced his retirement at the beginning of 1963, he had remained active and deeply involved in the technical advancements of the industry.

In a retrospective article on the helicopter industry written for *Canada Commerce Magazine* in 1984, Igor Sikorsky praised Carl Agar's courage. He wrote:

> A flying craft remains useless unless there also exist other pioneers with courage, foresight and energy who can visualise the usefulness of a flying machine and fulfill the final stage of development of the craft by putting it to work to prove its value and thus assign to it its rightful place in our modern life.
>
> Carl Agar, to my mind, is one of the most brilliant and outstanding pioneers of this type.[54]

Early in the year, Okanagan Helicopters formed Canadian Helicopters Overhaul (CHO) Ltd. under managing director Gordon Askin who had been Okanagan's chief engineer. This new company's maintenance and overhaul facility, which included stores, workshops, hangars and offices, covered 20,000 square feet (6,100 square metres) and housed the most up-to-date equipment. Its 70 aircraft engineers and component specialists were headed by Rod Fraser as chief inspector and Dave McLean as superintendent of maintenance. Okanagan's overhaul facility had already been servicing a wide range of machines from the Bell 47s, 204Bs and 206s to the Fairchild Hiller 12 and FH-1100, Sikorsky S-55, S-61 and S-62 and the Hughes 269 and 300, but CHO would now service the machines of other operators from Canada and the US as well. Many of these operators had fleets of just two or four helicopters and welcomed contracting out major overhauls to reduce their need for hangar space and spares. CHO offered them engine and component overhaul and radio installation and repair. It also provided conversions for fire suppression, aerial spraying systems, aerial line stringers for hydro-line cable and a new device developed by an engineering firm retained by Okanagan—an extension cargo hook that was under the directional visual control of the pilot. In addition, the new company offered field-training courses including a five-week Bell 204 airframe and engine course and a two-week Allison engine course run by Howie Gatin, an experienced Okanagan instructor.

On March 1 Okanagan began operating a six-month Panarctic Oils contract on Melville Island, Northwest Territories. Two of the company's turbine-engined Bell 204Bs and a Hiller FH-1100 were airlifted by Pacific Western Airlines (PWA) C-130 from Prince George to Resolute Bay where they were re-assembled before being flown to Melville Island. Pilot Bill Janicke accompanied the helicopters and then flew one of the Bells north to the seismic exploration site off Graham Island. The temperatures, which hovered around -40 to -60°F (-40 to -51°C), would have been difficult for piston-engine helicopters

◄ Arnold H. (Barney) Bent, flight instructor on T-6 Texan/SNJ/Harvard. PHOTO COURTESY OF KEVIN BENT

◄ Igor Sikorsky in control of the S-48, later known as the S-51. The British version, built under licence, was known as the Dragonfly. PHOTO COURTESY OF SIKORSKY HISTORICAL ARCHIVES

▸ A Bell 47 on a mining operation at Downie Creek, BC (north of Revelstoke) in 1957. OKANAGAN HELICOPTERS PHOTO

▸ A Fairey Rotodyne was ordered by Okanagan Helicopters in 1958 as a potential candidate for an inter-city helicopter service (Vancouver, Seattle and Victoria). In 1959 when the British government cut costs, forcing the merger of several companies, Fairey Aviation merged with Westland Aircraft. The Rotordyne was discontinued due to cost-cutting measures and technical difficulties and terminated in 1962. Had it been successful it would have carried 57–75 passengers at a cruising speed of 200 knots (370 km/h) and carried 8 tons (7 metric tonnes) of freight. OKANAGAN HELICOPTERS PHOTO

▸ A Hiller UH-12E with new paint scheme in Prince George, BC, in 1960. Okanagan Helicopters experimented with a number of paint schemes to find one best suited to their work in the North. PHOTO COURTESY OF JACK MILBURN

◂ Bell 204B with another paint scheme.
PHOTO COURTESY OF JACK MILBURN

◂ Okanagan Helicopters' S-55, on the Arctic coast in the early 1960s. PHOTO COURTESY OF JACK MILBURN

◂ Okanagan Helicopters' 204B on floats services a Shell Oil rig in the Tofino area, Vancouver Island, in 1967. PHOTO COURTESY OF JACK MILBURN

▸ Pilot Alexander "Buist" Clarke flies Bell 47J-2 CF-OKJ at Rubble Creek, BC (southwest of Garibaldi Lake) in 1968. PHOTO COURTESY OF ALAN CAMPBELL

▸ Universal Helicopters was incorporated in March 1963. On October 11, 2013, they celebrated their fiftieth anniversary. PHOTO COURTESY OF BILL TURNER

◂ A Bell 204B with another new paint scheme in Prince George, BC, in 1970. PHOTO COURTESY OF JACK MILBURN

▴ S-58T on oil rig support in Canadian Arctic. OKANAGAN HELICOPTERS PHOTO

◂ Okanagan Helicopters' Sikorsky S-58T provides transport service between Kangerlussuaq and Maamorilik on the west coast of Greenland in 1974. OKANAGAN HELICOPTERS PHOTO

▸ Arriving at Maamorilik, Greenland, with supplies. OKANAGAN HELICOPTERS PHOTO

▸ A Bell 204B heads out over the Fraser River from the Vancouver International Airport in 1973. The photo was taken from inside a Bell 206. OKANAGAN HELICOPTERS PHOTO

▲ Okanagan Helicopters' Sikorsky S-58T CF-OKG starts a new contract in Thailand in 1974. OKANAGAN HELICOPTERS PHOTO

▲ Okanagan Helicopters crew enjoys a meal at the Shell Oil camp in Gamba, Gabon, in 1976. From left: Marty Battick, Austin Douglas, Keith Hull, Bill Schabes. PHOTO COURTESY OF BILL SCHABES

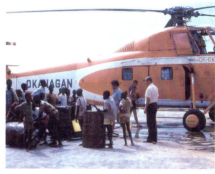

◂ Okanagan Helicopters crew at a Union Oil facility in Phuket, Thailand, in 1976. PHOTO COURTESY OF TONY COALSON

▴ Okanagan Helicopters crew supervises the refuelling of S-58T in Suriname in 1975. PHOTO COURTESY OF BILL SCHABES

◂ Associated Helicopters' Bell 47D-1 CF-GSL at an early bush camp in northern Alberta in the 1950s. Associated was sold to Okanagan Helicopters in July 1977, but continued to operate independently. PHOTO COURTESY OF TELLEF VAASJO

▸ A Dominion Pegasus Bell 206 works on the CN Tower in 1976. Toronto Island Airport is visible in the background. PHOTO COURTESY OF DOMINION PEGASUS HELICOPTERS

▴ Baby orca Miracle being airlifted to a Victoria, BC, aquarium in 1978. OKANAGAN HELICOPTERS PHOTO

▸ Captain Mac Forgie (at the door), Woody Brinston (on the stairwell) and Barney Reifel (looking up at Forgie) work in Goose Bay, NL, in July 1979. PHOTO COURTESY OF THE AUTHOR

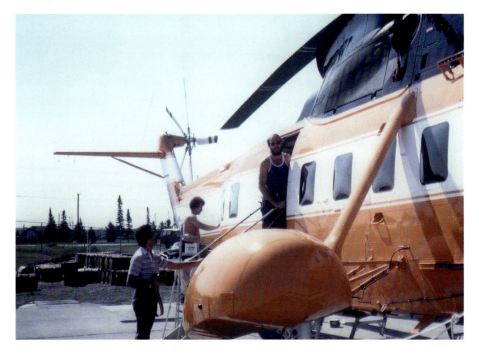

▸ As part of the LOREX project, Okanagan's seven specially equipped Bell 206Bs (JetRangers) were based at Resolute Bay on Cornwallis Island. They fanned out across the northern islands and were often on the northern ocean ice in 1979. OKANAGAN HELICOPTERS PHOTO

THE LATE 1970S   IX

▲ Cape Aldrich on Ellesmere Island, the most northerly point of Canada, in 1977. OKANAGAN HELICOPTERS PHOTO

◂ S-61 heli-logging, northwest of Toba Inlet, BC, in 1978. OKANAGAN HELICOPTERS PHOTO

▲ Warming up an S-61 on a cold morning in Inuvik, NT. The town lies on the Mackenzie Delta about 124 miles (220 kilometres) inside the Arctic Circle. The temperatures in January range between -22C (-19F) to -31C (-23.8F), making it challenging to keep machinery operating. OKANAGAN HELICOPTERS PHOTO

◂ The Most Reverend F.D. Coggan, Archbishop of Canterbury, fishing for salmon on the Kemano River in 1978. OKANAGAN HELICOPTERS PHOTO

▸ The Concorde and Universal Helicopters' Bell 206 at Gander International Airport, NL, in 1978. PHOTO COURTESY OF BILL TURNER

▸ S-61 C-GOKH lands on the Norfolk islands to refuel during a ferry flight from Australia to New Zealand. The islands issued a commemorative stamp to mark the first helicopter landing and the two hundredth anniversary of manned flight. Pilots: Captains Bill Schabes and Roy Webster. PHOTO COURTESY OF THE AUTHOR

▸ The crew of S-61 arrives at Vancouver International Airport after a ferry flight from Ireland in 1976. From left: Captain Jack Jaworski, engineer Chuck Taylor, Captain Pierre Looten. OKANAGAN HELICOPTERS PHOTO

▸ Bell 212 C-GDVG on the rig *Penrod 74*, offshore Puerto Princesa, Philippines, in 1979. PHOTO COURTESY OF THE AUTHOR

THE LATE 1970S   XI

◂ A drip torch suspended under a Bell 206 JetRanger ignites slash in preparation for reforestation. OKANAGAN HELICOPTERS PHOTO

◂ Helicopter and crew at work on a polar bear count north of Saglek, Labrador, 367 miles (591 kilometres) north of Goose Bay, NL. The count was carried out under the federal government's Polar Continental Shelf Program in 1979. The bears were tranquilized with a dart before being weighed, tagged and released.
PHOTO COURTESY OF GEOFF GOODYEAR, UNIVERSAL HELICOPTERS

▸ Esso's rig 3 on an artificial island in the Beaufort Sea in the western Arctic. The photo was taken from the cockpit of an S-61 in 1979.
PHOTO COURTESY OF THE AUTHOR

▴ Polair's converted DC-3 on an ice strip at a polar camp in May 1979. PHOTO COURTESY OF WAYNE ORYSCHAK

▸ Captain Wayne Oryschak and Okanagan Helicopters' Bell 205, the first commercial helicopter to reach the North Pole, 1979.
OKANAGAN HELICOPTERS PHOTO

▴ Engineer Ernie Tymerick at Okanagan Hekicopters' North Pole base camp in 1979.
PHOTO COURTESY OF WAYNE ORYSCHAK

▸ The Polar Continental Shelf's LOREX project required Okanagan Helicopters to station a number of helicopters across the Arctic, including this Bell 205 at the LOREX camp at the North Pole. OKANAGAN ANNUAL REPORT, 1979

◂ Buddhist monks bless a new Sikorsky S-76 in Songkhla, Thailand, in 1979. PHOTO COURTESY OF TONY COALSON

◂ A Bell 206 on contract to BC Forest Service for cone picking uses a hydraulic pruning device in 1980. OKANAGAN HELICOPTERS PHOTO

◂ Captain Tony Coalson flies an S-76 off Songkhla, Thailand, in 1979. PHOTO COURTESY OF TONY COALSON

▸ Three Sikorsky S-61s off Newfoundland, approaching the entrance to St. John's harbour. Two had flown support role for Esso in the Flemish Cap and the third supported a Texaco drill ship. OKANAGAN HELICOPTERS PHOTO, COURTESY OF ROBERT CROCKER

▲ The crew takes a coffee break at the Cottontail Ranch, Nevada, while on a ferry flight from Florida to Vancouver in Okanagan Helicopters' new S-76 in the early 1980s. PHOTO COURTESY OF JEAN BAINE

▸ This pilot, in a Bell 206, performs a typical landing for the Mountain Flying School course in the Okanagan. 1980. OKANAGAN HELICOPTERS PHOTO

◂ Okanagan Helicopters' Mountain Flying School located at the Penticton Airport in 1983.
PHOTO COURTESY OF THE AUTHOR

◂ Captain Jim Neill with Bell 212 C-GBPH at the Esso camp, Tuktoyaktuk, NT, March 1986.
PHOTO COURTESY OF JIM NEILL

▴ Moving a drilling rig from Tuktoyaktuk to a new site on an artificial island in very limited daylight hours, with temperatures between -30 and -40C (-22 to -40F) and winds around 10 mph (16 km/h). OKANAGAN HELICOPTERS PHOTO

◂ A Sikorsky S-76 loaded into a Lockheed C-130 Hercules for a contract in Southeast Asia. Upon arrival in Singapore the machine was reassembled and flown to Songkhla, Thailand. The Hercules also contained a Bell 212 that went on to Bombay, India. OKANAGAN HELICOPTERS PHOTO

▸ S-76 undergoes a crew change on the flight line in Songkhla, Thailand, in 1981. PHOTO COURTESY OF TONY COALSON

▸ S-76 landing on a Unocal drill ship, *Robray Tender 3*, in the Gulf of Thailand, in 1980. OKANAGAN HELICOPTERS PHOTO

◂ Captain Owen Shannon in an S-76. The people waving in the distance are Vietnamese refugees stranded without food or water on the island of Koh Khra, 60 miles from Songkhla, Thailand. The UN had asked Okanagan pilots to report the refugees' presence so that supplies and rescue could be arranged. PHOTO COURTESY OF OWEN SHANNON

▴ Vietnamese refugees arrive in Songkhla, Thailand, in 1980. PHOTO COURTESY OF GRAHAM COWLEY

▴ Vietnamese refugees receive water from Hotel Samila staff in Songkhla, Thailand, 1980. PHOTO COURTESY OF GRAHAM COWLEY

◂ Vietnamese refugees were taken by road to a camp outside Songkhla, Thailand, the day after they landed on the beach, in 1980. PHOTO COURTESY OF GRAHAM COWLEY

▸ New recruits undergo Search and Rescue training offshore of Halifax, NS, in 1981. OKANAGAN HELICOPTERS PHOTO

▸ S-61 C-GOKH lands at Invercargill Airport, New Zealand, in 1983. PHOTO COURTESY OF DEV ANDERSON

◂ The Indian Air Force's MIL-8s also supported the offshore program operated from Juhu, Bombay. PHOTO COURTESY OF THE AUTHOR

◂ WS-51 Dragonfly at Sri Lanka's Katunayake Air Force Base in 1981. PHOTO COURTESY OF THE AUTHOR

◂ A Sikorsky S-76 lands on the ice just north of Tuktoyaktuk, NT, in 1983. OKANAGAN HELICOPTERS PHOTO

▲ While en route to Vancouver from Venezuela on October 7, 1983, S-61 CF-DWC with a crew of four crashed in a heavily wooded area near West Palm Beach, Florida. Crew member Egan Agar suffered serious back injuries. The cause of the crash was the separation of part of the main rotor blade. PHOTO COURTESY OF PHILIP BERNARD

▸ S-61 CF-DWC crash. PHOTO COURTESY OF PHILIP BERNARD

▸ A 1984 Okanagan Helicopters promotional photo of a Sikorsky S-61. OKANAGAN HELICOPTERS PHOTOS

◂ A Sikorsky S-61 departs from an oil rig near Halifax, NS, in 1985. PHOTO COURTESY OF JOHN MCINTYRE

▴ CF-OKP hot refuelling at -30C (-22F) on the Panarctic contract on King Christian Island in the High Arctic in 1984. PHOTO COURTESY OF THE AUTHOR

◂ Captains John McIntyre and Jim Neill stand in front of their helicopter near Sable Island, southeast of Halifax, NS. PHOTO COURTESY OF JIM NEILL

◂ The rig *Moliqpak* operates in the Beaufort Sea an hour's flight north of Tuktoyaktuk in the 1980s. In winter, fixed-wing Twin Otters would land on the ice alongside the rig. PHOTO COURTESY OF THE UNIVERSITY OF SASKATCHEWAN LIBRARY, ARCHIVES AND SPECIAL COLLECTIONS, DOMMASCH HANS FONDS

▸ Okanagan Helicopters' first Bell 214ST (Super Transporter) C-GSYB, pictured here, crashed off the coast of Newfoundland on March 13, 1984, in Placentia Bay, with the loss of four passengers and two crew members. OKANAGAN HELICOPTERS PHOTO

▴ S-61 C-GOKH at Dyce Airport in Aberdeen, Scotland, ready for ferry trip to Vancouver, BC, in 1987. PHOTO COURTESY OF JIM NEILL

▸ S-61 C-GOKH in Narsarsuaq, Greenland, en route to Vancouver, BC, in 1987. PHOTO COURTESY OF JIM NEILL

▸ S-61 CF-OKH stopped in Kulusuk, Greenland, for refuelling while on a ferry trip from the UK to Canada. The next leg took them to Narsarsuaq, Greenland. Pilots Jim Neill, Rocky Rochfort and engineer Joe Zorenc, May 8, 1987. PHOTO COURTESY OF JIM NEILL

◄ New Year's Day, 1984 in Tuktoyaktuk, with a temperature of -25C (-13F). Okanagan Helicopters crew members pose alongside friends from Beaudrill. PHOTO COURTESY OF JIM NEILL

◄ Arthur Cox's painting of Bell 47 CF-FZX landing on a BC glacier appeared in the November–December 1980 issue of *West Coast Aviator*. PHOTO COURTESY OF ARTHUR COX

◄ Canadian Helicopter's Bell 212 C-GOKL, still in Okanagan colours, with the US Navy's nuclear submarine USS *Spadefish*, which visited the Sound Surveillance Systems (SOSUS) site 50 miles (80 kilometres) north of Greenland in 1988. PHOTO COURTESY OF DALE SIMPSON

▸ Conning tower of the nuclear submarine USS *Spadefish* in January 1988. PHOTO COURTESY OF DALE SIMPSON

▲ The captain of the USS *Spadefish* got an aerial view from the helicopter in 1988. PHOTO COURTESY OF DALE SIMPSON

▸ USS *Spadefish* in 1988. PHOTO COURTESY OF DALE SIMPSON

▲ The SOSUS camp in 1988. PHOTO COURTESY OF DALE SIMPSON

as was demonstrated later when a DC-3 crew had to start pre-heating their aircraft at 5:30 AM in preparation for a 9:00 AM takeoff. By the following year Panarctic Oils had discovered one of the largest gas fields in the Arctic Islands at Drake Point on Melville Island. These and later discoveries established significant reserves of natural gas.

In July pilots Fred LeGrice and Al Eustice and engineer Dick Mack were assigned to a long tour in the Hudson Bay area to work with an offshore drilling rig belonging to the Canadian subsidiary of the French petroleum company, Elf Aquitaine. Later in personal correspondence, Al described their flight from Vancouver to Churchill, Manitoba:

> After lengthy preparation, we departed VFR in two 206As with the hope of reaching the BC–Alberta border [in one] day. Flying astern and level with Fred at about 5,000 feet [1,525 metres], Dick and I cruised comfortably along in the smooth air [until] just west of Nelson, BC. Believing I was having mechanical problems, I turned abruptly to Dick and said: "Why are we climbing?"
>
> Dick looked rather puzzled. A second later we realized Fred was going down and we were going up. We followed Fred as he performed a classic autorotation into a creek bed, having just dealt with an engine failure.
>
> Dick made some comment about me being half asleep on the job.
>
> [What followed was a] typical Okanagan Helicopters recovery mission: an S-58 in play to move helicopter to Nelson . . . Crew works all night and we are on our way [again] the next day.[55]

Between July and October the crews faced erratic winds on the long trips over the hazardous pack ice and open water from Churchill on the west shore of Hudson Bay to the Pen Islands—a distance of 220 miles (354 kilometres)—and then an additional 120 miles (193 kilometres) out to the rig. When the weather cooperated, they spotted pods of beluga whales and numerous polar bears.

Okanagan further built its reputation for remarkable rescues in 1968 when a company S-58 from the Prince George base came to the rescue of a single-engine Piper Cherokee, which had skidded on a frozen lake when bad weather forced it to land. The S-58 lifted the aircraft off the ice and flew it to the Prince George airfield.

1968 ANNUAL REPORT
The company's top management was overhauled in 1968 after Glenn McPherson retired as company president and managing director and was replaced by Ian Kennedy, a World War II veteran and chartered accountant. By now Okanagan and its subsidiaries employed 150 people in Vancouver, Montreal and its 18 operating bases across the country. Revenue hours had declined during the year by 5,000 hours, in large part due to a cooler summer with fewer forest fires.

Al Eustice had served in the RCAF as a commissioned aircrew radio officer. He started flying commercially in 1959 from Campbell River for BC Airlines, which had a collection of amphibious aircraft, but when Vancouver Island Helicopters sent a Bell 47G-2 to Campbell River to assist in a search for a missing aircraft, he got his first helicopter ride and became convinced that helicopters were the future. He joined Okanagan in 1966. During his time with the company, he held many positions from line pilot, Campbell River base manager, operations manager VFR and manager of OK Heli-Logging. When Okanagan was bought out by Canadian Helicopters, Al's post with the company was that of vice-president of systems safety. He was recognized by Transport Canada and presented with the aviation safety award for service to industry.

1969

In 1969 Okanagan took on a 50-mile-long (80-kilometre-long) power-line construction job that ran north up Indian Arm, a steep-sided glaciated fjord branching off Burrard Inlet, to Alta Lake, near Whistler, BC. A Bell 204B and a smaller Hiller UH-12E delivered steel tower sections, each of them 15 feet (4.6 metres) tall, that they lowered and held in place while ground crews positioned them and bolted the sections together. The completed towers stood 300 feet (91.5 metres) high.

As the company was considering replacing its Bell 47G-3s and 47Bs and its Hiller UH-12Es, in June the Bell 204B was evaluated for survey work on a 17-day mining survey in the Ross River area of northern BC. This larger Bell machine demonstrated greater stability because high temperatures, high winds, downdrafts and turbulence had less effect on the larger helicopters with the result that they could provide a higher degree of accuracy on survey projects.

Starting with Shell Oil Company's operation offshore from Tofino on Vancouver Island and the previous year's Panarctic Oils contract on Melville Island, Okanagan and its subsidiaries were now making a name for providing support for major domestic oil and gas projects and drew the attention of companies such as Amoco, Elf Aquitaine, British Petroleum, Chevron, Esso, Mobil, Shell, Tenneco, Texaco, Total Eastcan and Husky Oil. The company pioneered precision landings on rigs, set a new standard in offshore flying and introduced instrument flight rules (IFR), the first helicopter company to be approved to do so by the Canadian Department of Transport. Its first IFR project for an Arctic oil company was an ice survey for Sun Oil Co., which was operating in the King Christian Island area during the winter darkness.

The eastern offshore oil field that Okanagan Helicopters serviced stretched from the continental shelf off Nova Scotia and Newfoundland, along the Labrador coast (AKA Iceberg Alley) and north as far as Davis Strait and Baffin Island. This rugged, inhospitable coastline presented some of the most challenging flying conditions in the world, with some drilling rig sites located as much as 244 miles (393 kilometres) offshore. One of Okanagan's S-61s, which was capable of handling a 6,000-pound (2,720 kilogram) payload, operated from the base in Sydney, Nova Scotia, and provided a daily service to a rig that was located 160 miles (260 kilometres) offshore. It was crewed by chief pilot Don MacKenzie, pilots Dave Whyte and John McIntyre and engineers Rocky Pearson, Chuck Taylor, Wally Boyle and Charlie Morin plus a dispatcher. The engineers had a reputation as pranksters. According to Chuck Taylor:

> Don MacKenzie would quite often be in a bit of rush for his flight and had an electric razor in his office desk to have a quick shave. Unbeknown to him, the engineers had removed the blades so for the longest time Don thought he was having a shave [when] in fact nothing was happening.
>
> The local man who was the dispatcher was known to have a bottle of rum stashed away in the radio room for off-duty occasions; again, the engineers were either hiding it in another location or replacing it with some foul liquid.
>
> Dave Whyte, who was a new co-pilot and recently married, arrived for his first offshore flight . . . along with his new wife to see him off. At the foot of the stairs, I said: "Dave, you had better give me your wallet, watch and any other valuables you might have." Dave's wife looked horrified and asked why. My answer: "Because these guys rarely come back after their first flight." The look of absolute horror was replaced with relief when the joke was exposed.[56]

1969 ANNUAL REPORT

Although Okanagan Helicopters remained the largest helicopter company in Canada and the third-largest in the world, by 1969 its fleet numbered just 45 machines, down from a high of over 60 five years earlier. This was mainly due to reorganization and consolidation and the phasing out of piston-engine helicopters. The company had also divested itself of the Fairchild Hiller FH-1100s when, after an accident resulting in the death of a California Standard employee, an important customer refused to accept them on any contract. Okanagan then turned to Bell 206A model JetRangers, ordering 11 for delivery in the following year, and introduced the new Sikorsky S-58T twin turbine.

By the end of the year, for investment reasons, Okanagan Copter Spray Ltd. was eliminated as a separate organization, and third-party work at Canadian Helicopter Overhaul Ltd. ceased due to increased internal demand. The company had created a flight safety officer post, and the International Union of Operating Engineers Local 115 had received certification to represent the company's pilots and engineers and negotiations had begun.

*

By the end of the 1960s Okanagan Helicopters was firmly established as an industry leader as the company had undertaken numerous innovations, thanks to its dedicated and experienced staff. It was the first helicopter company to install hydro towers; it also pioneered long distance ferry flights, support for offshore oil rigs and forest fire control. No longer merely a Canada-wide company, it had begun to move offshore.

Financial review 1960–69. Profits and losses as noted in the company's annual reports:

1960	$261,549
1961	$90,034
1962	($171,068)
1963	$237,146
1964	$293,419
1965	not available
1966	$119,400
1967	$462,132
1968	($25,695)
1969	($207,240)

Chapter Four

THE EARLY 1970S

1970

There was important news from helicopter manufacturers in 1970. Sikorsky announced that its S-61N and S-61L models had now transported four million passengers. Bell Helicopters began marketing the 212, its first commercially available medium-sized helicopter, with a demonstration tour throughout the United States and Canada. The 212 featured a heavy-duty airframe with a PT6 Twin-Pac engine built by United Aircraft of Canada and rated at 1,800 shaft horsepower, which provided the power to make height-velocity restrictions virtually non-existent.

In its own fleet Okanagan Helicopters converted three Sikorsky S-58s to twin engine S-58Ts to increase heavy lifting capacity; the first of these machines was contracted to support firefighting services in the Prince George area. Okanagan took delivery of the 11 new Bell 206A JetRangers ordered the previous year, and the elimination of the company's remaining piston-engine helicopters was completed when the last S-55 and spares were sold to Carson Helicopters of Pennsylvania.

In March 1970 Okanagan's fleet remained at 45 and consisted of the following:

15 Bell 206As	11 Bell 47s
3 Sikorsky S-58Ts	2 Sikorsky S-61s
10 Hiller UH-12Es	1 Hiller FH-1100
2 Bell 204s	1 Beech 95 Fixed-wing

As in previous years, Okanagan crews were involved in several rescue operations. The first, which was documented for *Outdoor Life* magazine by Gordon Gosling, occurred in January after Harvey Cardinal, a trapper, hunter and guide in the Fort St. John area of northern BC, tracked a grizzly bear through the thick brush. He carried an old .303 military Lee–Enfield rifle. When he failed to return by nightfall, his friends began to worry, and the following day a search party followed his tracks for a couple of miles into a tangled thicket where they found his body. Worried about another encounter with the bear, they promptly left the scene, drove to the nearest phone and called the Fort St. John RCMP. Several police officers drove to the scene with Fish and Wildlife Branch officer Jack Mackill; they determined that the attack had been so sudden that Cardinal had not had time to release the safety on his rifle. He was killed with a single blow of a forepaw to the side of his head. Concerned that the bear was nearby and would attack again, Mackill and the Mounties quickly retrieved the body and returned to Fort St.

◂ A new Bell 206A in air ambulance configuration attends to a derailment on the Canadian National (CN) Railway line northeast of Smithers, BC. PHOTO COURTESY OF JACK MILBURN

John. It was agreed that the bear had to be destroyed: "Whatever its reason for attacking, now that it had killed and fed on a human, the odds were great that it would repeat the performance," Gosling wrote.[57]

The next day three armed conservation officers climbed aboard an Okanagan Bell 206 flown by the company's Fort St. John base manager, Maynard Bergh, who had previously flown them on game counts and predator-control missions. Maynard flew them to the scene, but tracking the bear from the air proved difficult as the terrain was covered with aspen and dense stands of spruce. The 206 flew just above the treetops, but the main rotor stirred up the light, fluffy snow, which filled in the bear's tracks within seconds. After four hours and 8 miles (13 kilometres), they tracked the bear to an isolated stand of spruce. The helicopter circled around again but no tracks came out of the stand. Finally the bear moved into a clearing. Gosling:

> To me, one of the most surprising things about that bear hunt was the way the grizzly reacted to the chopper. All the while we were tracking him, I had visualized him running at top speed to get away or turning on us . . . But he did nothing of the kind. He showed neither anger nor concern. He just walked away and even after we started shooting he did not hurry.

It took three shots to kill the bear. Afterwards Maynard landed the helicopter, and the conservation officers climbed out for a closer look at the animal, but that was when one of the officers walked back along the side of the machine, and the still spinning tail rotor struck him on the side of the head, taking out a section of his skull "about a half inch wide and three-quarters of an inch long."

> [He] was unconscious and for a minute we thought he was dead. When we saw that he was still alive, we gave up all thought of checking out the bear and loaded [the officer] into the chopper for the half-hour flight to Fort St. John. Fortunately the fragile rotor . . . wasn't seriously damaged and the chopper could still fly.[58]

He was flown first to the local hospital and from there to Vancouver where prompt medical attention saved his life. He made a full recovery.

After the bear's carcass was brought in for examination, the conservation officers found that it was a very old, battle-scarred male in poor condition. In spite of this, there was no evidence of malnutrition and tests for rabies were negative. Why it was not in hibernation during the frigid January weather remained a mystery.

This incident demonstrated the value of the JetRanger in evacuating seriously injured victims to hospitals capable of providing specialized treatment. As a result, the company converted one Bell 206A to IFR to enable it to fly at night, allowing for 24-hour emergency coverage. It was also equipped with a new water/alcohol injection system used on commercial jet transport for additional power during landing and takeoff.

The second rescue incident of the year took place in May when a CN Rail train derailment in a remote area about 25 miles (40 kilometres) northeast of Smithers caused a number of serious injuries. Ambulances were dispatched from Smithers but the Bulkley River, which at that point runs between the highway and the railroad track, blocked access to the site. Fortunately, only a few days earlier Okanagan's new ambulance JetRanger had been assigned to the closest base, and it was dispatched with pilot Jerry Freeman at the controls. He placed two of the injured in the litters or rescue baskets and the third in the helicopter next to him and flew them directly to the Bulkley Valley District Hospital in a time of only 35 minutes. All three survived.

The third rescue event of the year involved managing pilot Don MacKenzie of the Sydney, Nova Scotia, base who saved fourteen people after he brought a disabled Sikorsky s-61 to a safe landing on an offshore oil rig. For his skill the Helicopter Association of America named him "Pilot of the Year." His co-pilot Jim Reid was also recognized for his skills and cool head during the incident.

1970 ANNUAL REPORT

Despite a slow-down in the economy, revenue for 1970 increased by approximately $125,000 over 1969. After two years as president, Ian Kennedy retired; John Pitts, who had become a company director in 1968, replaced him. The annual report stated that Okanagan had a staff of 131 spread over 18 bases and sales offices from Vancouver Island to Nova Scotia, but the report also singled out a number of staff members:

- Egan Agar, Carl's son, had joined the company after serving with the RCAF where he flew Sabre fighter aircraft. During his time with Okanagan, he was involved with rescues during serious flooding conditions in northern BC. He also had a wide range of experience in mining and power-line projects, accumulating over 7,700 flight hours in both fixed-wing and helicopters.
- Radio dispatcher Max Hoover, using the single-sideband (HF) system, kept daily contact with the bases and aircraft operating in western Canada. Max, call sign VXU215 Vancouver, was a committed salmon fisherman, known to smoke his salmon in an old fridge outside the hangar.

◂ Bud Tillotson trained many helicopter pilots from around the world during his time as chief flying instructor at Okanagan's Mountain Flying Training School in Penticton, BC. He was one of the pioneers of the training program. By 1969, he had accumulated more than 10,000 hours of which 7,000 were on helicopters. OKANAGAN HELICOPTERS PHOTO

- L.G. (Jim) Reid, an S-61 offshore captain, was one of the first helicopter pilots in Canada to be trained on IFR. He operated from the Okanagan's Sydney, Nova Scotia base on offshore Atlantic operations. By 1970 he had flown 10,000 hours in both fixed-wing and helicopters.
- Stu Smeeth, who had been with the company over 20 years, was in charge of Okanagan's component overhaul facility that covered everything from rotor heads to engine mounts.
- Mark Valpy, the Prince George base engineer conducted in-house mechanical training for pilots. By 1970 he had instructed 17 pilots.
- L.M. "Bud" Tillotson, chief flying instructor at the Mountain Flying School, trained in the RCAF in the 1940s and joined Okanagan in the late 1950s. By 1970 he had more than 10,000 hours flight time with 7,000 hours on helicopters.

1971

Early in the new year Okanagan took possession of the first-off-the- production-line Bell JetRanger 2 with pilot Don Broeder accepting the logbook from Bell's vice-president of commercial marketing. It had already proven itself by landing with three people onboard at an altitude of 12,500 feet (3,810 metres) in the Himalayas and then, with fuel planning, four passengers at the 13,000-foot (3,960-metre) level. Okanagan's first assignment for this machine with its light turbine 400 shaft horsepower Allison engine was heavy lifting in the hot, dry mountainous region of southern BC. It was next sent to the company's Revelstoke base, approximately 250 miles (400 kilometres) northeast of Vancouver as the crow flies, in the midst of 8,000-foot (2,440-metre) mountains with a timberline at the 7,000-foot (2,135-metre) level. This area has heavy rainfall in the summer

▸ An S-61 lands in the Universal Hangar in Goose Bay, NL, in 1981. The aircraft was working for an offshore drilling site operated by Total oil company off the Labrador coast. This main base for Universal was on the commercial side of Goose Bay's airport. PHOTO COURTESY OF UNIVERSAL HELICOPTERS

when the temperature can reach as high as 95°F (35°C). Most of the new JetRanger's work here was in mining and forestry with a great deal of sling work at high elevations. With its cooler engine temperature and increased power, it was a great improvement over the Bell 47G-3B that it replaced. It now worked alongside the JetRanger 206A model, one of the 22 acquired in 1970–71, which was used primarily for ambulance work.

In February 1971 Okanagan acquired all the shares of West Coast Helicopters Ltd., formerly owned by Westcoast Transmission Co. Ltd. of Vancouver. The company then sold off Westcoast's fleet of four Bell 47s and one FH-1100 to Trans North Turbo Air Ltd. of Whitehorse, Highland Helicopters Ltd., Lift Air and a private owner.

About the same time Okanagan purchased Universal Helicopters, which had been founded in Carp, Ontario, in 1963 by partners Russ Bradley, the founder of Bradley Air Services (known today as First Air), Gary Fields and G.H. "Herb" Johnson. Its original fleet consisted of a Hiller UH-12E and a Brantly B-2. Three years later Herb had moved the company to Gander, Newfoundland, where they worked with Eastern Provincial Airways (EPA) to provide helicopter services to complement EPA's fixed-wing bush

▲ Universal Helicopters' Bell 47 sits on floats aboard the research ship *Baffin* in 1969. PHOTO COURTESY OF UNIVERSAL HELICOPTERS

◂ New aircraft maintenance engineer Norman (Norm) Noseworthy, second from left, works in Moncton, NB. Photo taken in 1969. PHOTO COURTESY OF NORM NOSEWORTHY

operation. They flew support to the Bay D'Espoir hydroelectric development as well as mineral exploration and environmental and wildlife contracts.

Universal Helicopters received a welcome gift at their Christmas party in 1970 when assistant manager Bob Brough received a telephone call announcing that they had won their first offshore oil contract. That contract off Prince Edward Island involved their Bell 47G-2, CF-IZX, flown by Dave Eagleston. The Bell 47 was later replaced by a 206A, CF-XSK. On March 29 S-61 CF-DWC (the Jolly Green Giant) arrived from Sydney to start another offshore contract.

After Okanagan's purchase of Universal, it continued to operate as a subsidiary for the next 17 years. However, the purchase added another 15 helicopters to the overall fleet, including four Bell 206As and eight Bell 47s as well as a Sikorsky S-55 and two Hiller UH-12Es while at the same time giving Universal Helicopters a broader range of operations, moving it from its existing VFR to IFR and providing more support for oil exploration off the East Coast.

*

In the summer of 1971, Okanagan formed a brand new subsidiary company, OK Heli-Lifts Ltd., and during the company's three-week experiment to see if heli-logging could be a viable venture, veteran Okanagan pilot Grant Soutar flew an S-58T with a payload of 5,000 pounds (2,200 kg) of logs for 2 miles (3 kilometres) from the slopes of the Redonda Islands, east of Campbell River, to a drop zone in Pendrell Sound. The machine was flown an average of five to six hours a day, hauling out around 1,400 logs per day. Although at first there was a problem with the operation of the hook to which the cable was attached, it was eventually solved by the Okanagan engineers.

That summer pilot Al Eustice reported to Tommy Gurr in Tahsis on Vancouver Island to work on a power-line construction project with the Hiller UH-12E. His first week was spent familiarizing himself with the local area, including the location of the power line. Al Eustice recalled:

> I knew Tom Gurr and looked forward to working with him. Tom was a very senior Okanagan pilot [and] had a wicked sense of humour. He was [also] check captain on the S-55.
>
> On Monday morning with the whole crew of linesmen, we assembled at an old log landing at the head of Tahsis Inlet. Tom covered the numerous safety and operational issues and introduced new crew members. He started by saying, "Al Eustice here will be flying the support aircraft this week. Some of you [may] recognize Al; up until two weeks ago Al worked in the shoe department of Woodward's store in Vancouver."
>
> I foolishly assumed that Tom would tell them that I had just got back from power-line construction on the Hudson's Hope project or that I had been with BC Airlines and knew the area we were working in well. I was in dead water as no one was about to fly with a shoe salesman. By noon Tom was still grinning, but I had convinced the crew that it was probably safe to fly with me.
>
> Tom did buy the drinks.[59]

Later the Bell 204B was brought in to replace the Hiller and became the workhorse of the project.

1972

On the night of March 13, 1972, the 473-foot (145-metre) freighter *Vanlene* was approaching Barkley Sound on the west coast of Vancouver Island when it ran aground on the rocks of Austin Island, rupturing its fuel tanks and losing its winches. After five days of attempts to re-float the ship using standard salvage methods, the salvage company contacted Okanagan to remove the cargo: 300 Dodge Colt cars. By this time the ship's stern was partially submerged and the ship was listing to starboard. When Okanagan's flight safety officer, Grant Soutar, veteran pilot Roy Webster and engineer John Hodgson arrived at the site in a Bell 204B, their first task was to lift a pump and hose onto the *Vanlene*'s deck so that the fuel from the ruptured tanks could be removed. Grant Soutar wrote the following report for Bell Helicopter's newsletter:

> There were approximately 150 cars available in five groups, all forward of the bridge. Most of the cars were water free and only those not touched by water were to be removed.
>
> By 2 PM the forward set of "goal posts" that held the booms and the ship's rigging had been dropped forward and so made the No. 2 hold available to the helicopter by using 100 feet [30.5 metres] of line into the hold while the aircraft hovered just above the other set of "goal posts." Thirty-four cars were removed and placed on a barge approximately one mile away on the first day.
>
> By 11 AM the following day the remaining boom and masts had been pulled overboard, and this then made it possible to get deeper into the ship without the requirement for another 100 feet of line. Forty-three more cars were removed to a larger barge.
>
> We began work the next day at 7 AM. By 2 PM the last 54 salvageable cars had been removed.
>
> An interesting requirement to obtain the eight cars in the third level down in the No. 3 hold was that the hatch opening there was only half the size of the upper hatch. This made very careful alignment of the car necessary prior to

◂ A Bell 204B salvaging cars from grounded freighter SS *Vanlene*, Barclay Sound, Vancouver Island. OKANAGAN HELICOPTERS PHOTO

rapid and continuous vertical movement. This became quite spectacular, and the movement of the cars from the lowest level internally in the ship through three hatches to the upper deck and clear of the ship was likened to squeezing a wet bar of soap.[60]

At Vancouver International Airport ground fog often presented challenges for the company's machines. As a result, that spring, when an s-58T was due to fly to Whistler to work on a new ski-lift tower, operations manager Dave Dunn booked a tug and a barge and had it dock near the Okanagan hangar. The s-58 managed to hover over to the barge and was then towed to an area of clear skies to continue on its way to the work site. In similar circumstances, a Bell 206A, booked to ferry heavy crates of cranberries later that year, was loaded onto a flatbed truck and taken to the work site. Elsewhere in BC, the company tried heli-logging near Yale in the Fraser Canyon and along the route of a power line from the Mica Dam, which spans the Columbia River north of Revelstoke.

On the East Coast the company assigned a second s-61 to its offshore Amoco Canada Petroleum Ltd. contract and signed a new contract with Mobil Oil Canada Ltd. Some three weeks into the Amoco contract, the s-61 was used on a medical evacuation flight to airlift a critically ill man from a ship 175 miles (290 kilometres) off the coast. The s-61 also serviced a semi-submersible rig 150 miles (240 kilometres) offshore. Starting in September the company extended the range of its offshore helicopters out of St. John's, NL, when one of them flew a 700-mile (1,120-kilometre) ice patrol.

In August Okanagan began operating a contract in Greenland, working under Greenland Air to provide regular transportation for the 300-mile (480-kilometre) trip between Kangerlussuaq and Maamorilik on that country's west coast where a major zinc-lead mine was under development. It was expected to produce 1,820 tons (1,650 metric tonnes) of ore a day. Initially Okanagan's contract required one s-58T with a second machine added for a six-month period in the spring of 1972. These machines, equipped with pop-out floats, often worked in temperatures of -40°F/C with winds sometimes reaching 90 mph (149 km/h). The Canadian helicopters were required to have safety notices posted in Danish. However, whenever Danish passengers came onboard, they would read the notices and burst into laughter. The crews never found out what caused their amusement. The crewing started with veteran pilot Harvey Evans and engineer Dave O'Neill who were based in Maamorilik, but the crews rotated every two months.

*

Ian Kennedy, who had retired two years earlier, died on October 26, 1972. He had joined the company in May 1958 and held the positions of vice-president, general manager and chairman.

1972 ANNUAL REPORT

In 1972, the company's 25th year of operation, Okanagan's revenues rose significantly and flight hours set a new record, up 26 percent over the previous year. The fleet had expanded again with the addition of two new Bell 204Bs, and in February the company had ordered 12 JetRanger 2s with upgraded Allison engines and included an option for an additional 10 machines. The acquisition increased the light-turbine fleet to 38 machines, making a total of 70 machines operating out of 25 bases extending from Vancouver Island to Newfoundland and as far north as Inuvik. Since the JetRangers had been successful in carrying out numerous rescues and medical evacuations, some of the new machines were fitted with ambulance kits.

1973

Okanagan Helicopters continued its involvement with the oil and gas industry in the Arctic and Northwest Territories in 1973 by constructing new hangars in Inuvik and Norman Wells. Additions to the fleet included an S-61N, two S-58Ts, 15 Bell 206Bs, and two Sud Aviation Gazelle helicopters. In Vancouver the company's one-storey office building caught fire. No one was hurt, but the technical records had to be salvaged by a team of office temps who copied the essential information from the blackened and brittle record cards.

Okanagan acquired two more companies. Haida Helicopters Ltd. had started operating as North West Helicopters in 1967, becoming Haida NW Helicopters a year later and Haida Helicopters in February 1970. Although based in Vancouver, it was owned by a Montreal trust company, which had made an unsuccessful bid to buy Lac St. Jean Aviation to get a foot in the James Bay Project. In 1973 their fleet consisted of two Hiller UH-12Es, a Hiller S14, two Alouette IIs, a Bell 205 and an SA 341G Gazelle as well as a Helio Courier fixed-wing aircraft. When Haida joined Okanagan, Ken Blackwood was the operations manager and Bob Fiedeldy the chief engineer.

Okanagan's second acquisition that year, Lac St. Jean Aviation of Quebec, which had been originally owned by Aurelien Cote and R. Simard, had started out as a fixed-wing bush operation that added a Hiller helicopter to its fleet. In 1966 it had been sold to a French helicopter company, Heli-Union, formed in 1961 with the backing of a pharmaceutical company. Heli-Union came to Canada with two Alouette IIs, later adding Alouette IIIs, to work on Montreal's Expo 67, Hydro-Québec's James Bay Project and a contract in Labrador. Heli-Union sent crews from France; among those who stayed on were Michel Perrier, Claude Chaput, Alain Verdes, Michel Raymond and Jean Tarvic. In a recent interview engineer Jean Tarvic, one of those original Heli-Union employees, recalled:

> I arrived in Montreal at the beginning of January 1966 and was employed by Lac St. Jean Aviation, which was then owned by Mr. Aurelien Cote.
>
> Mr. Cote, who also owned a transport business, had the opportunity to see helicopters working while on a visit to the USA. He sold some of his trucks to buy Bell 47 helicopters. At the time an Alouette II (1408) was also in the fleet with Mr. Couturier as pilot and Mr. Mondion as engineer. In addition, Lac St. Jean Aviation leased an Alouette from Heli-Union, which was flown by Heli-Union pilot Luc Desaulnier and myself as the engineer.
>
> We did film work along the St. Lawrence River for Radio-Canada [CBC's French-language service] as well as carrying out demonstration flights. However, our main activities were Hydro-Québec contracts, mostly in support of the James Bay Hydro project with operations out of the Matagami base... The fleet consisted of an Alouette II (CF-VKN), an Alouette III (CF-POH), and a Bell 47 (CF-HTJ).
>
> It was bitterly cold in Abitibi with our camp on the frozen Rupert River; we were surprised one morning to find that the mercury thermometer had broken. The mechanical thermometer worked, but it could only read [down] to a maximum of -50°C and our temperature was well below that. Everyone in the camp quickly dove back into their sleeping bags; we never did know the true temperature that day.
>
> Another big memorable occurrence! An Alouette had an engine failure on a frozen lake; we could not find the cause of the engine failure, so after two

snowstorms, another turbine arrived and we were able to change the engine. The closest vehicle access was 500 metres [1,640 feet] away, so the engine in its container had to be pulled in by three large Ski-Doos. No heat was available at the work site, so engineers had to take turns warming themselves in a faraway truck. The new engine was partially installed and the pilot took the risk to fly off the lake to about two kilometres [one mile] away so we could complete the work. I strongly thanked the pilot but his name escapes me.[61]

On the international scene, Okanagan submitted a bid in response to a proposal call from Thai Airways for a helicopter service transporting tourists from Bangkok International Airport to Pattaya. At the same time Thailand was opening up offshore oil work for a number of companies such as Amoco Thailand Petroleum, Triton Energy, Tenneco, British Petroleum and Union Oil. Okanagan had meetings with Gulf Oil and Union Oil of Thailand and sent its chief pilot to Union Oil's head office in Los Angeles, while Dan Dunn, the company's operations officer, went to Thailand to assess the operational conditions for a possible start-up in January/February 1974.

1974

The Salmon Airlift operated again in 1974. This time the federal Department of Fisheries contracted the company to operate an exclusive Bell JetRanger service to assist the salmon from Babine Lake past obstacles that were preventing them from reaching their spawning grounds on the upper reaches of Pinkut Creek. The flight facilities were rather primitive: the passengers were loaded with dip nets into converted firebombing buckets, which did not give them much swimming room but did provide aerated water. It was only a five-minute ride, and once on the spawning grounds, they were unceremoniously dumped into their new surroundings. This service was estimated to have carried over 17,000 adult salmon in a period of just three weeks.

In Vancouver that summer there were wild scenes of helicopters and fast cars zooming among skyscrapers for the movie *Russian Roulette*, which was based on the Tom Ardies novel *Kosygin Is Coming*. The story follows the exploits of a Mountie, played by George Segal, who becomes involved in a KGB conspiracy to kill Soviet premier Alexei Kosygin when he visits Vancouver. Although the identification on the helicopter was RCMP, the machine came from Okanagan Helicopters and was piloted by Grant Soutar and Glen Rankin. Colin Nel of Okanagan's marketing group, who also took part as an extra in some of the flying scenes, managed the complex scheduling of the helicopter.

In eastern Canada, in the face of increased concern about pollution in the St. Lawrence River, the Quebec government's environmental protection service awarded Hélicoptères Canadiens/Lac St. Jean Aviation a five-year contract to pick up water samples every month from spring to autumn from Kingston on Lake Ontario and Percé on the eastern tip of the Gaspé Peninsula. The float-equipped helicopters collected the samples about a mile offshore and then rushed them to a laboratory at Rivière-du-Loup for analysis.

The company's activity in the High Arctic increased after Imperial Oil encountered natural gas while drilling in the Beaufort Sea. Okanagan supplied many of the helicopters involved and carried out the first night-slinging using a Sikorsky S-61L model. The company was also called in to provide support for a Sun Oil study tracking ice movement in the King Christian Island area, approximately 73 miles (117 kilometres) from the magnetic North Pole. Scientific instruments installed in the ice had to be checked periodically to

CHAPTER FOUR—THE EARLY 1970S

ensure they were functioning; the challenge lay in returning to the exact locations in the darkness and severe weather conditions of the Arctic. During this period the Okanagan fleet established another first for operating on an ice station by using an IFR equipped S-58T model, which led to the development of precision-instrument flying techniques for year-round Arctic use.

Pilots and engineers faced many challenges in the Arctic, and in the following passage, pilot Owen Shannon describes his introduction to the "sub-zero temperatures, blowing snow, noise and confus[ing] wind[s]" of his first day of flying there and the quiet heroism of his young engineer, George Hartmire, who "went the extra mile" to get them safely back to their base:

> We were en route to Eglinton Island from Rae Point, located on Melville Island, NWT, ... about 730 miles [1,182 kilometres] north of Inuvik. We had chosen to cross a 2,000-foot [615-metre] ridge of ice caps before descending a long inlet on the west side of Melville Island. The weather seemed to be cooperating and the anticipated ridge seemed clear, with rocks for reference amidst the snow-covered rising ground. At this height a change occurred. I adjusted the speed as the rocks started to disappear and white became more apparent. I had made the decision to turn back as I had a sudden loss of reference, no horizon, no depth of field and no ground reference—nothing at all except for one black speck in a world of white.
>
> I had been in the Arctic for two days. This was my first trip, having spent the last four months working in the Canadian Rockies after completing my mountain flying helicopter course at ... Penticton. I was an Arctic newbie and was in the process of learning some brand new skills in this desolate environment. I had a total of 10 hours Arctic time then in my two days ... It consisted of flying [at] less than 500 feet [150 metres] ... from Rae Point to Drake Point to Sherard Bay and all working camps [in between] for Panarctic Oils Ltd. I had two long days of slinging and moving personnel in a Bell 206 on floats in temperatures of 22°F (-5°C) with a visibility of less than a couple of miles with fog patches and blowing snow.
>
> My preparation for the Arctic was not particularly detailed. Apart from a Global Navigation System [a land-based forerunner of GPS] and ... some warm clothing—that was it. Most other newbies had the advantage of the summer weather in which to work into the approaching winter conditions. Bob Batchelor, an experienced Arctic pilot who I was replacing, gave me an excellent handover, briefing me while he was waiting to board the plane I had just arrived on. When I mentioned that this was my first trip to the Arctic, I remember him shaking his head in disbelief and telling me not to go flying until the icing conditions discontinued, which currently were a daily feature. I was about to learn of the many weather-related condition changes in a very short time.
>
> On September 8, my third day on the job, we were tasked with assisting Associated Helicopters' Bell 204 located on Eglinton Island for a couple of weeks. The weather had improved to a visibility of 10 miles [16 kilometres], so a direct routing was planned covering 170 miles [272 kilometres] taking about one hour and thirty-five minutes flying time. Little did we know what was in store for us.
>
> We were well over halfway to our destination when we encountered the world of white. The black speck was a rock about a foot high just ahead of my foot pedals. I had no time to look at anything else but to hold that rock in my

vision—and bump!—we were on the ground. My engineer, George Hartmire, and I looked at each other with question marks hovering about our heads: "What the #*!! happened there?" Without realizing it, we'd slowed down to less than a walking pace as the reference points had disappeared—no time to turn back—and literally we were on the ground. Lady Luck had produced the second of her contributions for the day. This was the whiteout I'd heard so much about, and the suddenness of it was a bit frightening.

We spent some time chatting about our options, which seemed to point towards shutting down and waiting it out. The question was how long would we have to wait? We had no luck trying to raise Rae Point on the HF radio, and with using the map we estimated that we were 150 feet [46 metres] below a pass and we were currently at a height of 1,850 feet [565 metres]. All we had to do was get on the top of the pass and down the other side, and we hoped we would be on our way. Simple for a couple of young, brave and naïve guys. The solution still stared us in the face and said: "Stay where you are."

George suggested that he walk ahead of the helicopter and I use him as a reference point. He checked the depth of the snow and, in his winter gear, started trudging ahead of the helicopter. I lifted the machine off the ground and started to follow; this idea lasted 10 seconds. Try as I might, George had just about disappeared. He soon realized what was happening and ran down the hill towards the helicopter waving his arms. I got the machine back on the ground without any damage; the floats must have been the saving grace—Lady Luck's third contribution.

We came up with another idea. The HF antenna on the Bell 206 JetRanger was a long stinger, probably about seven feet [two metres] in length, which protruded out of the nose. George would grip the end of the antenna and I would fly or—more like—skid the machine along following George. It worked; it bloody well worked even if it was a slow process. I thought how white is white with nothing but the blade tips and George as the reference. It was like we were suspended in white. I couldn't help feeling sorry for George out in the cold . . . He was bent over, holding on to the antenna; he looked like he was hauling a sledge surrounded by blowing snow kicked up by the rotors and the loud engine noise. Slowly we climbed the gradual rise and after some time we were on the ridge, but we did not seem to be descending. George climbed back in for a break while we tried to figure this out. It looked like we were on a ridge that was between the two inlets and needed to turn north or south to go down. North was more [the] direct [route] to our intended course, so George grabs the antenna and almost immediately we started to descend. Pretty soon things were not right as the terrain began to steepen to a point where it was difficult for me to keep the helicopter at George's slow pace. He actually turned and held us in . . . position by pushing on the nose. It was surreal. This hooded guy, whose face I could not see beyond the iced-up edges of his fur-lined hood, [was] leaning against the nose of the running helicopter in a total whiteout. I was concerned that there might be a cliff behind him that he could not see. This was not a good situation.

Very cautiously I lifted off without zinging the tail rotor (Lady Luck's fourth contribution—or was it Freddy Baird's snow landings and take off instructions on Apex Mountain near Penticton?). Using George in his crouched position for reference, I managed to get the machine turned around. We had another breather for George, then off we went again to the top of the ridge, hoping that the descent on the other side was more gradual.

We made it to the top again and I was able to contact Rae Point via the HF radio. They had been trying to contact me for some time, wondering where we were. Our ETA for Eglinton Island had long since come and gone. I explained our predicament and also explained that we would need more fuel once we got out of our present conditions as we had been flying and skidding for nearly three and a quarter hours. The call was interrupted as George suddenly stopped walking and made a dash back and quickly got in the front passenger's seat. Once inside, he gasped "Polar bear!" I looked around, but being in a milk bottle I saw nothing. "Tracks," he said. This was serious. I envisioned our walking the helicopter exercise as over . . . [and the] unimaginable consequences if this weather continued. There was no way George or I, for that matter, were going to get out of this helicopter if there was a polar bear around.

As we sat chatting and thinking this out, I happened to glance at the compass and saw that instead of pointing south as we had been since our last turn, we were in fact pointing east. I suppose that when I was on the radio to Rae Point I may have taken my eyes off the compass and had likely turned east via a 270-degree turn to the right. This might have explained the tracks—we may have passed over our own tracks and George might have mistaken his own footprints for those of a bear. After some convincing, George jumped out and indeed confirmed that they were his footprints.

It was back to walking again and we soon descended . . . this time in a gradual manner. After a short period it was a relief to see the rock reference reappear. Knowing George must be pretty tired, I had him sit on the floats outside my door with his hand clasping onto my arm. If we started to go too fast, he would give my arm a squeeze, and this was how we skied the helicopter between the rocks, toboggan-style, until a ceiling appeared and the visibility was good enough to fly again. We both chuckled over it.

Once on the coast, we found a good spot to land and informed Rae Point of our position, then we shut down and had a rest waiting for fuel. As relieved as we were, it was years later before I realized how lucky we had been. George did comment that this was not in his job description and immediately fell asleep. He was able to get it as it took nearly three hours . . . [before] . . . Sandy Donaldson arrived in an Associated Bell 212 with some food and fuel.

Sandy mentioned the weather as being typical [for] this time of year around the ice caps. He had taken the long route around the west of Melville to avoid the conditions that we had just come through. What you can learn from Arctic old-timers.

Footnote to this story: as we lifted off after refuelling, the Eglinton Island base informed us to make all speed as the Associated Bell 204 had just crashed. The engine had failed just after their engineer had hooked up a sling load of fuel drums. Somehow the pilot managed to topple away from the engineer who dived for cover amidst the remaining fuel drums. He was shaken but not seriously hurt, thank heavens.

George never did get any recognition for his walking endeavour, which he richly deserved. Possibly such exploits were considered all in a day's work . . . Nothing further was said about our adventure, and luckily no incident reports were written up. As far as I was concerned, George was number 1 on my list of

Lady Luck contributions that day. Perhaps similar accolades were needed for the Associated engineer that day.[62]

Over the years Okanagan Helicopters came up with many innovations that helped improve efficiency in the logging industry. One device was the drip torch used for slash burning to clear forest undergrowth and provide fertilizer for the new trees. It was a sled-type apparatus slung under the helicopter and consisted of a tank containing a jellied fuel (40/60 mix), a pump and a delivery hose with a nozzle controlled by the pilot. The pilot worked a designated area and, starting at the centre, flew about 20 or 30 feet (six or nine metres) in a circular path, dropping blobs of fire from the hanging drip torch. Ground firefighting crews were on hand to control the spread of the fire.

Okanagan was involved with a five-week study of heli-logging in the Port Alberni region of Vancouver Island with MacMillan Bloedel and the Tahsis Company. The project compared hauling logs to a water-dump area versus hauling to a dry sorting ground. Environmentalists and the Department of Fisheries were concerned about saltwater dumping because of the large amount of debris that remained in the water. The project also looked at harvesting previously fallen logs from second-growth areas. The experiments, successful from Okanagan's point of view, proved that heli-logging was not only economically viable but also practical. However, the logging companies were not entirely convinced, and the unions were not on side about the new technology.

During the year Okanagan also held a seminar in Prince George for pilots, forest rangers and their assistants to develop a closer working relationship between those battling fires on the ground and those battling them from the air. By using audiovisual fire simulations, the pilots and rangers reversed roles so that they could become aware of each other's responsibilities and problems.

*

Okanagan became involved in the James Bay Project in northern Quebec in 1973-74. This project had begun in 1959 when a team from the Shawinigan Water & Power Company investigated the potential generating capacity of the James Bay region. At that time it was projected that Quebec's electrical energy needs would double every ten years. By 1965 Hydro-Québec had focussed its attention on the five major rivers flowing into James Bay. The initial development proposal, concentrating on the Nottaway, Broadback and Rupert rivers, was for seven power stations with a combined capacity of about 5,500 megawatts of electricity, which studies indicated would meet all of Quebec's future needs.

The SEBJ (Société d'énergie de la Baie James) project was officially launched in April 1971, but it faced an immediate controversy: the area was inhabited by several thousand people from the Cree First Nation, and the drainage basin would cover about 108,750 square miles (175,000 square kilometres) or about 11 percent of the province, much of it their ancestral lands. On November 15, 1973, after a long court battle, Judge Albert Malouf granted the local Cree and Inuit an injunction to stop the project. Two years of negotiations followed before the James Bay and Northern Quebec Agreement was finally signed, providing for the construction of three dams on the La Grande River: LG-2, LG-3 and LG-4. Helicopters and light bush planes had continued exploration of the sites during this period, and by late 1973 over 60 helicopters were working in the region to complete the many environmental and hydrological surveys that were required. At that time air traffic control in the region was virtually non-existent, with only basic weather reports provided by a small team of Department of Transport radio operators. Fortunately, as the project progressed, communications and air traffic control were vastly improved, and gravel strips replaced ice runways.

Due to their versatility, helicopters flew more hours on the James Bay Project than their fixed-wing counterparts, accumulating 215,000 flight hours between 1973 and 1980. About 200 helicopters were used over the life of the project with approximately 45 on site at any one time. They included Bell JetRangers, Bell 204s, 205s and 212s for medium lift, Alouette IIs (known affectionately as "the old cement mixer"), a Bell 47G-3B (with its turbine power it was capable of lifting its own weight), a Hughes 500, and Sikorsky S-55s and S-58Ts with the occasional S-61 and an S-64 Skycrane for heavy lift. While helicopters and small fixed-wing aircraft served the remote sites, the larger transport aircraft were required for heavy equipment, and in 1973 SEBJ also acquired a civilian Lockheed C-130 Hercules with its short takeoff and large load capabilities to provide year-round service.

Okanagan was represented on the project by three of its subsidiaries: Lac St. Jean Aviation, Sept-Îles Helicopters (purchased in 1975) and Hélicoptères Canadiens. This group of companies set up a string of bases in the region, including Matagami, Chibougamau, Quebec City and Baie-Comeau and built a new maintenance facility at Montréal–Dorval International Airport. Captain Bill Schabes, who flew helicopters for Okanagan at James Bay in 1974, recalled:

> In the early part of the SEBJ project the laser survey was introduced. Rather than cutting survey lines through the bush (initially five hydro lines were planned running from camp LG-1 south), the helicopter was used to establish the direction and turns required for the hydro lines. The Alouette II was used for this job because of its power and stability. Tellurometers and theodolites were set up at known survey points, preferably on high ground. Then the helicopter was sent to wherever the hydro lines made a change in direction. The helicopter was equipped with a strobe light to which the operator of the Tellurometer took aim. When the helicopter was at the correct location, it had to hover until the distance and angle were established. Then the operator on the helicopter dropped lead weights with streamers through the trap door in the floor of the helicopter. The ground crew then had to locate these lead weights and cut a small clearing where a laser was set up, which sent a vertical beam straight up. Then the helicopter had to return to the location and hover over the laser beam, which was captured by a mirror mounted forward of the nose and the final reading was taken. This method of survey greatly sped up the process of finalizing the hydro lines. However, the job was very specialized and only a few pilots could do it. The comical part about this was that any company that worked in Quebec had to have crews (pilots and engineers) who lived in Quebec and spoke French. However, it was so specialized and Hydro-Québec did not want to pay for the training of the additional pilots the contract stipulated [so] all crews had to fulfill the above requirements except Glen Patterson and [me].
>
> Later on in the contract I was checked out on the Bell 205A as well as the S-58T and was mostly involved in sling work.[63]

On the international scene Thailand's Department of Civil Aviation approved the application of Sky of Siam Airlines to act as the agent for Okanagan Helicopters, which supported Union Oil with the Sikorsky S-58T CF-OKJ for a period of three months, ending in February 1974. Other contracts signed in 1974 based Bell 212 CF-OKL in Songkhla in southern Thailand on a Tenneco contract and Bell 212 CF-TCQ (ex-N83179) in Phuket for Esso.

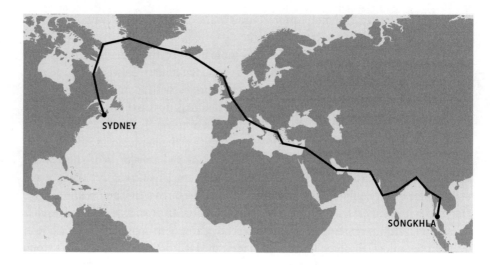

► The route that S-61 CF-OKM flew from Sydney, NS, to Songkhla, Thailand, a distance of 12,659 statute miles (20,368 km). The flight covered sixteen countries and was completed in less than one hundred hours over thirty days. 1974.
SOURCE: OKANAGAN HELICOPTERS

▲ Don Jacques, the pilot of a record-setting long-distance ferry flight, in 1973.
OKANAGAN HELICOPTERS PHOTO

During its contract negotiations for offshore work in Thailand, Union Oil requested a helicopter larger than the Sikorsky S-58T and signed a contract for Okanagan's S-61 C-GOKH to be based in Songkhla. Because the machine was needed in short order and dismantling and shipping would take too long, Okanagan decided to ferry it from Canada, leading to another world record for the longest ferry flight of a commercial helicopter: 12,659 miles (20,368 kilometres) was completed in 98 hours. The crew consisted of Okanagan's chief pilot, Don Jacques, pilot Bill Janicke and Okanagan engineers Dan Lemire and Chuck Taylor. They reported the long flight relatively uneventful, other than routine problems with custom clearance (tedious in many countries), snow and icing conditions over Greenland, Iceland and—surprisingly—Lebanon, as well as sand storms as high as 8,000 feet (2,438 m) above the deserts of the Middle East. They also experienced some problems with refuelling and difficulty obtaining permission to fly at a helicopter's lower ceiling in the volatile Middle East where low flying aircraft were easy targets.

Starting in Sydney, Nova Scotia, in early February, this historic flight touched down in 16 countries spanning the North Atlantic, Europe, the Middle East and the Far East. Their route took them from Halifax to Sept-Îles, Quebec, then on to Frobisher Bay (now Iqaluit) on Baffin Island followed by an IFR night flight to Sondrestrom in central Greenland, 60 miles (100 kilometres) north of the Arctic Circle. Heavy ice accumulated on the machine as they descended through a stratus layer off the coast of Greenland, luckily with no negative consequences. The weather closed in for the tricky flight over the Greenland ice cap slopes, but by flying at 12,000 feet (3,692 metres) they were able to escape the clouds and blowing snow before descending to land at Kulusuk airport on an island off the east coast of Greenland. When the crew learned that the town of Angmagssalik, about 15 miles (24 kilometres) away, had been locked in by the winter ice and had not received Christmas mail because of aircraft problems, the Okanagan crew loaded up the ton of mail and delivered it to the very grateful population. The flight continued to Reykjavík, Iceland, then to Vágar in the Faroe Islands and on to Aberdeen, Scotland. There all the Arctic survival gear was removed for shipment back to Canada.

From Aberdeen they continued to Lyon and Nice in France before heading to Rome, Brindisi and Athens, then on to Iraklion on the island of Crete and Beirut in Lebanon. At this point, due to poor weather, high minimum altitudes and local hostilities, they changed their route. Pilot Don Jacques recalled being "told that the Iraqi Air Force had been strafing and bombing the Kurds and [we] were advised that feelings in the area were running pretty high against overflying aircraft such as ours."[64]

From Damascus, Syria, they flew over desert terrain where they faced wind-whipped sand storms before landing in Al Qaysumah, Saudi Arabia. Here the crew had to borrow aviation fuel from a local company due to lack of fuelling facilities before they proceeded to Bahrain and to Dubai in the United Arab Emirates. Temperatures went from freezing in Lebanon and Syria to 95°F (35°C) in Dubai. The final leg took them to Karachi, Bombay (Mumbai) and Calcutta, then through Burmese air space to land at Rangoon (Yangon) before heading for Bangkok and the last 589 miles (942 kilometres) to Songkhla. This historic flight broke the record set ten years earlier by the Okanagan crew who flew the first commercial helicopter across the Atlantic from Montreal to Gatwick Airport in England.

Further on the international scene, Okanagan won an offshore drilling contract in Gabon, West Africa. During the contract pilot Jack Milburn and the crew of an S-58T were suddenly pressed into service by the chief of state and ordered to fly to the village of Bitam, near Gabon's border with Equatorial Guinea and Cameroon. This was a flight of 380 miles (612 kilometres) that took them over dense jungle, and they had to make stops for refuelling at prearranged sites, finally arriving at Bitam where crowds of people with flags awaited the arrival of Gabon's President Omar Bongo.

In his log Jack Milburn wrote:

> Shortly after we arrived, a turboprop landed with President Bongo, followed by a [Douglas] DC-6B and three Harvard fighter planes armed with rockets and machine guns. Soldiers with camouflaged uniforms were armed with machine guns and rifles.
>
> The Okanagan S-58T was supposed to fly President Bongo to the border village for a meeting with the Equatorial Guinea president to discuss some disputed territory in an area bordering both countries. However, the S-58T was so loaded with wine and food for the dinner meeting plus other government officials that the president had to fly in another aircraft.[65]

After much shuffling of people and food, the mission was accomplished and the following day, the S-58T and crew flew back to its base in Gamba.

1974 ANNUAL REPORT

By 1974 Okanagan Helicopters and its subsidiaries had expanded to 36 bases across Canada, and its new ventures in the international field included contracts in Thailand, Cambodia and Gabon. The company added S-58Ts, S-62s, S-61s and 206Bs to the fleet as well as its first S-61L (land) model, CF-OKB (originally registered as N304V), which was purchased from Los Angeles Airways where it had provided transportation from downtown Los Angeles to Disneyland. The machine was then contracted out to MacMillan Bloedel in the Port Alberni region of Vancouver Island.

By the end of the year construction was completed on Okanagan's new two-storey office building on the north side of the hangar at Vancouver International Airport. It replaced the facility gutted by fire the previous year.

1975

On February 1, after a long negotiation process, Okanagan finalized the purchase of Dominion Pegasus Helicopters (DomPeg), a major Bell operator headquartered in King City, north of Toronto. It became another of Okanagan's wholly owned subsidiaries, allowing the company access to the Ontario market and a larger share of the Quebec market. The original company, Dominion Helicopters, had been formed in 1967 by Jack Fleming, a respected helicopter pioneer, and Bob Gillies, the owner of Inspiration Helicopters (later Pegasus Airlift) of Burlington, Ontario. Dominion had operated an air-taxi service at Expo 67 in Montreal, using both the piston Bell 47J model and the first turbine JetRanger to operate in Canada; between April and October of that year the company's eight helicopters had carried over 100,000 passengers. By the end of the 1960s, however, the majority of Dominion's work involved mining and oil exploration plus a federal government contract to provide support for oceanography, wildlife counts and land surveys on the polar continental shelf. The company suffered a notable accident in 1968 when the tail rotor fell off the s-55 that pilot John Schultz was flying near Marathon in northern Ontario. Luckily the trees broke the helicopter's fall, and once it had tumbled to the ground, Schultz managed to crawl away from the wreckage, pulling out the engineer just before the fuel tank exploded.

By 1972 Dominion had become the second-largest helicopter company in Canada, and Gillies approached Fleming about merging it with his own company, Pegasus Airlift. The new company, Dominion Pegasus, which was incorporated with Jack Fleming as chairman, Jim Plaxton as president and Ernie Grant as vice-president, was a subsidiary of Charterways Co. Ltd., but Charterways went into receivership in 1974, leaving DomPeg open to acquisition by Okanagan. The deal added 35 machines to Okanagan's fleet including 26 Bell 206Bs, six Bell 47Gs, a Bell 205A and a 212 (IFR) plus an SA 341G Gazelle.

Okanagan gained a further foothold in the eastern market when it bought Sept-Îles Helicopters, which was founded by Jacques Blouin and his brother, Jean-Guy, in October 1969. The company had later sold off part of its operation to Dominion in order to concentrate on a contract with the Quebec North Shore and Labrador (QNSL) Railway, which ran daily iron ore cars to a deep-water port on the Gulf of St. Lawrence. Sept-Îles' six Bell JetRangers, operating 100 hours a month, inspected the 350 miles (563 kilometres) of rail line, transported maintenance crews and equipment and provided emergency medical evacuation services.

By 1975 about 20 percent of Okanagan's revenue was coming from its overseas contracts in Mauritania, Morocco, Burma, Thailand, the Philippines, Cambodia, Haiti, Guyana, Suriname, Zaire, Singapore and Peru, and most of these were oil exploration contracts. For example, the Burma operation consisted of two Sikorsky s-58Ts working for the French oil company Total. In Thailand one Sikorsky s-61 was on contract to Union Oil, while two Bell 212s (C-GOKL and C-GOKX) were on contract to Esso, and in the Philippines one Bell 212 was contracted to Amoco. In Peru a Bell 205 worked on pipeline construction near the headwaters of the Amazon. On these international assignments it was not just the aircrews who had adventures. Charlie Heap, the avionics field-maintenance man operating out of Singapore, had a memorable flight out to a base in the Philippines:

> There were Bell 212s located in Singapore, Tavoy in Burma and Puerto Princesa on Palawan Island in the Philippines. Also Sikorsky s-58Ts were in Akyab [in] the northern part of Burma [and] Sikorsky s-61s in Songkhla, Thailand. The logistics of supporting these various aircraft at the spread of locations was nightmarish to say the least. Communication and travel to and from was often awkward and complicated by the requirements of the different countries involved.
>
> On one occasion in Singapore I received a message from Puerto Princesa that the [helicopter's] ADF [the main navigational aid] was not functioning as a goat had chewed off the antenna. What a predicament! Friday, May 9th, I found

myself, complete with a new piece of antenna, wire and tools in a briefcase and a trusty AVO [amps, volts, ohms] meter on my way to rectify the problem. The ticket was for travel via Manila and a stopover at the Hilton Hotel... Little did I know or suspect that it could have been my last supper that evening, for tomorrow, the 10th was, to say the least, a day to remember... The Hawker Siddeley HS 748 operated by PAL [Philippine Airlines] left on time [for Puerto Princesa]... The morning was clear and sunny. I sat a couple of rows back from the cockpit door peering out of the window to my right... soon we were airborne and the wheels up... What was that loud bang? The announcement from the pilot was in a language I didn't understand, but I had a good idea it meant we weren't getting to our destination as planned; instead we might try to return to the airport... I thought this is not a good situation to find myself in as I peered out the window at the homes that were passing underneath and getting ever closer. Another announcement from the pilot! Still [I] didn't understand [but] thought it's time to put [my] head down between the knees as the ground was really getting close. Soon some trees passed under [us] almost brushing the fuselage and in a short time the propeller I had observed earlier began to change shape as the tips curled backwards... The cockpit door swung open and a large volume of paddy field mud came shooting into the passenger compartment. Luckily, it passed me by. Some rows back was a man searching for his glasses [which] I managed to retrieve as they went by me at some speed during the deceleration period. I sat waiting for the mayhem behind me to calm down and for the children on board with their parents and the odd bag with various chickens and other livestock to evacuate. Eventually the cabin attendant appeared from the cabin door and the only part of her that was not brown from the paddy mud was her eyes. Seeing me, she shouted, "Come on, get out!" and placed her hand firmly in the middle of my back, leaving a big muddy imprint on my lovely white shirt.

Having escaped from the aircraft and moved away, I observed a young fellow sitting on the bank of a ravine very nearby... I approached him and asked, "Are you okay?" With a look that I shall never forget, he turned his head and said, "That was my very first airplane ride." [I replied:] "Gee, I am sorry, but they don't usually end up like this." I often wonder what became of that young man...

The skill of the ex-Air Force pilot was commendable. Unfortunately, he received the only injury, a cut on his forehead. Some months earlier a similar accident not far away from this location resulted in fatalities because the aircraft hit trees... The crew and a collection of passengers at some distance from the wreck were engaged in a collective giving thanks to the Almighty. A passenger from England, a rep for a [pesticide company] was busy searching through his briefcase and said: "I don't know what [they're] up to, but I know what I need." He produced a bottle of fine whiskey and we both had a good swig. I think I should be excused for drinking on duty in such circumstances...

Philippine Air Force helicopters were a welcome sight, and not long after interrogations we were, courtesy of PAL, booked into the Philippine Village Hotel.[66]

Two days later the passengers were reunited with their luggage, and the following day the airline provided a special flight to Puerto Princesa where Charlie Heap was met by Bob Johnson, Dave Eagleston and "some Amoco people." He had no problem repairing the antenna, and a test flight out to the oil rig proved everything was in order. But Heap had one more hurdle before he got out of the country:

Upon exiting the Philippines for Singapore on Sunday the 18th there was a flurry of activity at the customs area and I was drawn aside. It appeared that the tools . . .carried in my briefcase and other things rang a bell or two . . . Explanations [were] accepted, I was escorted back into the lineup for boarding . . . Next problem! [67]

1975 ANNUAL REPORT

With expanding commitments at home and abroad, in 1975 the board of directors authorized the purchase of 10 new Sikorsky s-76s but later increased this to 23 with the first delivery scheduled for June 1979.

Chief engineer Davey McLean was awarded the "Maintenance Man of the Year" by the Helicopter Association of America "for distinguished contributions to aviation safety through good practice in the field of helicopter maintenance." Davy had trained in the RAF and served through World War II before coming to Canada where he was employed by Canadian Pacific and Queen Charlotte Airlines; he had joined Okanagan Helicopters in 1953.

1976

Okanagan's eastern subsidiaries were active in both the domestic and international markets in 1976. Bell 206 CF-PZG was sent from Montreal to Port-au-Prince in Haiti, departing on Saturday, March 27, and arriving three days later. Dominion Pegasus had a contract with the Guyana Defence Force for a Bell 206 and a 212 working in an area bordering on Suriname, Brazil and Venezuela, which required pilots and engineers on a two-month rotation. Captain Bill Schabes recalled some of his adventures there:

> At the start of 1976 I went to Vancouver to get checked out on the Bell 205A-1 . . . by Tommy Gurr and Grant Soutar. Five days later I was on my way to Georgetown, the capital of Guyana, formerly known as British Guyana. I was met by Fred Baird, whom I was replacing . . . The camp where we were based was in the interior, about 120 [nautical miles (222 kilometres)] from Georgetown . . . There was an airstrip which was regularly visited by military Caribou, a present to Guyana from Canada. The reason for our presence was to supply transportation for a survey team studying the possibility of a power dam project, plus slinging supplies for building permanent housing, etc. Due to the elevation, we could not start flying until about 11:00 in the morning . . . when the fog lifted . . . However, for the rest of the day we hot refuelled and flew until evening. The trees were all about 150 feet tall [46 metres] and map reading was useless. This was before the days of GPS [so] we flew compass headings plus time to find the various helipads in the jungle where test drilling took place.
>
> Linden Burnham was then prime minister of Guyana, [which was] considered a communist country with close ties to Cuba and Fidel Castro. He also had a small helicopter division with a [man with the] last name of Gillespie in charge [so] it came as somewhat of a surprise when we received the request from the PM's office to accommodate Mr. Burnham at the end of February for a tour of a proposed dam site and various helipads near some of the villages. On the day Woody Brinston, my engineer, and I showed up with our helicopter

CF-AOT at the official residence, landing inside the compound. This particular Bell 205 had electric extendable steps, which looked impressive. The red carpet was rolled out and Mr. Burnham and his entourage came . . . aboard. I was informed that a security officer would be my co-pilot. Captain Gillespie in his Alouette III was to depart ahead of us and make sure all the landing sites were secure . . . We departed from the residence and headed towards [our camp in the interior]. Partway [there] we got hit by one of those tropical showers that only people who have been to the tropics can appreciate. Shortly after we got into this heavy rain, the engine fire warning light came on suddenly. What options did I have? I had only one engine! Make an emergency landing into 150-foot trees? No. Ignore it? Well, someone might notice it, so another no. I gingerly reached up and pulled the circuit breaker. The light went out and I waited for something to happen but nothing did . . . As I found out later from Woody, it was not uncommon for the engine fire warning light to come on during heavy downpours . . .

As we came out of the rain, I tried to call Captain Gillespie with no response. The rest of the tour was uneventful. In the evening I returned to Georgetown without any other issues, and Mr. Burnham thanked me personally. As for Captain Gillespie, he did return safely well after us and admitted that he had got lost and never landed at any of the sites he was to inspect. At the end of February, Fred Baird returned and replaced me. My next tour was to Suriname . . .

In Suriname, formerly known as Dutch Guiana, Dan Dunn and Fred Moore from Okanagan's Operations and Marketing Division had set up a company called Suriname Helicopters with a Bell 206B. Mel Barton and engineer Carlos DeCampos flew it from Toronto through rain, fog, sleet and snow to Miami where it was dismantled and stowed on board a DC-6 for the flight to Georgetown and then on Suriname. Bill Schabes continued:

The Canadian registered helicopter CF-PON was transferred to Suriname Registry [as] PZ-HAC. This was the first helicopter registered in that country. [It arrived] in March of 1976, and I ferried the helicopter from Georgetown to Paramaribo. The transfer of registration was completed by April of that year and I was the first helicopter pilot in Suriname with a Suriname licence. [But] the Department of Transport . . . would not give me licence #1 but instead gave me #7 with the explanation that the numbers 1 to 6 would be reserved for Surinamese.

Our flying was limited to some drill moves and flying government officials into the interior, and it became evident that this was not going to be a money-making venture. In June of 1976 the Bell 205A CF-AOT was brought in from Guyana to haul a water tank externally from Afobaka to a village called Kabalebo. Due to a short shaft failure, that Bell 205 crashed into the jungle.[68]

Captain Bill Yearwood provided more details on the 205-crash story:

Fred [Baird] was flying the 205 one day when the transmission input drive shaft failed and he went down in dense jungle. Bill Schabes found him and Woody Brinston climbed down steel cables hanging on the 206 hook . . . he cut a clearing with a dull machete and Bill flew them out. Fred had a broken back and remained a paraplegic for the remainder of a very full life.[69]

Captain Bill Schabes continued his recollections of life in Suriname:

> One of my most memorable flights was in January 1977 when we received a call from the Canadian Embassy in Georgetown, Guyana, asking if it was possible for us to fly to a football field on the outskirts of Kourou in French Guiana and pick up Mrs. Rogers, the wife of the Canadian ambassador, who had been hurt during a boat trip to Devil's Island, the infamous penal island that [was the setting for] the book *Papillon* . . . The Bell 206 was converted to the stretcher configuration, and we flew Mrs. Rogers from Kourou direct to Georgetown.
>
> By February 1977 it was decided to close the operation down. I flew the machine to Georgetown . . . where it was dismantled and airlifted back to Miami and then flown back to King City, Ontario. Deregistration was not done [quite] the way it was done normally. Just before crossing into Guyana from Suriname, I landed in a clearing, removed PZ-HAC and stuck on CF-PON and instantly [it] became a Canadian-registered helicopter.
>
> A year or so later unrest started in Suriname and the military seized power. All the Dutch installed politicians were removed and many lost their lives.[70]

In the Philippines, Al Eustice was asked by the Philippine Airline Development Council [PADC] to accompany two pilots to assess the terrain of a proposed power-line route in Northern Luzon. He was advised to meet the flight crew at their hangar where a light aircraft would depart at 8 AM. He was on time but had to wait an hour for the flight crew and the aircraft, a Britten-Norman Islander.

> En route to the destination, we flew through some very narrow, steep valley terrain where the crew elected to fly through the middle of the valley, which limited the ability to complete a 180-degree turn without some difficulty . . . We landed on a dirt strip adjacent to the shoreline and were picked up by a truck for a long ride through the jungle with two check points . . . [where] the watchmen appeared to be armed with sporting rifles. After what seemed like hours of viewing a variety of proposed towers and operational sites, we returned to a small village with a store and a canteen. No one seemed particularly friendly. We had a cold drink and headed back down the mountain to the landing strip. Back at the aircraft I asked the pilot why the crew on the road carried rifles; their response—which took a time to grasp—was because "We are in guerrilla territory. They don't like the government." My estimated ransom value must have been low.
>
> Back at the aircraft we climbed into the later afternoon . . . sky filled with tropical thunder. The somewhat casual flight crew seemed to delight in the proximity of the lightning as we headed south on a very bumpy ride back to Manila.
>
> There is a time-honoured procedure for arrival back to the hotel room following a long difficult day in the field: wash your hands and get to the mini-bar ASAP. That cold San Miguel tasted so good.[71]

On the home front, Okanagan Heli-Logging began an experiment in heli-yarding for a number of companies including MacMillan Bloedel, Tahsis Co. Ltd. and Richmond Plywood Corporation Ltd., which involved transporting logs from the forest to an area of level ground to facilitate loading onto the trucks for transportation to lumber mills. They demonstrated that this method could also be used in steep terrain and unstable ground where building roads would damage the watershed.

In Vancouver, as in most major cities, construction cranes on top of skyscrapers were—and are—a common sight. Usually the disassembly process takes a crew of six about two weeks to complete. On one particular Sunday in 1976 pilots Grant Soutar and Roy Webster, flying an S-61L, dismantled a crane on top of a 29-storey hotel in about 90 minutes and 11 trips. The loads, which ranged between 3,000 to 7,400 pounds (1,360 to 3,357 kilograms) and up to 95 feet (29 metres) long, were transported to a waterfront area about four blocks away.

In March when Captain Pierre Looten and the crew operating an S-58T in Hopedale, Labrador, were confronted by 80 mph winds, they secured the machine by attaching a 45-gallon (170-litre) drum to the tail wheel and adding more tie-downs to the blades. When the wind subsequently gusted to 100 mph (130 km/h), the helicopter started to rock from side to side, forcing the crew to crawl along the ground in order to run a cable from the tail wheel to a camp building. They also fastened a cable to the nose of the helicopter and attached it to another nearby building before crawling back to safety. Fortunately, by morning the winds had moderated. Some of the blades had been damaged, but the tie-downs had held and the helicopter was saved. The crew, however, were nursing bruises after being bowled over into a pile of 45-gallon drums.

Sept-Îles' Bell 206, CF-POC, on contract with the Canadian Wildlife Service in the Eastern Arctic, was used in the polar bear–tagging program that year. Pilot Dale Simpson recalled:

> Once we had located our camp and set it up, we would offload as much as we could, including the rear doors. [We] flew around 300 to 400 feet [91 to 122 metres] above the ice, looking for pressure cracks. This was where the seals would come up, [and] quite often you could spot the bear tracks. The biologists wore special brown lenses . . . so they could see the tracks. If we had a tracking device on board, we could find the bears quite quickly. The biologists would be in the back on the right hand side and would fire the tranquilizer gun when the bear was five to 10 feet [1.5 to 3 metres] away. The gun was a .22 and the tranquilizer dart was about six to eight inches [15 to 20 centimetres] long. After being hit, it was nothing for the bear to run for 5 minutes and still cover nine miles [14 kilometres].
>
> Once the bear was down, we got out the tripod [to weigh the animal], and then the biologists would take samples of hair, fat, look at teeth, tag the ear . . . Radio-tracking collars were placed on the bear—today [they're] GPS collars.
>
> Once back in the helicopter, we would wait until we saw movement before flying off. Females and cubs could not be left because of possible hypothermia [and] also wolves or arctic foxes, [which] would kill the cubs while mum was asleep. We would sometimes see fox tracks around male bears, but they never went too close.[72]

In the spring of 1976 United Technologies quarterly journal, *Bee Hive*, carried an article on Okanagan Helicopters' Halifax offshore operation titled "Rotocraft Support for Sedco H," which caught some of the difficulties of oil rig support work:

> The men drift into the hangar through a side door in ones and twos, carrying small suitcases or duffle bags. After threading their way through the light planes . . . they move into a tiny, spartanly furnished waiting room where the aroma of coffee replaces the fuel and oil smells of the hangar. The only decoration in the room is a hand-lettered sign taped to the wall above the coffee pot announcing that this is the "Sedco H Coffee Shop" . . .

▲ A helicopter approaches the rig Sedco H, 180 miles (290 kilometres) off Halifax, NS, in 1976. OKANAGAN HELICOPTERS PHOTO

Most pay no attention to the bustling activity on the other side of the room's single window where the smaller aircraft are being moved so that the big yellow and white Sikorsky S-61N helicopter with the distinctive hummingbird on the tail can be rolled outside. These men... are returning to work. Their jobs are on the *Sedco H*, an oil drilling rig anchored in the North Atlantic Ocean off the coast of Nova Scotia, 180 miles [289 kilometres] from this hangar at Halifax International Airport. Okanagan Helicopters Ltd. will take them there...

In a cubbyhole of an office adjacent to the waiting room, pilot John McIntyre is on the radio getting the latest weather forecast from the rig, a forecast that is updated hourly. If the winds at the rig are above 70 miles per hour [112 km/h] the flight will be delayed. Although 86 mph [138 km/h] winds and 30-foot [nine-metre] seas were reported the night before, the report today is good.

S-61 pilots Pat Miskell and Brian Small, dressed in orange flight suits, head for the apron to give the helicopter a final once-over. The machine is meticulously maintained by five engineers assigned to the Halifax base...The helicopter has airline-type seats, but they are hidden by the heavy orange immersion suits that have been laid out for the passengers. The suits are uncomfortable to wear and difficult to put on, but the men make no complaints. The waters of the Atlantic are freezing cold in February, and the suits could save their lives in the event of an emergency water landing. The S-61 also carries two inflatable, 12-man life rafts whose bright yellow containers make them easy to spot...

By the time the S-61's rotors are beginning to turn, Okanagan engineer Charlie Morin slams and locks the aft stairs door, and the helicopter taxies onto the runway... The helicopter lifts from the ground, turns its nose southeast and heads over the rugged Nova Scotia countryside...

Miskell, who began flying helicopters while serving with the US Coast Guard and has been with Okanagan for three years, climbs steadily to get above the turbulent air that buffets the helicopter. By the time a cruising altitude of 5,000 feet [1,525 metres] is reached, the S-61 has passed through several snow squalls and patches of thick fog and is over the ocean... Once the helicopter reaches altitude, the flight smooths out and many of the passengers begin dozing off, perhaps lulled to sleep by the steady drone of the engines and the kind of boredom fostered by routine repetition...

An hour and a half after takeoff, the rig comes into view... *Sedco H* is a triangular-shaped, multi-decked platform that sits atop three massive, 35-foot [11.5-metre] diameter caissons or legs and appears at first to defy all the nautical rules... The dominant feature is the drill derrick which towers 180 feet [55 metres] above the main deck... The rig is approximately 350 feet long and 385 feet wide [107 by 117 metres], with the main deck 146 feet [44.5 metres] above the footing bottoms... At the forward end, or bow, are the helicopter pad, the crew quarters, the galley and the offices.[73]

Farther north, a funny thing happened on the way to Goose Bay, Labrador. Bill Henderson was checking out the new pilots on the Bell 205 when a call came in from Olympic Helicopters of Montreal that one of their Bell 206s had made an emergency landing due to engine failure just north of Goose Bay. Could the Okanagan 205 sling it back to Goose Bay? Bill thought this would be a good chance for one of the new pilots to try flying with an underslung load. He set off with the new co-pilot and an engineer. They got to the site and the engineer got the slings attached and the 205 lifted off with the 206 dangling below. The co-pilot was just observing and not doing the flying; however, he did have his hand on the co-pilot's cyclic. He turned to Bill and said, "What's this red button for?" The 205 shot up into the air, minus the 206. He had released the machine, which needless to say was a write-off.

On landing back at Goose Bay, they met the Olympic Helicopters' engineer who inquired about the 206. Bill told him they'd had an electrical malfunction and had to release it in the air. The engineer said, "That's good. We'll probably get more money from the insurance than what it's worth." Everyone was happy except the new co-pilot who did not live that one down for a long time. The moral to this story: don't press red buttons!

*

On September 16, 1976, a Sikorsky S-58T that was on a test flight over North Vancouver after a major maintenance inspection crashed, killing Okanagan's chief pilot Don Jacques and pilot Merv Hesse. Don had recently completed a marathon flight from Canada to Thailand in an S-61.

He had joined Okanagan on January 5, 1955, after taking his helicopter pilot training course in Penticton. For the next three years while he was on the company's charter roster, he established the limits for the degree of slope for a Bell 47G-2 on floats. In 1964 he received an award from Sikorsky for his role in the Granduc Mine disaster rescue operation. Appointed Okanagan's chief pilot in 1966, he became responsible for setting flying standards, pilot training and check rides and was instrumental in pioneering civilian helicopters IFR operation in North America with the Sikorsky S-61. He perfected vertical reference flying techniques for the erection of steel transmission towers and procedures for operating in the -76°F (-60°C) total darkness of the Arctic winters. While chief pilot, he saw the fleet expand from 50 to close to 150 helicopters.

Don became the first western pilot to get first-hand experience on Russia's flying crane, the Mi-10, when he was on a visit to Russia to assess it for use in northern Canada's mining operations. He also enjoyed gliding and made a test flight in a glider owned by University of British Columbia students from their launch site at a Fraser Valley airstrip with a student sitting on his shoulders. Don left behind a wife and six children. Included among the tributes was an unpublished obituary that read in part:

> He was a true professional, who possessed extraordinary talent in his chosen field and who earned great respect for himself and for his contribution to the industry.

The following year at the Helicopter Association International convention he was posthumously named Pilot of the Year.

Merv Hesse was one of the special breed who had earned his wings as a bush pilot. Before joining Okanagan, he and mechanic Heinz Kallweit had started their own company, Northern Mountain Airlines, but they ended up with two aircraft and a lot of debts. In October 1968 he sold his share and joined Okanagan Helicopters. At the time, he had 10,000 hours fixed-wing and 142 hours in helicopters.

Merv was also a graduate of the Okanagan Mountain Flying School in Penticton and initially worked at the Prince George base. He also flew in the Fort St. James area until he obtained his IFR rating. Then in March 1975 he joined the South East Asia operation, flying a Bell 212 from Rangoon to a drilling site off the Burmese coast. On his return to Canada he worked on forest fire suppression in Ontario and on charter work in BC. Merv left behind his wife, Chris, six children, his parents, and two brothers in New Glasgow, Quebec.

Part Two

As a member of the RAF I was trained as an air radar mechanic, but that position gradually evolved into aviation electronics or avionics, which included air radar and communications, flight instrumentation and autopilot and electrical systems. When I left the Air Force for civil aviation, I specialized in rotor aircraft, and in June 1977 I was hired by Okanagan Helicopters as an avionics engineer, remaining with the company until the late 1980s. During that time my job took me all over Canada and to India, Sri Lanka, Malaysia, Thailand and the Philippines. I worked with some of the best helicopter crews in the world, and it is their adventures as well as my own that I tell in Part Two of the Okanagan Helicopters story.

Chapter Five

THE LATE 1970S

1977

Okanagan's most noteworthy mission of 1977 began quietly in June after fisherman Bill Davies found a baby orca swimming erratically in Menzies Bay, off Vancouver Island, suffering from gunshot and propeller wounds. Davies befriended the young female and began feeding her by hand then contacted the Vancouver Aquarium, which, in turn, contacted Bob Wright of Sealand of the Pacific in Victoria. Wright decided to bring her to Victoria for treatment, and after six months of close calls and several minor miracles, she was declared healthy. By then she had been appropriately named Miracle. At 250 pounds (567 kilograms), she had outgrown her temporary home in a hotel swimming pool and needed to be moved to the Sealand site.

Officials at Sealand contacted Okanagan, and the company dispatched a Sikorsky S-58T, flown by pilots Roy Webster and Michael Dick with engineer Eugene Austin while Grant Soutar handled ground coordination. Miracle was kept damp for the six-minute

◂ Baby orca Miracle being transported by helicopter to an aquarium in Victoria, BC, in 1978. OKANAGAN HELICOPTERS PHOTO

◂ Associated Helicopters crew performs survey work in the 1960s; Bell 47 CF-GSL is pictured in the background. PHOTO COURTESY OF TELLEF VAASJO

▸ A geologist, supported by Associated Helicopters in July 1953, surveys an outcrop along Scatter River, BC. CF-GSL, pictured here, was their first Bell 47D and was later modified to include a third seat, making it a 47D-1. PHOTO COURTESY OF TELLEF VAASJO

20-second flight in a purpose-built, fleece-lined sling suspended under the helicopter. Hundreds of spectators lined the beach as local television crews filmed the unusual airlift. One spectator reported the whale kept lifting her head trying to look at the helicopter to see where the noise was coming from. Sadly, after a few years in captivity Miracle drowned when she became entangled in a net that made up part of her enclosure.

Meanwhile, in the spring of 1977 the annual seal hunt had started around the remote town of St. Anthony in northern Newfoundland, igniting the outrage of many groups and celebrities such as actress Brigitte Bardot, all of them intent on bringing enough publicity to stop the hunt. The machines of Universal, Sept-Îles and Lac St. Jean Helicopters were chartered by a variety of organizations including the media, Department of Fisheries and Greenpeace until the growing number of helicopters and fixed-wing aircraft on the scene made flying there very dangerous. One DomPeg pilot said it was a bit like a mini-Battle of Britain with helicopters. Rules of engagement had to be implemented to prevent accidents; aircraft had to maintain separation or be subject to fines and risk the loss of licences and withdrawal of their operating certificates.

*

Okanagan and its subsidiaries undertook a number of new ventures during the year. In Ontario, DomPeg started trials for an air ambulance operation using a Bell 212. And in Toronto a Bell 205A-1 was used to install an 11-foot (3.6 metre) rod that measured wind speed and air temperature on top of the 1,815-foot (553-metre) CN Tower, which at the time was the world's tallest free-standing structure. Pilots Chad Murray and John Carnie

A geophysical surveyor in northern Alberta with Associated Helicopters' first machine in the background. PHOTO COURTESY OF TELLEF VAASJO

hovered above the tower and gently lowered the rod into a three-inch (7.5 cm) diameter hole where it was locked in place by John McLernon, an employee of the Atmospheric Environmental Service.

Later that year five specially equipped, Vancouver-based Bell 206B models were assigned to Resolute Bay on Cornwallis Island, north of the Arctic Circle, along with a dozen pilots and engineers. This was the beginning of a multi-year contract for the Polar Continental Shelf Program. The helicopters would become a lifeline over the vast northern region where scientists were carrying out hydrographical and geological surveys, studying plant and animal life and ice movement.

In Alberta the mining giant Luscar Sterco Ltd. awarded Okanagan a contract to fly miners from the town of Edson, Alberta, to a coal mine 39 miles (63 kilometres) away. The 32-passenger S-61 with its airline-style interior was fitted with IFR equipment, while microwave landing systems were installed at the Edson base and the mine site, enabling flights in almost all weather conditions and any time of the day or night. A round trip, including loading and unloading, usually took 50 to 55 minutes. When fully operational, the S-61 carried up to 288 people a day, logging about 2,300 hours and over 25,000 miles (40,235 kilometres) a year.

In July Okanagan purchased Edmonton-based Associated Helicopters from the Neonex International Group. The original company, Associated Airways, had been formed in 1945 by wartime buddies Thomas Payne Fox and David C. Dyck as a charter airline; they serviced northwestern Canada with one de Havilland Tiger Moth trainer and a four-passenger de Havilland Dragonfly. By 1950 they had moved into a new enterprise, Associated Helicopters, with Rex Kaufman as president. They purchased their first machine, a used Bell 47D, CF-GSL (serial no. 24) for $19,000, but since they had no one trained to fly it, Bell organized a temporary crew with Chuck Magner, an American World War II veteran who

Surveyors unloading CF-GSL on early Associated Helicopters' contract in northern Alberta in 1953. PHOTO COURTESY OF TELLEF VAASJO

already had over 1,000 hours on helicopters. The engineer was Gustaf Henkie from Long Island, New York. In late June, after they had reassembled and test flown the machine, they went north to Fort Vermilion for their first job before moving on to a job at Hay River and then to Slave Lake for a contract with a geophysical company.

At that point Tellef Vaasjo, who had joined Associated Airways as a pilot in 1949, was asked if he would be interested in transferring to helicopters. He trained with Magner that fall and by December 15 had accumulated 17.5 hours dual and 16 solo. After clocking up 133 hours on flat-land jobs, he was sent to the very mountainous Pine Pass–Azouzetta Lake area of BC on a geological survey. Vaasjo recalled: "The fact that we kept the aircraft running during the subsequent very steep learning curve was pure luck."[74]

To increase revenue, the following year the company modified CF-GSL to make it into a three-seat machine, and in May, Vaasjo and engineer Gordy Cannam went north to begin work for Imperial Oil on a gravity-meter survey on the Steen River. In 1952 Associated sent Jack Hook and Rod Taylor in a small truck to Fort Worth, Texas, to pick up a new Bell 47, CF-FGC, which had an additional 30 horsepower; as soon as it arrived in Edmonton, it was sent north for the Imperial Oil job. The following year the company added a third Bell 47, CF-HAQ, and began to recruit additional staff. The hiring guidelines specified a minimum of 1,000 hours accident-free fixed-wing time with bush experience, good navigation skills and experience flying in adverse weather conditions. Vaasjo, as the first instructor of the company's in-house training program, required an endorsement on his licence and went to the Department of Transport. When he told them what he needed, the official asked, "Where's your licence?" He handed it to him, the official endorsed it and, presto, he was a helicopter instructor. No exams needed.

By the end of 1955, the fleet had grown to eight Bell 47D-1s and the company had moved its headquarters from Edmonton's hangar number 10, built in 1947 for Trans-Canada Air Lines. The following year Associated sold its fixed-wing service to Pacific Western Airlines (PWA). With the introduction of larger helicopters to the commercial market in 1964, Associated paid $7,000 for CF-JTI, one of the RCAF Sikorsky S-55s that had been used on the Mid-Canada Line, and Vaasjo went to Okanagan's Vancouver base to be checked out on it by chief pilot Don Jacques. Then he and Associated engineer Dean Roads, who had previous experience on the S-55, ferried the machine back to Edmonton where it was put in the back of the hangar; in the spring it was rolled out and sent to the town of Slave Lake to help with serious flooding and then on a contract for firefighting in the Caribou Mountains area, northeast of Fort Vermilion. In 1966 CF-JTI was sold to Eldorado Aviation, which re-sold it to Buffalo Aviation in Fort Smith where it eventually became derelict. It now stands outside Calgary's Hangar Flight Museum painted in Associated's colours.

During the 1970s the Mackenzie Delta, Tuktoyaktuk, Beaufort Sea and Inuvik areas became increasingly active with oil exploration and drilling, putting Associated in competition with Okanagan and Bow Helicopters. But in these extreme temperatures Associated had an advantage over the competition because their Bell 206 had an air-heating system that had been designed and approved by the company to keep its crews comfortable. The air was bled off the jet-engine compressor at a temperature of 500°F (260°C) and cooled by adding outside cold air before being brought into the cabin, and a muffler reduced engine noise. The standard Bell fuel-burning heater was not designed for Arctic temperatures. In 1969 Associated had become part of Neonex, a conglomerate owned by the Vancouver entrepreneur Jim Pattison, and at the annual Neonex meeting in Vancouver in 1977 Pattison informed Associated's directors that Okanagan Helicopters wanted to buy the company. He promised, however, that it would only change ownership with their approval. For over a quarter of a century Associated had battled Okanagan, sometimes in fierce though often friendly competition, and they had even helped each other on occasion. Tommy Fox and Carl Agar had, in fact, been good friends, but after discus-

◂ Associated Helicopters' hangar was located at Edmonton Municipal Airport in 1968. ASSOCIATED HELICOPTERS PHOTO

sions Associated's directors turned down the deal. But when they returned to Edmonton, Kaufman had a call from John Pitts, president of Okanagan, requesting a meeting. Pitts came to Edmonton, met with the directors and outlined a plan to amalgamate the two companies with each one operating independently but in co-operation. Further meetings took place in Vancouver. After intense negotiations they agreed to the arrangement, and on July 7, 1977, Associated became part of the Okanagan group. The relationship worked well for both companies, giving Okanagan flexibility with equipment and allowing Associated staff a chance to move into Okanagan's International Division and to fly a wider range of helicopter types.[75]

In 1977 Okanagan also signed a contract to service three exploration rigs in waters off the Republic of Ireland. Initially two Bell 212s and an S-58T were leased to Irish Helicopters, followed by three S-61s. On May 16, S-61 CG-OKA began a ferry flight to Ireland from Okanagan's King City, Ontario, base with pilots Pierre Looten, John McIntyre and Kelly Hague, and engineers Jack Robbins and Elwood Schmidt. The S-61 headed first for Fort Chimo in northern Quebec and went from there to Frobisher Bay (now Iqaluit). The flight continued via Sondrestrom in Greenland to Reykjavík, the Faroe Islands and Aberdeen, Scotland, before finally landing at Shannon where it was to be based. One of the Okanagan engineers recounted the following conversation while he was operating from Shannon Airport:

> We realized that our helicopter, which was bright orange, was not the most popular colour in southern Ireland. One day I was talking to an airport employee when the S-61 landed. This Irish guy said to me: "What a terrible colour for a helicopter." To which I replied: "But it is an Irish helicopter company—O'Kan Agan." He replied, "Oh well, if it's Irish, that's all right then."[76]

Another incident at Shannon resulted in a slight disagreement with the aircrew of KLM Helikopters. When one of the Okanagan S-61s landed at the airport after a trip out to the rig, the engineers began the required maintenance while the flight crew, still wearing their aircrew shirts and captain's bars, changed into shorts and started scrubbing the tail boom where the exhaust stack vented. A KLM captain came over and told the Okanagan aircrew that they were demeaning their captain's status by performing menial tasks that should be left to their engineers. The Okanagan crew replied that they worked as a team and helped wherever they could and suggested that KLM might adopt the same policy. As a result of this exchange, there was no love lost between the KLM and Okanagan flight crews.

Other international events that year included positioning Bell 212 C-GOKL in Bombay to support operations of the Oil and Natural Gas Corporation (ONGC) of India and starting a joint venture with Brambles Industries Ltd. of Australia, a supply-chain logistics company. The new company, named Okanagan Australia Ltd., provided specialized services to the petroleum industry in Western Australia. Meanwhile, an Okanagan S-61 that was sent to New Zealand for an offshore contract operating out of Invercargill was the first to fly in that country. It arrived as deck cargo on the *Hobart Star*, protected by "cocooning," a technique developed in World War II that involved spraying the aircraft with a protective membrane. In Central America Okanagan crews started a contract servicing a drill ship 80 miles (128 kilometres) offshore in the Caribbean using an S-58T ferried from Vancouver to Puerto Cabezas, Nicaragua. In the Middle East Okanagan sent two Bell 212s and crews to Hurghada, about 250 miles (400 kilometres) south of Cairo, on contract to Esso Egypt to support a drill ship operating in the Red Sea. Farther east, a Bell 212 and a 206A went on contract to Texas Pacific Oil Company in the Bay of Bengal, off Bangladesh.

◄ Associated Helicopters' S-55 CF-JTI was chartered to fight fires in the Caribou Mountains and Fort Vermilion, AB, area in 1964. Here, firefighters transfer from a de Havilland Beaver to the S-55. This machine is now at the Hangar Flight Museum in Calgary, AB. PHOTO COURTESY OF TELLEF VAASJO

1977 ANNUAL REPORT

By the beginning of 1977 Okanagan Helicopters had added its sixth S-61 to its inventory, for a total of five S-61NS, or nautical models, and one S-61L, land model. During the year the company purchased an additional 16 Bell 206s, 4 Bell 205As, and 2 Sikorsky S-61s, bringing the fleet to 128 helicopters. Despite all this activity, 1977 was not a good year for the Canadian helicopter market because of intense price competition and increased operating costs, which led to disappointing financial returns.

1978

On April 19, 1978, Okanagan Helicopters entered into a refinancing arrangement with two banks in order to extend the company's outstanding debt to coincide with the life of its aircraft and to improve its working capital, which would put the company in a position to take advantage of new opportunities as they arose. As a result of this arrangement, during that year the company ordered 21 of a new generation of Sikorskys, the 12-passenger S-76. This acquisition would not expand the fleet; it was intended to launch the process of replacing the company's older helicopters.

Meanwhile, Okanagan's new subsidiary, OK Heli-Logging Ltd., was getting underway with two S-61L models, CF-OKP and CF-OKB, purchased from Boise Cascade and New York Airways, and the Bell 206s CG-OKJ and CF-CQE. Later S-61 CF-JDK replaced CF-OKP. The company also reached an agreement with Evergreen Helicopters of McMinnville, Oregon, to lease a Sikorsky S-64 Skycrane, which was able to handle underslung loads of 20,000 pounds (9,070 kilograms). The OK Heli-Logging crew consisted of five pilots, one crew chief and two engineers. In good weather a normal workday for them was often over 16 hours, and an assignment could last up to 25 consecutive flying days with as many as 275 flight hours. A typical run involved delivering logs to tidewater, which was usually some distance from roads or land sorting areas, in a turn-around time of three minutes or less with an average load of 7,000 pounds (3,175 kilograms). In 1978 the machines carried a total of 28,760 cubic units in 1,770 flight hours. Logging manager Walter Palubiski recalled:

> Initially a high percentage of our ground crew came from Victoria. I guess the word spread quickly among the university students that we were looking for help. Later people came from communities near our operation like Campbell River. Few, if any, of the university applicants had any logging experience so we had to train them ourselves. Despite their inexperience they proved to be very willing, hard workers who were enthusiastic about working with helicopters—there was a form of romanticism attached to it. It wasn't unusual for these people to come in at the end of the shift and enquire about the day's quota. Relations between the ground and aircrew were extremely good, a necessity in heli-logging.
>
> As in any situation where morale is very high, there were the practical jokes. It was necessary for the man on the ground to take out rain gear and food since he was going to be out for up to twelve hours at a stretch. Sometimes a pilot would spot a chokerman's lunch sitting on a stump and would very precisely drop the 60-pound [27-kilogram] hook on it with inevitable results. The airwaves would be usually filled with comments that did not bear repeating. We had to put a stop to that.[77]

Many helicopter crew assignments were far less arduous. The Terrace base manager, Dave Newman, had the honour of flying the Archbishop of Canterbury, the Most Reverend and Right Honourable F.D. Coggan, and his party on a fishing trip on the Kemano River, about 360 miles (580 kilometres) north of Vancouver. The Archbishop was visiting the Canadian North to celebrate the anniversary of the first Anglican service held in North America, and he had been invited to visit Terrace by a personal friend, the Right Reverend Douglas Hambidge, Bishop of the Diocese of Caledonia. Newman flew the group from Terrace to Kitimat and then on to Kemano, following the power-lines route through the Coast Mountain Range. He later recalled:

> While flying en route, we saw mountain goats on various mountain slopes and were able to give the Archbishop a good view . . . [It was] the first time he had seen them . . . The fishing? It wasn't a very good day, and we have to let out the secret: the Archbishop posed with a salmon that was caught by another fisherman and was "borrowed" for our picture.[78]

In Alberta, Okanagan crews continued to provide flights to the Edson mine, carrying 67,544 passengers over the course of the year. Crews flew 95 percent of the more than 4,000 flight hours scheduled for their "Miners Air Express"; most of the remainder were not completed due to icing conditions, heavy fog or other poor weather conditions. Only 28 trips were cancelled due to mechanical problems.

Although as an avionics technician I was based in King City, Ontario, I also covered Nova Scotia and Newfoundland and Labrador where the company provided aircraft for operations out of Grand Falls, and for an offshore contract out of Cartwright until the end of October. I remember being in Goose Bay, Labrador, in July that year to rectify some avionics problems and to add installations to the fleet. On completion of my work there, I would normally have taken an Eastern Provincial Airways [EPA] flight to Gander, but it so happened that a Bell 206 came down from Nain in northern Labrador en route to Gander. The pilot, Carlos DeCampos, asked me if I wanted to fly down with him. It was a trip of approximately 500 miles (800 kilometres), a great opportunity to see the country at low level rather than 26,000 feet (7,925 metres).

Just before leaving, I had to attend to an avionics snag that delayed our departure, but Carlos still felt we had enough daylight to make Gander. We took off and flew southeast, and I admit I thoroughly enjoyed watching the landscape go by, especially the wildlife—caribou, moose, deer and the odd black bear. We arrived at Lourdes-de-Blanc-Sablon airport to refuel, then flew across the 17-mile (28-kilometre) Strait of Belle Isle to St. Barbe on Newfoundland's west coast. I was amazed by the number of small settlements that were nestled into the side of the cliffs and the small fishing outports with harbours full of the famous dories and other fishing boats of various sizes.

By the time we turned inland from Rocky Harbour heading for Deer Lake we were beginning to lose the light and, as we flew over the town of Deer Lake, we spotted a lamp flashing toward us. Carlos thought it might have been the Universal Helicopters base trying to contact us using an Aldis lamp. We descended only to find that we were over the local drive-in movie theatre, and the flashing was from the film projector. We climbed away quickly, probably leaving a lot of locals wondering about the special effects. We carried on to Gander, which was another 129 miles (208 kilometres) away. By now it was getting quite dark but, since it was such a clear night, we could see the car headlights on the Deer Lake–Gander road and the big searchlight that identified Gander International Airport. We did an air traffic approach and landed outside the Universal Helicopters Hangar, 505 miles (813 kilometres) from Goose Bay. It was probably one of the best flights that I have been on during my time in the helicopter industry.

At that time Goose Bay was a very active airfield with a military presence, including a permanent detachment of RAF personnel, and was used for fast jet, low-level flying training for the militaries of a number of allied countries. The base's two very long runways—11,000 feet (3,352 metres) and 9,500 feet (2,895 metres)—also made it a major diversion airfield for trans-Atlantic emergencies. The previous year a Lockheed SR-71 (AKA Blackbird) had declared a pan call, which unlike a mayday means there's no immediate danger to life or the aircraft, but the situation is urgent. The aircraft was a high-altitude reconnaissance machine capable of flying at Mach 3.3, and when the captain had declared the pan over Greenland, he asked Goose Bay to sweep the runway before he landed. The sweeper had only managed to get part of it cleared when the SR-71 appeared over the airfield. All emergency services were activated, but he landed safely and taxied over to the domestic terminal instead of the military side. Needless to say, it attracted lots of attention. People snapped pictures until the RCMP arrived and began confiscating their film. The aircraft was soon towed to a secure site awaiting a special crew that would fly in to solve the problem. This particular aircraft had claimed the speed record from New York to London in September 1974 in a time of one hour, 54 minutes and 56.4 seconds.

But there were other incidents involving military aircraft at Goose Bay that summer. One afternoon one of Universal's Bell 206s landed with a very irate pilot, Carlos DeCampos. This mood was very unusual for him as he was normally very mild mannered, but as he had been returning to Goose Bay, two RAF Jaguars had flown on either side of him at very high speed, rocking the 206 violently and scaring the pilot and his passenger. When Carlos landed, he went to the office and advised the authorities of the incident and demanded the culprits be reprimanded.

After he calmed down, the phone rang and Paul Williams, Universal's base manager, shouted to Carlos that he had a call. Carlos took the call but nearly broke the receiver as he slammed it down and cursed. He came into the crew room and told us that the call had come from one of the RAF pilots, who said, "Just to let you know, old chap, we did see you." The comment only added fuel to Carlos' anger.

In October the King City base had a frantic call from Sudbury where steelworkers at the Sudbury mine had gone on strike. The mine management had hired DomPeg to take essential personnel past the picket lines, but that operation had come to a halt as someone had stolen the headsets from both of DomPeg's Bell 206s; without these the pilots could not contact air traffic and the machines had to be grounded. The strike, which lasted from September until the following June, had a devastating impact on the town. At one point the hangar was under police protection because of concerns about sabotage to the helicopters, which were also used as air ambulances.

In Quebec, Hélicoptères Canadiens of Montreal was involved in successfully erecting a radically new hydro tower designed for the transmission line at Hydro-Québec's James Bay Project (SEBJ). Stronger than conventional structures, this tower, called the Chainette, was simpler and cheaper to construct, easier to maintain compared to the guyed and rigid V-towers, and lent itself to helicopter construction techniques since the weight of all the components was within the limits of the S-61. On a test installation the helicopter transported the mast to the site of a pre-installed footing, then hovered and held the mast in place while the ground crew anchored the guy wires in just four and a half minutes. The new Chainette also eliminated cross arms, which made up about 50 percent of the old-style tower's weight, and replaced them with a system of crossed steel cables, designed somewhat like a suspension bridge. Hydro-Québec estimated that the installation of these new towers by helicopter saved them about $25,000 per mile.

Whenever the Montreal base was short-staffed, I was sent to work on the SEBJ contract. The entry point was La Grande, about 620 miles (1,000 kilometres) north of Montreal, and this was where they issued everyone with a kind of credit card, which was used for accommodation, food and travel around the site. The territory was so vast that SEBJ had its own internal airlines to transport people and equipment around the camps. I guess between Lac St. Jean, Sept-Îles, Hélicoptères Canadiens, and DomPeg—all Okanagan subsidiaries—there must have been between 15 and 20 helicopters located at the various camps, and it became my job to travel to camps LG-2, -3, and -4 to fix any avionics problems.

On one trip of about six days, I ended up at LG-3 and was told I had to wait a few days for a flight out. I found one of our Bell 206s was scheduled to leave for Chibougamau, about 110 miles (177 kilometres) to the south, and pilot Luc Pilon was more than happy to have some company on the trip. The weather was warm and quite sunny when we left. Our flight plan had us crossing the La Grande watershed, flying along the cutline, which at this time had no hydro pylons, until it intersected with the road to Chibougamau and then making a left turn toward the town.

However, as we flew down the cutline, the weather started to deteriorate and a thick blanket of fog enveloped us. Being in a helicopter, we could hover about 10 feet [three metres] above the ground and fly quite slowly, but I looked out through the bubble from the co-pilot's seat, with increasing concern that another helicopter might be coming the other way. As the fog became thicker, we reduced our speed to a crawl. Every so often we crossed a small lake and then had to find the cutline again. Did it continue straight or veer off to the right or left? It must have been hard on Luc as he concentrated on the flying while peering through that thick fog. Meanwhile, the fuel gauge, which was on my right on the instrument panel, was slowly sinking toward the red, and Luc told me to watch it and as soon as it registered empty to let him know. We would have to put down and walk out. Just as he said that, he spotted a quarry to our left where some guys were working. Luc landed and told me to keep the throttle in idle while he climbed out. They gave us some diesel fuel that would at least get us to Chibougamau, which was not far away.

(Diesel is much the same as the Jet A fuel used in turbine engines, so all the helicopter pilot would need to do was have the diesel flushed out afterwards.)

We continued on down the cutline until it intersected with the road. Luc turned the helicopter toward what he thought was the town when suddenly through the fog we saw the huge radio antenna of the local AM station directly in front of us. He pulled up on the collective and soon we were back in thick fog, but we'd missed the radio mast. Looking down, I could just make out the white lines of the main road. Suddenly a car went past, and Luc brought the helicopter gently down until we were by the side of the road. After he got his bearings, we set off once more for Chibougamau, found the base and landed. Just as we were getting the helicopter covered up for the night, a pilot from Hydro-Québec came over and asked us how the cutline was as he was heading up to LG-3.

We checked into a motel, and I headed straight for the bar for the biggest glass of whisky they would serve me. Luc asked me if I wanted to fly with him to Montreal the next day, but I declined and took a Quebecair Fairchild F-27 instead, followed by an Air Canada flight on to Toronto and home. I often wonder if, had I been with a less experienced pilot, things would have turned out differently.

In the late 1970s Luc started his own company, Nipissing Helicopters, with one helicopter operating out of North Bay, Ontario. He is now president of Helicopter Transport Services, which operates two fixed-wing support aircraft and over 60 helicopters worldwide.

Later that year the base at King City was closed down and the crews were transferred to a new facility at Montréal–Dorval International Airport, which now became the eastern headquarters for DomPeg, Hélicoptères Canadiens, Sept-Îles, Lac St. Jean and Universal Newfoundland. The move allowed the company to provide full support for the SEBJ project in northern Quebec.

*

Okanagan continued to be active on the international scene in 1978. In Thailand, Bell 212 C-GOKY was assigned to support Amoco Thailand's oil support vessel *Diamond Dragon*. A second 212 was sent to support Texas Pacific Thailand's drill ship *Tainron*, which operated out of Songkhla. In the Philippines, Okanagan started operations for Cities Service in Puerto Princesa; for that job a Bell 212, re-registered as PR1677, was flown down by Jack Milburn and engineer Jim Broadbent.

Farther south, Okanagan S-61 C-GOKH, with captains John Grey and Gene Burelson and engineers Chuck Taylor and Harold Michaels, set a record for a flight from New Zealand to Australia, crossing 2,000 miles (3,219 kilometres) of water with prearranged refuelling stops at Lord Howe and Norfolk islands, two very small dots in the middle of the Tasman Sea. To commemorate the event, the Norfolk Island government issued a stamp showing the Okanagan S-61, the first helicopter to land on their territory. From Australia the S-61 was then shipped back to Canada by sea.

Associated's Bell 212 CF-AHX, which was destined for Morocco, left Montreal via KLM to Amsterdam where it was reassembled by engineer Gordon Brown with the help of the KLM Helikopters staff. Then with Roy Webster at the controls, the helicopter headed off for a contract in Agadir. Meanwhile, the company signed a dry lease for a Bell 212 with Abu Dhabi Aviation to be used for an oil support contract. In the UK the company also supplied a dry-leased Bell to British Executive Air Services (BEAS), based at Baginton, Coventry. These dry-leased helicopters did not carry Canadian crews.

In Ireland Okanagan pilot Pierre Looten returned to his headquarters in the town of Cork one day after completing the ferry trip from Hell. He recalled:

After inflicting misery on our part of Ireland for three consecutive days, the snowstorm died, leaving ice and deep ruts on the streets of Cork. When I pushed open the door of our small office, I soon realized there was not going to be any comfort there after the bitter cold outside: most of the power lines laden with ice had snapped and there would be no light or heat again today. But power was not the only thing missing: the employees at the country's telephone company had gone on strike a week earlier, and I had lost all contact with headquarters of my company in Toronto.

However, being an eternal optimist, I had been trying to dial Canada every morning, hoping for some miracle. And now it looked like I had come very close to one! A voice answered from the other side of the ocean. I recognized Bonnie, our Ops secretary: "Oh Pierre, I am so glad you called! Please go immediately to Madrid. You are booked at the Hotel Majorca; you will meet Dave O'Neill there and . . ." Bzzz went the telephone line again, a familiar sound over the last week, the line cut again by an overzealous striker.

I had been in the lovely city of Cork for over a month with my friend Brian Small . . . flying a Bell 212 to and from an oil rig for the Marathon Oil Company. The weather had been horrendous, almost as bad as our famous "Newfie" one: wet snow, gale winds, freezing rain, thick and sticky fog—you name it.

A trip to Madrid was indeed tempting but what did my company want me there for? To my knowledge Spain was one of the rare countries we had not yet put on our operating map. Bonnie, a . . . forever happy middle-aged lady, had a wonderful sense of humour, which she used to play practical jokes on and about everyone and everything. But Madrid? For sure, she would not have dared this one . . . or would she? Well, off to the passenger terminal to get an airline ticket to Madrid: it was just my luck that there was a flight in a couple of hours . . . After an hour's flight and a taxi ride, I was sitting on one of the deep couches in the lobby of the Hotel Majorca, dumbfounded. There was no reservation here in my name and they had never heard of Dave O'Neill. Rehearsing some chosen words in my head for the telephone call to my company, I checked my watch to calculate the time in Toronto. And in the date window here it was: Friday, April 1—April Fool's Day! I had been "had" by yet another of Bonnie's practical jokes! Ice down my spine—next flight back to Cork—too late for one today—one night in Madrid, and of course this whole episode would not be allowed on my expense account. I would have to pay for it . . . Bonnie's message had sounded genuine, urgent enough, but it had contained no details and, above all, no reason for the sudden trip. Oh, Bonnie, I thought, I owe you one, and it will be a good one, you can be assured of that!

As my mind had already started working on the subject, I heard a familiar voice behind me. "Hi, Looten!" I turned to face Dave O'Neill and immediately felt relief. I knew he had been in Canada only days ago, and Bonnie would have pushed her joke a little too far sending him all the way to Madrid for nothing. Dave is an engineer and a very dear friend of mine. He dropped his suitcase, fell into the armchair next to me and proceeded to tell me the reason for the trip. Unknown to me, a company helicopter had been here the whole winter, a Sikorsky S-58T, on contract to a small oil company. The contract was over and the helicopter was needed back in Canada—and needed yesterday, as usual. A space had been reserved for it on a cargo ship due to leave Bremerhaven in the north of Germany the day after tomorrow at 16:00! We had to cross the whole of Europe with a relatively slow aircraft in one and a half days! I had no maps of the itinerary, no contacts in Germany, no money, only one Shell fuel credit card with a question mark on its validity date. We did not even know where the aircraft was located in Madrid and whether or not it was in a serviceable state. As for tools, Dave had only what he was able to carry in his suitcase: a set of screwdrivers, a pair of pliers, some locking wire and not much else. Here I think it is worth opening a parenthesis. In those wonderful days, the company would hire you and immediately place all its faith in you: "Here is a job to be done, we know you can do it, go! Make plenty of money for us, try not to kill yourself and see you when the whole thing is over." The actual flying was usually the easiest part of the assignment. A pilot or an engineer had to double as customs clearing agent, diplomat, public relations officer and do all the other tasks associated with setting the job up and seeing it through to completion. This attitude sometimes led to confusion and frustration but developed in the crew a very exciting sense of involvement and initiative, which is rarely found now in our days of highly compartmented spheres of responsibilities.

But let's go back to the eve of our ferry trip across Europe. Dave and I were sitting in the lobby of the hotel, slowing digesting the enormous amount of things we had to do in about 36 hours of allotted time with two thousand kilometres [1,245 miles] of totally unknown territory to cover. As neither of us spoke Spanish, we decided to telephone the air traffic control tower: all international airport controllers are supposed to speak English, and the one who answered our call did very well indeed. "Yes, your helicopter CF-LWB used to fly in and out of the international airport. However, it has not done so for a while. And it was hangared at the northwest end of the airport in a big, old grey hangar. Yes, you can buy maps and charts at the Civil Aviation office, but it is closed now for the weekend and won't open again until . . . next week. You might find some at the local flying club!"

Dave and I decided to start the next day at a very early hour. At 6:00 o'clock we were in a taxi, trying to explain to the driver we wanted to go to "a big, old, grey hangar at the northwest end of the airport!" Was this a good omen for the rest of the trip? Without hesitation he took us to the exact location, and as we stopped at the gate, we could see the big orange nose of our helicopter with the funny "nostrils" of its engine air intakes. At least we had found the aircraft.

That it had not flown for a while [was obvious]; it was surrounded by boxes, cases and bits and pieces from other aircraft and covered in dust. But we had no time for aesthetic concerns. We pulled it out of the hangar. While Dave checked the numerous oil levels and pumped grease into where it was needed, I walked over to the local flying club. It was not open yet, but a young boy was washing the floor of the office. I had learned Italian at school, and by adding a few A's and O's to it, I managed to explain that I wanted to buy some charts for the trip. Either the boy did not understand or he did not have any maps or the authority to sell them, but for a few pesetas he let me lift off the wall a chart that covered the north of Spain and enough of the south of adjoining France to show my next refuelling stop. I also used the telephone to file my flight plan to Biarritz, just over the border.

Back at the helicopter, I started and ran the engines for a few minutes so Dave could check everything for leaks; there were none, thank God and Pratt and Whitney of Montreal for building these wonderfully powerful power plants! It was barely 8:00 AM and we were ready to go.

The trip to Biarritz was smooth; clearing customs was a breeze. Had we made mountains of our lack of resources and preparation? Could this be a good sign that the rest of our trip was going to be uneventful? Well, not quite!

At the airport office they did not have any aeronautical charts for sale. And no, I was not allowed to "borrow" the one that was pinned on the wall either! But because the officer was a good man, he would let me have a Michelin road map he had in his car. As fast as I could, I copied on it all the navigation and communication frequencies I would need.

Back at the aircraft I was faced with a real crisis: our tanks had been refuelled to the brim from the Elf Aquitaine pump, the only one there. We had a Shell credit card, which was accepted by all refuellers in the world—except the Elf Aquitaine man in Biarritz, France! And he would not take US dollars either or my personal Visa card: we would have to go to the bank. Which opened next Monday at 10 o'clock! And he proceeded to "defuel" our aircraft, sucking back the fuel he had put in it. We had 45 minutes in our tanks when we had landed, and that's what we were left with when the operation was completed. According to him, there was Shell fuel in Bordeaux. That was about thirty minutes away, not much of a margin, but we had no choice.

Here I must make a pause and explain a stupid decision of mine, which was about to cause me numerous problems: I was born and raised in France, but I had never flown there. My military training was done in Morocco and, after my time in the Air Force, I had almost immediately emigrated to Canada where all flying until recently is done using the English language. I don't know any of the proper terms for "flying" in French but, because I was so proud of overflying my country for the first time in my life, I decided to use my mother language. And that was about to make my life very difficult!

Dave and I had no problems getting to Bordeaux, but when we arrived in the vicinity of the airport with precious little fuel left, we were told there were some jet fighter exercises in progress and instructed to "hold at check point Golf." Holding means flying around and over a particular spot on the ground, hence burning fuel. And having no aeronautical charts of the area, I had no idea where "check point Golf" was. However, I started orbiting and advised the control tower I could not do this very long. I was told the jet exercise "would be over . . . in a half hour or so," well beyond my remaining autonomy! I declared an emergency, asking for immediate landing. The controller sent the jets away and cleared me to land right away, but I could judge by the tone of his voice that I was in trouble. And indeed, I was instructed to present myself at the airport office with my licence and on the double! "Your licence please," which I produced. "No, your French licence." "I don't have one." "You do not have a licence?" The controller's voice had gone from its official I-am-going-to-get-that-one tone to one of total disbelief as if to say: this guy is flying that big helicopter and he has no licence? He is a madhouse case. And he looked around as [if] to see if he could summon some help in case I went into total seizure or unpredictable acts of madness.

"No, I do not have a French pilot's licence, but I have a valid Canadian one. And you have it in your hands. And I am Canadian."

"Oh, you are Canadian but you spoke French on the radio." In his mind, I am sure, passed visions of [Canada as] thousands of square miles of frozen wasteland . . . a country of lawless adventurers where if one decided to go flying, one did so in total disregard of any laws . . . With contempt—or was it pity?—he handed me back my documents and advised me to get out of Bordeaux as fast as I could. I never spoke French again for the remainder of the trip!

All this had . . . wasted time and our aircraft was not equipped for night and instrument flying. We would have to be on the ground again when night came. Also the weatherman had told us to stick to the west side of France as the east and northeast were, for the time being, subject to fog and bad visibility. Above all, I wanted to avoid Paris and its region; with no proper map, flying through it would have been professional suicide!

With careful navigation and a bit of luck, we would make Tours that night. So loaded with as much fuel as we could carry, we were on our way again. And speaking only English, we breezed through all control zones without any further trouble. Arriving at our destination as night was falling, we parked our aircraft and reported to the airport office.

And there and then started the most incredible part of our trip. When I remember it almost twenty years later, I can't help but be amazed at the odd series of events that led to the next few hours. Dave and I were tired and very hungry . . . We had so far survived on a chocolate bar and a bottle of cola we had bought at the Madrid flying club. So, at the airport office and after the usual landing formalities, we asked the officer in charge to be so kind as to telephone the closest hotel and reserve a couple of rooms for us. Which he did with much kindness. When we also inquired about a taxi, he told us that the suburbs of Tours where the airport is located were very quiet and typically French; this was Saturday night, remember, and at this time of day people were well into their first aperitif, followed by a few more before eventually they would proceed to the dinner table—a ceremony not to be disturbed! And the rule went for taxi drivers as well . . . "But if you guys can wait, my shift will be over in about a half hour. My wife will come and pick me up and we would be delighted to give you a lift." We thanked him very much and settled to wait . . . Right on time, a car came to a stop in front of the door. He turned the building lights off, locked the door behind us and introduced us to his wife, a very pretty young lady.

As we were driving to Tours, Dave started yawning, mainly from hunger and the long day behind us but also because he could not understand much of the conversation as it was conducted in French:

"I hope this hotel has a restaurant. We have not had anything to eat the whole day!"

"No, it does not . . ."

"Oh, could you stop at a restaurant somewhere? We will find our own way to the hotel after we have had something to eat."

"I am afraid there are none, but . . ." Husband and wife started a *sotto voce* dialogue, which I was unable to understand because of the noise of the car. Then, turning to us again, [he said], "My wife says it will be no problem preparing a snack for you. Nothing fancy, a potluck kind of thing if you don't mind . . ."

I cannot get over the kindness of this couple: they did not know us an hour ago and now they are inviting us for dinner at their home! I accept the offer after consulting with Dave . . . And a few minutes later we are sitting in the living room of a very comfortable apartment, sipping wonderful Anjou sparkling wine. Two young children are lying on the carpet watching cartoons on the television, their mother has locked herself in the kitchen while her husband explains to us that he has worked a double shift to accommodate a colleague and he is very tired.

"Have another glass of wine. Isn't it good?" It is indeed but on our empty stomachs . . .

We are now well into the second bottle of wine and, despite quite a bit of noise in the kitchen and the adjoining dining room, there is still no sign of our sandwiches.

And that is when the lady of the house enters and announces, "Gentlemen, supper is ready!" The children are first on their feet. We unfold from our armchairs, find the ground a bit unsteady. And we all proceed to the dining room. There, I cannot believe my eyes: the table has been set for a wedding banquet or is it for Christmas? White tablecloth, sparkling silverware, three glasses per setting. A big loaf of crusty French bread and an expensive looking bottle of red wine, which our host opens immediately. We are invited to sit down in front of this beautiful example of French hospitality. In the middle of the table a large plateful of escargots: these obviously are the hors d'oeuvres, and if they set a trend for the main course, we are in for quite a meal.

All of a sudden, Dave does not seem to be frustrated anymore by the conversation that he cannot understand: it sets his teeth in motion, devouring the snails at much higher speed than the legendary pace of them. Then comes saucisson Lyonnais, a delicious sausage cooked in a bread crust and served with crunchy fries. I cannot remember this ever tasting that good! We are so busy eating that we have hardly noticed the two children slipping off their chairs. They are now lying on the carpet sound asleep. A plate of assorted cheeses comes next. And another bottle of wine! "You don't eat cheese with a Bordeaux. You need a wine with more body, more—how can I say—strength," and [our host] uncorks what looks like a pretty dark Burgundy. Do we need more strength? He sure looks like he needs a good sleep. And sure enough, as I turned to Dave to remark on the delicious taste of one of the cheeses, I hear a thump. Our host has fallen asleep, his head has missed his plate by a centimetre and is now resting on the table cloth. He has simply passed out, here and now! . . . But his wife does not seem to be concerned at all.

"He does this quite often, you know; he goes to sleep right in the middle of his meal. He has worked for 24 hours and he must be very tired. If you gents could excuse me for a minute, I will put him to bed." And she is back in no time with a large cake and box of ice cream in her hands! We are both exhausted; we have been up since five o'clock in the morning. It is now very late and we have to depart early tomorrow if we want to make Bremerhaven in time. Dave looks at me with despair in his eyes as we eat a slice of cake each so as not to offend the young lady.

I ask for a very last favour: "I think it is time we left. Would you be so kind as to call a taxi for us?"

"No taxis at this time of night. I will give you guys a ride to the hotel, no problem!"

French drivers have acquired a worldwide reputation: when they are sitting behind the steering wheel of their cars, they know only two speeds—stop and full blast! A Frenchman myself, I think this reputation is not deserved, or let's say it could be shared by many other countries' drivers. Try a taxi ride in Rome, for example, or Bombay or Bangkok. No, most French drivers conduct themselves quite safely on the streets and roads of this world. [But] not this one! Our young lady negotiates the streets of Tours as if the town was going to be hit by an atomic bomb any minute now. I hear a moan from the back seat. Instinctively Dave has adopted our "Bombay position." When sitting in a taxi in that city, he has turned around and [looked] through the rear window. He . . . is not interested in the sight of the end of his life!

As we are taking yet another sharp turn to the right at just under the speed of sound, my eyes are only fast enough to register the obstacle as we hit it: a huge pile of sand, right there smack in the middle of the street! In a relatively smooth fashion, we come to a complete stop. On top of it. I thought I had seen the usual sign just around the corner indicating that the street was closed to traffic, but at that speed, no time to warn our driver. The car engine has stalled. There is no traffic at all in the streets, especially the ones blocked by piles of sand. There is not a sound until Dave gets out of the car and says, "Now what?" The car is resting on its belly, the wheels a few inches from the sand. I turn to our host. "Would you have a shovel in the trunk of the car?" Well, no, she does not have one.

But the wines we drank have left enough gray cells intact in my brain that I might have a solution to our plight: this car, a Citroën, has a hydraulic suspension which, among other advantages, allows the driver to vary the height of the car above the ground. I start the engine, place the proper lever in the "high" position. Did I feel the car rising? If so, then the wheels are now back on firm ground, right? Very carefully I engage the clutch, the car goes down the slope. We are back on terra firma! A few minutes [more] and we are pulling up in front of our hotel. The car has barely stopped and [Dave] . . . is walking through the entrance door with his suitcase.

It is now around midnight. If we want to make Bremerhaven in time, we will have to get airborne again at daybreak. As I walk around to the back of the car to pick up my suitcase, I almost bump into our brave driver. "The night is still young," [she says.] "Let's go for a drink and then . . ."

I never heard the end of the sentence. I was backing away, almost scared, thanking her profusely. But today I wished I had known at least her name, maybe her address to say thank you again, [and] in a more sober way tell her she was so kind to a couple of lost Canucks. And so lovely.

It is again very early in the morning. We are back at the airport, still stunned from the previous night. But our tanks have been refuelled, the weather man predicts tailwinds and good weather for the rest of our trip. Our only problem: I still do not have a proper map. And I will have to fly carefully around Paris and land in Amsterdam, which is our next refuelling stop!

No, I cannot lift the map off the wall but, yes, I am welcome to copy a few more bits and pieces of information on my old Michelin road map. The trouble is it stops just short of Amsterdam! In those days, [photocopiers] were rare indeed, and all I can do is draw my own chart on a blank sheet of paper, hoping that I will not have to divert from it for any reason. We breeze through the west part of Paris, the north end of France, barely notice Belgium. It is now time to call Amsterdam: "Amsterdam tower, this is helicopter Charlie Whiskey Bravo, two thousand feet, ten miles southwest landing Amsterdam for fuel."

"Charlie Whiskey Bravo, maintain two thousand feet, proceed to checkpoint Delta, call at Delta."

Well, here we go again: I do not have a clue where Delta is, fuel is low and this is a big airport! This time, let's play dumb: "Amsterdam, hum, our chart just flew out the window, we do not know the position of Delta and, hum, we are very low on fuel, but we do have the airport in sight." I will not repeat here the comments buzzing around the airwaves from all the airliners trying to land in Amsterdam. Most of them are not very kind and a few even frankly rude. But we are instructed to land. And, of course, to present ourselves at the airport office, immediately after landing—with our pilot licence! Sound familiar? Never in my flying career have I ever had to present my pilot licence so many times to the authorities in such a short period of time! Unlike the Bordeaux controller, this one is not on the verge of apoplexy. Rather phlegmatic actually when he discovers I hold a Canadian licence . . . as if my citizenship suddenly made the reason [for] the incident very clear. And he proceeds to tell me that this particular helicopter flew through Amsterdam last year, crewed by Canadians and created havoc in the flow of traffic. He knows. He was on duty that particular day!

"I don't know what the matter is with you guys . . . but get some fuel, give me a call when you are ready, and by the way, here is a map that should see you safely all the way to Bremerhaven for your sake. And ours too." We are off again. The rest of the trip is totally uneventful, dull by comparison. As we are cleared through the Bremen control zone, the tower, aware of our destination through our customs clearing agent, advises us to land on the docks at the Bremerhaven harbour. Easy enough: it has been cleared and its access blocked by a couple of police cars.

It takes us an hour to remove the main blades and make the aircraft ship-shape for the trip. During this period, ground crew has started loading the ship with brand-new cars destined for export to Canada, we suppose. An uninterrupted convoy of BMWs and Mercedes are driven right into the ship's belly. Then comes our turn. But we have no tractor! So our helicopter is—in a very unceremonial manner—towed by a Volkswagen Beetle and disappears into the gaping mouth of the ship. Within a few minutes this is closed and the ship leaves the port.

All of a sudden, Dave and I feel exhausted; the excitement, the lack of sleep and proper meals, but above all the satisfaction of having "done it" by the skin of our teeth! As I bend down to pick up my suitcase, [Dave says], "I don't know about you, Looten, but I am going to the best hotel in town and I am going to have a meal to match!" And that is exactly what we did. When I phoned head office that night and gave Pat Aldous, our boss, a resume of the trip, his answer, as always, was very simple: "Eh, I knew you could pull it off. Well done!" And it felt so good . . ."[79]

The Okanagan operation in Ireland ended in September 1978. S-61 CF-OKM was flown to Marshall Aerospace in Cambridge, England, where it underwent Civil Aviation Authority (CAA) modifications and was then assigned to a contract operating out of Peterhead, north of Aberdeen, Scotland. A second S-61N, C-GOKH, was ferried to Songkhla, Thailand, by captains Dave Whyte, Jack Jaworski and Tony Coalson and engineer Marty Battick. These flights had now become routine and planning was down to a fine art. They arrived in Songkhla on August 20 and immediately started a Union Oil contract.

Pierre Looten returned a third S-61, CF-OKA, to Vancouver, 5,000 miles (8,045 kilometres) away, via the northern route in 48 hours flight time over four and a half days. It was the first direct flight from Europe to the West Coast of Canada; previous marathon flights had been from eastern Canada to Europe. With the weather very cloudy and foggy, three-quarters of the trip was flown on instruments at an average 115 mph (185 km/h) and altitudes between 1,000 and 2,000 feet (305 and 610 metres). The flight path, departing from Shannon, took them to Stornoway in Scotland, the Faroe Islands and then Reykjavík where they overnighted before going on to Kulusuk on the east coast of Greenland. During the flight over Greenland, the crew experienced heavy cloud and icing conditions. Captain Pierre Looten recalled:

> We tried to make it over the ice cap, but the clouds were 5,000 feet [1,525 metres] and the rotors were icing, so we turned back and headed around the south tip of Greenland. It delayed us for the better part of a day.

After Godthåb (now Nuuk) on Greenland's west coast and then Frobisher Bay (now Iqaluit), their next stop was Coral Harbour on the west coast of Hudson Bay, then Churchill, Prince Albert, Revelstoke and finally into Vancouver. Pierre Looten described it as:

> . . . a fairly routine trip. The crew took 50 pounds [23 kilograms] of groceries on board, and [we] had our fill of canned food, dried fruit, cookies and cheese. We overnighted in whatever accommodation they could find in those remote areas with unfamiliar names.
> A world record—I never thought of it that way. It was an enjoyable flight, although we are a little tired.[80]

Okanagan had been working in India since 1975, and in late 1977 another helicopter from Ireland, Bell 212 C-GOKL, was sent to Bombay with captains Dale Simpson and Kelly Hague on a one-year contract. Engineer Frank Kearney caught a British Airways flight and met the machine on its arrival at the Juhu airfield, which was just two kilometres from Bombay's Santacruz International Airport (now Chhatrapati Shivaji). At that time airport authorities had posted a "Notice to Airmen" (NOTAM) advisory regarding confusion between runway 09/02 Santacruz and 08/26 Juhu. The proximity of Juhu Airport's runway, which was just 3,750 feet (1,143 metres) long, to Santacruz's runway, which was a full 14,752 feet (4,400 metres) long, had caused a few problems over the years. On July 15, 1963, a British Overseas Airways Corporation (BOAC now BA) Comet had landed at Juhu by mistake. It had taken nine days to remove as much equipment as possible in order to fly it out. And on December 24, 1972, a Japan Airlines DC-8 had overrun the Juhu runway and been damaged beyond repair.

But more recently Bombay had seen a worse air tragedy. On the night of January 1, 1978, an Air India Boeing 747, VT-EBD, had taken off from Santacruz International Airport destined for Dubai. Approximately 1.9 miles (three kilometres) out over the Arabian Sea, the pilot made a scheduled right turn and returned to normal flight level. Soon after, however, the plane rolled to the left and never regained its normal flight path. The cockpit voice recorder revealed a conversation between the captain and first officer about a discrepancy between the attitude indicators, which are vital to the flight crew in inclement weather and nighttime conditions to provide horizontal and banking information. The aircraft plunged into the sea, killing all 213 people on board. Okanagan's Bell 212, C-GOKL, having been recently posted to Bombay as standby for rig medical evacuations, was scrambled to the scene to look for survivors. The helicopter crew flew over the area using high-powered searchlights but only found debris floating on the surface.

*

Okanagan was also active in Central and South America in 1978. In March the company signed a contract with Panama Exploration to use an S-58T while Aerotecnica Ltd. of Brazil awarded an additional contract. S-61 CF-DWC (re-registered as YV-323C) and Bell 212 C-GPKX (re-registered as VY-322C) made the ferry trip to the town of Maturín, the centre for the development of the Venezuelan oil industry; they were accompanied by three Venezuelan trainees. For both helicopters this marked the start of a long contract with Aerotecnica.

In November 1978 a DomPeg engineer, who was in Guyana on a contract to maintain the Guyana Defence Force's Bell 212s, learned that one of the 212s had flown to Jonestown, a community known as the Peoples Temple Agricultural Project led by American cult leader Jim Jones, in northwest Guyana and had been grounded there due to a compressor stall. The engineer was flown in to evaluate and fix the problem at the same time US Congressman Leo J. Ryan was conducting a fact-finding tour of Jonestown to investigate allegations that US citizens were being held there against their will and that there were human rights violations and social security irregularities.

While the DomPeg engineer was working on the 212, Ryan and his party returned to their aircraft, a de Havilland Twin Otter, but as they attempted to board, the occupants of a nearby trailer owned by the Peoples Temple opened fire, killing Ryan and three members of his party and seriously wounding five other persons. Once the shooting stopped, the engineer, who had taken cover in the jungle, returned to the 212, quickly completed the repairs, and the 212 made a dash back to Georgetown to raise the alarm. In the aftermath of the shooting, it was discovered that a cocktail of cyanide, sedatives, tranquilizers and Kool-Aid given to members of the Peoples Temple community had resulted in the death of 912 people.

1979

In the spring of 1979 the first of the S-76 Spirits, ordered a year earlier, finally arrived directly from the factory, and on May 5 *Sikorsky News* reported:

> Delivery of the first Spirit Helicopters to an international operator was completed last month when Sikorsky turned over three aircraft to Okanagan Helicopters Ltd. of Vancouver, British Columbia, Canada. The aircraft contained two new features—a sliding cabin entrance door on the right side and a cargo hook system for external lift operations.
>
> Okanagan, which has ordered 21 of the new 12-passenger transport category helicopters—the most by any operator—ferried the aircraft to Montreal where they were placed aboard a Northwest Territorial Airways C-130 transport for shipment to their working locations in the Far East and Australia. The aircraft will be placed into service supporting offshore oil operations in Thailand and Australia.[81]

A fourth S-76 was delivered within the month.

On the domestic front in the spring of 1979 Captain Owen Shannon completed a two-year posting as base manager in the town of Golden, BC, which is nestled in the Rocky Mountains and surrounded by Banff, Jasper, Yoho, Glacier and Kootenay national parks. Pilot Vic Corrie established the base in 1975, and Shannon reported that Corrie had worked there . . .

... without a hangar [in] mid-winter temperatures [that] could dip to -10°F [-23°C] and lower. There was a need for blade covers, heated blankets and internal heaters to protect the helicopter from winter conditions [and make it] ready to fly each morning. Okanagan management in 1976 budgeted sufficient funds for building a new hangar, and Vic supervised the construction before handing over the baton to me.

Much later Owen Shannon wrote a report on these years, describing "a time when standards were less rigid: if you felt you could do the job safely, then you went ahead and did it. If you were not sure, then you asked for assistance."

There were 15 Okanagan bases in BC and NWT (Mackenzie Delta area) during the height of activity in 1977. Each base [was unique], typified by its location, local industry and terrain. Common to all the bases were the customers from BC Forestry, BC Hydro, wildlife [organizations], BC Tel and Fisheries while to a lesser degree . . . work in mining, surveying, rescue services and air ambulance. Some [extra] challenges [faced by] . . . base pilots and engineers were jobs such as assisting the spawning of local salmon due to local rivers being blocked by rock falls . . . Each base has its own story about . . . the work involved building up customer and community relations.

 Life at an Okanagan base in Western Canada during the 1970s was just about everything a helicopter pilot could wish for—varied tasks, community lifestyle, full days, home most nights and more. [Flying from our] location took us into very isolated areas, often miles from roads or river access . . . up some valley laden with magnificent spruce or cedar trees that required inspection, up and down glaciers for photographers or the mountainous slopes for skiers. We also landed on mountain peaks to drop off technicians who serviced communication towers or earthquake monitoring stations. It was comforting to know that Max Hoover in Vancouver was monitoring the flights and always in communication [through] HF radio. He was always there and if you did not report in as expected he was looking for you right away.

 Company flight monitoring was a pretty loose arrangement by today's standards, but [there was] a combination of base monitoring done by Kathy Johnson in Mica Creek and air-to-air communications [that] worked very well. On one occasion, Cranbrook reported Rolfe Ganong as missing. Max organized a search using local base helicopters and they spent several hours searching the valleys where [Rolfe] had been working. The thought of one of our pilots and colleagues in trouble became the main priority and other pre-planned jobs were put on the back burner. A very apologetic Rolfe called off the search later in the day. [He] had dropped in on his family and forgotten to advise [the base]. It showed that the system worked in an emergency.

 Summers were a very busy period and daily flight hours were high in many cases . . . Winter, however, tended to be more relaxing and gave us time to tidy up the base, get jobs around the hangar done and catch up on maintenance and servicing. During the summer a single pilot base could hire a local to help man the base HF radio, deal with customers and generally keep the base area tidy. . . . The bases during this period used the Bell 206B with the Allison 250-C20 engine, not known for a lot of power at altitude but enough as long as mountain flying techniques were carefully [followed]. . . . The skills [they] taught [at the mountain flying school] kept me out of serious trouble for the next 30 years. Without this training, it would [have been] impossible to work safely in the BC mountains; you are constantly having to deal with convection [currents] caused by warm air . . . figure eight recces, cirque and saddle landing techniques, up drafts, down drafts and even bald eagles who tend to soar in the lower and upper flowing air currents . . .

We were often able to use the long line for some jobs and [in one case] I had . . . to use a three hundred-foot-long [91.5-metre] line to recover a snowmobile from a narrow gully near Mummery Glacier. Slinging jobs varied and in some cases minimum down drafts and manipulation of the underslung loads were essential for safety. A regular load was concrete used for building the footings of ski lifts, gravel for national park trails and fire equipment for crews isolated by tall trees.

The hot dry summers brought the forest fires where helicopters were an essential tool alongside the fixed-wing water bombers. Tasks included positioning rap attack teams (first responders and very essential), water bombing [and] supplying the fire watch stations located on the tops of mountains . . . I remember Bob Thurston (Thirsty Bob) and I doing a quick course on "Sky Jennie," repelling and flying each other as we descended down a 150-foot [45.5 metre] rope under the supervision of our repelling friend. This gave us a better understanding of the forestry rap attack crew's job and the reason for the occasional jerk on the line . . .

The lumber companies required firefighting assistance, but they also had other tasks, which involved flying over treed areas to identify the tree types using aerial photography. The actual volume of timber in these forests required the helicopter to place crews near a block of trees every morning and pick them up later in the day at a predetermined rendezvous point. Their principle task was to sample the trees for timber content, age, etc . . .

New inventions and techniques were developed locally . . . often at the request of the customers. One such item was the drip torch, which . . . allowed BC Forestry and lumber companies to slash burn large areas already logged off and to clear the old roots and offcuts (slash) in preparation for replanting . . . The acceptable conditions for this type of operation [were] dry combustible slash [and] no wind with firefighting precautions in place. A block would be marked out and the pilot would begin setting on fire the centre area and then fly and drip the ignited fuel in ever increasing circles outwards to the edge of the marked block. I remember torching a block as large as 600 acres [240 hectares]—a pyromaniac's heaven. Convection heating drew heat and smoke into the centre of the block, thus lowering the possibility of setting fire to the neighbouring trees.

BC Hydro work entailed tasks such as power transmission line construction, power line patrols (checking for broken insulators), survey work, etc. When I was asked if I could land on two wooden cross [beams] between two power poles about 60 to 80 feet [18 to 24 metres] above the ground, I couldn't see any reason why not. The BC Hydro guy wanted to nail number plates to the cross pieces without having to climb each set of poles. This was over a five-mile [eight-kilometre] stretch of isolated power lines in mountainous terrain. I cannot remember if the actual power lines were in place at the time. The cross pieces were sturdy 6 x 12 [-inch, 15 by 30–centimetre] lumber less than a couple of feet apart, and I had just enough space to position the helicopter skid gear between the two vertical poles. The Hydro guy intended to lean down from the back seat, place one foot on the cross pieces for support and hammer four nails into the number plate. I asked if he had done it before and he said, "No, but there's always a first time for everything." We had a trial run in front of the hangar... He then demonstrated how he was going to do it. It was a good thing that the 206 had the versatility of high and low skid gear. We had fitted the low skid gear. It was obvious he had given it a lot of thought, and he accepted that he would have to slide partially off the seat and out the door to [get in] position to do the nailing. Anyway, he proved he could bend down enough with the safety harness... I insisted that another person sit in the back with him to supervise, hand him the equipment [and] also talk to me on the intercom so I would know what was going on.

Positioning the helicopter on these cross pieces and having the back seat directly above the centre of the cross piece took some getting used to, too. It was touchdown, hover and balance and, with the door removed, I had to look behind to get a reference for positioning and note his nailing process. The other passenger acted as the observer and explained the movements as they occurred. Once we got into the rhythm we covered a power pole every four to five minutes. Normally it [would] have taken several men to carry the gear and days to accomplish this project...

There were also those jobs where you [had to get] used to the waiting game; [sometimes] it took all day for a token amount of flying. The water survey was one of them. [It was carried out by] Environment Canada, the department responsible for monitoring the country's fresh water. The water resources crew used special equipment to record water levels and volume. It was time-consuming work setting up a line across streams and rivers for measuring [and it] involved wading in... and taking recordings every few feet for a certain period of time. Once completed, it was a case of packing up all the equipment and flying to a new location, sometimes not far away, to go through the same process. In winter, snow levels were recorded... in order to calculate spring runoff and using these recorded levels to compare with past levels. All this information became valuable, especially regarding climate change.

The job for the pilot [often] was long and quite boring unless you took an interest in what was being done; if not, a good book was essential... During the winter [I would] perfect [my cross-country] skiing while waiting. In the summer time mosquito repellent was essential.

We were regularly involved with photography. Being located in the Rockies gave us a spectacular scenic landscape. I flew Norman Kezier from the BC Department of Travel [Ministry of Tourism] around the Golden area while he took some spectacular photography. I never got tired of viewing these areas and they certainly reminded me of my own country, New Zealand. I also had the opportunity to provide the camera platform for some documentaries [of] the Columbia Icefield...

I was privileged to fly visiting celebrities around the local area... One of my favourites... was an old timer in Golden, Ed Feuz, who was originally from Switzerland... He was the first man to climb over 70 peaks in the area while working as a guide for the Canadian Pacific Railway [CPR] out of the Rogers Pass area... As we climbed out of Golden, ahead of us was a beautiful sunrise with colours [spread out on] the new alpine snow. Feuz was spellbound and interested in everything around him. At 93, he was dressed in his traditional Swiss climbing gear, hiking boots, long socks, jacket and tie; unfortunately the headset replaced his traditional hat. As we flew north, he had great delight in naming all the peaks in sight ... [His] flight was sponsored by HTV [Harlech Television], a Welsh station that was documenting an expedition by a British climbing team ... After spending a short time with the TV crew and climbers at the base camp (Great Cairn Hut), it was time to head home. But not before we climbed the mountain [Mount Sir Sandford] by air and Mr. Feuz pointed out the route that he and his fellow guides had taken with [American mountaineer] Howard Palmer [in 1912] ... [Now] looking over the glacier, Mr. Feuz was shocked at how much it had shrunk in size ...

One drizzly grey day I was asked to do a job in Yoho National Park, a 25-minute flight from Golden. I had to land at the park headquarters and pick up a film crew and fly them to the Burgess Shales, the Cambrian fossil fields just above the town of Field, population 300. I had to wait for them to complete their job and then return them to park HQ. The weather cleared enough, and we landed at the fossil fields for the filming. The Burgess Shale, recognized for its ... well-preserved fossils of marine organisms that lived over 500 million years ago [has been] designated by UNESCO as a world heritage site. After shutting down the machine, I decided to watch the filming. It was obvious that one of the team, a guy named David, knew what he was talking about as, with no notes, he explained the creatures illustrated on the rock he was holding and was scurrying around to find other rocks with different ... creatures and explaining more details ... Later we made our way back to the helicopter and he asked me if I visited the area very often. I told him it was my first visit [and] he bent down and after a brief search handed me a rock ... He pointed out the symmetrical indents on the edge indicating some sort of marine creature. It was not until several years later that I saw [him] on TV. [Sir] David Attenborough was instantly recogniz[able] and I realized how lucky I had been to meet him ...

All bases provide ambulance and rescue services on demand ... The Golden base had its fair share of these [when I was there between] 1976 and 1978 [including] retrieving a badly injured forestry worker, [casualties of] traffic accidents in the Kicking Horse Pass, [and] a shooting victim, [flying] him to a hospital in Calgary in the middle of the night via the moonlight on the snow and car headlights on the Trans-Canada Highway. Unfortunately there were few lights on the return trip at 0200.

About this time Glacier National Park introduced a mountain rescue procedure pioneered by [Banff] parks staff[er] Peter Fuhrmann and [Okanagan base pilot/manager] Jim Davies ... The method was known as HETS (Helicopter External Transport System). It was a method whereby a park ranger and [his] equipment were carried on a long line beneath the helicopter to the scene of a climbing accident. Once on the scene, he would attend to the injured person, place them on a stretcher and then, attaching them under the helicopter on a special harness, fly [with] the victim to an area where an ambulance would be waiting ... By helicopter, rescue was achievable within a couple of hours once the alarm was given.

At this time the procedure was not regulated by the [Ministry of Transport], but this did not mean it was done without an enormous amount of training. Many hours were spent flying park rangers out of the Rogers Pass HQ to and from various peaks around Glacier National Park to ensure the rangers gained confidence in the system, the equipment and the pilot. [Later] the Parks people felt another pilot should be trained in case Jim Davies was [unavailable]. I was given the nod... I quite often had park rangers dangling 60 feet [18 metres] below me. The communication was... by the use of a radio with a microphone installed in their helmet to reduce wind and helicopter noise. We learned quickly that turns made at speed were not good for the ranger [dangling] under the helicopter due to the G-forces. It was important to keep the ranger comfortable at a reasonable speed and height above the terrain. I do remember two mountain rescues using the park rangers' long line. Bruce McKinnon and I rescued a school teacher who had broken his leg in a fall while climbing in the Albert Canyon region of the Selkirk Mountains. We [also] flew out [his] companion who had stayed with him while another went for help.

The other rescue was in August 1977... I went to Mount Owen late in the afternoon to pick up a fall victim [after] climbers called in to report that they had heard calls for help. One of the climbers [had come] across a single climber on a 8,900-foot [2,712-metre] ridge. [By] gestures [he] indicated that another person was stranded in the snow some 500 feet [150 metres] below... I noted an area on a snowy ridge that could be used. I had to return to Golden for fuel [and] to pick up a St. John Ambulance assistant, Dave Stewart, and I also informed the RCMP. Dave and I had worked together on other accidents in the past. Arriving back on the scene, we discussed a recovery procedure. I then wrote it out on paper, and... managed to drop the instructions to the climber below. I needed him to cut away and level the snow on the ridge so that he could climb on board the helicopter with little difficulty. He read the note, waved and I went to an area where I could remove the back door. I returned to the ridge where I was able to rest the skid on his side and he climbed aboard...

During this period there were [also] some heartbreaking accidents involving avalanches in both the Selkirk and Purcell mountains. On February 16, 1979, Barry Holmes, my Bow Helicopters competitor and friend... came by and asked if I had any means of providing lights with the use of a generator... a number of skiers from the Swiss National Team had been buried in an avalanche and lights were needed to search for them. We had been out with these guys the night before sharing a few schnapps. Also, sadly, one of them was the

◂ Bell J-2 CF-JYQ was introduced to heli-skiing by Okanagan in 1962. The J-2 began production in 1956 and on July 13, 1957, became the first US presidential helicopter when D.D. Eisenhower flew in an H13J (J-2). OKANAGAN HELICOPTERS PHOTO

brother of a local guide from Golden. Seven of the ten lost their lives in that avalanche...

The mid- to late seventies was a period when heli-skiing was being promoted by a number of companies. One in particular, Canadian Mountain Holidays, had already established a beautiful lodge in the Bugaboos, a range in the Purcell Mountains... Okanagan flew a number of winter skiing contracts with helicopters positioned at the lodges that were sprouting up... It was not uncommon for the Golden-based helicopter to be called in to help... During the summer months [there was] heli-hiking using the lodges as the main bases.

One of the methods we used to satisfy our local clientele was non-revenue flights. We would take customers on a local fishing trip... into areas that normally were very difficult to access [or take] a customer's relative who was visiting for the first time... for a sightseeing tour. Though seldom abused by base personnel, there were occasions when it came in handy. I was introduced to this perk by a senior pilot we will call W. We were flying out of Revelstoke when our wives were inbound from Kelowna for the weekend by car; unfortunately [the car's] engine overheated near Sicamous. A passing truck driver who stopped to help them said it looked like a water pump problem. On receiving the call, W informed the girls to stay put as he would be in the area within minutes. We jumped aboard the base helicopter, tools in hand, and arrived at the site about 15 minutes later. We removed the water pump and were all back in Revelstoke in time for a beer and dinner. The next day we flew to the site, installed a new water pump and the car was driven home. The company bean counters never heard [about] this.

My time at the Golden base finished in 1979. Okanagan had started a heli-logging division using the bigger Sikorsky S-61L models, and it gave a lot of pilots who only had light single [engine] helicopter ratings [a chance] to move into the left seat of a 61... After my time in heli-logging [and] my IFR endorsement, [I] then went into the International pool flying the Sikorsky S-76 in Thailand. The Golden base was a great experience; it challenged my management and flying skills [and] offered a very wide range of jobs.[82]

▸ A Bell 47 in the early days in BC's mountain terrain. OKANAGAN HELICOPTERS PHOTO

CHAPTER FIVE—THE LATE 1970S

As a result of the dramatic increase in oil and gas projects in the late 1970s, by 1979 Canada's East Coast was in high gear with Okanagan operating seven heavy and two medium helicopters to ferry personnel and equipment for major companies including Esso, Texaco, Chevron, British Petroleum, the Eastcan Group and Elf Aquitaine. In addition, Universal Helicopters had two S-61s, CF-OKP and C-GOKZ, on contract for Esso operating out of St. John's while Okanagan had a leased Greenlandair S-61 at work out of Gander. Five machines were on contract again that year for the seal hunt out of St. Anthony, Newfoundland. All of these projects meant that the company's engineers worked very long hours, and one anonymous engineer put pen to paper to write about a typical day in his life:

> We were getting two S-61s ready for a new offshore oil project due to start in St. John's in the spring... and working out of Halifax International Airport. The machines, CF-OKP and C-GOKZ, [needed] a lot of modifications, both mechanical and electrical. The crew included contract sheet metal techs, avionics and AMEs [aircraft-maintenance engineers].
>
> Our hotel was located in Dartmouth, about 20 miles [32 kilometres] from the airport... We were working out of the IMP hangar and one problem we had was meals. The only food available was at the Halifax International Airport food outlets, which were some distance away. With the workload and the weather, we were often hungry and [had to] arrange for someone to do a fast food run.
>
> One day we finished about 9:00 pm, and by the time we were back at the hotel, the restaurant was closed. To say the least, we were famished... The restaurant offered to make us some sandwiches, but we felt we needed a more substantial meal. One of the staff told us about a pub... about three blocks away. I think there were about eight of us. We located the pub and ordered a beer; the waitress brought over menus and mentioned a daily special—steak and fries for $1.99—which we all ordered. When it arrived, we were amazed how thick it was as were the fries. One of the crew said to the waitress, "How can you serve such a good steak and only charge $1.99?" Her reply in that wonderful Maritime accent was: "Lord Thundering Jesus, bye, it's amazing what falls into Halifax harbour." The steak was so good and we were so hungry we ordered another. We did return the next night but, alas, no steak for $1.99. It was back to hamburger and fries.

In Labrador the company had a contract for a Bell 212 to operate between Nain, Hopedale and Goose Bay. During one flight I took there the weather deteriorated, and our 212 had to divert to Davis Inlet, a small Inuit community about 37 miles (60 kilometres) north of Hopedale. It consisted of a number of homes, a Hudson's Bay store built in 1925, a small RCMP detachment, a nursing station and a school. (In recent years this community has been in the media due to social problems resulting from alcohol and drug abuse.) We landed near the nursing station, and the RCMP officer who met us told us that the only accommodation was at the nursing station. We got the machine battened down in case of high winds, which were well known in this area, and headed off to the nursing station. There were four of us—pilot Alec Calder, the co-pilot whose name escapes me, engineer Frank Kearney, and me, avionics. The word had got out that there were new people in town, so we had a welcoming committee made up of the RCMP officers, the Bay manager and an employee of the telephone company who was in the area to upgrade the system. The nurse was a young Scottish lass from just outside Glasgow who was on a one-year contract with the Grenfell Mission, which had been providing medical services along the coast of Labrador since the 1890s. Since most of these places were too small to need a full-time doctor or hospital, the Mission hired contract nurses, mainly from Britain because they were also experienced midwives.

Being very inquisitive, I asked about the jobs the people did in this small isolated place, and the nurse told us about numerous incidents in this troubled community. Someone said how awful it must be for a young woman to be confronted by this, to which she replied, "This is nothing compared to the emergency room at Glasgow Infirmary on a Saturday night after the pubs close." She mentioned how inventive the locals were when it came to repairing anything and told us about a local man who had stayed in the Mission overnight. Over a coffee, she had mentioned to him that the washing machine was broken, and parts would not be coming from Montreal until sometime the following week. He looked at it, took it apart and jury-rigged the motor to get it working until the part arrived.

The next morning the weather improved so we got away and flew to Hopedale for fuel before going on to Goose Bay.

*

In the Arctic, Esso and Elf Aquitaine expanded their search for oil with a summer program on Brevoort Island, the site of an early warning radar station off the eastern coast of Baffin Island that had been in use until the 1960s. In addition, Okanagan had a contract for the polar bear study with the Canadian Wildlife Service in Northern Labrador and Baffin Island. However, the most interesting of the company's Arctic contracts in 1979 was the LOREX (Lomonosov Ridge Experiment) Expedition to conduct a geophysical survey of the land beneath the Arctic Ocean. Robert Peary had been the first person to reach the North Pole in 1909, while Richard Byrd and Floyd Bennett were the first to fly over it in 1926. Forty years later two Canadian expeditions had flown in and spent a few days, but the LOREX expedition of 1979 was the first large and certainly the longest expedition to visit the vast ice-covered ocean at 90 degrees north. As the Polar Continental Shelf Program was supplying the LOREX expedition with logistical and air support, Okanagan Helicopters, which

▸ Okanagan Helicopters' Bell 205A C-GOKR, the North Pole workhorse, in 1979. PHOTO COURTESY OF WAYNE ORYSCHAK

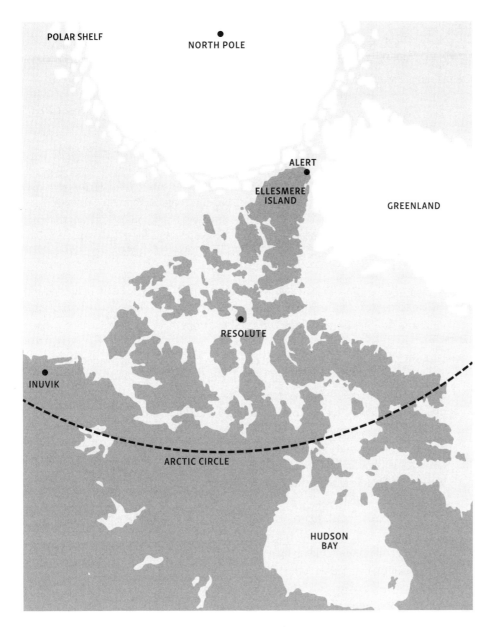

▸ In 1979 Okanagan had seven specially equipped Bell 206s on contract to the federal government to ferry scientists conducting a wide range of research projects across the northern islands for the Polar Continental Shelf Program.
SOURCE: OKANAGAN HELICOPTERS

was in the second year of its contract with the Polar Continental Shelf Program, also became part of the LOREX Project, operating from Resolute Bay on the south coast of Cornwallis Island, one of Canada's most northerly communities. Other support bases were located at Alert, at latitude 82 degrees 30 minutes north, about 500 miles (815 kilometres) from the geographic North Pole, and at Thule Air Base, operated by the US Air Force in northern Greenland. Air support consisted of a military Lockheed C-130 Hercules that provided para-drops to the main base camp with backup supplied by a Wardair de Havilland Dash 7.

The expedition, sponsored by the Department of Energy, Mines and Resources, was staffed by 32 Canadian scientists and support workers, who were studying the Lomonosov Mountain ridge near the North Pole as part of their research on plate tectonics. Their experiments included seismic seabed profiling, ice floes, heat flow, geomagnetic sounding, coring and bathymetry, which is the study of the depth to the ocean floor. Throughout the two months of research, the ice varied from six to ten feet (1.8 to three metres) thick, and temperatures hovered around -2°F (-30°C). The crew accommodations were special Arctic tents that could withstand very high winds and temperatures as low as -58°F (-50°C), and stoves inside the tents that kept them at a cozy 70°F (21°C). Ice movement saw the camp drift some 160 miles (257 kilometres) during the two months of the project. Captain Wayne Oryschak, who was part of the Okanagan crew, and kept a log:

> Bell 205A [C-GOKR] left Vancouver on March 19 [1979] with Captain Mike McDonagh and [me as] co-pilot, along with engineer Jim O'Connell heading for Yellowknife, a distance of 1,470 miles [2,370 kilometres]. The next stage was from Yellowknife to Cambridge Bay, just 531 miles [855 kilometres], and then on to Resolute Bay, 444 miles [714 kilometres] away. By March 30, [we] were en route to Alert, a Canadian military base and weather station, 682 miles [1,998 kilometres] from Resolute and 1,061 miles [1,709 kilometres] from the geographic North Pole. Mike McDonagh . . . returned to Vancouver, leaving [me] with OKR to continue on the contract.

The Bell 205 with Captain Oryschak and engineers Jim O'Connell, Ernie Tymerick and Mal McConachey joined the main scientific campsite on the ice. Their job was to transport personnel and supplies from there to two satellite camps.

> On April 2, [we] arrived at the LOREX camp, which was located at the geographical North Pole. The main base was built on thick ice at 88 degrees 38 minutes north and 172 degrees 18 minutes west. The two satellite camps, "Snowshoe" and "Iceman," were located about 60 miles (100 kilometres) from the main camp. What was unique about this was it was the first time a commercial helicopter had landed [at] the North Pole. This was three years before Australian adventurer Dick Smith landed his Bell 206 JetRanger in his epic around the world pole-to-pole journey. The news media erroneously indicated that Smith's helicopter was the first . . .
>
> From April 2 until June 1, OKR provided the support line to the main base camp and the two satellite camps. During this time [we] suffered severe weather conditions, including high winds, which left open water between the tented camps. I stayed with the helicopter right through to June 2 when I flew the machine back to Alert, then Resolute and finally Tuktoyaktuk where it remained to complete some local contract work [around the] Beaufort Sea.[83]

The LOREX 79 Polar Expedition resulted in Okanagan adding another aviation first to an already long list of accomplishments. Without fanfare or media coverage they just got on with the job and then moved on to the next project.

Farther south, Okanagan was one of the first companies to experiment with Bell's 214B BigLifter. Derived from the famous UH-1 (Huey), the 214B had a single Lycoming engine and operated well in both high temperatures and high-altitude conditions. With its cruising speed of 130 knots (240 km/h), it was capable of carrying an underslung load of 6,720 pounds (3,062 kilograms). In the 1979 season, logging on Cortes Island, off the east coast of Vancouver Island, the machine took out approximately 65,500 cunits (a cunit is 100 cubic feet or 30 cubic metres of wood) in 46,277 flights. Engineer Sandy Forbes was a member of the first Okanagan crew to work on the new 214B-1:

> [When] it was decided the 214 might be just the machine for [heli-logging], the company sent Bruce Croft and myself on the engineer's course and Dev Anderson, Dan Hayse and Don MacKenzie on the pilot's course.

Before the new machine, C-GJNU, went logging, it was sent up to Terrace to work for BC Hydro doing some heavy lifting to see what it could do. Bruce spent the first tour with C-GJNU trouble-free and on my arrival had nothing but good things to say about the machine.

About a week into my tour Dev Anderson reported [that] the clutch/freewheel had slipped on him that morning, and he was convinced of that by the banging sound it made during the occurrence. Dev, being an S-61 man, had experienced this [problem] on the Sikorsky. I was a Bell engineer and had never experienced [it] so I wasn't convinced. Up we go to induce the problem. Sure enough, a banging noise and shudder happened, but I noticed the engine instruments fluctuating during the banging. After phone calls to Frank Ranger and StandardAero [SAL] in Winnipeg, [we] decided it was a compressor stall, so Bob Cameron from SAL flew out to Terrace. Bob and I worked day and night [to] fix the problem. Now we needed a ground run. Dev came in, started the engine, and halfway through the start it flamed out. Not good but we decided to try another start. Same thing. Dev sticks his head out and says, "You guys probably left a plug in the fuel line." Bob and I were exhausted after working long hours to fix the problem, [and] we didn't need to hear that, so [I] gave [him] a piece of my mind.

I give him credit. He went in the hangar and left us alone. Bob turns to me and says, "You know, he may be right. When you are tired, you miss things." We took a few lines apart and, sure enough, there was a plug in a line. We took it out, called Dev for the ground run, and everything worked beautifully. I felt bad about my outburst, but at the time I didn't say a thing about it.

Three or four years later, Dev and I were sitting in the... bar, and I asked him if he remembered the time in Terrace with C-GJNU when we had the compressor problem. He said he sure did and how I had given him a piece of my mind. I then told him that he had been correct—we left a plug in the line. We both laughed for about 10 minutes.[84]

Although C-GJNU spent that summer logging on Cortes, in the end it was demonstrated that the 214 was too small to be economical. However, by 1979 OK Heli-Logging had three dedicated Sikorsky S-61s. Two were ex–New York Airways machines: CF-JDR had been converted by Boise Cascade in Idaho and CF-JDK in the Vancouver hangar. An additional S-61, CF-DWC, was added in September. This was logging in a big way with the heavy lift machines working full-time at various locations. The company was the successful bidder to take out timber from Kingcome Inlet on the mainland coast with a camp and heliport set up at Protection Point. At the same time the company took on an operation for Weldwood of Canada in Toba Inlet, about 100 miles (160 kilometres) north of Vancouver.

OK Heli-Logging was providing S-61 training for its pilots and engineers. One of the S-61 training captains was Terry Wolfe-Milner, an ex-Canadian Navy pilot who had flown for Bristow Helicopters out of Sumburgh in the Shetland Islands and had offshore experience in the North Sea. In December 1975 while he was still with Bristow Helicopters, he and his first officer had responded to an emergency call in an S-61. Loaded with winch gear and emergency equipment, they flew out to recapture a 490-foot (149-metre) tower that was adrift. He and his crew were also involved in rescuing two seriously injured men from an oilfield supply vessel after an explosion. For these heroic acts Wolfe-Milner and his crew were awarded the Queen's Gallantry Medal for bravery.

Many of those who "went logging," however, soon moved on to obtain their IFR ratings and transferred to International. In the end the company was unable to meet the demand for heli-logging crews as the result of these internal transfers and started recruiting from the UK. In their first year on the logging crews, these newcomers operated either out of Toba Inlet or in the Thompson Sound area on the northeast corner of Vancouver Island. After six weeks in the logging camps, they were flown back to the UK for two weeks off. When their terms ended, many opted to immigrate and became permanent residents. Logging engineer Dave McKay:

> Okanagan advertised in the *Press and Journal* newspaper [Aberdeen] in the spring of 1979, and the interviews were held in Dyce [Scotland], although mine was done by telephone as Shetland was fogged in for a few days at the time. I joined in June and a few weeks later Neil Watts, Paul Hicks and Dick Maynard joined; sometime later Trev Castle joined, followed by Dave Shand. [The] initial contract was for six months with extensions; the pay was $2,000 per month and $3 per hour flight with 100 hours guaranteed.
>
> When we worked in Vancouver, we stayed at the Skyline Hotel [near the airport]. The job . . . was two weeks on and one off. Al [Eustice] was the president [of OK Heli-Logging] . . . and Terry Dixon and Jim Smithson ran the operation. John Lee was [chief engineer] with Pete Jenkins as his deputy.
>
> Sometimes in the summer, logging would have to be shut down and then we went tramp steaming across Western Canada on fires or steel setting; although this [was] hard work, it was really enjoyable, a great way to see the country.[85]

Trevor Castle, logging engineer:

> I first found out about heli-logging while reading an advert in a helicopter magazine while on a rig in the North Sea with Bristow Helicopters. Okanagan [was looking] for heavy lift engineers. I phoned Okanagan Helicopters in Vancouver from the rig . . . and was put in touch with personnel and HR. Then two days later in Aberdeen I had a phone call from Al Eustice asking me what helicopters I had worked on . . . I was informed that Okanagan Helicopters would get back to me. In the meantime I moved to Exeter as an engineer on Sea Kings from Westlands that Bristows had the contract for . . . Al came down to Exeter and we had the interview in the bar of the hotel he was staying in . . . The more beer I bought him the better the contract! [86]

Jim Neill, logging pilot:

> I was hired by Al Eustice to work for OK Heli-Logging in January 1979 and my first assignment was the S-61 pilot ground school. This was taught by a training engineer from Sikorsky in an ATCO [portable] trailer at Agar Drive [Okanagan's Vancouver airport office]. I had been flying for ten years and [worked] a few years before that as an engineer, [but] this was the first job I had in the helicopter business that was one week off at home every two weeks. It was great! I said goodbye to staying out for four months at a time [and] living in a tent without a break the whole summer.
>
> It wasn't until May 17 that I had my first flight in the cockpit of an S-61 and that was taking off from JFK in New York with Dev Anderson. Okanagan [had] purchased two S-61Ls from New York Airways (C-GJDR and C-GJDK) to use as logging helicopters. Along with Dev and Mike McDonagh as the training

pilots, Bill Ross, Bill Yearwood and myself flew the aircraft to Montreal with the help of our engineers Barry Stone and Gary Griesel. After spending a day in Montreal stripping the airline interiors out of both aircraft, we added another pilot, Dave Eagleston, and departed for Vancouver.

Most pilots [who] started in the logging division had to fly the Bell 206 on logging support for a few months to get experience... This entailed flying out the rigging crew every morning and landing them on prepared helipads on the hill. During the day we would sling bundles of chokers to the riggers from the log landing area, which improved our vertical reference skills. The 206 was also the medevac helicopter as well as being used to support the tree fallers.

At the end of the logging day we would pick up all the riggers and fly them back to camp. The worst part of this job was picking up the riggers when the logging helicopter called the day for bad weather. Somehow they always seemed to leave it until the hill was completely socked in. Furthermore, they would always log until last light, and you ended up bringing your last crew back to camp after dark. Having said all that, I did the same thing when I was flying the logging helicopter.

I received my S-61 type rating from Mike McDonagh on July 26 on C-GJDR but did not pull my first log off the hill until August 23 flying with Terry Dixon in Ramsay Arm. I should say at this time that Terry Dixon and Jim Smithson as logging training pilots on the S-61 had a lot of guts to ride with a bunch of pilots that had less than 15 hours on type. You have to understand that most of the pilots that came to OK Heli-Logging had flown nothing bigger than a JetRanger and had little or no long line experience. We all started out with 140 feet [43 metres]... OK Heli-Logging leased these helicopters and brought in some of their pilots to help teach us how to log and keep the production up.

If we were working around the treeline and the 140-foot (43-metre) line was not long enough to keep us away from the standing timber, we would change to a 170- or even a 200-foot [52- or 62-metre] long line. Most of us were struggling with 140 feet of line, and having to change to a 200-foot was just one more degree of difficulty we didn't need. I remember coming in for fuel at the end of logging cycle after changing to the 200-foot line, and misjudging my height, I took the corner off our cabin roof. As it turned out, no one was hurt, but it did wake up the engineer who was having a nap.

The majority of the pilots that started with OK Heli-Logging around the time I did went on to fly the S-61 and many other types... Some pilots, including myself, went on to the IFR Division, domestic and international.

I remember Reg Rivard [senior managing pilot] saying that the Bell 206 pilots being checked out on the S-61 to work for logging were very lucky as this was not the norm for pilots moving up through the ranks at Okanagan. It would normally take years to get a seat in this aircraft. I came back to logging for a short stint years later as a training pilot as the pay was much higher than in the IFR Division. However, the pilots coming on board then had lots of medium- and long-line experience... and caught on a lot faster than we did. I am not saying we didn't have our tense moments as they all had to find out the hard way. If you want to be fast, you have to start off slowly. Believe it or not, that was the hardest lesson to learn.

I remember when I went back [to] logging, one of the IFR pilots asked me why. I told him because I can. Logging is not an easy skill to master, and to date [it's] the hardest job I've ever done with a helicopter. And yes, even flying IFR in the Arctic.[87]

By 1979 Okanagan's offshore oil exploration operations stretched from the North Sea to the South Atlantic and east into the Indian Ocean, the Gulf of Thailand and the South China Sea. In addition to the North Atlantic contracts, which operated out of Halifax, Nova Scotia, and the North Sea contracts out of Aberdeen, Scotland, the company remained active off Bombay, Songkhla, Puerto Princesa, and Exmouth in Australia as well as Rio de Janeiro and the Orinoco Delta from the Venezuelan town of Maturín.

Completed contracts off Iceland, Bangladesh and New Zealand were replaced by others, such as Okanagan Australia's contract with Esso for S-61Ns. Once Bell 212 CF-DVG had completed its contract with Abu Dhabi Aviation, it was ferry-flown to Portugal for an offshore contract operating from Oporto. When the Rio de Janeiro contract finished, pilots Fred Shuman and John Carnie with engineer Norman Noseworthy ferry-flew their helicopter back to Halifax where it was destined for a new oil support contract.

As a result of contracts coming to an end and new contracts being signed, many of the pilots and engineers who signed on with Okanagan saw a large slice of the world. While I cannot claim to have outdone Phileas Fogg and his faithful servant, Jean Passepartout, I did circle the world on one of my trips for the International pool, albeit it took me 84 days. In January 1979 after only a few weeks at home, I left Montreal on yet another international trip. My first port of call was a return to Bombay where we had five Bell 212s supporting India's west coast oil and gas industry. Most of the year these helicopters flew VFR, but from June until September, which was the monsoon season, the pilots needed IFR and all their avionics in working order. I cleared snags as they came along, installed a new weather radar in one machine and carried out some cockpit cosmetics.

Among the items I had brought with me were some new David Clark headsets with good noise cancelling capabilities. Unfortunately I was not able to bring enough to refit all the machines so some still had the old ones. One afternoon when one of the 212s returned from the field, the pilot came over to me complaining loudly about the old headset. He was determined not to wear it ever again and proceeded to throw it into the deep grass. The next morning he reappeared beside the helicopter demanding one of the new headsets, but all the new headsets were already flying, and suddenly he realized his dilemma: no headset, no flying. I advised him he would have to retrieve the one he had thrown away and recommended that he take a stick with him to ward off a possible cobra attack. That got him worried. Eventually he paid one of the hangar cleaners to get it for him. The cleaner found it all right—covered in dew and slugs. The pilot had no choice; he had to fly.

After six weeks I moved on to Singapore where I had spent time as a kid and later with the RAF in the 1960s, but I was disappointed that the colourful old areas I remembered had been replaced with skyscrapers and modern shopping centres. The next day I caught a Thai Airways charter for the crew change flight to Songkhla, where the company had just introduced the new Sikorsky S-76s to the Union Oil contract. I had never been near an S-76 so it was a big learning curve. I had two main problems: the factory-installed electrical-wiring harnesses were too short, so removing instruments was a real challenge, and the new electrical connectors and Kapton wiring required special tools and a glove for handling the wire assemblies. (The latter was made of a material that has turned out to be excellent for removing stuck jar lids!) I managed to work my way slowly through some of the avionics problems with a lot of help from our engineers and the Sikorsky rep, Joe Brolio.

After two weeks I returned to Singapore, checked at the office for telexes from Vancouver and learned my presence was required in the Philippines to clear an avionics problem on a Bell 212 operating out of Puerto Princesa. One of the engineers who met me at the airport filled me in on the snags—the pilot was unhappy because he had been without an ADF for a week—and when the machine landed, the engineer and I started work. We dealt with the list of snags quickly, and I made arrangements to return to Singapore and—hopefully—home as I had been away for over nine weeks. Alas, it was not to be.

Back in the Singapore office it was "Songkhla calling, Songkhla calling." I was needed to deal with more S-76 problems. Arriving there on the crew change, I worked well into the late evening and did what I could. The next day I advised Vancouver that they would have to purchase some specialized equipment to support the S-76 avionics.

In Singapore again I was asked to meet a 212 on a ferry flight from Bombay to check for electrical or avionics snags before it carried on to Songkhla. It turned out that there were only a few niggling things, which I fixed quite quickly, but the machine did have a weather radar problem, which would have to be fixed before the monsoon season. I didn't have any spares, but I learned that Heli-Orient, the Bell distributor for Southeast Asia, had a large avionics repair shop in Singapore. Taking the unit with me, I asked if they could do a quick turnaround and was surprised to find that the avionics manager was an old RAF friend whom I hadn't seen in over 10 years. He gave me first priority, took me to the local flying club for a good curry lunch, and the radar was waiting for collection upon my return. The 212 got away and easily made Songkhla by early evening. Back at the office, I found a telex from Vancouver asking me to stop in on my way home via Hong Kong and San Francisco.

The next day after a stopover in Hong Kong, the group of us that were called for boarding were seated in the forward cabin with the rear doors closed. After the meal, another passenger and I took a walk toward the rear of the aircraft to see what was going on. That's when we discovered that the other passengers were Vietnamese refugees en route to the US.

I flew on to Vancouver and called my wife. At head office I learned that even the company had found it hard to keep track of me as I moved around Southeast Asia. I gave my report to the various departments, especially regarding the S-76, but I indicated I was not very happy with these frequent, long international trips. I was wined and dined, got a night's sleep, but then before leaving for Montreal, I was asked to return to head office where I was offered a two-year posting in Singapore.

After 84 days of travel I landed in Montreal. However, I was soon on my way to Florida for the S-76 course. In late June we were scheduled to fly to Singapore via Hawaii, but because the monsoon season had arrived in Bombay, we went east instead of west and spent a very soggy five weeks before finally moving on. Oh, the joys of the International pool.

By the time my two years in Singapore were up, I was looking forward to snow and asked for a transfer out of International. The company kept their word. Within a few weeks of arriving in Vancouver, I was sent to Tuktoyaktuk—in October with more snow and cold than I could have wished for.

1979 ANNUAL REPORT
In 1979 the company had introduced a new navigation system, Ontract 3 VLF (Very Low Frequency) Omega on several machines. This forerunner to GPS gave the aircraft's true position once synchronized with worldwide ground stations, greatly assisting flight crews, especially those flying out over the Atlantic to find oil rigs. By this time the company had accumulated one million flying hours and increased its fleet to make it the largest in Canada.

Although late equipment deliveries had created difficulties with some contract start dates, the company had experienced a significant improvement in revenue and net profits as oil price hikes from the OPEC countries had caused a dramatic increase in the number of domestic and international oil exploration projects. The annual reports for the decade tell the story:

1970	Balance at year-end:	$950,506
	Working capital at year-end	$669,532
1971	Balance	$860,153
	Working capital	$305,080
1972	Balance	$1,767,994
	Working capital	$513,295
1973	Balance	$2,623,936
	Working capital	$563,919
1974	Balance	$3,017,718
	Working capital	$1,804,139
1975	Balance	$3,869,824
	Working capital	$1,930,567
1976	Balance	$4,987,000
	Working capital	$2,726,000
1977	Balance	$6,189,000
	Working capital	$3,852,000
1978	Balance	$7,032,000
	Working capital	$813,000
1979	Balance	$7,761,000
	Working capital	$4,612,000

Chapter Six

THE 1980S

1980

At the start of the last decade of operations under the Okanagan name, the company continued to expand its fleet. Three more Sikorsky S-76 Spirits were delivered, and the company put in an order for seven Aérospatiale AS-332 Super Puma, a new 17-place helicopter with a cruising speed of 140 knots (259 km/h) and a lifting capacity of 8,000 pounds (3,628 kilograms). That spring Okanagan's senior managers also visited the Bell plant in Fort Worth, Texas, to see the Bell 412 and the 214ST (Super Transport). The 412, though basically a 212 with a four-bladed rotor system, had an upgraded Pratt & Whitney twin pack and a Sperry autopilot and communication systems. With a cruising speed of 130 knots (240 km/h) at 80 percent torque and a gross weight capacity of 11,550 pounds (5,239 kilograms), it had a fuel consumption of 750 pounds (340 kilograms) per hour. The 214ST with capacity for 18 passengers was able to hover at near gross weight on one engine. Okanagan ordered one of each to be delivered the following year. The other big news of the year was Okanagan's option on Boeing's 234 Chinook heavy lift, a tandem rotor machine.

As the fleet expanded, the Vancouver and Montreal engineering bases had to increase staff and resources to keep up with the many machine types, each with distinct maintenance and inspection procedures. In Vancouver the old facility on Agar Drive, which housed the head office and a hangar, was already overcrowded and lacked sufficient storage space for all the new parts and equipment. Since overhauling the dynamic components (rotor heads, blades, transmissions and gearboxes) of the helicopters was a major part of keeping the fleet operational, it was deemed time to open a separate maintenance facility in Richmond. The new facility, located away from the main airport in a new industrial complex on Viking Way, had 26,000 square feet (2,415 square metres) of space, making it large enough to accommodate state-of-the-art component overhaul facilities with upgraded tooling and equipment plus an engine-repair shop capable of overhauling the Allison 250-C20 engines in the Bell JetRangers and the General Electric T58s in the S-61s. Previously, all this work had been contracted out. During the year the component shops began the process of obtaining S-76 certification as well. The new facility also had space for stores, technical records, engineering planning and data processing as well as a safety and survival division. As new specialized communications and navigation equipment enabled aircraft to operate more precisely under IFR conditions in the Arctic and offshore, the Vancouver office—with input from the company's field engineers—developed a computerized system for tracking component replacements.

It also became necessary to institute an efficient system to cover an AOG (Aircraft On Ground) status system since the route between Viking Way and Agar Drive took about 25 minutes by car each way.

In March the company decided that its newsletter, *The Okanagan Reporter*, needed a facelift and expansion to keep employees better informed about staff changes and events in domestic and international operations. The challenge to find a new name was put out to staff. A panel of seven judges unanimously agreed on *RotorTales*, a name submitted by the manager of eastern operations, Dick Everson.

On the domestic front the BC Forest Service hired a Bell 206 to gather spruce cones in the Williams Lake area. The job had to be carried out in August when cones are at their best for reforestation purposes. Bert Warttig, the local base manager, described the operation as a "natural" for the Bell 206 helicopter:

> With the helicopter doors removed, the "clipper" stands on the outside skids, well strapped in by a safety belt. The helicopter hovers, the tree is topped using a hand-held hydraulic clipper, and the four-to-five-foot [1.2-to-1.5-metre] top is pulled into the cabin. When the cabin is full, the machine flies back to the base where the pickers take off the cones.
>
> The helicopter is in constant radio contact with the ground personnel who select the "plus" trees to ensure that the cones being brought in are of good quality.
>
> [This year's] cones were harvested at the 4,000-foot [1,220-metre] level in the Horsefly Range District at Bill Miner Creek and also at a logging site near Tisdale Lake . . .
>
> Cone gathering by helicopter is proving less costly than the conventional method of falling the trees from the ground. And, of course, a tree that is clipped continues to grow unharmed.[88]

West Coast logging operations continued under contracts with several major companies. The largest operation was in the Quadra Island area where production was about 150,000 cunits, or about 55 percent of the timber harvested during the year. The OK Heli-Logging staff came up with some thought-provoking statistics at the end of the year:

- If the lumber from all the logs extracted during the year was used to build a house, it would be 3 million square feet (278,709 square metres), cost $150,000 and have payments of $1,875. (Note: this was at the time of 20-percent interest rates.) The crew decided they would hold an open house for 6,000 persons, strictly BYOB.
- If the S-61s' annual fuel consumption was used in a car, it would last 347 years.
- If the S-61s were holiday aircraft, they would fly around the world twice with 85,288 ascents and descents for sightseeing.
- If the cargo had been gold instead of logs, it would have had a value of $1,440,420,000,000.

※

In 1980, *Professional Pilot* magazine named Penticton's Mountain Flying School "the most respected mountain flying course in the world." Since it began operations in 1954, the school had been training civilian and military pilots from all over the world. In 1980 the course cost $350 per hour plus fuel. Company-sponsored students were guaranteed employment after successful graduation, while independent pilots had an advantage over their competitors when looking for work. Don MacKenzie, Okanagan Helicopters chief pilot, who was interviewed for the story in *Professional Pilot*, described the course:

> The mountain course introduces the pilot to confined area work, sling and vertical reference—which is working with a long line—water bucketing and so on. We like to put these young pilots in a situation where they are working with senior pilots so that the school practicum is basic training. The advanced training would be done at Vancouver or Montreal where we have the IFR equipment . . . About 16 pilots were trained last year as company pilots . . . The usual number of [commercial] pilots trained each year runs between 15 to 20. The school also trains around 40 military pilots in advanced mountain courses. There are eight instructors and 14 check pilots who offer everything from initial training to check rides, but the heart of the school is the mountain course, which can be a three-month, 100-hour ordeal.[89]

On Blackcomb Mountain, part of the famous Whistler Blackcomb Ski Resort, Okanagan crews, using the heavy lift Bell 214 C-GBHC, finished the construction of 150 towers for seven chairlifts then cleared several ski runs in the Whistler area. The tower-construction technique used here was designed by Lift Engineering, and though it took more helicopter time, it was still much quicker than traditional methods. The helicopter slung each of the tubular towers to its site and nursed it into a prepared hole where it was temporarily guyed up for support. The helicopter then bucketed in about eight yards (7.3 metres) of concrete, one yard at a time, and placed it around the base to form a mass footing for permanent support. Kyle Steele, marketing rep, reported: "It's very demanding work with two pilots working at two-hour stretches, and thanks to the engineers, the 214 serviceability was excellent. They are to be commended along with the flight crews."[90]

In August at Glade Hill, near Castlegar in the West Kootenays, Okanagan S-61 pilots Dev Anderson and Walter Ramsey were manoeuvring an 80-foot (24-metre) section of steel tower into place at a construction site when the guideline snapped and the tower lurched sideways. The pilots managed to steady the helicopter and stabilize the tower long enough to enable seven workers to climb down to safety at ground level. Pilot Dev Anderson praised the steadiness of his co-pilot and added a special tribute to Okanagan senior pilot Roy Webster who had been his instructor in power-line construction: "Roy taught us to always allow a margin of power for emergencies . . . and it was that bit of power we had in reserve that allowed us to hold the tower in place." When Workers' Compensation Board spokesman Roy Peterson, an accident prevention officer, presented commendations for bravery, he said, "You kept your cool and did what had to be done to save those seven men . . . We are proud to award you certificates of commendation under our Bravery Awards Program.[91]

In the Arctic, Okanagan undertook the colossal task of moving a 5,000-ton (4,535-metric tonne) oil-drill rig in temperatures hovering between -4 and -22°F (-20 and -30°C) and only two hours of semi-daylight. The rig, previously used in Dawson Creek in northeastern BC, had been trucked to Hay River then flown by Hercules transport to a staging area on Pullen Island, Northwest Territories. The next step was to move it to a new exploration site on an artificial island at Issungak, northwest of Tuktoyaktuk on the Beaufort Sea, a task that took two S-61s, a Bell 212 and a sub-contracted S-64 (Skycrane) the next seven days. They flew from 7:00 AM until 8:00 PM to move the dismantled rig the 17 miles (27 kilometres) from the staging area to the artificial island. The two S-61s, which are capable of transporting loads of about 7,000 pounds (3,175 kilograms), then remained on site to support the drilling operation until mid-summer, flying a continuous shuttle

▸ Okanagan Helicopters' international operations in 1980. SOURCE: OKANAGAN HELICOPTERS

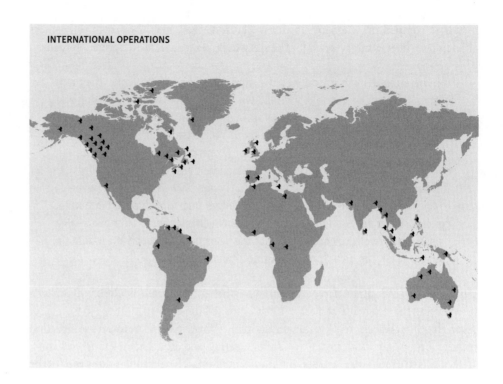

in which they carried drill stems, fuel, portable trailers and everything else needed at a drilling work site for 70 workers.

In Ontario, pilot Jim Lyon of Dominion Pegasus Helicopters made national headlines when he rescued an eight-year-old Boy Scout who had been lost for two days in the hills of Killarney Provincial Park on Georgian Bay. Jim spotted smoke, which led the police dog rescue unit to the site.

The beginning of 1980 saw the responsibilities for the company's International Division, which had been split between Vancouver and Montreal, moved entirely to Vancouver with J.C. Jones, previously general manager of Okanagan Australia, in charge. At the time of the announcement of this move, about 20 twin-engine IFR helicopters were supporting offshore operations in Australia, Thailand, Venezuela, Philippines, India and Brazil.

Okanagan Australia was supporting the exploration activities of Phillips, Esso and Woodside Petroleum with a staff of 38, including five at head office in Perth, and 33 in field bases at Exmouth, Derby and Sale on the west coast. The small town of Exmouth, 900 miles (1,450 kilometres) north of Perth, had a population of 2,500 at that time and was primarily a US/Australian military base. Derby, farther north along the coast, lies in an area of intense cyclone activity with temperatures ranging from hot to very hot all year round. The two S-76s located there supported the Phillips/ Woodside rig *Sedco 471*, and their Okanagan crews joked that in the swarms of flies they had to put up with, some of the flies had more flying hours than their chief pilot, Dave Whyte. There was also a temporary operation at Eucla on the Great Australian Bight off the southern coast of Australia where the crew lived in the only hotel in town and had to contend with sand storms and limited fresh water.

Meanwhile in India, Okanagan's Bombay base had been expanded to include three Bell 212s under contract to ONGC; they serviced eight drilling platforms, two drill ships, a pipe-laying barge, a derrick barge and a tanker, the *Jawaharlal Nehru*. The base manager and base engineer resided permanently in Bombay. The first Indian national to join the company was engineer George Desouza who had recently completed a Bell 212 course in

◂ CF-BHF on floats, still in Bow Helicopter colours, Juhu Airport, Bombay, 1980. PHOTO COURTESY OF THE AUTHOR

Fort Worth, Texas. In May he was joined by an ex-Indian Air Force captain, Cavas Panthakay, who had been a commissioned officer for 16 years. He had flown a variety of fixed-wing aircraft and helicopters including the Hindustan HT-2 primary trainer, the North American T-6G Texan, Brantly, Bell 47G-3, Aerospatiale Alouette III and Mil Mi-8. He also had high-altitude flying experience on the India–China border in the Himalayas.

The monsoon season on the west coast of India runs from June to September, exactly the period I was stationed there in 1980 to service the machines. During that time it rained heavily every day, often with severe flooding. Unfortunately, in the early S-76s, the inverters were located on the left wall of the rear baggage compartment and covered with wire mesh for air circulation for cooling. However, the engine deck was not fully sealed, and in the monsoon season the rain ran down the baggage compartment walls, causing the inverters to shut off intermittently with the result that the pilots would lose the attitude indicator and the horizontal situation indicator (compass). It was another year or so before Sikorsky sent out a modification team to seal the engine deck.

▴ Captain Tony Coalson poses with his helicopter on a rig off the east coast of Thailand during monsoon season in December 1975. PHOTO COURTESY OF TONY COALSON

We had one pilot who would snag the avionics equipment in his machine just for the heck of it. I hate to admit it, but when he would show up with a complaint, I would spout some technical mumbo-jumbo, and he'd walk away happy. One day I was up to my armpits in snags when he came over to tell me that one of the panels in the cockpit of Bell C-GOKL had a hole in it that did not look very professional and would I do something about it. Just what I needed with all the major problems during monsoon season!

Later in the year C-GOKL was due a 1,000-hour inspection where the helicopter is taken apart, major components are changed and modifications are carried out. We also catch up on insignificant snags, so this time when I finished the regular work, I took the offending panel to my avionics shop. I could see that at one time there had been a switch in the hole the pilot was complaining about, but it had been removed. I stripped the panel of all its old paint, sprayed it matte black, installed a three-way switch with no attached wires, and labelled the three positions: Off, Ground Mode and Flight Mode. Across the top I put "Flt Mode Synchronization: Insure switch is in Flight Mode before takeoff," reinstalled it in C-GOKL and forgot about it. Some months later when the check pilot came to Bombay, he asked me about the switch, and I told him the story behind it. He laughed and told me that the pilots were putting it in flight mode before takeoff. He decided to leave it. I have no idea how long it stayed like that.

On yet another of my trips to Bombay, I met two pilots who were new to the company, Donovan (Don) Wright and Brian Chung, both from Jamaica. Don was Caucasian and Brian was Chinese but both spoke with strong Jamaican accents since their families had lived there for many generations. They had immigrated to Canada where they were hired by Hélicoptères Canadiens to work on the James Bay Project before they transferred to International.

I was very intrigued with Don's stories of life in Jamaica, and one topic that came up was the subject of *obeah*, which is related to folk magic and spiritualism throughout the West Indies. One day while he was doing his walk around the helicopter before his flight, I jokingly asked him if *obeah* was okay for today's flight. He looked up at the clear blue sky and said, "I don't know, mon. It would all depend on the way the bones fell on the ground." He got in and set off for the rig.

Later in the hotel restaurant, I asked one of the cooks if the next time he was doing chicken he could keep the bones for me after they had been boiled down. The following day he gave me a bag of clean white chicken bones, which I spray-painted many bright colours then put into a multicoloured cloth bag with a string tie that I found in the local market.

I now had the perfect set-up for Don's next flight. I said, "Captain Don, I have the voodoo bag to predict your flight conditions." The side doors of the helicopter were always open until start-up so all the passengers were looking at us. Don replied, "Well, mon, let's see what the *obeah* will bring." I shook the bag and dropped the bones on the helipad. We both looked down at them. Don said, "Well, it looks good, but maybe a bit of turbulence on the way and a good menu for lunch."

When Don returned later, he was chuckling. Some of his passengers had told him they thought the helicopter was supposed to have special electronics for flying out to the rig, not a bag of chicken bones. At first he had spun them along about the workings of *obeah*, but finally he told them about having weather radar with the beacon mode, ADF, etc. It was probably a good thing that he explained all the avionics on board, otherwise the word might have got out that Okanagan was relying on black magic for trips to the oil patch.

Another of the pilots flying for the company out of Bombay was Captain Vinay Bhatnager, who was born in India and served as a pilot in the Indian Navy, flying Hawker Sea Hawks and later helicopters. He had immigrated to Canada in 1976:

> Fortunately my Indian Navy flying time on helicopters [was] recognized, so I just had to do 10 hours [of] flying training with a Canadian training school and take a check ride. But before [I could do] that, I was second mate on the ships that sailed in the Great Lakes, and I made enough there to pay for my helicopter training. On completion, I landed my first job flying the Aérospatiale SA 315B Lama for National Helicopters in Montreal [before] I joined Hélicoptères Canadiens, then a subsidiary to Okanagan. I flew mainly in the James Bay Project to get my hours.
>
> By 1979 I decided to take my IFR training with the hopes of transferring to the International Division. The criteria was . . . a Class 1 IFR ticket, which I got, and in 1980 I went into the International pool. I guess with coming from India, Bombay would be as good a place [as any] for my first tour. I remember the Christmas [of 1980] very well. One of our avionics techs whom I had got friendly with called me on Christmas Eve and asked what I was doing. He got me down the street with him, and we rounded up the local chokra boys [street kids]. [We] took over a local restaurant and paid for their Christmas dinner. Their facial expressions were worth a million dollars. After that we never had any trouble with the local [beggars] when we left the hotel. In fact, the [chokra boys] would escort the guys and their wives down on the beach and you were never pestered by others.[92]

◀ Graham Cowley, a Union Oil paramedic, helps hotel staff care for Vietnamese refugees on the beach, Songkhla, Thailand, 1980. PHOTO COURTESY OF GRAHAM COWLEY

At the end of two onerous assignments for the International Division, Okanagan's Vancouver hangar crew faced the challenge of loading both an S-76 and a Bell 212 into a C-130 Hercules for a trip to the Far East. Bell 212 C-GBHJ, ex-Bow Helicopters, had worked in the Arctic for six months, so before it could be transferred to International operations, it had to have a 1,000-hour inspection, conversion to IFR and installation of pop-out floats—all of this in an impossibly short time. At the same time Vancouver had taken delivery of a new S-76 slated for Thailand. Although the crews had not worked on this type before, they installed an auxiliary fuel tank, changed two engines, assisted a Sikorsky team in the modification of the tail boom then carried out routine maintenance. After that they dismantled both machines to make them as small as possible and secured them on wooden pallets to facilitate loading and unloading. It was not the first time that Okanagan had shipped helicopters by air, but it was the first time they had sent a 212 and an S-76 together. Using a scale model of the loading configuration, they rehearsed the loading operation meticulously beforehand, but nobody breathed easily until the 76 was winched into the fuselage of the Hercules. Two Okanagan engineers, Frank Kearney and Michel Perrier, accompanied the helicopters to Singapore. On arrival Michel joined the crew in Songkhla with the S-76, and Frank flew with C-GBHJ on to Bombay.

During late 1979 and early 1980, the Songkhla operation supported Union Oil's offshore oil field, which included the rigs *Robray 111*, *K2*, *Glomar 111*, *Scan Queen* and *E.W. Thornton*. The rig crews were shuttled by a Thai Airways' Hawker Siddeley HS 748 between Seletar Airport in Singapore and Songkhla on the regular Monday and Thursday crew change flights; at Songkhla they transferred to the Okanagan S-76s, which flew them out to the rig. This was the period of the exodus of the Vietnamese boat people in the Gulf of Thailand, and on one occasion the Okanagan crew and other members of Songkhla's expat community were enjoying their usual Saturday night barbeque at a local hotel when they noticed the staff disappearing over the seawall onto the beach. The expats followed them and discovered a refugee boat with about 40 people—women, small children and a few men—on board. They were in a poor state, all very dehydrated and obviously hungry. Captain Tony Coalson remembered:

▲ Vietnamese refugees with a child, Songkhla, Thailand, in 1980. PHOTO COURTESY OF GRAHAM COWLEY

The hotel bar was a semi-open-air affair with a small wall looking onto the beach. Miss Tha, who was the hotel manageress, was all dressed up that night in a nice long evening dress, and she came over and said that a boat was on the beach full of people. We all ran out and saw Miss Tha in her long dress out on the beach helping these bedraggled Vietnamese refugees . . .

Many refugee boats headed for the rigs where they knew they would get help. Although the oil company boats were obliged to rescue them, the companies did not allow the refugees on the drilling platforms for safety reasons.

The refugee camp in Songkhla had about 7,000 refugees and was run by a character, Joe Devlin, a Roman Catholic priest. Father Devlin had spent time in Vietnam, including five years living in the Mekong Delta. When South Vietnam fell, he was one of the last Americans to leave. He returned to the US briefly but went back to Thailand in 1978 to help with the refugee program.[93]

Captain Owen Shannon added:

I remember numerous refugee boats coming into the area around the old Samila beach . . . The Thai Navy had placed a party of troops on Koh Khra [Island] to intercept the Thai fishermen bringing refugees there for their pleasure. [There were] reports of men killed, ladies raped. Unfortunately the seas that monsoon season were consistently huge and would not allow a boat close enough to shore to allow food deliveries . . . [We] made at least two trips there to deliver rice . . .

During the same period the UN set up a large barge complete with tents on it to accommodate refugees arriving in the Erawan Field. When they did arrive, they invariably opened the sea cocks on their boats, and the Union Oil boats were obliged to rescue them. However, no doubt to the disappointment of the Vietnamese, they were not allowed onto the platforms or drilling rigs. They were instead delivered to the barge, and when a total of 100 or so occupied the place, the UN would send out a boat from Songkhla to pick them up.

One day while on the *ELQ* [one of the rigs], a weather front came through from the southwest, preventing us from taking off. We sat there running (no time to shut down or tie down) being thrashed around by winds up to 45 knots [83 km/h] and heavy rain. Just before the visibility closed in, we saw the barge being swept with large waves and tents . . . blown off by the winds . . .

Minutes later when the barge came back into sight, it was bare. Being too far away to see if any folks remained on board . . . we flew slowly over it . . . and were happy to see at least a dozen very wet Vietnamese and were assured later that no one had been lost . . . The only other thing that remained on that steel deck was the frame of a toilet on the back.[94]

In the Philippines the Phillips Petroleum contract involved servicing the semi-submersible rig, *Penrod 74*, which operated between Puerto Princesa and Cebu City. Unfortunately, after a year it hit a reef and had to be towed to Cebu for repairs, putting the Okanagan crew on standby. However, in that one year of operation, the Bell 212 C-GDVG had flown 550 hours, almost exclusively supporting *Penrod 74*. Doug Trann, Cebu base engineer told *RotorTales*:

We had a memorable flight recently—an emergency medi-vac for the military. We left Puerto with five people on board to supposedly pick up an injured person on an island 150 miles [241 kilometres] offshore. After much juggling, we returned with nine bodies—six alive, three dead. Live grenades can be dangerous!⁹⁵

1980 ANNUAL REPORT
The year saw the first promise of contracts with China when John Pitts, president of Okanagan Helicopters, joined the Canada China Business Council that visited Beijing, Shanghai, Guangzhou and Guilin and met with senior government officials in each location to discuss the offshore oil and gas projects underway along the Chinese seaboard. Later in the year a delegation from the People's Republic of China visited the Okanagan Helicopters' Vancouver headquarters and toured it and the Viking Way overhaul facility.

The annual report for 1980 showed profits up over the previous year: the balance at year-end was $9,117,000 and working capital $3,040,000. The company had 904 staff members and a fleet of 161 machines, including 30 belonging to Associated Helicopters, which was celebrating 30 years of operation. The fleet was composed of the following:

AS 350 AStar 3	Bell 212 14
Bell 206A 8	Bell 214B 3
Bell 206B 96	Sikorsky S-58T 4
Bell 206L 2	Sikorsky S-61L 4
Bell 204B 4	Sikorsky S-61N 11
Bell 205A 4	Sikorsky S-76 Spirit 8

1981

Offshore work continued to be an important part of the company's operations in 1981 and with it the company's Survival, Search and Rescue (SAR) Division, which maintained the latest survival equipment based on information from both the Royal Navy and the US Coast Guard. John Pedriel who had trained with the Royal Navy as a search and rescue crewman, eventually becoming an instructor, had formed this division in 1975. In 1981 he completed the US Coast Guard's SAR Management Survival School course in New York, becoming the first Canadian civilian to graduate from this prestigious college. Okanagan's survival section, located at the Viking Way facility, had responsibility for evaluating and purchasing equipment, such as the compact survival packs containing concentrated food and water purification devices, and for carrying out regular inspections on fire extinguishers, floats, electronic location transmitters (ELTs), life rafts and survival suits. In addition to these duties, they put on two-day courses to train crews for land and sea survival. The first day of the course was spent in the classroom learning theory while the second focussed on water survival including techniques for launching and sustaining life aboard survival rafts. A course for survival on land was held in Penticton and covered first aid for minor injuries and snake bites, finding potable water, operating solar stills, building shelters and finding food, including identifying edible plants.

On March 2, 1981, Williams Lake base pilot and long-time employee Bert Warttig and three passengers were killed in the crash of a Bell 206 in the mountains of south central

Bert Warttig, originally from Kenora, Ontario, began his aviation career in 1949 at age 15 when a local company, Parsons Airways, hired him as a ramp helper. After he moved into the hangar to assist the engineers, the owners were so impressed with him that they lent him the money for his commercial pilot's licence. In the five years Bert flew with Parsons he accumulated approximately 4,000 hours in aircraft ranging from de Havilland Fox Moths to Douglas DC-3s. Some of his experiences were recounted in H.P. "Hank" Parson's book, *The Trail of the Wild Goose*, published in 1978. But Bert's real passion was to fly helicopters, and in the fall of 1959 he applied to Okanagan Helicopters for pilot training and was accepted into the January training course along with classmate Don MacKenzie. He spent his first year flying off a supply ship in the High Arctic servicing DEW Line sites. Bert and his wife, Elaine, set up Okanagan's base in Williams Lake in 1967, and for two years it consisted of Bell 47G-3, Bert, Elaine and their home telephone; a new facility was built there in 1969.

In 1973 Bert flew a new Bell 206B JetRanger, CF-OAM, from Fort Worth to Williams Lake, and over the next seven years he amassed 5,000 hours herding sheep, fighting forest fires, picking cones, slash burning, patrolling power lines, flying geologists and carrying out search and rescue and emergency flights. (On one occasion, a baby was born in the helicopter en route to the hospital.) Bert also developed flying techniques that became standard practice. As an instructor, he trained many Canadian armed forces pilots, and because he had the ability to put his students at ease with his calm air and sense of humour, he brought out the best in them.

BC. The passengers, Harold Mitchell, Wes Prediger and Nels West, were biologists with the provincial Wildlife Service on a bighorn sheep survey. A search began the day of the crash in the area of Tyaughton Creek, a tributary of the Bridge River north of Gold Bridge, but the helicopter was not located until June when it was found in the Yalakom River area, north of Lillooet. The delay was attributed to fresh snow in the crash area at the time of the initial search.

In the 1980s the personnel at Okanagan's base at Port McNeill on the northeastern tip of Vancouver Island took the initiative in developing new projects for their Bell 206. One was a reforestation operation involving tree selection, and later, base manager Pete Barratt and local forestry officials published a booklet detailing the procedures and safety factors for this type of operation. The base was also involved in the fishing industry. The 'Namgis First Nations had a hatchery near the upper end of Nimpkish Lake where they raised chum and sockeye salmon. Workers caught the mature salmon returning to spawn in early fall to strip them of their eggs and sperm, then the Port McNeill 206 was chartered to transport the eggs and sperm to the hatchery where they were mixed to facilitate fertilization and deposited in trays for hatching. At the end of the summer the 206 moved the fry from the hatchery to pens about 24 miles (38 kilometres) away at the lower end of the lake where the fry were fed for about two weeks before being released. The program had a success rate of 98.5 percent.

The same Bell 206 did road reconnaissance for forestry companies, transported CBC and BC Telephone crews servicing mountain-top repeater sites and carried out long-line cement pouring and shake-hauling contracts. With timber on Vancouver Island and the West Coast mainland at altitudes of 120 to 220 feet (37 to 67 metres), all sling work in the area required the use of long lines and two-way communications. During the fire season the Bell 206 was frequently chartered by Forestry to fly a patrol near the fire perimeter to check for the hot spots. With the helicopter at about 200 feet (61 metres), a cameraman took shots out of the right rear door with an infrared camera connected to a monitor, while an operator watched for hot spots as they were pinpointed on a map. Fire crews were then dispatched to deal with them before they could flare up and restart the fire.

*

In Alberta, the operation using S-61s CF-OKB and C-GROH to ferry work crews to the Luscar Sterco mine site 40 miles (64 kilometres) south of Edson was still in full operation. The helicopters made 10 round trips Monday to Friday, flying seven hours on a weekday, dropping to four hours on weekends; by the end of May 1981 CF-OKB had flown 2,084 hours. One of the challenges for the Edson operation was that the S-61N model had been designed to function close to sea level, but the altitude at the Edson mine's landing pads was about 4,000 feet (1,220 metres). The mining company had dealt with landings at the mine-site end of the trip by installing a lighting system, a microwave landing system and non-directional beacon (NDB), which worked in conjunction with the ADF fitted to the aircraft. These navigation aids combined with the Okanagan pilots' skill allowed the operation to continue in all weather with a flight completion rate of 97 percent.

In the Drayton Valley of Alberta logging pilots Jim Smithson and Jim Neill placed a 410-foot (122-metre) chimney designed to disperse noxious fumes from a gas plant. The operation, which set a height record for this type of guyed structure, was part of a growing trend to call in helicopters when conventional building methods were not feasible.

The Ontario Air Ambulance Corporation had started with one helicopter in 1977, but the value of the program had been demonstrated the following year when that helicopter's quick response had saved the lives of a number of children injured in a school bus crash near Barrie. In 1980 the provincial government approved the expansion of the program by the addition of two fixed-wings—a Cessna Citation in Timmins and a Beechcraft Super King Air 100 in Sioux Lookout—and two helicopters. One of these was Toronto Helicopters' Bell 212 air ambulance, which became known as "Bandage I," a nickname that was bestowed by a young patient at Toronto's Hospital for Sick Children. In 1981 Dominion Pegasus, operating from Thunder Bay, began using Sikorsky S-76 C-GIMT (aka Bandage III) on its contract with the province to provide support in medical emergencies in remote communities. C-GIMT had been modified to air ambulance configuration at Okanagan's Montreal facility. It was particularly valuable because of its speed, its smooth, quiet flight, and its range of 400 nautical miles (741 kilometres) with a 30-minute reserve. As an IFR machine, it was able to fly in all weather conditions and had an advanced FM communication system, which linked paramedics at the scene to physicians at Toronto's major hospitals. It also had an unobstructed cabin, which could easily accommodate stretchers and medical equipment, and a landing-gear system that enabled it to approach airport ramps for loading and unloading patients.

In the Northwest Territories, Captain Randy Klohn was flying S-76 C-GMQD 16 miles (26 kilometres) northwest of Tuktoyaktuk on September 26 when he had an unusual sighting. He filed the following report:

Aircraft Incident Report
Dome Petroleum Ltd.
A/C Type: S-76
Date of Incident: 26-9-1981; GMT: 04.30; Local: 22.30
A/C Reg.: C-GMQD
Crew: Capt. R. Klohn; Co-Pilot: D.M. Fleming
Route: Tarsnit to Tuktoyaktuk; Posn: N 69.30; W: 133.30
Visibility: 20 miles (32 kilometres);   Cloud Cover: 1/10th
Alt.: 1000 ft. (305 M.); Flt Phase: Cruise Descent.
Capt. Randy Klohn S-76 C-GMQD:

At approximately 22:30 local time, 16 miles northwest of Tuktoyaktuk, a white light was observed paralleling our course. It appeared to be 4 to 5 miles away at our 4 o'clock position.

The light turned towards us and accelerated rapidly. A red light was observed at the 7 o'clock position and a blue light at the 1 o'clock position, relative to the bright white light (about the same illumination as an aircraft landing light.) [600 watts.] It lit up the inside of our helicopter and drew the attention [of] our 5 passengers.

Within a matter of seconds, a collision appeared imminent and we initiated a climbing left turn. The light followed us through a 45 degree heading change, remaining at our 4 o'clock position. We extended our searchlight and turned back on course towards Tuk. The lights moved away from us, perhaps 100 yards [90 metres], and continued to parallel our track, still at our 4 o'clock position. We observed a layer of fog in front of the white light, as was also present in the beam of our own searchlight.

We then contacted Tuk air radio and asked if there was any other traffic in our area and advised them of the light. From this angle the red light appeared below the white light. No blue light was visible. Tuk air radio contacted the Tuk DEW station and [they] replied that our helicopter [was the only aircraft in the area].

At approximately 5 miles back from Tuk we lowered our landing gear and turned on the landing light. The white light then moved behind us and followed us at our 6 o'clock position. We were in contact with MOT [Ministry of Transport] and the company flight watch, who saw only one set of lights on approach. On a prearranged call, we turned our landing and searchlights off, and the light behind us also went out. From the ground only our position and anti-collision lights were visible.

On short finals, I observed a widely dispersed light on the horizon in the direction from which we had just come. After landing, while standing beside the helicopter, we saw a beam of light (like a searchlight) flash straight up on the horizon, west of Tuk.

On a second flight, one hour later, no boats or ground vehicles were seen in that area. Five minutes after departure another similar beam was seen in the same area by one of our base engineers.

Signed: Randy Klohn and
Dale Fleming[96]

In an email from 2010 Randy Klohn added more details to his memories of that night:

A Schlumberger [Oilfield Services] employee working in the pipeline yard that night reported that he saw the same series of lights appear over Tuk hamlet in a layer of clouds. No shape or sound, only three lights. They moved back and forth for several minutes and then streaked out to sea. Five minutes later the helicopter appeared and landed. The light then reappeared over the hamlet for another few minutes, then went out.

I filed a report with Tuk Flight Service Station by telephone that night (all Canadian FSS offices have these UFO sighting forms). I also filled out a MUFON UFO sighting report (some civil UFO sighting agency out of Toronto) at the suggestion of Steve Smith who lived in Toronto at the time. Several months later, a report came back describing an identical intercept on a S-76 going into Aberdeen, exactly 1 GMT hour later and 5,000 miles away—go figure![97]

On a more down-to-earth note, the Phillips Petroleum contract in Western Australia ended in February, and a Transport Canada inspector was sent to check out the Australian pilots to evaluate them for Canadian licences, which would allow them to work anywhere in Okanagan's operational fields. As a result, five Bell 212 pilots joined the crews at Juhu Airport in Bombay. One of the Australian S-76s, VH-IMZ, was transferred from Australian registration to Canadian as C-GIMZ and ferry flown from Perth to Bombay over nine days to provide additional support for the ONGC offshore oil field. A second Australian machine, S-61 VH-IMS, arrived in Vancouver by ship after 17 days at sea and was re-registered as C-GOLH. It was then dry-leased to a UK company and ferried by captains John McIntyre, Didier Moinier and Bev Preater and engineers Marty Battick and Ken Malkin. Taking off on January 29 from Montreal, they flew to Fort Chimo, Quebec, and across Labrador to Godthåb, Greenland, then Reykjavík, the Faroe Islands, Sumburgh in the Shetlands, Aberdeen and finally Cambridge in England where it was handed over to Management Aviation for that company's North Sea operations.

A third Australian S-76, VH-IMK, was ferry-flown from Perth to Songkhla by pilots Brian Small and Dave Whyte and engineer Marten Hobbs. With extra fuel in three 45-gallon (170-litre) drums, the aircraft's range was stretched to 600 miles (966 kilometres), extending its flying time to six hours. The 3,404-mile (5,478-kilometre) journey, completed in five stages at an average speed of 139.5 knots (258 km/h), started at Jandakot Airport, south of Perth, and took them to Broome, then to Bali, with a stop for Indonesian customs at Kupang, Jakarta, then on to Singapore and finally Songkhla. Their speed came under scrutiny in Bali when air traffic asked them to slow to a minimum approach speed as they were gaining on the jet traffic. Later when taxiing to the parking area, they were asked to confirm they were a helicopter!

On December 31, 1981, I arrived back in Bombay just in time for the end-of-year partying. All the Okanagan crew had been invited to a New Year's Eve party at the home of the Rolls-Royce representative just down the beach from our hotel. The guest list also included aviation people from the many other airlines staying at the hotel at the time, among them the crews from a number of Eastern Bloc airlines such as Aeroflot, which had very large crews for the size of their aircraft. We joked that they were there to keep an eye on each other and all the other crews, but they were not friendly and didn't mix. However, they seemed to do a good black market business in t-shirts, which were cheap in Bombay, but the good party members often ended up wearing ones emblazoned with the American eagle or other incongruous symbols of the capitalist West.

The Czech Airlines crew had been moved out of the hotel to a crew house because, we suspected, they were getting too friendly with the Westerners. However, one of our pilots had made friends with some of the Czech Airlines crew and went along to their crew house to tell them that they were invited as well. They declined due to an early morning flight.

Lots of expats and locals also attended the party, and the New Year was duly piped in with "Auld Lang Syne." Three Japanese cabin attendants who flew for Air India were fascinated by the piper in his kilt. This was an entirely new experience for them. Eventually everyone drifted home or back to the hotel in the early hours of the morning.

The Okanagan pilot who had gone to the Czech crew house lived in a small town in southern Ontario, and about a year later he was at home on time off when the phone rang. It was the Soviet Embassy in Ottawa asking what he had been doing at the Czech crew house on December 31, 1981. Totally astonished, he hung up. I guess Big Brother really was watching.

Okanagan's Bombay operation always had one early bird flight that had to take off at 6:00 AM, while the others were scheduled as required. Because they flew out of Juhu, these machines did not have to clear customs. However, if they had to divert due to weather or if they arrived after dark, they had to land at the international airport where clearing customs could take three days or more. Needless to say, as this threw off the company's schedule for days, it was avoided whenever possible.

Around 3:00 PM one day a 212 arrived at Juhu but had to return immediately to the field to respond to an emergency. It was going to be touch-and-go whether it got back before dark. The engineers organized the refuelling and did a quick maintenance check; the captain did his external checks while the co-pilot, whose job it was to file the flight plan, decided to save time by giving it to a hangar sweeper to deliver to the tower. The machine got away and just managed to get back to Juhu before dark.

The following day Okanagan's base manager, Steve Birchall, received the following memo:

> Sir,
> Please be advised that in future when filing a flight plan, it has to be presented to the appropriate air traffic assistant or controller by one of the following: the captain of the aircraft, the co-pilot of the aircraft, or the minimum of an

engineer. We cannot accept hangar sweepers, fuel lorry drivers, store men or clerical assistants.

Signed
Senior Air Traffic Controller

On one of my trips to the Philippines, I was in Puerto Princesa on Palawan Island to repair the avionics of Bell 212 C-GDVG, which was supporting Phillips Petroleum's semi-submersible rig *Penrod 74*. After clearing up a number of snags, I found that the problems with DVG's ADF persisted. Since the ADF was necessary for operating offshore, the pilot, Earl Neil, suggested that I fly out with him to see the problem first-hand and have a look at the VHF base radio on the rig while I was there.

For Okanagan to operate in the Philippines, the company had to take on a local partner and one member of the flight crew had to be a local. Okanagan's partner was Philippines Resource Helicopters, which provided three pilots—Ray Acedero, Toto Cammacho and Rafael Castro. On this trip Earl's Filipino co-pilot would be Ray Acedero, and when they set off the next morning, I was looking over their shoulders to see if I could detect anything abnormal. On landing at the rig, C-GDVG's crew was told that there had been a terrible accident, resulting in the death of an employee of Schlumberger Oilfield Services, and it would be necessary for the helicopter to fly the body to Manila. Okanagan's flight crew wanted to fly back to Puerto Princesa to pick up equipment for the long flight, but they were told there wasn't time as the rig had no means of refrigerating the body and it needed to be sent to a proper facility in Manila immediately.

The crew strapped the body bag into the rear of the aircraft, we grabbed some water and set off for Manila, 567 miles (816 kilometres) away. However, we had to stop to refuel at a cache on Coron Island about 245 miles (390 kilometres) from the rig. When we landed, Earl and Ray realized that C-GDVG's emergency fuel hand pump was in the Okanagan storeroom at the Puerto Princesa airport. As the helicopter usually only travelled back and forth to the rig, it had been removed to make more space for cargo. Now the problem was how to get the fuel from the 45-gallon (170-litre) drums into the fuel tanks. A crowd of inquisitive locals appeared, most of whom had never seen a helicopter up close. Luckily, Ray Acedero was able to explain the problem to them, and one man went away and came back with a length of clear plastic tubing. The next question: who was going to syphon the fuel? There was a very good chance of swallowing a mouthful. Once again Ray came to the rescue by offering the man who brought the tubing some money if he would do it. Fortunately this fellow was an expert, and before we knew it the fuel was going into the tank—and he did not swallow a drop. He was more than happy with the 500 pesos (about $10 US) Earl gave him.

We landed at Manila airport just before dark. The waiting ambulance quickly removed the body and left. Then we took stock of our situation. The fuel tank was just about empty again, I had about $50 US, we had no passports, no change of clothing and no hotel reservations. But we did have Ray. He got hold of his company manager, Chippy Grey of Philippines Resource Helicopters dispatch, who booked us a hotel, picked us up, and gave us a subsidy to cover expenses.

After a meal and night at the hotel, we were back at the airport the next morning to a refuelled C-GDVG ready for the return flight. We also had a loaner portable fuel pump on board. Back at Puerto Princesa our engineer, whose name escapes me, had been worried because in all the panic we had forgotten to ask the rig to let him know what was going on. (Personally, I think he was more worried that the avionics guy was servicing *his* helicopter.) The ADF behaved perfectly all the way to Manila and back.

1981 ANNUAL REPORT

Over the course of 1981 the boom of the previous year evaporated, and at year-end the Annual Report advised that the economic outlook was not encouraging. Inflation had reached 12 percent and a new federal energy policy had curtailed activity in much of the oil and gas industry. Because of high costs and slow markets, the company's before-tax profits had declined to just 60 percent of the previous year: balance at year-end, $9,532,000; working capital, $2,938,000. In an attempt to address the storm hovering on the horizon, management began developing plans to divide operations into several independent profit centres and sell off the older helicopters.

1982

On January 22, 1982, the board of directors of Okanagan Helicopters Ltd. accepted an offer from Calgary-based Resource Service Group (RSG) of $15 for ordinary shares and $9 for convertible shares, making RSG the company's majority shareholder. RSG, a nationwide company, had diverse interests including steel fabrication, hydro supplies and mines. It also had direct ties to the oil and gas industry where it provided services through transportation and the production, sales and maintenance of heavy equipment. RSG's chairman, John Lecky, had held shares in Okanagan for many years and had served on the board of directors. Two weeks after RSG's offer was accepted, Pat Aldous was appointed president of Okanagan Helicopters, replacing John Pitts, who had become president in 1970 and had been instrumental in expanding the company's fleet and its international operations. John Lecky became the new chairman of the board.

At a farewell party for John Pitts held on February 26 in Okanagan's Vancouver hangar, he was presented with a PADL (power assisted, dual line) fishing rod, designed and built by Erik Eiche, who was both a machinist and a sheet-metal technician. The February edition of *RotorTales* reported that it was "a dual line ... to catch twice as many fish in half the time. The rotor motor engages to provide lift once the line extension exceeds 35 pounds." Pitts went on to become the president of the Richmond-based aerospace company, MacDonald, Dettwiler and Associates (MDA). He died in Vancouver on February 3, 2006.

Okanagan's new president, Pat Aldous, a chartered accountant, had come into the Okanagan organization in 1967 as a member of the audit team in the twilight of Carl Agar's administration. He became the company's secretary treasurer in 1972 and went into operations as the general manager of the Western Division a year later. He was then selected to open an international operation in conjunction with a UK company, but due to irreconcilable differences between the partners, that plan was aborted and he returned to Canada. As operations manager of the Eastern Division, he had responsibility for the purchase and integration of Haida and Lac St. Jean into the Okanagan family in 1973. He had been vice-president of operations for three years prior to his appointment as president. (Pat was also a rugby player and represented Canada as captain when the Canadian team toured Wales in 1971.)

This change in ownership and administration, which was only the beginning of the bigger changes to come for Okanagan Helicopters, was followed very shortly by the most tragic event of the year—the loss of the *Ocean Ranger*, a self-propelled, semi-submersible drilling rig, in the Hibernia field on the Grand Banks, 166 miles (267 kilometres) off the coast of Newfoundland. On the night of February 15, the rig was hit with an extreme weather event that created waves over 55 feet with some as high as 70 feet (17 to 21 metres).

According to the investigation, a rogue wave smashed a porthole, and as water poured in, the rig developed a ballast control problem. At 12:52 AM local time, the crew sent out a mayday as the rig was listing badly on its port side. At 1:30 AM its last radio transmission was sent, advising that the crew was taking to the life boats. The *Ocean Ranger* sank about an hour and a half later.

Soon after the distress call, two Okanagan s-61s stationed in St. John's, Newfoundland, were scrambled to attempt rescue. In the midst of one of the worst storms to hit the area, the engineers had to chip the ice away to open the hangar doors, and even towing the helicopters out onto the apron was difficult because the high winds sent both the helicopters and the tractor skidding across the icy apron. By 3:00 AM, one of the helicopters was airborne, with the second close behind, and by 4:30 AM they were over the area, but the *Ocean Ranger* and its crew of 84 had vanished.

At daylight the following morning the Canadian Armed Forces began their search of the area, but there was no sign of the rig. The bodies of 22 crew members were recovered; all had drowned while in a hypothermic state. Later that day, 65 miles (105 miles) east of the *Ocean Ranger*'s last known location, a Russian container ship, the *Mekhanik Tarasov*, was hit with the same storm conditions and, after listing dramatically, sank, losing 32 of its 37 crew members.

On March 8, W.L. Mason of Mobil Oil Canada sent the following letter to Pat Aldous:

> On behalf of Mobil Oil Canada, Ltd., I wish to commend the actions of your helicopter crews in St. John's during the recent tragedy with the *Ocean Ranger*. Their quick reaction under adverse conditions and their persistent attempts to locate possible survivors in the most hazardous flying conditions deserves the highest praise and indicates a level of professionalism second to none in the world.
>
> While it must have been frustrating not to have been successful, their efforts are sincerely appreciated by all in Mobil. Would you extend to the crews our sincere gratitude and a hearty "well done."
>
> Sincerely
> W.L. Mason[98]

The machines were flown by Michel Durin and Kerry White in the first s-61 and Bob Jarvis and Bruce Hutchings in the second. The hangar crew who battled the adverse conditions in order to deploy the s-61s were pilots Gary Fowlow, Ken Steele and Don Bauder, and engineers John Hulan, Dean Gale and Woody Brinston.

That spring, as the industry continued to decline, Okanagan closed its Montreal facility and leased it to Innotech Aviation, an aircraft maintenance and refurbishing company, keeping only a small storage area and office for the company. Then, since Quebec operations had been running at a loss for two years, at the end of the year when the company's contracts with the James Bay's Project and the Québec Cartier Mining Company were terminated, the base at Chibougamau was also closed. Meanwhile, there were changes ahead at Luscar Sterco's operation in Edson, Alberta, as the reduction in coal sales had prompted the company to re-evaluate the s-61 helicopter shuttle operation there.

During the year, Okanagan gradually sold off 15 Bell 206B models and 2 206L LongRangers, and as the number of contracts for the Bell 212s declined, there was speculation that some of them would also be sold. Instead, the company purchased two 16-passenger, twin-engine, IFR Bell 214STs, which were particularly suited to offshore work. The first of these machines went to Halifax in anticipation of the start of a new Mobil contract.

The second replaced S-61 C-GROH, which returned to St. John's to support the rig *West Venture*. In Halifax a new Shell contract started in mid-October with the arrival of the rig *Sedco 709*; it was serviced by S-61 C-GOKZ, which had just completed the Petro-Canada project in Labrador.

Other additions to the Okanagan fleet in 1982 were the first two AS 322 Super Pumas that had been ordered two years earlier from Aérospatiale in Marseille, France. A medium-sized, twin-engine helicopter, it was smaller than the S-61, but it had more powerful and reliable engines and was able to carry 17 passengers or a load of 8,400 pounds (3,810 kilograms). All of Aérospatiale's machines destined for North America were shipped to New York and then sent by land freight to a finishing centre in Texas. As Okanagan already had contracts for both of its Super Pumas, they were ferried to Vancouver soon after, and Aérospatiale sent four technicians from Texas and three from France to finish the required modifications. Working alongside them, Okanagan avionics technicians stripped out the existing equipment, leaving only the instrument panel, and carried out a completely new installation to meet IFR requirements for offshore operation. This included new instrument landing systems, automatic direction finders, colour weather radar systems with beacon mode, distance-measuring equipment, high-frequency radios for long-distance communications, intercoms and hoist rescue systems. C-GQRL was assigned to a contract with Dome Petroleum in Tuktoyaktuk; C-GQYX went to Associated Helicopters for a contract on Ellesmere Island.

When C-GQRL arrived in Tuk, it still required a major sheet-metal modification that had to be done by a factory-trained technician, and he arrived along with a French technician a few days later. The tech rep from Texas was of Vietnamese origin and spoke both English and French; the French technician spoke only French. After they had checked into camp, they were given a tour of the facilities, which were first class, but according to one report, when the French tech was told by the tech rep that, like most camps in the oil business, the camp was alcohol free, he became very agitated.

When the Super Puma came back from its last flight of the day, the two were taken to the hangar to start work. The company had been told that it would take 24 hours over two days to complete the modification, but the French technician managed to do it in 18 hours straight with the tech rep bringing food and liquids (non-alcoholic, of course) to the hangar. When he finished the job, he quickly returned to camp, packed and caught the first Kenn Borek Air Twin Otter to Inuvik where, according to rumour, he booked into the hotel—licensed, of course.

*

On the West Coast, Okanagan's Viking Way engineering-support facility began undertaking third party component overhaul in 1982. Its first customer was the Canadian Coast Guard's Prince Rupert-based S-61. It also handled the Coast Guard's Sea Island, Richmond base hovercraft, as its engines were similar to those of the S-61.

Also on the West Coast, Okanagan partnered with Canadian Mountain Holidays to offer one-week heli-skiing holidays. The skiers spent part of their first day in safety briefings about skiing and conduct around helicopters. Then, subject to the daily weather forecast, the group skied either high elevations or tree runs. For this enterprise Okanagan provided a Bell 212 or a Bell 214, which hold a maximum of 14 people. To facilitate landing in powdery snow and to provide greater stability, the machines were equipped with skis running the full length of the skids. A special rack attached to the helicopter fuselage on the pilot's side carried skis and poles. The shuttles were coordinated by radio between the guides, the helicopter crews, the lodge's operations centre and the helicopter base.

In heli-skiing, the greatest danger was—and remains—avalanches, so the guides carried emergency equipment, and the skiers were required to wear avalanche radio beacons to locate them if they became buried. The deep snow and mountainous terrain were challenges not only for the skiers but also for the pilots who faced updrafts and downdrafts, sometimes so strong that they could send the helicopter out of control. However, Okanagan's experienced mountain pilots were able to deal with these conditions by recognizing the features of the terrain and changes in the helicopter's performance and use the drafts to lose or gain lift. Another concern for the pilots was that powdery snow looks flat with no distinguishing features but it is often very deep. As a result, the landing sites on the ski runs had to be marked with five-foot (1.5-metre) stakes with red flags attached to provide reference points and indicate wind direction and velocity.

All of the pilots assigned to the heli-skiing operation were required to take a refresher course at the Penticton Mountain Flying School, which in 1982 was conducted by Wayne Grover. The school also provided on-site training in the areas to which the pilots were assigned. The engineers maintaining the helicopters faced the problems of bad weather, deep snow, darkness and the lack of hangar facilities at the ski lodges. And in addition to their regular maintenance, inspection and overhaul schedules, they also were expected to assist the skiers when the helicopter was ready to do a run.

Many of the mountainous areas of BC are prone to avalanches in winter, threatening road traffic as well as the lives of skiers and backcountry recreational users. In the past, artillery guns were positioned along major highways, aimed at areas of extreme risk and fired by remote control, but by the 1980s helicopters had become part of the operation. Okanagan crews worked with clients such as BC Hydro and the avalanche teams from the Whistler Mountain Ski Corporation whenever snow threatened their sites or the service roads connecting them to highways.

For these avalanche-control contracts the company used a Bell 206, which in addition to the pilot carried a three-man team—a recorder, a shot-preparation tech and a bombardier who held a government-issued blasting certificate. Each had specific tasks, and they kept in constant communication through the intercom system. The recorder directed the pilot to the site of the potential avalanche then used a stopwatch to record the time of the burning fuse, placement of charges, detonation and results. The shot preparation technician was responsible for the explosives, which were placed in an aluminum casing with fuses already crimped before loading into the helicopter. He placed the igniter on the explosives and passed the prepared charge to the bombardier who sat beside him in the rear of the machine. The bombardier, secured by a spotter's harness, directed the pilot into a precise hover, fused the explosive charge, pulled the igniter and released the device into the snow.

During this procedure, the following dialogue would take place:

Bombardier: "First shot is lit."
Recorder: "First shot lit; stopwatch started."
Bombardier: "First shot is away; second shot is away..."
Recorder: "Time."[99]

When the recorder called, "Time," one and a half minutes had passed since the first fuse was lit, and it was time for the helicopter to move away. The number of charges depended on how many could be dropped within the time limit. Afterwards, the pilot circled and gained altitude so the avalanche team could observe the results of the explosives.

*

In May 1982 the City of Edmonton, owner of the municipal airport's hangar number 10, built in 1947 for Trans-Canada Air Lines, decided not to renew Associated's lease there. On May 27, the company moved to a new hangar nearby and waited for their old home to be torn down. Instead, ten days after all the stock had been moved out of hangar 10, the roof caved in, and the main door fell down.

Associated experienced more changes that year when both Rex Kaufman and Jack Hook retired. Chief engineer Jack Hook had been with the company since the early 1950s. Rex Kaufman had joined the original Associated Airways as an accountant and in time became vice-president and general manager. He was later appointed president and retained this position after the Okanagan takeover. If Rex had one claim to fame, it was probably that he was the only accountant without a helicopter pilot's licence in North America who had carried out an acceptance check on a pilot of a Bell 47D-1. It seems that when the pilot arrived for the checkout, only Rex and the secretary were on site, so Rex, who was always willing to do whatever was necessary, did the checkout.

In the north, Universal pilots Geoff Goodyear and Ken Drover participated in a gyrfalcon count for the government of the Northwest Territories. As a result of similar assignments in the past, they had become known as experts on conducting northern wildlife surveys. Also in the north, Okanagan leased an Aérospatiale AS 355 TwinStar from Era Helicopters of Alaska to support a seismic program in the Hudson Bay area. The machine and crew were based onboard a ship and flew between Puvirnituq and Churchill.

Okanagan was once again the successful bidder for the Panarctic Oils contract to move ice camps in the Lougheed, Graham and King Christian islands of the High Arctic. This contract, which began once the ice reached 8 feet (2.4 metres) thick, required a Bell 212 and an S-61 to move all the equipment needed to set up three drilling camps. Two complete crews serviced this contract so that, weather permitting, the first crew began flying at 8:00 AM and finished at 6:00 PM. The machines were then refuelled without shutting the engines down, while at the same time the engineers carried out routine maintenance. This was usually accomplished in the space of two hours with external power on, inverters running and a Herman Nelson heater to prevent the transmission from freezing. At 8:00 PM the second crew began its shift and flew until 6:00 AM when more maintenance was carried out. The previous year when the weather had been good, the job had been completed in 27 days.

In 1982 Okanagan's International Division had 29 helicopters operating in Scotland, Brazil, India, the Philippines, Sri Lanka, Thailand and Venezuela, and a staff of approximately 100 pilots and engineers from many nations. All of the pilots in the International pool had Class 1 instrument rating, while the engineers usually had two or three factory and civil aviation endorsements on medium and heavy lift helicopters. By 1982 most of the company's international contracts involved support for offshore petroleum exploration and production. During the exploration stage the helicopters acted as a shuttle service, ferrying personnel and equipment between the shore base and the offshore rigs. In the production phase they moved technicians and material from platform to platform around the gas or oil field; it was not uncommon for a machine to make up to 70 landings a day.

In India, Okanagan had four Bell 212s and a new S-61 leased from Bristow Helicopters. At Juhu Airport they operated out of an old World War II hangar they shared with the Indian Air Force, which also provided helicopter support for the Bombay oil field with Russian Mi-8s. Every evening as soon as the helicopters returned, Okanagan's engineers began work on the machines in the hangar, which was equipped for major servicing.

However, the Canadian crews faced challenges with the delivery of parts because Indian customs would routinely quarantine essential components until ONGC posted a bond. These delays often led to the grounding of much needed helicopters for days and sometimes weeks, and at times the engineers struggled to keep the required number of helicopters in service for the day's production. For Okanagan staff in Canada who had not been stationed at one of the international bases it was often difficult to appreciate this kind of challenge.

Preparation for flights destined for the Bombay High oil field, located 99 miles (160 kilometres) off the coast, started daily at 5:00 AM to allow the engineers to conduct inspections and the flight crews to check freight manifests and flight plans. Once the passengers and freight were on board, the captain conducted a safety briefing for the passengers, and the flight crew settled into an IFR routine because of the haze or inversion layer obscuring the horizon. With no topographical checkpoints, the offshore reporting points, designated as Alpha, Bravo, Charlie, etc., were based on a combination of time, ground speed, bearing and navigational beacons—when these were available.

While in the field or flying to and from the base, the pilots were in constant radio communication with the dispatcher who monitored delays or problems that occurred during the day. In April 1982 *RotorTales* provided its readers with a typical radio positioning report to a rig on that oil field:

> [Pilot:] *Penrod 74* [the name of the rig] Oscar Kilo Lima [OKL, the aircraft's call-sign] by Alpha [a checkpoint] 10:00 [the time] 3,500 feet [altitude] [1,067 metres], estimating Bravo [the next checkpoint] 10:30 hours . . . Charlie [operations are normal] . . .
>
> [Rig Dispatcher:] Roger, Kilo Lima . . . I checked you by Alpha at 10:00 hours, the altimeter setting is 2998 and winds are 020 at 10.
>
> The pilots usually replied in very polite tones, knowing that if they are pleasant to dispatch, freshly made doughnuts and coffee would be waiting for them on arrival.
>
> Pilot: Thank you, sir. Oscar Kilo Lima.[100]

Information on the number of passengers and types of freight was also relayed during the flight. On the final approach, the rig advised the crew that the heli-deck was clear and prepared for the landing. After the helicopter arrived at the rig, it remained there for the rest of the day as a production-support machine controlled by the rig dispatcher who co-ordinated its movements around the field and instructed the pilot regarding routes and stop-off points. Although the helicopter was flown out to the rig in IFR conditions, once on the field, weather permitting, it reverted to VFR, which required only one pilot, giving the crew the chance to split the workload.

On one occasion at the Juhu base, the crew carried out a 1,000-hour inspection on a Bell 212, which involved removing the tail boom and all the compass wiring and the flux valve, the electro-magnetic device that senses the horizon by using the earth's magnetic field. Re-installing it was very time-consuming because the compass has to be "swung" for accuracy. To do this, the helicopter has to be flown to an area on the airfield that is free of metal buildings or interference from metal objects. The avionics technician is positioned in the centre of a circle with his calibrated master compass on a tripod. The pilot then rotates the helicopter at 30-degree intervals around the technician while he takes compass shots. Using a mathematical formula, the technician determines the amount of the helicopter's compass error and records it on a new compass card that is then installed in the helicopter.

One morning I was carrying out one of these compass swings at Juhu airport. Nearby some local women were cutting down the long grass. How they did it I will never know because the area was full of cobras. One of the women had a little boy with her, and he drifted over to watch the helicopter moving and me performing my duties. Eventually we had the compass swing completed, so I waved the boy over, took his hand and put him in the back of the helicopter. I told pilot George Aiken and his co-pilot to take us for a ride around Bombay, so off we went. Well, the young lad had eyes the size of saucers. When we landed back at the Juhu hangar and the blades had stopped, I let him out and the first person he saw was one of our Indian engineers whom he ran over to and started to talk very excitedly in Hindi. George then took him into the hangar and gave him an Okanagan hat and some pictures of the helicopters and off he went. I never knew if his mother had noticed him missing. George said that the sad thing was that the lad would go home and no one would believe him.

In Madras in southern India the company operated out of the hangar belonging to the Madras Flying Club, which had been established in 1929. The club did not have flight simulators or link trainers but trained pilots using a beautifully maintained de Havilland DH 80A Puss Moth, and they hired a number of locals to lift and move it around to demonstrate roll, pitch and yaw while the trainee sat in the cockpit. Over the door of what had become the stores room was an old sign, "Tiffin Room," which may have dated from the 1940s when it was an RAF station, as "tiffin" was the Anglo-Indian term for the midday meal.

Cobras were everywhere, including among the parts in the stores room, probably because of the considerable gap under the door. One engineer had a specially cut stick, which he used to great effect when searching for parts there; he would hit the stick against the spares boxes and watch the cobras slither out so that he could then rummage through the spares in relative safety. With no hangar facilities, it was not uncommon for the engineers to go out to the helicopter in the early morning to start their daily inspection and find three or four cobras curled up under the belly of the helicopter by the hell hole. The pilot and the engineer would then have a discussion on how to solve this problem. Usually they paid a local to deal with the snakes.

Next to the stores was a piece of ground covered in brambles with a metallic object in the middle. On investigation the Okanagan crews discovered that it was a complete Bell 47 that had been imported years ago without the necessary import documents. So there it sat. From their own experiences, the crews were well aware of India's tough import restrictions.

June is the hottest time of the year in Madras with temperatures hovering around 105°F (40°C), and one day when I arrived there to deal with an avionics problem, the machine arrived back from the oil rig, and the two pilots got out soaked with sweat. The co-pilot, Ron Ellard, I had met a number of years before when we worked for another company. The pilot, whose name escapes me, was older, probably in his late 50s and not very sociable. It seems that the rig had agreed to provide our crews with food they had difficulty getting locally, and Dennis Cox, a British contract engineer who was part of the Okanagan crew, had been trying to get the pilot to bring back some milk for his tea, but he always kept it for himself. On this day the pilot had a bulging flight bag, and I asked Ron to distract him so I could get access to the bag. It was full of food and cans of milk. I removed one and replaced it with a tin of hydraulic fluid. After hiding it in my bag, I worked on the machine and, with Dennis's help, fixed it.

Afterwards we returned to the hotel with the precious can of milk. The pilot went to his room and was not seen again until the following morning, while the three of us,

Dennis, Ron and I, set off for a local curry house. The bell captain hailed a cab, gave the driver instructions and we were on our way. The taxi driver asked if we were British. When I replied yes, he proceeded to sing "D'ye Ken John Peel," a march past of the old Border Regiment, which had spent the years between the late 1800s and World War I in southern India. The driver then informed us that his great-grandfather and grandfather had been batmen to officers of the Border Regiment.

We arrived at the restaurant and gave the taxi driver a good tip because he had kept us entertained. The building was an old colonial hotel, and the restaurant appeared to be a mess hall with lines of tables filled with locals all enjoying their dinner. We sat down. A server came and put down banana leaves in front of us while another server came along with a trolley and put down rice and curry. We tried to ask for utensils to no avail. Looking around, we realized that all the other diners were using their fingers very adeptly. They had the last laugh watching us slopping curry all over ourselves.

At 5:30 the next morning the three of us got into the back seat of the car, leaving the front for the captain. When he got in, he said, "I suppose we have a comedian in our midst. This morning I went to make my tea, and not having my glasses on, I proceeded to pour in what I thought was milk. When I tasted it, it was disgusting as the can of milk was a can of hydraulic fluid."

"Oh no!" Dennis said. "I think we must have yoghurt in the transmission."

Ron, as the new co-pilot, was in for a bad day.

After the machine got away to the rig, Dennis and I went off to the airport for some breakfast. I love Indian food, and in the morning I would regularly have a dosa, a curry-flavoured crepe made of rice and lentil batter. Afterward, we returned to the flying club and tackled the paperwork. I nailed a piece of wood to the bottom of the door to keep out the snakes, and Dennis and I set about reorganizing the stores.

On a hill at the far end of the runway was a building that looked like a church, and despite the heat, we decided to investigate. It was a lot farther away than we expected—talk about mad dogs and Englishmen! It turned out to be one of the seven churches founded by St. Thomas after he went to India in AD 52. About 20 years later he was martyred while praying at this site. The Portuguese arrived in the mid-sixteenth century and erected a cross at the site; the existing church originates from approximately two centuries later.

A nun took us to see the orphanage nearby and gave us a tour. Most of the children were girls who had been abandoned by their families. Sadly, the nuns could take only 30 babies at a time and could not keep them beyond age six. If they were not adopted then, they were back on the streets. After Dennis and I returned to the airport, the machine came back with no snags, so we put it to bed and returned to the hotel. We mentioned the orphanage to the rest of the crew and organized a "whip-round." Because it was difficult to get money through the Indian banking system, all we could raise was 12,000 rupees, about $250 Canadian, but that would go a long way at that time.

I returned to Madras on several occasions and came to appreciate its historic atmosphere. Entering the hotel we stayed in, the Taj Connemara in the centre of the city, was like stepping back to the days of the Raj. It was built in 1854 and named by an Anglo-Irishman, Sir Henry Pottinger, who held the post of governor of Madras from 1848 to 1854. Just around the corner was another piece of Victorian history, Spencer & Co. department store, built in 1863–64. As you went in, a young boy, dressed in a khaki uniform, met you at the door with a basket and accompanied you around the store, putting in the items you wanted to buy. When you were finished shopping, you went over to a clerk sitting at a high desk. He figured out how much you owed and asked for the rupees. If change was required, he put the money in a brass container and through a series of ropes and pulleys, hoisted it to a cashier located up in the roof who would make the change and send it back down the ropes and pulleys to the first clerk. The boy followed you out carrying your basket, and you were expected to give him a few rupees for his work.

Some months later we were moved out of the Taj Connemara into the new Hilton, which was nearer to the airport and still under construction. One evening the Okanagan crew decided to visit the bar, which had just opened. The only other customers were four white guys with punk hair-dos and lots of metal face ornaments. Over a beer and a chat we found out they were a punk rock band and had come to Madras to give a concert. The next morning the foyer of the hotel was crowded with the conservatively dressed young men and women of the Mormon Tabernacle Choir, who were appearing in the same concert. It wasn't until several years later when I was watching TV that I realized that punk rock band had been Bob Geldof and the Boomtown Rats. In 1984 Geldof co-founded a charity group, Band Aid, that raised money for victims of the famine in Ethiopia. In 2005 he put on another charity concert, and for his services he was invested by Queen Elizabeth II as an honorary knight of the Order of the British Empire.

In Sri Lanka, an S-76 on an offshore contract gave pilots Jack Milburn and Peter Hort a fright. They were flying on a straight and level course in cruise mode at about 167 mph (270 km/h) when suddenly they heard a loud bang—the pop-out floats had deployed. They managed to get control of the helicopter, declare an emergency and land safely. The problem, discovered by an Okanagan Australia avionics engineer, had been caused by the wire bundle for the float test panel chafing against the weather radar tray. Eventually, with all the vibration, it had broken, causing the floats to pop. This was another case of the very tight wire bundles in those early S-76A models causing problems for engineers.

In early 1982 Okanagan's contract in Thailand was confirmed for a further three years with the addition of an S-61, but on April 30 one of the company's deadliest accidents occurred there, taking the lives of Captain Malcolm (Mac) Forgie and twelve passengers. He was flying the S-76 back to Songkhla from the rig when it had a tail-rotor failure and crashed into the Gulf of Thailand. Mac had joined Okanagan in February 1975 as an engineer, working on Bell 206s, and gone on to become a pilot and offshore captain on the S-58T, Bell 212, S-61 and S-76. He had come up through the Eastern pool and done tours in the Arctic and Eastern Canada before joining International and undertaking his first assignment in Maturín, Venezuela. Mac had been the base manager in Songkhla since February 1981. He was highly respected by both colleagues and customers.

Elsewhere in Southeast Asia, Bell 212 C-GDVG was flown from Manila to Singapore and then onto a drill ship in the harbour; from where it was ferried to a rig off the coast of Salalah in southern Oman. When engineer Rudi Riccardo arrived in Oman, he discovered the machine needed an engine change, but his challenge was to find a space and the equipment necessary to carry out the job. He approached Airwork Services, a civilian contractor servicing the Sultan of Oman's helicopters and fixed-wing fleet. The company, run by British ex-servicemen, had a hierarchy that was hard to get through, and the staff was not very helpful. But as Rudi left the hangar wondering where to try next, his luck changed—and it was all because of a boyhood friendship.

Rudi came from an Italian family that lived in Ethiopia for many years. His interest in aviation began when as a kid he spent school holidays on an uncle's isolated farm where he helped with the maintenance of his uncle's small plane. On leaving school, he went to Perth, Scotland, to enrol in the three-year program at Air Service Training to become an aircraft engineer; from there he could go on to obtain a UK Civil Aviation Authority (CAA) aircraft engineer's licence. The students came from all around the world, and Rudi became friendly with a lad from Oman. After his three years Rudi obtained his engineer's licence and was hired by Bristow Helicopters, first in Redhill and later Aberdeen. In the meantime the situation in Ethiopia had deteriorated, and Rudi's family moved to Australia. Rudi followed and was eventually hired by Okanagan Australia. When the company shut down in 1981, he joined Okanagan's International pool.

Now here he was in Oman, and as he was walking away from the Airwork Services building, a window opened and a familiar voice shouted, "Rudi, what are you doing here?" It was his Omani friend. As one of the first Omanis with aircraft engineering qualifications, he had become the officer in charge of aircraft maintenance for the sultan's air force in Salalah. From that point on Rudi had hangar space, tools, equipment, manpower and the use of an air-conditioned office.[101]

When the overhaul was complete, the Bell 212 stayed with the rig as it was towed to the Bombay High oil field. However, during a storm the rig came adrift and wallowed almost to the toppling point, losing all but one of its towlines. The Okanagan crew on board, Captain Pierre Bock and engineer Dennis Cox, recalled being spread-eagled on the heaving deck trying to ensure that the helicopter stayed secure.

1982 ANNUAL REPORT

Late in the year United Helicopters Ltd. (Bristow Helicopters) of Redhill in the UK submitted a proposal to purchase 49 percent of Okanagan Helicopters' common shares for $20.8 million. While negotiations with Okanagan's new parent company, RSG, were successful, the agreement was subject to the approval of the Air Transport Committee, which turned it down; they ruled that the transaction would unduly restrict competition and was not in the public's interest.

Not including the Associated Helicopters operation, the company's total flying hours for 1982 declined significantly to approximately 75,000 from 89,700 in 1981 and 91,600 in 1980.

1983

The economic news continued to be dismal in 1983. Depressed markets in the oil industry led to cuts in exploration and drilling, impacting both domestic and international helicopter contracts, although the situation in Southeast Asia was somewhat more stable than that in North America where non-oil and gas work was also scarce. Due to the downturn in the coal market, Edson's Luscar Sterco Mines cancelled the S-61 helicopter transport service; over the life of the contract Okanagan had carried 750,000 passengers on 35,000 flights without incident.

One positive note for the company in 1983 was the expansion of the Viking Way facility to full capacity in order to handle the repair and overhaul of Bell 206, S-76 and S-61 engines. Company engineers were able to complete a major overhaul on a General Electric CT58 engine for Dome Petroleum in a record 58 days.

That spring an Okanagan Bell 205 tested a new emergency multiple person rescue apparatus (EMPRA) developed by Gem Industrial Sewing Ltd. and Dart Aero Systems, Inc. in response to a number of incidents both at sea and on land that had required the rescue of multiple persons. In the past, crews had been able to move only one person at a time by using the winching system. The EMPRA device was capable of holding 15–20 people, and, as its flotation collar was level with the water, it was easy for survivors to roll or crawl into the basket. In addition, its trawling procedure gave helicopters the ability to scoop survivors into the basket, and the collapsible sides and open top ring made it easy for survivors to get out when the helicopter landed. The EMPRA's reflective paint made it visible both day and night.

In a tragic event on April 1, 1983, a Piper PA-24 Comanche with four persons aboard crashed while en route from Edmonton to Vancouver. The pilot, Mike Ruwald, had reported an engine malfunction to the Abbotsford control tower, giving his position and advising that he was attempting to rectify the problem. When the aircraft suddenly lost power and altitude, he sent out a mayday, and minutes later the aircraft slammed into the side of Chehalis Mountain at the 5,300-foot (1,615-metre) level. The Rescue Coordination Centre (RCC) at Comox on Vancouver Island was informed and they picked up an Emergency Location Transmitter (ELT).

A Canadian Armed Forces Aurora aircraft pinpointed the signal to the east side of the mountain, about 60 miles (100 kilometres) from Vancouver, but because the crash occurred late in the afternoon, search and rescue personnel were unable to reach the site before dark. In bad weather early the next morning the crew of a Comox-based Boeing Vertol CH-113 Labrador helicopter made several approaches following various valleys, but although they were unable to reach the crash site, one of the crew members spotted three people standing outside a snow cave. They had survived the crash, a major snowfall overnight and sub-zero temperatures, but now the Vertol's crew were concerned that their wash could trigger an avalanche or blow the survivors right off the side of the mountain. The obvious solution was a smaller helicopter, and the RCC contacted Okanagan Helicopters. The company dispatched a Bell 206L LongRanger, a more powerful version of the JetRanger, flown by Terry Dixon, one of the company's most experienced pilots. Arnie Macauley, Search and Rescue (SAR) technician recalled:

> Terry shows up with the LongRanger and a couple of slinging cables. Luckily he had also stopped at Abbotsford to pick up Craig Seager, another of our SAR techs. We sure needed Craig, as it turned out. Anyway, we jury-rigged a Billy Pugh [a large mesh scoop/cage rescue device] on a cable underneath the helicopter, and Craig Seager and George Makowski got in it. I rode in the cockpit to direct Terry.
>
> We took off with the Billy Pugh hanging below us, and Craig and George swung out three thousand feet or so [900 metres] over the valley. By this time the mountain was covered in cloud, there were ice crystals blowing around, and we could hardly see a damn thing. But we had [all] the luck in the world. I found this ridge rock that I knew led up to where the people were, so we followed it and found them.[102]

When Arnie located the ridge, the helicopter was slightly less than three hundred feet (90 metres) below the crash site. In order to reach the site, Terry had to manoeuvre extremely close, entailing a slow, climbing hover with the tips of the blades only a foot from the mountain. Had the machine drifted too close and the blades touched the cliff face, the helicopter would have exploded in a fireball and the crew would have died instantly.

Pilot Terry Dixon's own comment about this stage of the rescue, published in the June 1983 issue of *RotorTales*, was:

> Flying in those clouds and snow conditions was like flying inside a ping pong ball.
>
> This is the sort of work our pilots like Jim Davies in Banff are doing routinely, [but] it's certainly not the type of work pilots normally find themselves faced with.[103]

According to Arnie Macauley, at one point during that slow, nail-biting climb, Terry turned to him and said:

> I'm getting nervous. Did you feel that?
> Feel what? the SAR tech asked.
> My heart. When I am nervous, I can hear my heart pounding.[104]

Arnie commented later that Terry kept the chopper as steady as a rock and never lost his focus. He flew the aircraft, kept an eye on the rotors, and slowly climbed the cliff face, while Arnie did his best to look out for Craig and George and watch the tail rotor so he could direct Terry if he lost reference. Arnie continued the story:

> He tucked the helicopter even closer it seemed and Craig and George were able to swing the net back and forth and jump onto the snow. They had their ice axes with them so got a good grip. If they hadn't, they would have fallen all the way to the valley floor.

When the rescue crew reached the wreckage, they found the three passengers alive and in relatively good condition, except for one broken arm sustained when the plane hit the mountain. Sadly, the pilot, Mike Ruwald, had died. As quickly as possible, the two women survivors were assisted into the rescue cage. George held onto the side of it and Terry took them down the mountainside while Craig remained with the injured man. Arnie recalled:

> Just getting out of there was dicey. The cloud was like soup and we could hardly see a thing. Terry felt that he couldn't just back down the mountain, but we had to back away from it. Then he did a pedal turn to his left while I tried to watch the ridge on our right. Finally we got out of there, popped through the cloud into clear air and whisked right down into the valley.[105]

On the ground, the two women were wrapped in electric blankets in the waiting Labrador, and then the LongRanger returned for the injured man and Craig. By that time the clouds had cleared, but it still took another hour and a half of circling in the clouds and falling snow before Terry was able to manoeuvre over the rescue site again and pick the two men off the ledge. Because the priority in search and rescue is to assist the living, the body of the pilot had to be left on the mountain. The survivors were treated at the hospital in Abbotsford and then released. By chance they ended up staying in the same hotel as the SAR techs.

Arnie Macauley told the rest of the story:

> Later that evening, I heard a tap on my door and when I opened it . . . [One of the rescued passengers] was standing there. She told me the RCMP did not have the equipment to get her husband's body off the mountain until the weather was better and she asked if we would bring him down for her. So George Makowski and I volunteered.
>
> The weather was good next day and this time Terry brought another pilot with him. George and I took some rescue tools and crash axes with us, and even then, it took us about an hour to get the body out. Because the plane had flipped when it crashed, it came down on [the pilot] and had broken his neck. We actually had to cut through the floor to get to him. When we had

◄ Terry Dixon receives the Star of Courage from Governor General Jeanne Sauvé at Rideau Hall in Ottawa on November 9, 1984, for conspicuous courage during the helicopter rescue of survivors of a plane crash near Chilliwack, BC. PHOTO COURTESY OF TERRY DIXON

the body ready to go, we collected . . . the log books, the luggage and anything else of value and put it into the big cargo net. Terry took this down first. Then he came back up with the Billy Pugh and George and I had a nice ride down.[106]

On Friday, November 9, 1984, with the SAR techs in the audience, Governor General Jeanne Sauvé presented Terry Dixon with the Star of Courage for "conspicuous courage in circumstances of great peril." George Makowski praised Terry for his quick response to their call for help and to their changing plans. The governor general then presented medals to George, Arnie Macauley and Craig Seager.

*

Associated Helicopters experienced two tragedies during 1983. In the first, Jack Lunan, the VFR chief check pilot and operations manager was killed when his World War II Harvard touched wings with another Harvard while flying in formation for the Western Warbirds Association over Oliver, BC. Jack had joined Associated as an aircraft-maintenance engineer in 1949 and went on to gain his commercial fixed-wing licence. Having logged over 10,000 accident-free hours, he had been a recipient of the Helicopter Association International's pilot safety award. In the second incident, engineer Ray Bolier, aged 27, went missing while on a contract for Petro-Canada in a remote part of Devon Island, Northwest Territories. He was presumed drowned after his canoe and gear were found at the bottom of a lake. He had been with Associated since 1980.

*

Helicopter operations on the West Coast were frequently based in remote areas, often in small settlements and logging camps, and occasionally even positioned on log booms. When required, engineering staff had to fly into these sites, which often meant transferring to a float plane for the last leg of the journey. That was why in the early summer of 1983 I found myself heading for a camp in Kishkosh Inlet off Douglas Channel about 60 miles (100 kilometres) south of Prince Rupert. As I was the only passenger, the float plane pilot had me sit in the co-pilot's seat. It was a beautiful day and the view was spectacular. I asked the pilot if he enjoyed flying float planes and if he wanted to fly something bigger, and he told me that he had flown for the airlines but found it boring after bush flying.

We had one call to deliver freight and mail to a camp off Pitt Island. As we landed, the pilot touched down very smoothly, pointed the de Havilland DHC-2 Beaver toward the dock and in five easy movements, cut the engine, stepped out on the float and then onto the dock, tied up the plane and kept on walking toward the office with the mailbag under his arm.

It took me only a few minutes to repair the helicopter I had come to service, but I had to wait until the following day to catch a flight on the logging s-61 to Prince Rupert and then a scheduled airline flight home. I couldn't get a flight out of Prince Rupert until Sunday, leaving Saturday a free day, but it was the local sea festival weekend and lots of events were going on around town. Unfortunately, the weather did not cooperate and the rain was jumping a good six inches off the ground. While waiting for the parade, I asked one of the Coast Guard guys if weather ever stopped a parade. "God no," he said. "If we let rain dictate to us in Rupert, we would never get anything done."

Okanagan assigned pilots Bill Yearwood and Stan Ulrichsen to a new contract at Nanoose Bay on Vancouver Island with the Department of National Defence (DND). The job was torpedo recovery, using s-61 CF-OKB modified with a special winch located in the centre deck of the main fuselage, and the search area was 100 square miles (260 square kilometres) of seabed in the Strait of Georgia, 30 miles (50 kilometres) north of Nanaimo. At this location the seabed has an average depth of 1,345 feet (410 metres) making recovery relatively easy. High-tech military equipment was used to track the approximately 300 to 400 torpedoes test-fired there annually, mostly by the US Navy. According to the crew, torpedo recovery was good fun—except when the winch cable broke and went up into the rotor system tearing up two blades. Fortunately, engineering was able to modify the winch system.

On the East Coast, on August 17, a "Central Flight Following Service" was introduced in Halifax to provide a centralized dispatch service for all aircraft working in the Scotian Shelf and Sable Island areas. Previously, each of the four oil companies had been operating its own service with aircraft reporting on different radio frequencies. The new service was the brainchild of Okanagan check pilot Pierre Looten who pushed for a system where all aircraft operating in the field would report to one dispatch centre on a special radio frequency. The goal was to provide 24-hour, seven-day-a-week combined support with three radio operators on duty.

In Newfoundland two new Bell 206s were contracted to survey a spruce budworm outbreak that had started in August in the Pasadena, Springdale and Badger areas. The purpose of the survey was to determine the budworm egg concentration and assess the extent of damage to spruce and fir trees. Meanwhile, in Ottawa the Air Transport Committee dismissed a complaint by Sealand Helicopters of predatory pricing against Universal Helicopters Newfoundland Ltd. The charges had been made after the Newfoundland government awarded Universal a two-year contract for five Bell 206Bs.

In the High Arctic, Bell 212 C-GOKX was contracted for the summer to Dome Petroleum to operate out of Hans Island, near Ellesmere Island, a beautiful but isolated area, as part of a scientific expedition. The study's focus was the ice floes, their speed and direction and the potential results of impacts on fixed objects such as oil rigs; the scientists hoped that with accurate information they would be able to prevent collisions. The Okanagan crew consisted of pilots Joe Hessberger and Mark Gilbert with engineer Guy Murrison.

Meanwhile, Associated provided a Bell 212 and Okanagan an S-61 for a new Panarctic Oils contract on Lougheed Island for November and December. This contract involved using the two helicopters to sling in supplies and drilling equipment to set up ice camps while two de Havilland DHC-3 Otters plus PWA's Lockheed C-130 Hercules came in with the heavier equipment. In addition, Okanagan won contracts with Esso for a Bell 212 in Norman Wells and with Gulf Oil in the same area. Although the rates were low, the contracts were secured in the face of stiff competition.

At Tuktoyaktuk all personnel travelling by helicopter to the offshore platforms of either Dome Petroleum or BeauDril of Gulf Canada Resources were put through a safety briefing and fitted with immersion (survival) suits before each flight. To make sure the passengers had the right-sized suits, the manufacturer, a Vancouver-based company, employed four young women to fit them. The women rotated every two weeks, and as a result, the Okanagan crews got to know all four of them well. Now it happened that one Okanagan pilot who often rotated out of Tuk loved to play practical jokes, not just on his fellow pilots but on engineers, oil workers, managers—everyone was fair game. On one occasion, another pilot—Captain C—who was very much a company man, became his target. Captain Joker selected a few assistants to contribute funds, which were then given to one of the young women along with a list of supplies from a particular store in Vancouver. She returned with them two weeks later, and it was then just a matter of waiting for Captain C to leave on the regular crew change. The day arrived and the crews heading home were joined at the airport by more well-wishers than usual.

Oil companies are known to buy only the best equipment, especially tools, and as a number had been stolen over the year, the company had installed a security system at the airport to detect the thefts. The joker had managed to get into Captain C's crew bag then mark it and had let security in on his plan. As the bag went along the conveyor belt, lights flashed and bells rang. The belt stopped and the security man asked the owner of the bag to identify himself. Captain C stepped forward and was asked to open it. The security man rummaged around and pulled out various pieces of sexy lingerie to a great chorus of laughter. Poor Captain C's last comment on boarding the Boeing 737 was: "When I catch the bastard who set me up, they'd better look out!" However, despite many attempts, he was never able to find out who was behind the prank.

Visitors—usually oil company officials, often environmental and marine consultants and sometimes government officials—passed through the camps in Tuktoyaktuk on a regular basis, but it was only that last group that we kept our eyes on. One summer day I was working with Ron Jackson on an S-61 parked between the Tuk airport building and the Dome Petroleum hangar. When the Dome Petroleum Boeing 737 landed and began unloading the latest crew change, Ron spotted a guy who had left the industry and joined the Ministry of Transport (MOT) in Edmonton. He was accompanied by a woman. Our first thought was they had come to do a snap inspection—there was no other logical reason for them to be there. As we were closing up the machine, Dome Petroleum's chief engineer, Al Schmitt, who was ex-Okanagan, came by heading for the hangar and we informed him. Then we noticed the two newcomers heading for our S-61 so we closed the doors, loaded up the truck and prepared to head back to camp. This caused the two to change direction and aim for the Dome Petroleum hangar when suddenly the hangar doors there started to close. Just then, we saw that one of our Bell 212s bringing passengers to the airport was about to land, so we signalled the pilot to go around again. We watched as the MOT officials gave up and headed back to the airport to get the bus to camp.

The next day it started—inspections, paperwork, equipment standards, flight procedures, maintenance control, quarantine areas—the list went on and on. Ron and I were working on the S-61 when they arrived in our hangar, and their first comment was how dirty the seat covers were. We explained that we were flying oil workers to and from the rigs and the seats were bound to get dirty, although we did send them to the camp laundry from time to time. Another comment was that the exit sign above the door was not centred and could cause confusion.

Our job manager was a very diplomatic guy and tried to pacify them, but everyone was glad to see them leave on the next crew change. Previous inspectors had given us no problems as they had been people who had worked in this environment and understood the challenges. Some months later when we got the report, there it was: dirty seats and the exit sign six inches to the right of centre. They had also picked up on a few other minor things. Then, of course, the memos arrived from head office. I often wondered why the MOT never sent its staff in January or February. Perhaps they had just wanted to get away from the office for a few days or pick up a University of Tuktoyaktuk (Tuk U) T-shirt.

The standards at the Tuk oil camps varied considerably. Some were first-rate with modern quarters, good food and even gyms. However, one camp was a lot smaller, had poor-quality food and few amenities other than a small library. According to a story that made the rounds, one Christmas day the non-flying Okanagan crews and engineers from the smaller camp, knowing that DEW Line crews were always happy to see visitors, decided to visit their site to have some seasonal cheer. When they returned to their camp later that afternoon, they were hungry, having missed lunch, and since the camp mess was closed and no staff was around, they took it upon themselves to find something to eat and proceeded to do some cooking. The supervisor came in and ordered them out of the kitchen, and the manager demanded they be removed from the camp immediately. The Okanagan crew at one of the better camps had to transfer to the smaller camp to provide coverage, and the banned crew moved to the better camp. One individual was heard to say, "When I get home, I'm going to cancel that damned gas credit card."[107]

*

With the international market saturated, helicopter rates dropped dramatically during 1983. British Airways Helicopters and Schreiner Airways of the Netherlands submitted tenders for contracts in India that were 18 percent and 25 percent respectively lower than Okanagan's bid. And British Airways Helicopters was offering rates that were 50 percent lower than two years previously. However, Okanagan was the successful bidder for an Esso contract for two Sikorsky S-76s to start the following year in China.

In India the company increased the number of nationals hired for the Juhu base, including pilots Ashok Tamahane and Duleep Nachia. Each had 15 years of rotary and fixed-wing experience in the Indian Air Force and had been flying the Bell 212 as co-pilots. They were sent to Vancouver on a training course to earn their Canadian commercial helicopter licences and Class 1 instrument rating.

In early September, crews from Okanagan Australia and the Royal Australian Air Force (RAAF) successfully airlifted 52 men from the jack-up oil rig *Key Biscayne*, which was sinking off the west coast of Australia. While under tow about 100 miles (160 kilometres) north of Perth, the rig had encountered severe storm conditions, causing its towline to break and leaving it adrift. Okanagan Australia was alerted by Esso to stand by with both its helicopters for a rig evacuation. When the rig's mayday came, the first helicopter, crewed by Frank Hillier and Nick Price, set out for its last known position, but while they were able to establish visual and radio contact, the weather conditions prevented them from rendering assistance. The evacuation began once the RAAF Search and Rescue helicopter and the second Okanagan machine, crewed by Dave Gibson, Nigel Osbourne and Robert Vaughn-Johnson, arrived. Between 11:00 AM and 1:00 PM hours, the three machines rescued 40 men off the listing rig, leaving a skeleton crew of 12 on board. Three hours later the remaining men were taken off, and the rig sank that evening. Esso and the 52 survivors expressed their gratitude to the crews for saving them.

In South America the declining value of the Venezuelan bolívar, foreign exchange control and falling world oil prices resulted in the termination of Okanagan's Venezuelan contract and the return of the Okanagan machines to Canada. The S-61 CF-DWC, ferry-flown by Capt. Jack Jaworski, co-pilot Jorge Aguay and engineers Philip Bernard and Egan Agar, was at 2,000 feet (610 metres) on its final approach into the airport at West Palm Beach, Florida, when it began having mechanical problems. It crashed into a nearby wooded area. Emergency services crews were amazed when they arrived to find three of the crew members walking around the wreck with the fourth already on a stretcher. In an interview in 2008 Phil Bernard remembered that crash clearly:

> In the early evening of October 7 we were making our approach into West Palm Beach. The pilot had both visual and verbal contact with the airport control tower. We were given clearance to descend from 1,500 to 1,000 feet [460 to 300 metres] and join [the] right hand base leg for landing. When Jack Jaworski lowered the collective control to descend, we all heard a loud bang that actually sounded like a gunshot from behind us. It was aft of the cockpit near the main transmission. After the initial shock all was quiet for a second. Time seemed to stand still, then the helicopter started to pitch wildly fore and aft. Jack managed to centre the cyclic and collective to maintain some resemblance of control of the wildly vibrating and pitching helicopter.
>
> I was told by eyewitnesses that as they watched the helicopter in the air, they saw a large object fly from the machine and then they heard the loud bang. We found out later that the object was half of one rotor blade that had separated. The eyewitnesses watched in horror as the helicopter fell out of the sky. Jack fought to maintain directional control with the tail rotor as there was little response from the main rotor control. The descent from 1,500 feet [300 metres] to the ground took about 30 seconds, although inside the helicopter it seemed a lot longer. As we were making the approach, I was standing in the entrance to the cockpit watching... Egan Agar, the other engineer, was standing behind me looking over my right shoulder. As the helicopter fell from the sky, Jack tried to head for an open area in an attempt to land, but as we got closer, he realized there was movement in the field and instinctively pushed the tail rotor control to steer the helicopter away. We found out later that it was a school field with children playing in it. After turning away, the helicopter made contact with some trees in an area adjacent to a housing complex. The trees were enough to break the fall of the machine. Although [it] was split into two pieces, there was no fire or explosion after impact. The pilots were out first through the left and right windows. The next thing I remember was sitting against a tree with Egan groaning in pain. We had managed to get Egan out of the cockpit window, but he had a broken back. He was soon attended to by paramedics.
>
> As the week progressed we were involved with a post-crash investigation. It was determined that the main rotor blade had failed due to a corrosion pit on the internal corner of the spar of the blade. Over time with successive flexing

▲ Engineer Philip Bernard stands on the top of S-61 CF-DWC. PHOTO COURTESY OF PHILIP BERNARD

of the blade it had failed. The separated pieces of the blade [were] found in the parking lot of a seniors' complex about half a mile away from the crash site.

This was certainly one adventure I would not like to go through ever again. Thanks to the flying skills and experience of Captain Jack Jaworski and co-pilot Jorge Aguay, we survived what could have been a catastrophic accident. Egan was admitted to the local hospital for treatment, which he responded well to, and after returning to Vancouver for a long rest and physiotherapy returned to work. Upon our unexpected landing in West Palm Beach, the S-76 which was travelling a short distance behind us, landed at the airport and the crew were instrumental in helping sort out medical, operational and travel needs.[108]

1983 ANNUAL REPORT
At the end of 1983 the Air Transport Committee in Ottawa released figures showing that the Canadian domestic aviation industry had been operating at a loss since 1981. Their figures showed that helicopter flight hours had gone from a high of approximately 551,000 in 1981 to 410,000 in 1982 and 350,000 in 1983.

1984

The industry continued its decline in 1984. Canwest in Alberta went into receivership, Kenting Klondike Helicopters and Liftair of Calgary sold 50 percent of their fleets, and Quasar Helicopters of Abbotsford, BC, was forced to take on direct bank involvement in its operations. By the end of the year, Heli Voyageur in Quebec would also be in receivership with its five 206B JetRangers auctioned off to companies in Mexico and Tennessee.

Okanagan Helicopters responded to this environment by cutting back to approximately half the number of people it had employed two years previously, closing branches and reducing the fleet. In the late 1970s as many as 50 Okanagan machines had worked in Quebec; now due to reduced flying hours and a cut in rates, the company ceased operations there, closing its bases in Montreal, Sept-Îles and Quebec City. Some machines, such as Bell 214ST C-GVZO, were returned to Vancouver; others were reassigned to short-term contracts elsewhere. On the East Coast, when Okanagan lost its contract with Mobil to Sealand Helicopters of Newfoundland, the Bell 214ST on the job there was reassigned to a four-month contract with Petro-Canada.

On the West Coast there was cause for optimism when the company's Western VFR Division won a summer contract with the US government for two Bell 212s and a 205 to conduct a survey of the DEW Line across the Canadian north. Another bright spot was the authorization of Viking Way as an Allison engine overhaul service centre, which allowed the company to undertake more third-party jobs, increasing its work load to approximately three times that of the previous year. It renewed contracts with the federal government for the repair and overhaul of the RCMP's Bell 206, the Coast Guard's hovercraft engines and the provision of components and engines for the Coast Guard's S-61 in Prince Rupert.

Henry Peare of Okanagan's engineering support group was honoured in 1984 for his contribution to the improvement of the overhaul procedures for Allison 250-C30 engines. He and his team of Yves LeRoi, Jurgen Funke and Matt Cawker developed the procedure after they realized that another operator had lost an S-76 when a failed turbine wheel caused an engine to shut down in flight. As a result of several similar incidents, an airworthiness directive (AD) was issued grounding all S-76s with less than 100 flight hours on their engines. Allison then adopted an amended form of the Okanagan team's procedure, but because Okanagan had implemented the change early due to the foresight of Peare and his team, the company's fleet was unaffected by the AD.

Early in the year Okanagan's S-61 C-GJDR headed south from Vancouver to appear in the Columbia Pictures' movie *Starman* alongside Jeff Bridges and Karen Allen, who were directed by John Carpenter. C-GJDR, which had been a logging machine and ferried mineworkers out of Edson, needed a complete makeover for its new role. Stripped of its orange colour scheme and painted military drab, it was also modified internally to look like a sophisticated command centre for a government law enforcement agency. Its crew consisted of Captain Rocky Rochfort and engineer Chuck Taylor who were responsible for its operation during filming, which took them to Las Vegas then to Winslow, Arizona, and from there to Nashville and Chattanooga, Tennessee. (Tennessee was the only state that would allow the movie moguls to start a forest fire!) Flying with Rocky was Jim Deeth from Jetcopters, Inc. of California who had previous helicopter filming experience. While C-GJDR was on lease there, Jetcopters provided Hughes 500s and Bell 206s for the production.

That same year OK Heli-Logging took on a job at the north end of Harrison Lake, 118 miles (190 kilometres) from Vancouver. Heli-logging operations cause severe vibrations on the machines, which in turn cause the wiring harnesses and connectors to separate, and as a result, at one point the S-61 was grounded because of a problem with its turbine inlet temperature (TIT), which indicates the temperature of the internal engine. Terry Dixon, our operations manager, and I flew there in a Bell 206 to fix it, and with us came the chief pilot of Era Helicopters of Alaska who wanted to observe the operation. The TIT problem was quickly fixed, but our return flight could not take place until the Era chief pilot was ready to leave. Driving out was not an option for Terry and me as Harrison Hot Springs, the nearest town, was nearly 40 miles (64 kilometres) away over a rough, one-lane logging road with the ever-present danger of running into wildlife or meeting logging trucks coming the other way.

The next day while we waited I had the chance to fly in the logging machine to see how it was done. I stood between the two pilots while they screamed down the side of the hill. In fact, I was looking down at the lake as we flew at it. As we came closer, the pilot flared the machine, dumping logs where a boom boat rounded them up.

The following day we boarded the 206 and were flown to the Harrison Hot Springs Resort where Terry's wife was to pick us up and run us back to Vancouver by road. The pilot landed in front of the hotel, which had a lot of open space, hovered there and turned the helicopter so it was facing the lake with the tail boom pointing toward the hotel, then the three of us got out and walked away. As the machine flew back to the logging camp, we could see someone running towards us from the hotel, waving his arms. It was the hotel's very irate catering manager.

"Do you realize that you have just blown over all the food and chairs and tables set up for the BC Socred [a provincial political party] convention?" It seems the premier and his entourage were due within minutes.

With his usual sense of humour, Terry said, "Well, I guess you aren't going to invite us into the bar for a beer then."

The catering manager was livid and told us in no uncertain terms to get off the premises. Terry managed to contact his wife and she met us at a nearby pub. As we were apolitical, we thought it was funny and raised our glasses, but we did have to explain to the Era pilot what had just happened. While the incident would not be in his report, he said he would take great delight in telling the story when he got home to Anchorage.

*

One of the major events in Canada in 1984 was Pope John Paul II's visit, which included a stop in Vancouver and a mass at Abbotsford Airport. Depending on the weather, the organizers decided that he would fly into Abbotsford either in an RCAF helicopter or an Okanagan Helicopters S-61. To prepare for this event, Okanagan brought in two S-61s from logging jobs and hired students from the Pacific Vocational Institute (PVI) aero-maintenance program to scrub and polish the machines over the weekend. Specially made interiors similar to a Boeing 737 were installed and by Tuesday morning the S-61s were immaculate.

The crews, made up of pilots Mike McDonagh and Dev Anderson and engineers Trevor Castle and Mike Clerk, were kitted out in new Okanagan uniforms. However, the weather was good on the day so the organizers decided that the Pope would fly with the military while Okanagan would carry the cardinals and other VIPs. Trevor Castle recalled the event 30 years later:

> After landing at Abbotsford both helicopters were [marshalled] to . . . a secured area within the airport boundaries, and of course for security reasons we were asked to leave the aircraft . . . Police with sniffer dogs went all over the helicopter, checking for anything that shouldn't be there. One of the dogs took off with my lunch, which was under the crew seat . . . with the handler in pursuit. If I remember rightly, we could not even look over the helicopter to do after-flight [checks and were] escorted to a gate into the public area.
>
> From there the pilots and engineers went and had something to eat and generally wandered around. We were given a . . . time to go back to the helicopters, long before the cardinals were finished, so we could start up and get everything ready, but [we were not allowed] back into the secured area . . . as we had not been given the special passes required . . . Eventually Dev called a few people and we were allowed in, but this, of course, took some time so everyone was waiting for us . . . We got in, started up as fast as possible, loaded up the cardinals with lots of apologies . . . and we all headed back to YVR.[109]

*

Three prospectors hired John Innes, Okanagan's base pilot in Smithers, BC, to ferry them to a claim approximately 70 miles (112 kilometres) into the bush. The weather at the site was around -25°F (-32°C) with clear skies, and although the prospectors were dressed for the conditions and the terrain, they opted to carry only light backpacks and no overnight survival gear. Later in the day when John returned to pick them up in Bell 206 CF-POM, only one of the men was at the rendezvous point, and John began an air search. Just as dwindling fuel and fading daylight were forcing a halt to his search, he sighted a flare in a wooded area. As he was unable to land there, he used a loud hailer to advise that he would return and drop overnight survival gear. By this time it was 17:15, well after dark and beyond flying in VFR conditions. Despite the late hour, he flew back to base and loaded up with parkas, sleeping bags, Ski-Doo suits, boots, matches, fire starter, flashlights, coffee, food and a radio. On the return trip under a full moon, he was accompanied by co-pilot Miron Smaha. Terry Grant, the base manager, was on the radio and had contacted Terrace base pilot Pat Casey to stand by in case of problems. At 7:10 PM by the light of a flare, John located the man in the trees again and hovered overhead while Miron lowered the survival pack; it came just in time as the prospector had been unable to start a fire.

Assured that the man would now survive the night, they set off to look for the third person. Before long they saw the flicker of a fire in a swampy area, and with the aid of CF-POM's landing lamp they were able to land and complete the rescue on what had become an extremely cold night. The three returned to base at 8:15 PM. At dawn John flew back to the site and picked up the man who had been out all night. Luckily he was in good shape and reported no frozen parts. The following day the same three men set off again to complete the job they had started, but in the process one man suffered severe frostbite and lost a couple of toes. John Innes was commended for safely completing the rescue mission.

Okanagan pilot Jim Davies was called out late one afternoon in Banff National Park after a 21-year-old climber dislodged a snow slab, which sent him hurtling down the face of an ice waterfall. He fell about 60 feet (18 metres) before his climbing companion managed to stop him. He tied the injured man to the slope using rope and screws and then scrambled down the mountainside to summon help. As the temperature was dropping, Tim Auger, the park safety warden, decided that, even though it was too dark to climb out, it was necessary to attempt an immediate rescue. The Bell 206 had only been used on three previous night-time missions, and those rescues had relied heavily on the expertise of the pilot.

On a reconnaissance flight Jim found the icefall clearly visible against the dark rock of the mountain. After equipping the helicopter with survival gear and medical supplies and attaching a 45-foot (14-metre) rope to the undercarriage, he returned with Tim and lowered the rope to the ground but found it was the wrong place. Luckily they heard the survivor's cry for help farther up the waterfall. Over the radio, Tim directed Jim to return to base and harness up another safety warden. They set him down about 500 feet (150 metres) up the waterfall, then Jim set Tim down 1,000 feet (300 metres) above his original spot. Tim soon found the injured climber, immobilized his leg with an inflatable cast, and secured him in a "genie bag," a combination of stretcher and sleeping bag. Then, along with one of the wardens, the injured young man was carried underneath the helicopter back to Banff. The RCMP and the wardens praised Jim Davies for his very skilful handling of this night rescue mission.

In the early spring of 1984 bad weather in Newfoundland shut down ferry service between Bell Island, Portugal Cove and St. John's. A shuttle service, which was initiated by pilot Frank Kearney and supported by both VFR and IFR crews using a Bell 206L, moved stranded people back and forth between their homes and St. John's. Meanwhile, Super Puma C-GQRL was supporting Husky Oil's rig *Bow Drill 3* off the coast near St. John's.

In the oil and gas fields off the coast of Nova Scotia, the Shell oil rig *Vinland* had a severe blowout and discharged natural gas. Well cappers from Texas with the support of Okanagan crews managed to rectify the situation, but the skill and professionalism of the helicopter crews didn't go unnoticed. Shortly after that, Captain R.L. Freehill, the master of the *John Shaw*, an oil rig located offshore from St. John's, sent the following memo to Universal Helicopters:

> As the helicopter departed from the rig today, the thought occurred to me that most of us take the helicopter service for granted. It might be appropriate to

relay to Universal Helicopters just how much we all appreciate the superb service provided.

Day in day out, choppers are heading our way, and discounting occasional cases of freezing rain and occasional socked in alternates, the helicopter is always there, often flying at or just above minimums. The pilots' professionalism is second to none and their willingness to accommodate freight and passengers at very short notice is very much appreciated. From all of us on the *John Shaw*, many thanks for providing such superb service.

Besides, we have the best meal on the coast.[110]

In the North the company was the successful bidder on an Esso contract based in Tuktoyaktuk to support a challenging winter exploration program in the Beaufort Sea. The contract started with two s-76s and a Messerschmitt-Bölkow-Blohm Bo 105 and later added an s-61. Okanagan had first evaluated the Bo 105 in 1975 and, based on Dome Petroleum's experience with it, had chosen it over the Aérospatiale TwinStar. This time, however, when Bo 105 C-GSTV completed its contract, it was flown to Yellowknife and then returned to the manufacturer. In the same area s-61 CF-OKM was on contract to a combined BeauDril (Gulf Canada Resources) and Esso operation.

In the High Arctic the annual Panarctic Oils operation began in November on Lougheed, Graham and King Christian islands. As in the past, this contract involved moving equipment and crews out onto the ice where the rigs had been set up for winter drilling. Associated Helicopters' Bell 212 C-GAHD was sent from Edmonton to Rae Point on Melville Island and was followed by s-61 CF-OKP. Weather permitting, this job would take from seven to 10 days and would require helicopters to fly as many as 20 hours a day and sling in total darkness while temperatures hovered between -4 and -40°F (-20 and -40°C).

Repairs and maintenance also had to be carried out in these difficult conditions, but at -22°F (-30°C) even small jobs such as changing a landing light became very challenging with frostbite an ever-present danger. Gloves could be removed only for a few minutes at a time. Another danger was the presence of polar bears, which were difficult to spot in the dark. In 1983 a polar bear had apparently watched a man come into the yard the same time every day until one day it grabbed him. Luckily someone driving a front-end loader was nearby and came to his rescue by driving at the bear, which dropped its prey, giving the victim a chance to scramble into the bucket. A local Inuit hunter hired by Panarctic shot the bear, which was found to be an emaciated female.

On one occasion, Peter Berendt, Jeremy Wilks and I were at the maintenance shack on King Christian Island, just a short distance from the main camp, when high winds and whiteout conditions suddenly enveloped us. We battened down the helicopter and scrambled into the shack to sit it out since we could not risk returning to camp. Blizzards in the region have been known to last for days, but the shack had sufficient survival rations and, with nothing to do, we exchanged life stories.

Engineer Peter Berendt was usually a very quiet man, but that day he told us that, of the many places the company had stationed him, he had loved New Zealand best, not only for the climate but also for the people. However, much of his work had been in the High Arctic, and at one time he had been on loan to Evergreen Helicopters in Alaska, working on the isolated north slope. Later he was sent to Greenland on a contract to keep a mine supplied and crewed. On one flight the s-58T developed engine problems halfway to the mine and had to make an emergency landing. The pilot brought the machine down safely, but they were stranded there for a few days. In addition to food and survival gear on board, they had the mine's supply of beer, but since he and the pilot were probably the only two non-drinkers on the contract, the beer was safe. Peter spent many more years in the High Arctic on just about every Arctic island and told tales of encounters with polar bears, grizzlies and even a wolverine.

The blizzard cleared after a few hours and we were able to return to camp, but I never forgot Peter's stories. By late December, after 150 flight hours, the Panarctic contract was completed, and s-61 CF-OKP flew to Rae Point for servicing before flying south to Tuktoyaktuk.

*

In 1984 Okanagan began its first contract in China, but before the Sikorsky s-76s were shipped there, the engineering department carried out research on a new monitoring system for the s-76's Allison 250-c30 engine that would record engine parameters and transmit the information after each flight to a central computer. During a flight all the parameters were fed to a computer on the helicopter, and when it landed, the disc was uploaded into a maintenance computer for observation. This helped reduce maintenance by identifying potential problems with individual components or systems before they failed. In time the system became more sophisticated, allowing an engineer to plug in a laptop and download the information. This early monitoring system was later developed into the health and usage monitoring systems (HUMS), which could provide information on the performance of engines, airframe, flight controls and electronics.

Part of Okanagan's China contract involved training Chinese pilots on the Sikorsky s-76, which of course meant using the services of a translator. It was challenging for everyone, including the Chinese helicopter pilots who had never flown turbine-engine helicopters. Ed Long, the ground school training supervisor on this contract, told *RotorTales*:

> China. Right away I was consumed with the thought of drab blue- or green-suited people gaping at me, a foreigner, in their midst. I had nightmares about teaching Chinese pilots through an interpreter simple things like "droop compensator anticipator" or "monobromotriflouro methane." Would the Chinese language be able to cope with the wonders of English [technical terms]?
>
> With these and many other stereotypic[al] ideas filling my head, I went to China. Boy, was I surprised to find that people spoke English (or a facsimile of it) and they had been allowed to wear clothes much like ours for the past couple of years. Moreover, the people were extremely friendly and courteous.
>
> "How do you do, Mr. Eddie Wong."
>
> "No, it's Long," I would repeat [to] no avail.
>
> So Eddie Wong began teaching seven experienced Chinese helicopter pilots who were keen to learn and who, to my surprise, asked the same questions that our pilots ask. Another myth shattered.
>
> Mr. Wu, the translator assigned to the course, was a recent university literature graduate who, understandably, had not laid eyes on a helicopter before, let alone [had access to] the technical language of the aircraft industry. However, Mr. Wu worked hard and did an admirable job.
>
> The training took place in Zhuhai where the Civil Aviation Authority of China (CAAC), the Chinese helicopter operator, had built a new facility to support their offshore oil industry. The town of Zhuhai is in an economic zone only 6 kilometres [3.5 miles] north of the mainland portion of [then] Portuguese Macau.

Two weeks into the ground school training, [pilot] Mike McDonagh and [engineer] Jean-Jacques Etter joined me with S-76 IMJ, and a week later [pilot] Dave Whyte and [engineer] Michel Perrier arrived with S-76 IME.

The flight training progressed with all cockpit communications going through Mr. Wu who, by the end of the training, [had] 100 hours on the S-76! . . .

People ask me what I thought of China. In two words: "under construction."[111]

In October on the other side of the world, Bell 212 CF-BHF was ferry flown to Belize to start a new contract. The machine started its journey in Halifax. Captain Joe Hessberger recorded that ferry flight for *RotorTales*:

Belize (in Central America) sounded better than Tuk or Bombay, and it certainly is a new experience. But let me tell you about the trip down here with Associated's Wayne Davis and Harvey Trace aboard 212 CF-BHF. We met in Halifax where we picked up BHF. Clearing customs was a piece of cake due to excellent preparation by Fred Nelson, our Logistics Support manager back in Vancouver . . .

Leaving Halifax proved . . . impossible due to strong winds right on the nose. Another try the next day was successful. Our point of entry into the US was Bangor, Maine, where . . . once again Customs was over in five minutes. Flying mostly VFR, we got as far as Wilmington, Delaware, that first day. Passing through New York was an experience I'll never forget. Easy. All radar vectors hand off to other controllers and frequencies. We flew right over the center of [John F.] Kennedy Airport. Jets everywhere.

Passing through the autumn-coloured northern states to the tropical seasides was a pleasure . . . The pleasure, however, stopped abruptly when we met up with Tropical Storm Isidore, centered over Gainesville and effectively covering all of Florida. No way to go but through.

We had already lost one day in Halifax, so the pressure was on. Forecast was for winds to 55 knots [100 km/h] and turbulence in Cb [cumulonimbus cloud]. So we filed IFR and, with the wind mostly abeam . . . using radar we skirted the biggest thunderstorms and got through Isidore relatively unscathed. That is, except for the fact that due to the heavy rain most of our electronics went on the blink! Once again the controllers were most helpful . . .

Next day . . . off early with CAVU [ceiling and visibility unrestricted] weather allowing us to fly at 500 feet [152 m] all the way down . . . to the Florida Keys and eventually Key West. Great view—took lots of pictures of houses, sail boats and [fine bikinis] on the beach . . .

Clearing out of the US was no problem, although the Customs man couldn't believe our next point of landing—Havana, Cuba. Topped up [the fuel] and fed at the airport café, we began the short hop to Castro's lair . . . All our papers were in order so we didn't really expect to be shot down. However, we were re-routed and that added about 40 miles. In Cuba all our navigation was done with ADF [automatic direction finder] as the VOR [very high frequency omnidirectional radio range] was not too strong and only suitable for an instrument approach at José Martí International Airport (Havana).

Upon landing at Havana we were immediately surrounded by officials and soldiers carrying machine guns and pistols. The paperwork was checked and the helicopter thoroughly inspected. I was then escorted to the flight planner by armed guards . . . We were then told that it was impossible to go via the route we had planned and "fuel was not available at San Julián Airport" and anyway we couldn't leave "cause the weather was bad."

So, mustering all my Spanish, which basically consisted of "buenos dias" and "por favor, dos cerveza"... I explained (with a little [cash incentive]) that if he did not let me go, I would have to return to the US and go via the Gulf of Mexico. That, I told him, would add an extra 2,000 miles [3,218 kilometres] and my boss would kill me, so would he please let me go straight across all those restricted areas just once and I would never ask another favour again, please sir? And he said okay.

But, the weather was [bad] and we couldn't go. Six hours later it was too late to go. So the kind man said we could spend the night at a nice house the military had. So, via squad car, we were taken to jail!

The next day... same performance, except this time I got to call the Canadian Embassy. "Duly noted" pretty well expresses their offer to help. However, with help from Uncle Sam's dollars, we had some success. After another night in jail we were driven to the airport in the squad car at 140 km/h [85 mph], and we finally took off that day.

Because we still couldn't land to take on fuel, we had to take the lids off the aux tanks and fill the empty space with fuel. That gave us an extra half hour for the leg from the tip of Cuba to Cancún, Mexico. Their parting gift was to shut off the NDB as soon as we passed it, which meant we had to fly the 125 kilometres [78 miles] from San Julián across the Caribbean Sea to Cancún without navaids. We made it with 40 minutes fuel to spare.

Even though we had another five-hour wait in Cancún, clearing Mexican Customs was an anticlimax—no hassle! An hour and a half later saw us down the Yucatán Peninsula to Belize City.[112]

The year also saw another marathon ferry flight across the Atlantic. This time it was an Aérospatiale AS 332L Super Puma model flying from Scotland to Newfoundland, but it was delayed by a transmission failure in Greenland. The machine was followed by a second Super Puma, C-GQCO, which was destined for a contract with Husky Oil off the east coast of Newfoundland.

1984 ANNUAL REPORT

At the end of the year the federal cabinet reversed the Air Transport Committee 1982 decision regarding Bristow Helicopters' investment in Okanagan Helicopters and approved that company's purchase of 49 percent of Okanagan's shares. Although Bristow now had a representative on the board of directors, the management of the company remained in the hands of the Resource Service Group.

1985

The outlook for the helicopter industry continued to be as unpredictable in 1985 as it had been in 1984. In the international market, Okanagan's contract in China was reduced to one S-76 and in Thailand to one S-61, but on a positive note, the company picked up work with Petro-Canada in Pakistan and with Petroleum Air Services in Egypt.

The domestic situation was somewhat brighter. In the north the Beaufort Sea and Mackenzie Delta contracts remained active with slight increases in flight time. Concerns about the reliability of the s-76, which had arisen after an accident involving Petroleum Helicopters International, eased, and Exxon extended Okanagan's contract for three s-76s rather than replacing them as it had planned. In Newfoundland the company began the year with helicopters sitting idle in St. John's, but Universal Helicopters won a contract for Super Pumas C-GQKL and C-GQGL, and by year-end its VFR division achieved more flight hours than predicted. In addition, the Newfoundland provincial government awarded Universal Helicopters a two-year contract for three Bell 206Bs and two Bell 206Ls. Okanagan also won short-term IFR contracts for oil field support operating out of St. John's and in the Hudson Bay area of northern Quebec.

*

The BC forest fire situation in the summer of 1985 was extremely serious, so Okanagan's announcement that its staff had designed and built a new water-bombing belly tank to fit the Bell 212 came as welcome news. This heli-tank had a 320-gallon (1,210-litre) capacity in two equal compartments for water and chemicals. The retardant was released through two sliding doors that operated independently, enabling the pilot to control the drop pattern. It was also able to off-load retardant through a hose to a tank on the ground while hovering above the tree canopy. The water tank could be self-loaded in one minute from a source as little as six inches (15 centimetres) deep and emptied in half a second with the doors fully open. Although its primary role was water bombing, the helicopter could also carry rappel crews to inaccessible areas and support them with directed drops or by filling their portable ground tanks.

*

Accidents took a heavy toll on Okanagan's crews and machines in 1985. On March 13 Bell 214ST C-GSYB crashed off the coast of Newfoundland very shortly after departing an oil rig in Placentia Bay, killing the crew of two and four passengers. The wreckage was recovered from the ocean floor some 100 feet (30.5 metres) below the surface and just one mile (1.6 kilometres) from the rig. The pilot was Gary Fowlow, Universal Helicopters' manager of operations. He had joined Universal in February 1975 and, on completing his training in Penticton, had been assigned to the Gander VFR pool. An outstanding pilot, he had progressed quickly to IFR status and in 1981 became Newfoundland's first offshore captain. He was highly respected for his management skills and his ability to relate to people and anticipate problems.

The second pilot killed in the crash was Frank Kearney from St. John's. Frank had joined Okanagan in January 1974 as an aircraft-maintenance engineer in the Montreal pool. He had held a number of positions including job manager, supervisory engineer and crew chief before transferring to the International pool with postings in Venezuela, India and Singapore. In 1981 he took the company flying course at Penticton, becoming one of the company's few pilot-engineers. He spent two years at the Nelson base in BC before returning to St. John's and Universal Helicopters where he took his IFR training. A respected pilot and engineer, Frank had a typical Maritime sense of humour and great rapport with the customers.

Just one week later and a little farther south, the crew of Okanagan's S-61 C-GOKZ declared an emergency and ditched in the sea near Sable Island, about 37 miles (60 kilometres) east of Halifax, while en route to the rig *Modu Sedco 709*. The 15 passengers and two crew members managed to get into the dinghies that were ejected from the helicopter on landing. The Rescue Coordination Centre in Halifax picked up the distress call and two Sikorsky CH-124 Sea Kings from Air Command at CFB Shearwater were on the scene shortly afterwards. The passengers and crew spent only about 40 minutes in the water, bobbing about in moderate seas with waves about four to six feet (1.2 to two metres) high, but when they were brought ashore, three passengers were hospitalized for hypothermia.

Shortly before the incident, C-GOKZ had been put through a 9,000-hour inspection and a total rewiring of the electrical and avionics systems, but the cause of the accident turned out to be the loss of the hydraulic fluid in the main gearbox. When it landed on the sea, it was intact and waterproof and would have required only a fresh water washdown and inspection to return to airworthy status. Unfortunately, during the salvage operation it was dropped while being lifted out of the Halifax harbour; it turned over, filled with sea water and sank.

Everyone in the company was saddened when on October 23, Okanagan's former chief pilot Don MacKenzie and the company's IFR check pilot, Mike McDonagh, were killed when their Bell 214ST crashed about half a mile outside Edmonton. Don had just celebrated 25 years with the company. Mike had 30 years of flying time behind him. Both were highly respected in the industry.

Don MacKenzie had spent the first 12 years of his life in Northern Rhodesia (now Zambia) where his father was a mine manager. The family came to Canada in 1945 and settled in Kelowna. In 1953 he earned his fixed-wing instructor's licence, but after four years with Canadian Pacific Airlines (CPA), he joined Okanagan Helicopters. He told the authors of *Helicopters: The British Columbia Story*:

> As a co-pilot in CPA I started out at $300 a month and worked up to $700. In fact, the captain's deductions were bigger than my pay cheque. That was the rule of thumb then. I joined Okanagan because a number of my very close friends were with them at the time, fellows like Don Poole and Jim Grady, and they persuaded me that helicopters had only been around a few years and that they were obviously the coming thing. That, plus the insecurity in the airlines at the time—there were lots of layoffs, a lot of moves back and forth—made me think this would be the right move.[113]

As it transpired, Don experienced a classic case of "out of the frying pan into the fire," as two years later he was faced with layoff problems at Okanagan. However, he weathered that storm and in 1969 was sent to manage the first IFR offshore operations in Sydney, Nova Scotia, using an S-61. The crew on the contract was made up of pilots Jim Reid, Rolfe Ganong, Fred LeGrice and Reg Rivard along with engineers Wally Boyle, Rocky Pearson, Chuck Taylor and Charlie Morin. Captain Reg Rivard told *RotorTales* in May 1985:

> Don did an excellent job organizing the new operation, which later expanded to Halifax and St. John's... As well as all the other start-up work, Don had an onerous job setting up the IFR procedures with the [Ministry of Transport].[114]

In 1975 Don returned to Vancouver as the first IFR check pilot, but after the accident on Grouse Mountain that claimed the life of Don Jacques later that year, he assumed the responsibilities of chief pilot. He told *RotorTales* in May 1985:

> I took on this job in 1975 just as the company moved into its tremendous growth period—the growth of the International, Northern and Eastern oil-based operations and the opening of the Montreal base were all part of it... I have also experienced... the great disappointment of being caught up in the

economic downturn and seeing long-time good people laid off in the past few years. I am naturally pleased to see the activity picking up again, albeit in a much more competitive market.[115]

Despite Don MacKenzie's heavy administrative role, he had time to fly both VFR and IFR, but on July 31, 1985, he resigned his position to pursue new business ventures, although he remained an operations consultant for Okanagan.

Don MacKenzie's replacement as chief pilot was Dave Whyte who had started his career with Okanagan in 1967 when Copter Spray hired him. A year later he trained on the Bell 206 and continued flying aerial applications until the Copter Spray ceased operations in October 1969. He spent the next two years in the light-helicopter pool then became base manager of Inuvik before moving on to the medium-equipment pool, flying the Sikorsky S-58T. In 1973 while based in St. John's, he became a captain on the S-61. Two years later Dave became involved in the development of Exxon's offshore operations in Malaysia, Burma and Thailand. Returning to Vancouver in 1977, he spent two years as the International check pilot before going to Australia to become chief pilot of Okanagan Australia Ltd., heading up IFR operations there until 1982. In 1983 Dave returned to Vancouver as the chief IFR check pilot, responsible for all the company's operations in the Beaufort Sea, High Arctic and the East Coast, and he remained in that position until he was appointed to replace Don MacKenzie.

In the spring of 1985, Okanagan's first female pilot, Lois Hill, was appointed base manager at Norman Wells, Northwest Territories. Originally from Toronto, Lois had wanted the challenge of bush flying and obtained her fixed-wing licence in 1972. In 1978 she got her commercial helicopter licence and qualified on the Bell 47G-2. She went on to take a maintenance course on turbine engines, and by 1979 had added the Hughes 500D to her licence and was hired by Terr-Air Rotary in Ross River in the Yukon. A year later she moved to Yukon Airways and flew the Hughes 500D, 500C and a Hiller UH-12E, mostly in support of mining exploration.

In 1980 Lois joined Okanagan, based in Prince George, BC. Within six months she had her endorsement on the Bell 206. In the spring of 1983 her husband was posted to Mayo in the Yukon, and Lois convinced Okanagan management that there would be enough activity in mining, forestry and government work there during the summer to open a base with a Bell 206. She spent her winters working from Norman Wells helping Lee Smith with the construction of a pipeline and an artificial island being built as the site for a refinery. When Lee decided to move on, Lois became his replacement. A second machine was added to the base and flight hours increased to 2,500 per year. It was not unusual to have as many as 10 helicopters in the area in the summer covering pipeline work, wildlife and seismic surveys and maintenance of remote telephone sites. Highly respected by the company and the major oil companies, Lois felt being a woman pilot was "no big deal."

On one occasion she was caught in a headwind and had to stop to refuel late in the day at a small landing strip between Mayo and Norman Wells. After refuelling, the engine would not start. Luckily, there was an old shack with an oil stove on site, and, being resourceful, she kept warm by pouring jet fuel into the stove, about half a cup every 20 minutes. She also brought in the battery to keep it warm but would carry it out to the helicopter every hour to try to make radio contact with no luck. The only sound around there was the howl of a nearby wolf pack. She was located the next day by Search and Rescue who found wolf tracks all around the shack.

There was one personal achievement to celebrate in 1985: Sean Kennedy, a Universal Helicopters apprentice engineer working out of St. John's, Newfoundland, received the 1985 Canadian Business Aviation Association award for outstanding academic achievement.

In Ontario s-76 c-gimt, aka Bandage 111, was called to the scene of a motor-vehicle accident near Terrace Bay, east of Thunder Bay. Initially, the victim was to be transported by ambulance, but when his condition became critical, an emergency call went out to the Okanagan base. C-GIMT was immediately scrambled by pilots Murray Bale and Jay Faulkner who landed on the highway where the patient was transferred to the helicopter and whisked away to Thunder Bay where surgeons were able to save his life. A Terrace Bay doctor told *RotorTales* that:

> The helicopter may have made the difference between life and death, and I was amazed at how well the helicopter was equipped and how skilled the flight and medical staff were. If we had taken the patient by road, it would have taken four hours and I don't think he would have made it, but the 25-minute flight saved his life.[116]

In BC, the town of Golden, nestled in the Rocky Mountains, became the subject of a feature in the August 1985 issue of *Playboy*, thanks to the efforts of pilot Don McTighe and Vancouver photographer Alan Zenuk. While not the centrefold subject, the town was featured in a three-page spread showing aerial views for a brewery ad.

By the 1980s log homes had become very popular in the BC Interior. The owner of one lakeside property in the Shuswap Lake area, approximately 280 miles (450 kilometres) northeast of Vancouver, decided that he wanted a log house but didn't want to build a road into his property. Instead, he hired Okanagan's Bell 205 C-GOKQ with pilot Dan Berry to move all the Douglas fir logs to the site of his new home. Once the building crew had prepared the logs, fully assembled then disassembled the house at their work yard, the logs were hauled by trucks to an inactive logging area near the building site and spread out on the ground in the order of reassembly. Each log had to be weighed and its centre of gravity marked. On the day, C-GOKQ moved 40 tons (36 metric tonnes) of logs in 50 trips in just over six hours of flying. Skilfully, the pilot manoeuvred his cargo through the forest and set each log in place, while the building crew scrambled to secure it before the next log arrived on site.

In another BC moving job, Okanagan s-61 CF-OKB with crew members Bob Coleman, Bill Ross and Phil Bernard helped the Canadian Museum of Flight move an ex-RCAF World War II Beechcraft C-45 Expeditor, CF-CKT, from Abbotsford Airport to its new home in Surrey. The trip lasted about 20 minutes with CF-OKB moving at a speed of 40 knots (75 km/h).

In the Arctic, weather is often unpredictable, making trips into the camps challenging. One morning in 1985 an in-bound Okanagan crew left Edmonton as usual on a regularly scheduled flight headed for Tuk. When the Tuk airport was closed due to weather, they were diverted to Inuvik, a smaller airport with few services, then after hours of delay the crew were transferred to a hovercraft to continue their journey down the Mackenzie River. This hovercraft was a British design on trial in the Arctic and consisted of a utility platform with big, four-bladed propellers located on each corner. The cabin was a collection of utility storage sheds that had been hurriedly kitted out with plastic garden chairs. When the engines started and the fans began turning, the passengers knew they were in for a long, noisy, sleepless night. It was time to put on ear defenders and pull up parka hoods as they headed down the Mackenzie River in the dark. Every so often the hovercraft stopped and seemed to manoeuvre to the left or right in the fog. Finally at 7:00 AM the big fans changed sound, the vessel slowed, and after a while they heard the sound of the front-loading ramp dropping onto solid ground. They had landed on the beach at the Tuk marine yard. Quickly grabbing their gear, they got out and changed places with the out-bound crews. After a quick breakfast at the camp they were off to work.

*

In 1985 after an absence of eight years, Okanagan Helicopters returned to Egypt with a Bell 212, which was operated from Ras Gharib, the main petroleum production centre for Egypt. It lies 141 miles (227 kilometres) south of Suez.

In July the company completed its 10th consecutive year of operations in India. While the market there remained relatively firm despite the cutbacks in the oil sector worldwide, it still presented challenges for operational resources. Okanagan now held approximately 50 percent of all the offshore contracts in the country, operating two Bell 212s and two Sikorsky S-76s for ONGC and two 212s for Oil India Ltd. Three more 212s were spread across the subcontinent with one based in Vijayawada, north of Madras, another in Kochi (also known as Cochin), south of Bombay, and a third in Calcutta. Other foreign operators there at the time were British Airways Helicopters with one S-61N and one S-76, Schreiner Airways (Holland) with two Aérospatiale SA 365N Dauphins, Heli-Union (France) with two SA 365N Dauphins and Elitos (Italy) with one SA 330 Puma.

On May 27 Okanagan pilots Pierre Bock and Robert McCall were called out to make an emergency flight in Bell 212 C-GBHJ to a fire on a living-quarters platform under construction in the Bombay High production field about 95 miles (152 kilometres) offshore. Around 4:30 PM the crew had sighted black smoke pouring out of the lower deck. The helicopter crew directed water from the firefighting vessel alongside the platform and then evacuated 26 people. Since the platform's heli-deck had not been completed and was obstructed by equipment, the pilot had to approach downwind to position the helicopter. After picking up 13 people at a time he had to back out the way he had come in.

A few days later the jack-up rig *Sagar Pragam* broke loose from its towing barge and was abandoned in heavy seas. Later in the day 14 crew members were put back on board to try to recommence the tow, but the rig broke loose again. Seven of the crew members were taken off by a Schreiner's SA 365 Dauphin, but Okanagan was called out at midnight to evacuate the remaining crew members because of fears that one of the rig's legs was about to break off. The pilot's first approach was unsuccessful due to the poor visibility. At that point ONGC requested that the helicopter wait on the rig until the generators were shut down, but the salvage crew felt that the rig was in immediate danger of sinking. As a result, the helicopter came in, picked up the men and brought them back to shore. Crew members were commended on a successful rescue under adverse conditions.

The Bombay base had a growing number of Indian nationals on staff including pilots Cavas Panthaky, Vijay Kumar, Ashtok Tamhane, Duleep Nachia, Uday Gelli, Nand Verma and Winston Ferreira, engineers George D'Souza and Nigel Reynolds, avionics technician George Hollis, and storeman Gilroy Mesquitta. During the year Okanagan added a contract in the Andaman Islands, which lie between India and Burma in the Bay of Bengal; for security reasons this contract required a Bell 212 (C-GOKY) fully crewed by Indian nationals. Captain Cavas Panthaky along with other Indian pilots and engineers were assigned to the contract.

In spite of Okanagan's 10-year history in India and the number of machines at work there, the company's managers were becoming concerned that the country was moving toward self-sufficiency in the offshore helicopter market. They were right. On October 15 Pawan Hans Limited (PHL), the Indian helicopter company, officially took over all the international helicopter contracts. They planned to use the Westland 30, recently introduced by Westland Helicopters as it seemed ideal for their purposes. Initially Westland sold PHL 21 of these machines through a British aid program at a cost of £65 million, but shortly after delivery two crashed and the rest were grounded. Normally these machines could carry 16 or 17 passengers, but in areas where the air temperature was often over 100°F (38°C), their range was limited to 38 miles (62 kilometres); unfortunately, all the ONGC fields were well over 60 miles (100 kilometres) offshore. As a result, the machines sat idle for years while talks between the Indian and British governments and Westland senior management took place. Nine years later, with no compromise in sight, Westland bought back the machines for less than £1 million. Though the failure of the Westland 30 was a setback, PHL did have success with their acquisition of 19 Aérospatiale SA 365N Dauphins.

In Thailand, in a special ceremony at the company's Songkhla base, Thai national Khachit Suebprom was presented with his first officer's bars and S-76 endorsement. A second Thai national, Major Wuthichai, completed his Okanagan-sponsored IFR training and joined the company. However, Okanagan's operation there was cut back when a dispute arose between the Petroleum Authority of Thailand and Union Oil.

That summer a Chinese delegation visited Okanagan's Vancouver facility for the second time in six years. The first visit had led to the contract with China for the S-76s. The 1985 visit focussed on power-line construction. The delegation was taken on a tour of the 500-kV Cheekye-Dunsmuir line running from the BC mainland across Texada Island to Vancouver Island and given a demonstration of tower assembling by company aircrew and BC Hydro staff. The delegation also toured the Vancouver hangar, the engineering support facilities and then, at their request, visited a McDonald's. Before they left for home, Chinese pilot Luo Zhau Jin, who had been trained by Okanagan, was upgraded to captain and presented with his certificate by Dick Everson, general manager of the Operations Division. Back in Zhuhai, Okanagan's support services were increased to include one S-76 on contract to Phillips Petroleum exploration on a well-to-well basis.

In late September, Okanagan returned to Pakistan for a contract, although this time they would be working from Karachi in Pakistan (formerly West Pakistan), rather than Bangladesh (formerly East Pakistan) where pilot Jack Milburn and engineer Ev Cameron had operated a Bell 47G-3 on an agricultural mission 21 years previously. The new contract, which was to service two new offshore oil and gas wells, was to start with one S-76, C-GIMG, which would be ferry flown from Zhuhai, China, by captains Larry Graham and Luo Zhau Jin along with engineer Bob Bickle and interpreter Wu Zheug Dong. They flew from Zhuhai to Guanzhou then on to Nanning near the border with Vietnam to refuel, a distance of 314 miles (506 kilometres). Their next stop was Kunming, another 385 miles (620 kilometres), which was to be their final stop before flying over the famous Burma Hump. Kunming, a university city with a population of 3 million, is nestled at the 6,000-foot (1,828-metre) level of the Himalayas, near the border with Laos. At this point the Chinese crew members left, and the Okanagan crew set about getting flight clearance. To their dismay there were no telex facilities, and the antiquated telephone system had all 3 million Kunming residents lined up to use it. The crew eventually managed to get a line out around 3:00 AM.

They were still waiting for clearance five days later when they were advised by Operations that a skirmish between the Burmese army and local drug runners was taking place nearby, and since their safety could not be guaranteed, they were advised to proceed to Hong Kong. Unfortunately, flying east to Hong Kong posed a new set of challenges. For one, they were not permitted to fly in China without a Chinese flight crew unless they were exiting the country. This would mean making a single flight of 733 miles (1,180 kilometres) at over 12,000 feet (3,657 metres). After consulting all the manuals, they came up with a time frame of five hours for a flight from Kunming to Hong Kong. The second problem was more difficult: China did not recognize single-pilot flights. They overcame this by promoting engineer Bob Bickle.

Once en route, flying VFR, they saw a large number of MiG fighters both on the ground and in the air due to friction between China and Vietnam. Chinese air traffic control continually asked about their fuel status because they were unfamiliar with a helicopter that was capable of flying more than 200 miles (321 kilometres) before refuelling. On landing in Hong Kong, the S-76 still had an hour and fifteen minutes of fuel on board and had flown at an average of 125 knots (230 km/h). In order to get the machine to Pakistan on time for the contract, in Hong Kong they got C-GIMG loaded onto a ship destined for Singapore. From there, they set off on another ferry flight—uneventful this time—that took them through Thailand, South Burma, Bangladesh and India, and they arrived in Pakistan just in time.

On April 1 two Universal Super Pumas took off from Aberdeen, Scotland, heading for Newfoundland on what had become a routine flight. C-GQKK was crewed by captains Alec Calder and Eugene Matthews with engineer Bob Pardy. The second machine, C-GQCB, was crewed by captains Pierre Looten and Damien Lawson and engineer Marcel Plante. They landed on April 2 at 7:00 PM in St. John's, having covered the 2,310 nautical miles (4,278 kilometres) in 17.6 hours on a route that took them via Reykjavík, Iceland, and Narsarsuaq, Greenland. The last leg from Narsarsuaq to St. John's may have been a world record over water—854 nautical miles (1,581 kilometres) in 6.3 hours at an average ground speed of 138 knots (255.5 km/h).

In 1985 the Royal BC Museum published *Helicopters: The British Columbia Story*, written by Peter Corley-Smith and David N. Parker, which recognized the significant role that helicopters have played in the development of the province; it was published with the aid of a grant from the Friends of the Provincial Museum. The Museum's next project was to find the right helicopter for a static display. The Bell 47B-3, the first commercial helicopter to be certified in Canada, was not a candidate because of a lack of parts, so they chose the Bell 47D-1 instead and located an airframe in the rafters of an old hangar in Edmonton. Then with many generous donations of parts from aviation companies, institutions and individuals across the country, they began the restoration.

Their next problem was finding enough volunteers with Bell 47 helicopter experience to complete the reassembly, and they approached Sam Sirna of the Coast Guard's helicopter division in Victoria, who was a pioneer helicopter engineer. He thought he could help in the off-season but suggested contacting Chuck Roberts, who also had Bell 47 experience, to investigate the possibility of having Chuck's British Columbia Institute of Technology (BCIT) students join the restoration team. Chuck and his students subsequently brought the machine to within 75 percent completion with all the main systems in place. At that point, since the school was moving to new premises in the old Canadian Pacific Airlines hangar, the Bell 47D-1 had to be moved to Victoria where it was handed over to Eric Cowden, an engineer then working for Vancouver Island Helicopters (VIH). Retired Coast Guard engineer Ian Duncan helped him, and together they dismantled the machine and sprayed it in the company's shop. There was still a considerable amount of work to be done: the hydraulics were missing, the battery box and junction boxes were unobtainable and the machine lacked doors. Art Johnson, also an ex-Okanagan engineer working for VIH, fabricated some of the missing parts—the doors were the most difficult due to the convex curves in the tubing. Six months later when CF-FZX was moved to the museum's basement, it was virtually complete and looked like the machine Carl and Alf had flown into Penticton on August 9, 1947. It remained on display from November 1988 to the autumn of 1989 as the centrepiece of an exhibit depicting the history of the oil and gas industry in British Columbia.

1986

As 1986 began, there was no end in sight for the turmoil throughout the helicopter industry. Due to the reduction in oil exploration in the Gulf of Mexico, one company, Petroleum Helicopters International (PHI) of Louisiana, which had a fleet of 400 machines, idled 100 of them and put 40 into long-term storage. In Canada, Sealand Helicopters cut salaries by five to 25 percent depending on position. To reduce its fleet, Okanagan returned S-76 C-GIMN to Sikorsky and sold another S-76 to lumber company MacMillan Bloedel. Its remaining Bell 214B went to Japan and the last 205 to a Norwegian helicopter company, completely divesting Okanagan of all Bell 204, 205, and 214B models. It retained 18 Bell 212s, including 10 IFR machines and eight VFR, four of which had only been recently purchased.

On the West Coast, heavy lift operations normally consisted of logging and hydro tower construction, but during the year the company also undertook a number of unusual jobs in downtown Vancouver. An S-61 was used as a crane for projects involving tall buildings—lifting a steel base and communications antenna onto the roof of the Pan Pacific Hotel, giant air-conditioning units onto office towers, signs onto the top of a new bank building and a 6,500-pound (2,950 kg) electrified "W" onto the top of a department store. Meanwhile, engineering support's service facility increased capacity again, making it the largest facility dedicated to helicopters in Canada. In addition to Okanagan's fleet, it now provided support to 150 third-party customers, representing 30 percent of the facility's workload.

Expo 86 in Vancouver gave Okanagan a chance to show off at symposiums held from August 5 to 10 at the BC Pavilion with a number of Okanagan managers hosting seminars; there were also arranged tours of the engineering support operations in Richmond. Okanagan's profile was raised further by the film *Discovery and Challenge BC*, which depicted the wide range of company operations set against a backdrop of beautiful BC scenery.

In 1986 Okanagan used a Hughes 500 for a contract with the Salmonid Enhancement Program's Quesnel River hatchery, about 200 miles (320 kilometres) southwest of Prince George, to provide airlifts on the Willow River, one of ten streams flowing into the upper Fraser River. This river was stocked annually with around two million fish, of which 1.2 million were airlifted by helicopter. As in the Nimpkish hatchery on Vancouver Island, the first step in the process occurred in late August and involved airlifting the eggs and sperm from returning adult salmon in separate coolers to the hatchery where they were mixed, placed in heated trays and left for three months to incubate. The fry were transferred to rearing ponds and fed until they reached four grams (0.1 ounce), then packed into holding tanks and trucked to a site for the airlift back to their spawning grounds on the Willow River where they were released to grow for another year before beginning their migration to the Pacific Ocean. The hatchery buckets used for the airlift here were similar to the Monzoon Bucket used to fight forest fires and were designed and constructed by special projects engineer Doug Reid, base engineer at Prince George.

In Ontario during the summer of 1986, 22 Okanagan machines were involved in fighting forest fires, spraying and other work. In Labrador, Universal Helicopters, which had been working for several years with game outfitters, participated in a caribou hunt using a Bell 206L that was able to haul as many as 14 field-dressed carcasses out of the bush. Pilot John Danby also airlifted an orphaned moose calf after it became separated from its mother in a forest fire in the Petty Harbour area, 8 miles (13 kilometres) south of St. John's.

In the north, Okanagan pilot Ed Pruss and engineer Pete Lavoie carried out a hydro survey in the Great Whale River area. After completion of the project, the Bell 212 was repositioned to Thunder Bay, Ontario; from there it was sent to Frobisher Bay (renamed Iqaluit the following year) and then across the Arctic to complete a contract for the federal government in Inuvik. During June and July, Esso sponsored courses on emergency survival at their base in Tuktoyaktuk for 200 members of their offshore drilling crews. The course included a section on helicopter rescue put on by Bob Ireland, Okanagan's safety and survival manager. Two 12-hour days in the classroom were followed by four days of practical training that concentrated on survival at sea, including a life raft drill in survival suits in Tuk harbour. Other topics included safety around helicopters, preparation of landing areas, loading, and the theory behind autorotation.

*

As usual, Okanagan crews participated in a number of rescue missions during the year. On January 10 a Cessna 206 was forced down in Hecate Strait, about 15 miles (24 kilometres) from Prince Rupert, BC. The local Coast Guard station picked up the mayday and asked Okanagan to join the search. The crew of Okanagan's S-61 C-GROL, pilots Fred Shuman and Neil Thompson and engineers Rob Cowherd and Paul Ladefoged, picked up the victims and brought them to Prince Rupert. The letter of appreciation from the Coast Guard's district manager sent to Okanagan's headquarters noted the skilful manoeuvring by the pilots and the daring rescue off the rocks by the flight engineers.

In another incident, Fort St. John pilot Craig Houston, flying on contract for Westcoast Transmission, rescued a worker who had been overcome by lethal sour gas at the Pine River Gas Plant. Craig, realizing the man's life was in danger, pulled him clear and gave first aid on the spot. By coincidence, at his own request he had taken the sour gas emergency course just a week earlier.

A third rescue began on August 22 when the base in Tuktoyaktuk received an urgent call from the RCMP detachment in Aklavik on the western side of the Mackenzie Delta. A critical situation had arisen at Shingle Point, a seven-mile-long (11-kilometre) gravel spit on the Yukon and Northwest Territories border, which was a favourite fishing and whaling spot for local people. A group of about 30 Inuit was stranded in an area that was at imminent risk of flooding. A fixed-wing rescue was impossible due to the poor weather conditions—visibility of only 100 feet (30.5 metres), winds at 55 to 60 knots (100 to 110 km/h) and blowing snow.

The call was answered by captains Jim Neill and Ken Steele who were flying an S-61 from Inuvik to Shell's oil rig in Shallow Bay. They refuelled at the rig and took engineer Phil McCully along to assist. Using radar mapping, they found the sandspit, which by then had washed out in several places, and spotted the group about three miles from shore. The S-61 landed on the only dry spot that was clear of the fishing camp. Once the passengers, mostly women and children, were on board, the S-61 airlifted them to the nearby Shingle Point DEW Line site. Mission completed, the crew flew back to the oil rig to complete their work.

*

After two and a half years flying IFR offshore, Wayne Grover returned to Vancouver from Halifax to become the IFR chief check pilot. During his 20 years with the company, he had held the posts of VFR chief flying instructor in Penticton and base manager at Inuvik and Nelson.

Senior design engineer Keith Sketchley was appointed a design approval representative (DAR), general category, by the Aeronautical Engineering Branch of the Department of Transport, giving him authorization to approve many of Okanagan's aircraft modifications. With his appointment, which was based on academic qualifications, work experience and knowledge of DOT regulations, Keith joined an exclusive group of approximately 95 DARs in Canada.

In November, Universal Helicopters' chief pilot, Bert Barr, was honoured in St. John's for his outstanding work assisting the Newfoundland government's Emergency Measures Division, the organization responsible for river ice blasting operations. With East Coast weather patterns changing, early thaws and rafting ice often caused serious flooding and forced the evacuation of riverside communities. The director referred to Bert as the river guardian, recognizing his contribution to making ice blasting possible using the Bell 206L.

*

On the international scene, the company added a number of new contracts including one with Shell in Thailand and another in Turkey for a Hughes 500D. However, at the same time, Okanagan's presence in Australia was finally winding up with the closure of the office in Perth and the departure of the last Australian registered S-76, YH-WXF (C-GIMY)—along with a variety of spare parts and tooling—via ship to Vancouver.

In Thailand, Okanagan had been operating from the Songkhla base for Unocal Thailand Ltd. (formerly known as the Union Oil of Thailand) since early 1974, and in 1986 the company still had one S-61 and two S-76s stationed there. Most of the flying involved moving oil rig crews on their regular rotations around the field to remote platforms, living quarters (LQs), processing platforms, an exploration drilling rig and a tanker that stored the oil before it was off-loaded to other tankers. The remaining flights were medical evacuations and the transportation of parts not sent by ship. The LQs housed about 100 people in five-storey structures consisting of accommodations plus a recreation area and offices. The processing platforms, which separated the natural gas from water and impurities, were connected to the remote platforms by underwater pipelines and their production wells. The gas, left in the ground until needed, was piped to Bangkok for domestic consumption or exported to Japan.

Okanagan's Songkhla base, located in the Unocal hangar at the Royal Thai Navy airport, was made up of an operations centre and administration offices. In 1986 the operation had 24 employees with base manager Pierre Bock and base engineer John Bourne stationed on site with their families and nine expat crews rotating on two-month tours. Local support was provided by a long-time employee, Thai engineer Komo Jak, and twelve other Thai nationals, pilots, engineers and logistics support. Crews faced the challenges of working in 75 to 95°F (25 to 35°C) heat and high humidity, but for the most part, the monsoon rains that came between October and January did not delay the operation of the IFR S-76s.

In Indonesia, Okanagan crews had started training local pilots and loadmasters for Mobil. The pilot-instructors there were Mike McNulty and Al McKay from Associated Helicopters' Edmonton base with loadmasters John Matthews and Dave McKay from Okanagan.

1987

In response to the prolonged bleak economic outlook, the decline in the number of commercial helicopter operators continued into early 1987. Quasar Helicopters went into receivership, Viking bought out Trans Quebec Helicopters, and Ranger Helicopters returned to more lucrative commercial projects from a training operation. Okanagan, however, which celebrated its 40th anniversary in 1987, remained the largest helicopter operator in Canada and the third-largest in the world with 123 helicopters and 527 employees. At the end of 1947 its predecessor, Okanagan Air Services, had one Bell 47B-3, CF-FZX, two employees and flew just 31.4 hours with a loss of $13,364.58. As part of the anniversary celebration, *RotorTales* issued a special edition covering the highlights of the company's activities, noting its many firsts. The company's quarter-century club of current and past employees, the newsletter reported, boasted a head count that was higher than the staff of most Canadian helicopter companies.

Changes, however, were in the air.

On February 1 Okanagan sold Universal Helicopters Newfoundland Ltd. The employees of Universal had made significant contributions to Okanagan Helicopters through good times and bad, and that relationship had given them the chance to work in other parts of Canada and abroad. The new owner was Harry Steele, whose association with Universal had been a long and happy one as he had served on the company's board of directors for many years.

Okanagan lost three helicopters in accidents in 1987, fortunately without any injuries to crew or passengers. Meanwhile, its VFR fleet expanded when 14 aircraft were acquired from the sale of Universal, and a number of others, including six AS 350 AStars, were purchased from other Canadian operators. The company also announced plans to phase out the Bell 206Ls. Staff designed and implemented a brand new computerized information system to provide data such as individual component costs, location of spares, inventory levels, back orders and much more. This new system also generated packing slips and AI 99 serviceability tags, considerably reducing the time spent on paperwork.

The 1987 Abbotsford International Airshow honoured the Canadian commercial helicopter industry. In addition to its usual program, the show included a display of the Hughes 500, a demonstration of helicopter firefighting techniques and Okanagan's new S-76 Ontario ambulance kit. In another honour that year the Canadian airline Wardair paid tribute to Carl Agar as part of their tradition of naming aircraft after well-known aviators. In announcing the name of their new Airbus A310, Wardair stated that they were proud to have their aircraft carry the name of such a widely honoured innovator in commercial helicopter aviation.

Also in BC, Okanagan announced plans for a scheduled heli-service from Vancouver to Victoria in direct competition with Helijet Airways' Bell 412 (later replaced by an S-76A) as well as the float plane services operated by Harbour Air and Air BC. Okanagan proposed eight round trips daily using a 24-passenger IFR S-61 out of Vancouver International Airport and from the harbour heliport to downtown Victoria. Licensing approval was expected by mid-July—but in the end the project was shelved.

The company also announced plans to develop air ambulance services in BC and Alberta, basing them in Vancouver and Edmonton. The proposed 24-hour seven-days-a-week operations called for Sikorsky S-76s outfitted to emergency medical services (EMS) specifications to transport patients, especially accident victims, from remote areas and small communities to major hospitals. Dominion Pegasus had been the first operator in North America to use the s-76 in this capacity, and between 1981 and 1987 it had accumulated over 5,000 EMS flight hours, some in very challenging conditions. The s-76 was particularly good for air ambulance work because its full IFR package and four-bladed twin engine, which had a top speed of 178 mph (287 km/h), a range of 411 nautical miles (761 kilometres) and a service ceiling of 13,800 feet (4,200 metres), allowed it to provide long-range service in all weather. Its roomy cabin accommodated two standard stretchers and up to four medical personnel plus space for much of the equipment found in an intensive care unit. Okanagan's engineers had designed an EMS interior that the company then made available to other operators in kit form or installed as part of a complete heli-ambulance package. While the EMS market in Canada was relatively small, it was growing rapidly in the US as light, single-engine helicopters were replaced by larger twin-engine types. The only drawback to Okanagan's proposed air ambulance service in western Canada was the lack of hospital helipads; the BC government was only in the planning stage for constructing a helipad at one Vancouver hospital and was still evaluating the idea of a rooftop helipad for another.

In 1987 Okanagan Helicopters again became the successful bidder for the Polar Shelf contract, which was now managed by a federally funded research agency that supplied support and transportation services to scientific agencies involved in studies of the Arctic Archipelago. Okanagan operated 17 VFR machines, the highest number of helicopters in the project's 28-year history. Crewing and maintenance was handled by Associated Helicopters in Edmonton, and the helicopters were spread from Tuktoyaktuk to Resolute Bay and included a number of outlying field camps. While the main base camps were comfortable, conditions at the field sites were basic and usually under canvas. Even between April and mid-August, the period of prolonged daylight when the project was underway, weather conditions could be cold with temperatures as low as -40°F/C and whiteout conditions were not uncommon. In 1987 because of heavy fog and melting ice packs, operations were suspended for a time around mid-May, but after the thaw, phase two of the research began with activities concentrated on the animal and plant life.

In Thailand, the company continued its operations at Songkhla and Surat Thani. Due to the influx of Vietnamese refugees, many of the oil rigs had now built facilities for refugees, and Owen Shannon, one of Okanagan's s-76 pilots, recalled an incident that occurred there on November 28, 1987:

> About 19:00 crew on the *Satun* LQ noted an Asian lady banging on the window of the mess. These guys were more than surprised as women were not allowed on rigs in those days. She quickly pointed to the waters under the adjacent CPP (a platform next to the LQ containing a condensate processing plant), and in the gloom they saw amidst the wind-born three-metre [10-foot] seas the wreckage of a fishing boat and struggling bodies. They sprang into action. They first threw all the life jackets on the rig [down to them], giving the folks something to hold on to. They then climbed within reach and started hauling the people out—not easy. Unfortunately, the 40-knot [75-km/h] winds and current soon saw many of these folks drifting out from under the rig.
>
> A crew boat was called to help out and started picking people out of the sea, but again this was not easy in the conditions and several were churned up by the props. The lights on the [crew] boat were only made to see the deck

where equipment was stored and not to see over the side. This was when [Captain] Randy Leitch and I were called to assist. We were on night stand-by on another rig, the *Erawan* LQ, and quickly responded, with the task of hovering above the work boat and using our searchlight to allow the boat crew to see the people in the water.

How crazy were we back in those days—hovering over water . . . in daylight was not easy, at night in the pitch black near impossible. Anyway, we did manage it for a while [as] the boat was picking up folks close to the SLQ, and it was lit up like a Christmas tree so we had heaps of reference. After some time though, the SLQ started getting farther away, and it became too demanding to hold position.

Randy had control of the searchlight from the left seat and I'd also given him the task of monitoring the RADALT [radar altimeter] while also giving me left/right/forward and aft instructions to keep us on location. We hovered at 300 to 500 feet [90 to 150 metres] or so but Randy's job was really difficult, especially when the refugees were washed under the boat . . . Occasionally we'd do a circuit just to take a break, and while getting back to location and to search for anyone hanging onto a life jacket, the little lights . . . stood out easily in the stormy seas.

We eventually had to call our part of the rescue operation off due to the need for fuel. [We] landed on the SLQ for this and quickly visited the medic's office downstairs to see how things were going. What a disaster. Vietnamese men, women and children dressed in heavy blankets, all sitting around the corridors in various stages of shock. Apparently the [refugee] boat, which had been tied up to a buoy close by, [had] decided they'd try and land the passengers on the rig. The boat got caught in . . . a big swell under a cross member of the rig, and when a wave came through, it rose up and was split in half, spilling 79 folks into the sea; 57 were rescued, 22 lost.[117]

*

The July edition of *RotorTales* brought news that dumbfounded the employees of Okanagan Helicopters. It came in the form of a statement by Okanagan's president and general manager, Pat Aldous:

> It has been decided to use an abbreviation of Canadian Helicopters as the name of the holding company that is intended to own Okanagan, Sealands and Toronto Helicopters. CHC Helicopter Corporation has filed a preliminary prospectus with the Toronto Stock Exchange for the purpose of raising $30 million. While the TSX reviews the preliminary prospectus, the proposed issue will be promoted with brokers to determine how attractive the issue might be. By July 31 the underwriters' position will be determined and final prospectus filed.
>
> Assuming that the necessary funds are raised to complete the transaction, it is proposed that I will continue as president of Okanagan Helicopters as well as participating as an officer, director and member of the executive committee of CHC Helicopter Corporation.[118]

The company's employees struggled to understand how a large company like Okanagan Helicopters with a worldwide reputation could be sold off to a small, struggling enterprise.

The man behind the purchase was Craig Lawrence Dobbin, a Newfoundland businessman who had started with one Bell JetRanger purchased to transport him and business associates to remote fishing lodges in Labrador and Newfoundland. In 1977 he purchased additional Bell helicopters and started Sealand Helicopters to take advantage of opportunities in tourism, fishing and oil exploration off the coast of Newfoundland.

Dobbin had then recruited James C. Jones, who at the time was the general manager of Okanagan Helicopters' IFR Division. J.C., as he was generally known, had come from the US in the early 1970s after serving with the US Army. He wanted to fly helicopters in a bush environment and was hired by Universal Helicopters in Newfoundland. His first job was chasing poachers on ice floes. Because his last two years of military service had been spent instructing fixed-wing IFR, he had easily qualified for Okanagan's IFR pool when the company acquired Universal. After graduating with an MBA from Dalhousie University in Halifax, he became assistant operations manager at Okanagan's King City, Ontario, base when Dominion Pegasus was added to Okanagan's list of subsidiaries. He was next transferred to Australia to set up Okanagan Australia Ltd., the company's joint venture with Brambles Industries Limited. Returning to Vancouver, he held a number of senior management positions with the company before Dobbin recruited him for Sealand.

To compete with Universal Helicopters' Sikorsky S-61s, Dobbin had purchased a fleet of Aérospatiale AS 332 Super Pumas. These helicopters incorporated a number of new design features, which included run-dry transmissions, thermal de-icing of the main rotor blades and advanced weather radar. They had a maximum speed of 185 mph (300 km/h) and could carry 19 passengers 229 miles (370 kilometres) offshore, making them ideal for the oil industry. Unfortunately, Sealand received its Super Pumas just as offshore oil production and exploration plummeted.

About this time Dobbin's company signed a contract with an outfit building a road through the dense jungle of Colombia, running from Caño Limon near the Venezuelan border to the port of Coveñas on the Caribbean coast. Before the contract got started, Dobbin sent several Super Pumas south, but they only made it as far as Aruba off the coast of Venezuela where they sat for weeks waiting for bureaucrats to process entry permits. When the machines did start work, the crews discovered they were required to ferry men and equipment to remote sites that were often attacked by guerrillas.

As a result of this fiasco, Sealand Helicopters experienced a financial crisis with Aérospatiale pressing for payment. Dobbin, however, managed to deal with that crisis and began looking for more lucrative contracts. Recognizing that the Ontario Ministry of Health's air ambulance contracts held by Toronto Helicopters and Dominion Pegasus were moneymakers, he submitted a proposal to Ontario Health but was turned down as the government preferred the S-76 over his Super Pumas. Things began to go Dobbin's way at last when he decided to buy Toronto Helicopters. The owner, Len Rutledge, asked for a $500,000 non-refundable deposit and a negotiation deadline of 90 days on receipt of the down payment. Surprisingly, Dobbin met his terms, and Toronto Helicopters became a part of Sealand.

Over his first hurdle, Dobbin then approached his financial backers about buying Okanagan Helicopters. At that time Okanagan, with more than 600 employees and a fleet of 126 helicopters, was three times the size of Dobbin's combined companies. Nevertheless he approached John Lecky, head of the Resources Service Group, which held 90 percent of Okanagan's shares, and Lecky indicated that for Dobbin to pursue the purchase of the company, he wanted a $1 million non-refundable deposit, a 60-day deadline and $25 million in cash. Dobbin put his proposal to his financiers, who could easily see that a combination of the three companies would create a monopoly in the Canadian helicopter industry and overseas, especially in the offshore oil market. When shares were offered to the public on October 12, Okanagan had assets of more than $100 million and a projected working capital of $33 million. The proceeds from that initial public offering had a target of $30 million including $15 million in convertible debentures and $15 million in common shares, which would be used to purchase 51 percent of Okanagan and repay outstanding debts. The remaining 49 percent would be held by United Helicopters, which was owned by Bristow Helicopters. The offering was very soon sold out, and Craig Dobbin took over Okanagan Helicopters.

The Okanagan name along with its distinctive orange colour and hummingbird logo soon disappeared, replaced by the Canadian Helicopter Corporation's red, white and blue livery and stylized hummingbird. Everything orange, including photographs and files related to the old company, was removed from the company's Vancouver office. Soon after, Okanagan Helicopters' licence number 883705 for a Class 9-4 charter non-scheduled international service using rotary-wing aircraft was cancelled.

Craig Dobbin died in October 2006, aged 70. After tackling the nearly impossible, he left a legacy of shaping CHC into the largest helicopter operator of its kind.

Epilogue

1988 AND BEYOND

While researching information for this book, I learned that one last operation was completed in 1988 by Okanagan pilots, Associated engineers and a Bell 212 machine that was still in Okanagan colours—though the new Canadian name was on its tail boom. It took place in the High Arctic.

When the Cold War started in 1947, the United States and its allies developed a sound-surveillance system to detect Soviet submarines transiting through an area called the GIUK gap (an acronym for Greenland, Iceland and the UK). It consisted of a chain of listening posts that operated from 1961 until 1991. In 1988 CHC had a contract with the US Department of National Defense to provide helicopter support to the scientists and technicians who were responsible for tracking these listening devices, which were all located 40 to 50 miles (64 to 80 kilometres) north of Greenland, with a second set halfway to the North Pole and a third located at the Pole.

This contract started in January 1988 in Edmonton when Bell 212 C-GOKL was loaded onto an RCAF Lockheed C-130 Hercules. With C-GOKL went its crew, which consisted of CHC pilots Dale Simpson and Bruce Swain and an engineer from Associated Helicopters. Their destination was Alert on the northern end of Ellesmere Island, the RCAF's most northerly base, a 2,200-mile (3,540-kilometre) flight. On arrival the helicopter was re-assembled and flown to the first ice station where a camp was set up. The technicians and

◂ Identification flags, Ski-Doos and equipment during the visit of the USS *Spadefish* to the Sound Surveillance Systems (SOSUS) site. The flags were used to check wind speed while the Ski-Doo and other equipment helped with locating, retrieving and replacing the monitoring devices, in 1988. PHOTO COURTESY OF DALE SIMPSON

scientists had to track the listening devices, which had been travelling for a year about 200 feet (60 metres) below the ice, moving at a rate of a quarter knot (0.5 km/h). This was before GPS, so the devices were tracked by mobile sonar equipment. The process involved the scientific crew dropping the sonar into cracks in the ice to pick up signals that allowed them to locate the listening device by triangulation. They pinpointed where the device would be in two hours using mathematical formulae involving currents, cut a hole in the ice and sent down a remote submarine. With its grappling device, the submarine hooked the cable that held the listening device, winched it to the surface, where technicians replaced its tape reels and returned the device to its location on the seabed. With the task completed, the helicopter crews moved the ice camp to the next location.

At the final location, the geographical North Pole, the team had a surprise visit from a nuclear submarine, the USS *Spadefish*, when its conning tower broke through the ice. The American team members had been aware of its presence but had not told the others. The submarine's captain and some crew disembarked onto the ice, and Okanagan's pilot Dale Simpson took the captain for a short flight to take photos from the air. Unfortunately, no visitors were permitted to board the submarine.

▲ SOSUS crew at USS *Spadefish*. They were not permitted to board the submarine, in 1988. PHOTO COURTESY OF DALE SIMPSON

*

CHC's head office remained on the south side of Vancouver International Airport at 4740 Agar Drive, just around the corner from 4391, the location of the original Okanagan Helicopters hangar and head office. Many Okanagan employees stayed on with CHC, and some are still with them. Others went off into a variety of new ventures (see Appendix 1).

By the end of 1988 CHC had acquired the fuel distributor Aero Flight Holding as well as Offshore Technologies Ltd., a flight-simulator company based in St. John's, Newfoundland. Early the following year, CHC purchased Ranger Helicopters of Ontario and Quebec-based Viking Helicopters, later adding Heli-Welders of Richmond, BC, Atlantic Turbines International of Prince Edward Island, and ACRO Aerospace, again in Richmond, BC, to the list of its companies. (ACRO was the original Okanagan engineering support division.) Associated Helicopters was soon merged into the domestic division of CHC along with Toronto Helicopters and Viking Helicopters.

▲ USS *Spadefish*, in 1988. PHOTO COURTESY OF DALE SIMPSON

Over the three decades since the takeover of Okanagan Helicopters, the changes have continued. On the international front, CHC bought British International Helicopters in 1994, followed by the purchase in 1999 of Helikopter Service Norway, which operated a fleet of 37 twin-engine IFR helicopters for offshore work and search and rescue along with a large overhaul and training department. However, in 2000 after a management buyout, Canadian Helicopters separated from CHC, although CHC retained part ownership. Five years later Canadian Helicopters became an integral part of the Helicopter New Zealand (HNZ) Group, which today consists of Canadian Helicopters (Canada), Norse Helicopter Services (Norway), Nampa Valley Helicopters (US) and Heli-Welders (Canada).

On August 18, 2004, in Penticton, BC, where it all started, former Okanagan Helicopters employees held their first reunion. It commemorated the 57 years since the arrival of Carl Agar and Alf Stringer in CF-FZX back in 1947. The reunion, the brainchild of Didier and Maxine Moinier, both ex-Okanagan employees, was attended by 325 people who learned about it simply by word of mouth. Josie Knight, a former senior Okanagan administrator living in Penticton, had negotiated a special rate at a hotel (in high season) as well as the use of the convention centre at no cost and free parking anywhere within Penticton. The reunion was a wonderful gathering of old friends—with one slight hitch: the name tags had been misplaced. At the meet-and-greet, people were heard saying, "I

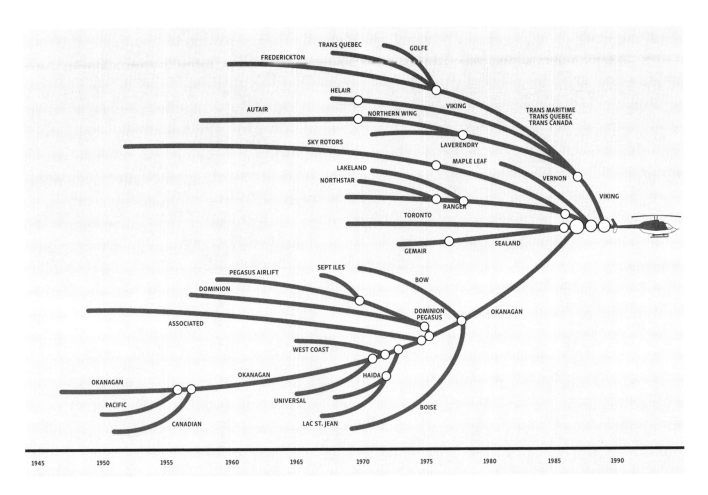

The evolution of Canadian Helicopter Corporation. SOURCE: CANADIAN HELICOPTERS CORPORATION LTD.

know the face, but I cannot for the life of me remember your name." The slogan of the reunion poked fun at the takeover: "Orange is really OK."

In February 2008 CHC was sold for a reported $3.7 billion to Connecticut-based First Reserve, a global energy and private equity investment company. By that time CHC had no helicopters operating in Canada, though it still had an impressive fleet of over 250 helicopters operating in more than 30 other countries.

Sadly, on May 11, 2016, the Canadian aviation magazine *Helicopters* carried an announcement that the parent company had filed for chapter 11, citing the dramatic slump in oil prices as the cause. However, on March 24, 2017, CHC Group (now operating from Irving, Texas) announced that it had concluded financial restructuring and emerged from chapter 11. The company has introduced a new logo that captures its Okanagan heritage with the hummingbird on an orange background and is making plans to celebrate the 70 years since Carl Agar and Alf Stringer arrived in Penticton in Bell 47 B3 CF-FZX to start crop spraying.

Appendix I

OKANAGAN PEOPLE

Captain Tony Adams was born and raised on the south coast of England, and his desire to fly was sparked by watching the RAF and the USAF planes towing Allied gliders over to France for D-Day. One Saturday afternoon instead of playing his usual game of riding the local freight trains in the stockyard with his best friend, he went to a rugby game with his dad, a World War I aviator. During the game, three German fighters swooped down and machine-gunned a train, blowing it up, killing the crew and his best friend. At 18 he joined the RAF for his two years of compulsory military service and was sent to Centralia, Ontario, and Gimli, Manitoba, for aircrew training, and as soon as his military service time was up, he immigrated to Canada. He found it impossible to get a flying job here, first, because all his military time had been spent on jet fighters, and second, because no Canadian company wanted a pilot who had no bush experience.

By working for a couple of years in an office and driving trucks, he saved enough to pay for a helicopter course and was then hired to fly a privately owned Bell 47G-2 and spent a season in the bush. With a total of 400 hours, he approached Okanagan Helicopters for a third time and was finally hired; his first contract was with a large mining company in Timmins, Ontario. When Canadian Helicopters closed its Toronto base, Tony was transferred to Montreal to begin 10 years of radio station traffic reports, first in a Bell 47G-2 and later in a Bell JetRanger. He went on to fly Sikorsky S-55s on the Mid-Canada Line. On one tour he flew out of the RCAF station in Winisk, a tiny ghost town in the extreme north of Ontario, where it was so cold that the S-55s were never shut down from the time they left in the morning until they returned at night; they had been clued in to this procedure after having a number of oil coolers blow. On one occasion he rescued chief pilot Don Poole from the Mackenzie River after his Bell 47G-2 was forced to land in a riverbed. Don had spent the night inside the machine watching the river rise. In 1973 Tony started S-61 training under Don MacKenzie and worked out of Halifax and Sydney, Nova Scotia, and St. John's, Newfoundland, on oil company contracts. In 1977 he was transferred to Halifax and was finally able to be home every night with his family. Unfortunately, this arrangement lasted only a few years; when East Coast exploration closed down, the crews were sent back to the Arctic. Tony Adams celebrated 25 years with the company in 1986.

Dorothy Agar, Carl's only daughter, received her 25-year service award in 1984. She had joined the company in 1959 as a records clerk and stenographer. Deaf from birth, Dorothy had attended special schools in Winnipeg, Montreal and Washington, DC, and completed secretarial training in Vancouver. She used a telecommunication device for the deaf (TDD) to communicate.

◂ Flying Officer Egan Agar of 444 Squadron poses with his Sabre Jet in 1960s Germany. PHOTO COURTESY OF EGAN AGAR

Egan Agar, Carl's son, joined the company in 1958 after leaving the RCAF where he flew jet fighters. He took his helicopter training in Penticton under Don Poole and Bud Tillotson and was then assigned to Shell Oil's contracts in northern BC, the Yukon and the Northwest Territories. In 1962 he worked at the Kamloops base, then moved on to become the Smithers base manager in 1965. He continued flying until 1975 when he lost his licence for medical reasons. From then on he worked on special projects, became a licensed aircraft engineer and worked on the S-61s in Edson, Alberta. He was seriously injured in the S-61 DWC crash in West Palm Beach, Florida, but after rehabilitation was able to return to work. Over his 25 years with the company he was a bush pilot, administrator, manager and engineer.

Engineer **Peter Berendt** was born in Germany but he and his sister were smuggled out in 1939 and sent to live with a family in Manchester. Because they were Jewish, few of their family members survived the war. In England Peter became an automotive mechanic apprentice and in 1944 joined the British Army. He immigrated to Canada after the war and spent five years in the Royal Canadian Navy where he was introduced to helicopters, working on the early Bell 47s and Sikorsky S-55s. His first civilian job was with Associated Helicopters in Edmonton. He joined Okanagan in 1958 as an S-55 engineer on the Mid-Canada Line contract and moved on to S-61s in the 1970s.

Ev Cameron, who received his 25-year service award in 1984, had started his aviation career in 1950 as an apprentice mechanic at Associated Airways. Within two years he had acquired his private fixed-wing licence and joined Hudson Oil Corporation as a crewman on the de Havilland DHC-2 Beaver. From there he went to PWA where he qualified for his aircraft-maintenance licence and spent 18 months on the DEW Line. In 1957 while working on the Mid-Canada Line, he met crews from Okanagan Helicopters. He joined the company two years later and trained under Davey McLean for a rotary endorsement on his engineer's licence. His Bell 47 and the Hiller UH-12E endorsements led him to team up with pilot Jack Milburn for Okanagan's first international contract, the eight-month-long agricultural survey in East Pakistan. In 1967 he took his helicopter flight training in Penticton from Bud Tillotson, Don Poole and Fred LeGrice and then returned to Revelstoke as one of Okanagan's first pilot-engineers. From there he moved to the company's base in Nelson as base pilot and stayed till 1976, when he decided to become a pool pilot, flying medium-sized helicopters. After getting his instructor's rating from Wayne Grover, he instructed military pilots as well as flying in the VFR pool on Bell 206s, 205s, 212s and 214s.

Ted Collins received his training in the RCAF between 1936 and 1946, and worked with Trans-Canada Air Lines and then Pacific Western Airlines. Ted came on board Okanagan Helicopters in January 1957 when the company realized a professional sheet-metal mechanic was needed on staff. He was a department of one until 1964 when Doug Stephens joined him. He was supervisor of the aircraft structures department for 27 years, retiring in 1983.

Rolfe Ganong, who was originally from New Brunswick, joined the RCAF in 1944 and completed his elementary flying training just before World War II ended. After being demobbed, he obtained his commercial fixed-wing licence. In 1957 he became a flying instructor and flew charters with Central Airways out of Toronto Island Airport; he joined Okanagan in January 1961 and was trained on the Bell 47-G2 by Jim Reid and completed his mountain-training course in Penticton under Bud Tillotson and Wilf Pinner. His first job was to ferry a Bell 47G-2 from Toronto to Tuktoyaktuk.

> When I landed at an airport in Marquette, Michigan, I was immediately surrounded by armoured cars and about 50 mean-looking soldiers all pointing

their submachine guns at me. The captain was livid and roared out that I was under arrest and my machine was impounded. It turned out that this airport had been designated a SAC (Strategic Air Command) base and security was tight ... After I showed him that it was marked civil airport on my map and showed all my documentation, plus pictures of my wife and children, he told me to get the hell out of there and he'd pretend it didn't happen. I said, "You bet!" and took off.

Rolfe flew the DEW Line near Tuktoyaktuk and later the Mid-Canada Line, flying S-55s out of Bird, Manitoba. In the mid-1960s he flew out of Dawson Creek then Prince George where the work included timber cruising, firefighting, power-line construction, mining, general construction and air ambulance—including one memorable flight when a baby was born aboard his S-55. In 1969 Rolfe qualified on IFR and was transferred to Sydney, Nova Scotia, where he flew on the Shell contract under Don MacKenzie.

I remember one memorable night ... when we were called out on a hurricane warning to evacuate the two rigs. The winds were blowing at 70 knots [130 km/h], making for tremendous waves. The support vessels would completely disappear in the troughs and come rolling up in a mass of white water on the next crest. The rig was pitching heavily. At daylight when the storm subsided and Don and I finished the evacuation, a call came from Shell to take all the workers back. Thank goodness Jim Reid and Reg Rivard were on hand to do that.[119]

After a job in Guyana, Rolfe transferred to Cranbrook, BC, as base manager/pilot to get back into mountain flying. In 1986 Okanagan honoured Rolfe Ganong for his 25 years of service to the company.

Pilot **Wayne Grover** was hired by the company in 1966 right after graduation from Penticton's Mountain Flying School and returned there as an instructor in 1974. Two years later he became Inuvik base manager but moved back to Penticton in 1977 to instruct again and became chief instructor on Bud Tillotson's retirement a year later. In 1983 Wayne moved to Halifax to fly offshore but was recalled to head office in Vancouver in 1985 to become the chief IFR check pilot. He left the company—now CHC—in 1993 and went to Alpine Helicopters in Kelowna. By retirement he had accumulated over 19,000 hours in the air.

In May 1980 **Max Hoover** (Mr. VXVU 215, his radio call sign), another long-time employee—and character—retired after 15 years in radio dispatch. He joined Okanagan in 1965 in Kamloops and two years later moved to Vancouver. There, starting every day at 6:30 AM, he transmitted to and received from all the bases in radio contact, obtaining serviceability reports, weather and operational status. At that time, long-distance communication was mainly by HF radios that bounced signals off the ionosphere, but Max was described as one of the best radio operators because he knew the optimum conditions for transmission and reception. He was also known as "Rusty, the Singing Cowboy" and performed many times on a Kamloops radio station as well as at the company's annual conference. On Max's retirement, Pat Aldous, vice-president in charge of operations, thanked him "for training him on the job" when he had arrived as a young accountant in 1969 to become operations manager. "Without 'Dad' Hoover's help, the job would have been much more difficult, if not impossible," he said.[120]

Davey McLean trained in the RAF during World War II and worked briefly for Canadian Pacific and Queen Charlotte Airlines before joining Okanagan as a bush engineer in January 1953. During his time with Okanagan he was a crew chief, hangar foreman, inspector, and technical instructor before becoming engineering manager. He retired in 1983 as vice-president of Engineering.

In 1984 Okanagan hired **Sherry Marshall**, its first female apprentice aircraft-maintenance engineer, for the base at Dryden in northern Ontario. The May 1985 issue of *RotorTales* reported that after graduating from high school Sherry had worked in a motorcycle shop for three years because she "loves machinery and is intrigued by things that really go fast . . . She bought her first motorcycle when she was 17 and, being mechanically inclined, had taken to repairing it herself."[121] However, she wanted to become a helicopter-maintenance engineer and took the two-year aircraft-maintenance program at Ontario's Canadore College, the only woman in her year. Although Sherry lost her job with Okanagan in the layoffs of September 1984, she was rehired in January 1985 to work in Vancouver in the VFR pool. One of her first assignments there was an exhausting tour of some of the BC and Alberta bases under the helpful wing of engineer Claude Paquette. Sherry Marshall went on to become an inspector for the Department of Transport.

"Gentleman" **Jack Milburn** was born in Clinton, Alberta, and raised in Prince George, BC. He joined the RCAF during World War II and saw overseas service in the Middle East and Far East. After discharge he went to the University of British Columbia and graduated with a degree in forestry but decided on a career change after he came into contact with helicopters. He joined Okanagan in January 1956 and spent his first five years in tented camps flying geological survey contracts. In 1961 Jack started a new base in Prince George. He was on the very first international contract in South Asia where, with engineer Ev Cameron, he flew a Bell 47J for eight months on an agricultural survey in East Pakistan. Before transferring to the Vancouver pool, he finished his international work flying offshore from Porbandar, 240 miles (385 kilometres) northwest of Bombay. He retired in 1983 after 42 years of flying, including 28 with Okanagan.

Fred Moore was a graduate of the Royal Roads Military College. He joined the RCAF as a pilot and served from 1950 to 1963, retiring as a squadron leader (major). During his military career, he was a distinguished test pilot and the youngest person selected to attend the USAF test pilots school at Edwards Air Force Base in California. On leaving the RCAF, he worked in sales and contracts for Northwest Industries of Edmonton, a company specializing in aircraft manufacturing, repair and overhaul. In 1970 he joined Okanagan Helicopters as marketing manager with responsibility for contracts, sales strategy and public relations. In 1986 when he was Okanagan's senior vice-president of marketing, he was elected to the board of the Helicopter Association International, which at the time represented over a thousand organizations from 41 nations. He was also a member of the Canadian Aeronautics and Space Institute and the RCAF Association.

Ruthanne Page became Associated's first female base manager when she was appointed to the Grande Prairie, Alberta, operation in 1980. With 2,400 helicopter and 600 fixed-wing hours in her logbook, she was one of the few experienced female pilots in Canada. She began her career in aviation as an avionics technician, then apprenticed as an engineer before obtaining her helicopter pilot's licence. She flew highway construction projects in the Yukon and Northwest Territories before joining Associated. In Grande Prairie, flying the new Aérospatiale AStar helicopter, she increased the company's business significantly and supported a remarkable 220 rigs within a 100-mile (160-kilometre) radius of the base.

Henry Peare began his apprenticeship as an automobile engineer with General Motors in Dublin, Ireland, and went on to serve in the RAF from 1943 to 1947. He joined the Rolls-Royce aero engine division in Derby, England, where he worked on both gas turbines and nuclear power plants. In 1966 he transferred to Rolls-Royce Canada, eventually becoming director of quality assurance before accepting a job with Okanagan's engineering division. He was chairman of the Eastern Canadian branch of the Institution of Mechanical Engineers and a design-approved representative on behalf of the DOT (Transport Canada). Because of his superior qualifications he was approved to develop and modify repair-maintenance procedures. He received a special award from the company in 1984 for his contribution to the improvement of the overhaul procedures for Allison 250-C30 engines.

Rocky Pearson trained as an aircraft-maintenance engineer in the RCAF and spent his last two years in the force on the Mid-Canada Line. On joining Okanagan in 1959, his first assignment as a pool engineer was back on the Mid-Canada Line working on Sikorsky s-55s and Bell 47s. In the 1960s Rocky joined pilot Don Jacques at the Kemano base looking after the s-55s and Bell 47s. After Kemano he spent a year and a half in Goose Bay, Labrador, then two years as base engineer in Terrace, BC. In 1969 he received his endorsement on the s-61, which qualified him to work on Okanagan's first IFR offshore contract in Sydney, Nova Scotia. During his time on the East Coast, he became chief engineer of the IFR Division. He returned to Vancouver in 1972 as hangar inspector, later becoming hangar foreman and finally the manager in charge of engineering support. He received his 25-year service award in 1984.

Frank Ranger joined Okanagan in 1952 as an engineer on the Kemano contract then went on to the Mid-Canada Line project in charge of the newly introduced s-58. In 1964 he became chief engineer for a major international offshore contract operating an s-61 out of Lowestoft, England. On his return home he became the hangar foreman at Agar Drive, Richmond. He left the company in 1973 but returned two years later as assistant to chief engineer Davey McLean. He ended his career with Okanagan as manager of warranty and rotable control, working with vendors and manufacturers. He retired in 1983.

Inventor par excellence, engineer **Doug Reid** and his research and development team contributed specialized tools for Okanagan's use, including tree clippers for forestry, drip torches, water wash kits, foot rests (attached to the skids) for the Bell 206, mirrors and improved spray equipment. He started his aviation career in 1952 with Central BC Airways and five years later transferred to their helicopter division, which was sold to Pacific Helicopters and merged with Okanagan in 1964. During his career, he was base engineer, chief engineer for northern bases, base manager and special-service manager. He was presented with his 25-year service award in 1984.

s-61 Captain **Jim Reid** marked his 30th year with Okanagan in February 1986. He was born in Windsor, Ontario, and raised in Toronto. He learned to fly in 1947, and his first job was with Central Airways at Toronto Island Airport, but he became fascinated with helicopters when he saw them flying into and out of the airport. Once hired by Okanagan, he was sent to Ladner, BC, for his basic helicopter training and then to Penticton for the Mountain Flying School under Don Poole and Don Jacques. For his first job he was based in St. John's, flying a Bell 47D, mostly for the Department of Fisheries and Wildlife. His 47 was also used as an air ambulance and kept busy servicing remote villages and cottage hospitals. In 1958 Jim transferred to the Sikorsky s-55 and flew on the Mid-Canada Line. Next he spent four years rotating out of Goose Bay, flying with base manager Reg Rivard on the s-58 to service the Pinetree Line. In 1965 Jim became one of the first Okanagan pilots to train on the Sikorsky s-61 then flew with Okanagan's joint-partnered North Sea venture. When the contract finished in 1966, he ferried the s-58 from Labrador to Vancouver. For the next few years he flew mainly high-latitude geological exploration work. Along with pilots Jim Grady and Reg Rivard, he originated offshore IFR flying using a Bell 204 to support Shell's rig off Tofino.

▸ L.G. "Jim" Reid, a Sikorsky S-61N captain, was one of the first Canadian helicopter pilots trained on instrument flight rules (IFR). Flying out of Sydney, NS, he had close to 10,000 hours of which 6,400 were on helicopters by 1969.
OKANAGAN HELICOPTERS PHOTO

Then came a transfer to Sydney, Nova Scotia, followed by a stint in Halifax. In 1975 Jim and other crews rotated out of eastern Canada to Shell's operation in South America. The following year he took over as Halifax base manager but moved after a year to become base manager of Okanagan's passenger service in Edson, Alberta, a position he held until 1980. In 1982 he transferred to the International Division. He told *RotorTales* in 1986:

> I've never considered flying as work, it's more a way of life—a way of life that nourishes a free spirit, something not many jobs can give you. I can't imagine anything I'd rather have done or any company I'd rather have worked for... Of all my flying, [Edson] was the most demanding job... During the latter part it was a full IFR operation, 365 days a year from 4:30 AM until midnight. We moved 600 people a day to and from the mine site with the aid of the first microwave landing systems. Even with these new IFR approach systems, it was frightening, flying in turbulent and icing conditions into the total black void of the foothills of the Rockies.[122]

In World War II **Reginald (Reg) Rivard** served as an air gunner with the RCAF on loan to the RAF. In 1951 while studying accounting, he decided to get a private pilot's licence; two years later he obtained his commercial and instructor's ratings. In 1954 he found a job with Canadian Helicopters (1948) Ltd. at their Toronto Island Airport base. When Okanagan bought the company, Reg became a line pilot, flying Bell 47s and S-55s on survey operations for the Churchill Falls hydroelectric project in Labrador. He was the first to fly a Bell 47 equipped with an electro-magnetometer, used for measuring the variations in the earth's magnetic field to detect ore deposits. During this operation, he flew all over northern Canada especially in the Yukon where they located the site that came to be known as "Asbestos Hill." Reg opened the base in Goose Bay, Labrador, flying support for the Pinetree Line of radar sites in the Sikorsky s-58. Next stop was Toronto and then Vancouver as manager of operations.

In the late 1960s Reg was sent to Sydney, Nova Scotia, where he worked alongside Don MacKenzie, flying IFR support for a Shell rig; later he took over from Don as base manager. In 1974, just as the James Bay Project was getting underway, he became Montreal operations manager. By the following year Okanagan and its subsidiary companies had 55 pilots, 30 engineers, eight staff and 49 helicopters operating in the James Bay area, which created some operational challenges, juggling helicopters and crews. After Montreal, Reg had a brief stint in St. John's as operations manager on the offshore exploration program. Recalled to Montreal, he took over the position of safety manager, replacing the retiring Grant Soutar. When the Montreal headquarters closed, Reg moved to Vancouver to continue in the same position. He celebrated 30 years with the company in 1984.

Jan Rustad was chief pilot and manager of the Penticton Mountain Flying School from 1983 until he retired on March 31, 2014, after 46 years of flying helicopters and 36 years at the school. During that time he completed the Mountain Flying Training Manual and the syllabus for all the courses. He was instrumental in convincing CHC to invest in a new facility, which was opened in 2012 in a new 20,000-square-foot (6,100-square-metre) building with all the latest training aids, modern classrooms, and a first-class hangar. The Eurocopter EC120B and the Bell 206 became the training helicopters of choice. Jan has been recognized by the civil aviation authorities of several countries and received awards from the military and industry for safety. He is a recipient of HAI's award for outstanding flight instructors.

Lloyd Siver, who came from a small farming community in Saskatchewan, joined the RCAF in 1952. After his initial flying training in Calgary, he became a flying instructor at CFB Trenton and continued instructing until he left the RCAF in 1959. After flying jobs with Trans-Gaspesian Air Lines and Quebecair, he took helicopter training, first with Tommy Gurr at Canadian Helicopters in Toronto and then at the Penticton Mountain Flying School under Bud Tillotson. His first job with Okanagan was flying s-55s on the Mid-Canada Line out of Brampton, Ontario. In May 1964 he transferred to Kamloops where he worked under base manager Jack Godsey until he took over that job in January 1969. In 1986 he claimed the record for the pilot with the longest posting in one location: 22 out of his 25 years with the company.

Okanagan's safety manager, **Grant Soutar**, retired in March 1980 after 23 years with the company. He had flown with the RCAF until 1945 and then with the Royal Canadian Navy where he flew Piasecki H-21s (Flying Bananas). On joining Okanagan in 1957 he flew an s-55, servicing the early-warning radar sites on the Mid-Canada Line. In the 1960s he became the base manager for Campbell River, running both the administration and flying sides; ten years later he was appointed safety manager and moved to Vancouver where he also acted as a check pilot. He was involved in the salvage of 400 Dodge Colts from the freighter *Vanlene* and was the first Okanagan pilot to fly in Southeast Asia. By the time he retired, he had flown in almost every area that the company operated. In the March 1980 issue of *RotorTales* engineer Barry Stone told the harrowing story of "Grant flying 500 miles [800 kilometres] . . . across the Gulf of Thailand with a burst appendix! And tough guy that he was, he was out of hospital two days later and bouncing back to the hotel in a trishaw."[123]

Aubrey Utting, the component shop inspector, had trained in the Royal Navy's Fleet Air Arm as an aircraft engineer. A keen sportsman, he had been a member of the

Navy's field gun crew in 1949 and became the Mediterranean Fleet's inter-service discus champion in 1951. His first civilian job was with Bristow Helicopters on a heli-whaling venture in Antarctica. He took the post with Okanagan in April 1960 and a year later brought his family to Canada. In 1985 he had this to share with *RotorTales*:

> I remember the years when we were away from May to September in the bush up in the Baffin Island area when we were working on the DEW Line. I liked the bush work best, but when I joined the component shop in 1974, under Stu Smeeth, I was happy to finally be home for dinner every night.[124]

Aubrey Utting celebrated his 25th year with the company in 1985.

In 1986 **Tellef Vaasjo**, president of Associated Helicopters, retired after 36 years with the company. He came from a farm near Cold Lake, Alberta, and on joining the RCAF, he was selected for basic flying training under the British Commonwealth Air Training Plan. After further training at Abbotsford, he was posted to the flying training school at Vulcan, Alberta, for multi-engine training and, on graduation in October 1944, to Prince Edward Island with the rank of sergeant pilot. On discharge from the RCAF he returned home to the farm and remained there until he joined Associated Airways in Edmonton in 1949, transferring to the helicopter division a year later. In 1970 he became a company director and vice-president before succeeding Rex Kaufman as president. He served a three-year term as a director of Helicopter Association International.

Over the years, Tellef Vaasjo witnessed significant technological improvements to helicopters, including increased lift to 8,000 pounds (3,630 kg) with an underslung hook, engines running for 3,500 hours instead of 300 before overhaul, and the ability to climb vertically with a load instead of using a technique that involved over-revving and bouncing along the ground or leaping off a cliff. He recalled that in the 1950s the Department of Transport (now Transport Canada) did not really think the helicopter industry would survive.

Bert Very joined the company in October 1957 and spent 26 years in the stores department, creating a master parts catalogue and inventory-control system. When Bert retired in 1983, Gerry Vanslyke, the company's engineering support manager, told *RotorTales* that "having Bert retire is like losing your favourite encyclopaedia... You know there is a lot of information stored up which is hard to find elsewhere."[125]

Engineer **Ray Williamson** was born in Calgary. In 1947 he joined the Royal Canadian Navy's Fleet Air Arm as a trainee aircraft-maintenance engineer and served aboard the carrier HMCS *Magnificent* before taking the Bell helicopter-training course. Later he was attached to the US Navy and then to the first RCAF Helicopter squadron at HMCS *Shearwater* in Dartmouth, Nova Scotia. In 1953 he joined Spartan Air Services in Ottawa where he qualified for his aircraft-maintenance licence with helicopter endorsement. Two years later he was hired by Okanagan as a field engineer and worked on contracts that took him from Vancouver Island east to Manitoba and north to the High Arctic. He was with Carl Agar on the search for the Trans-Canada Air Lines North Star that killed 59 passengers and three crew members when it crashed near Chilliwack, BC, on December 9, 1956, and was part of the team searching for Okanagan pilot John McNulty and engineer Peter Berendt when they were missing for a week north of Great Slave Lake. From 1957 to 1962 he worked on the Mid-Canada Line operating first out of Dawson Creek, BC, then Cranberry Portage, Bird and Winisk, Manitoba. In 1963 he was appointed base engineer in Kamloops and in 1975 became a field inspector. After he had completed the Sikorsky S-76 course in 1980, he joined the International Division for operations in Australia, China and Thailand. In 1986 celebrated his 30th year with Okanagan.

Alan Winter retired from Okanagan in 1986 after 15 years of offshore flying on the East Coast. Al was a World War II fixed-wing pilot who stayed on in the RCAF and transferred to helicopters in 1950. When he was assigned to the Mid-Canada Line he met helicopter pilot Roy Webster who had joined Okanagan upon leaving the RCAF and specialized in setting hydro lines through the Rocky Mountains. Having flown heavy helicopters on Search and Rescue in the Maritimes, Al was well qualified to move to Universal Helicopters' IFR offshore division. His first contract was with Amoco out of St. John's. In 1975 he moved to Halifax on the Mobil contract and worked there until his retirement.

Captain **Bill Yearwood** grew up in British Guyana on a sugar plantation with an airstrip for the crop dusting and corporate aircraft belonging to Booker Aviation of England. He hung out at the airstrip, occasionally getting invited to go for a ride. In 1970, when he was 16, he was sent to finish high school in Toronto, where he sold his motorbike to finance flying lessons at Central Airways. He got his private pilot's licence followed by his commercial licence, float rating and commercial helicopter endorsement then set off across Canada looking for a flying job. When the best he could get was flying tourists over Niagara Falls, he took more lessons, got his instructor rating and a job "teaching unsuspecting new students." In Montreal he applied to Hélicoptères Canadiens-Lac St. Jean, which by then was owned by Okanagan Helicopters of Vancouver. There was no helicopter available there to do a check ride, but chief pilot Pierre Looten said they would call him. When two weeks passed, he phoned them, only to be told they had never heard of him.

> The next morning I drove to Montreal and filled out another [application]. I got to see Pat [Aldous], but he said they only did check rides in Penticton. Two days later I showed up in Penticton... Bud [Tillotson] called Pat and he couldn't believe I had done that. There was a class of Canadian Armed Forces pilots... and Bud said it would be a week or more before he could get to me. I got permission to sleep on the couch in the hangar and that night washed and waxed both helicopters. [I] pushed them out... and had them sitting on the ramp gleaming when the real pilots and engineers turned up. Fred Baird took me up for a check ride first thing. He told Bud he thought I could make... money for Okanagan... He said some guys [they] see would make more money for [Okanagan] by working for the competition. I got a Bell 206 type, mountain and operational flight training and was sent off to James Bay... My first job there was moving a drill with a 206A. I got it done just short of running out of fuel... I flew over 1,000 hours every year for the next four years in Quebec, Newfoundland and Guyana, SA. Fred Baird continued to mould my flying and work habits. We worked hard and had fun doing it...
>
> When I came back, I worked out of King City as a check pilot for the Eastern Division. I also spent winters instructing new pilots in Penticton. In 1977 I only had two days off and that work streak ended in a crash in Lake Okanagan while trying to teach glassy water landings. A main rotor blade came into the cockpit and the [Plexiglas] cut me across my face. Thirty years later I investigated a similar accident [while working for the Transportation Safety Board] except the person seated where I was was decapitated.[126]

Appendix II

WHERE ARE THEY NOW

Many pilots, engineers, administration staff and managers stayed on after the takeover to provide their expertise to the new CHC. In 2014 a few were still there. Others, having learned their trade with Okanagan, left after the takeover but continued to contribute their talents and skills to the Canadian helicopter industry.

- **Pat Aldous** and pilot **Dave Whyte** bought Alpine Helicopters in West Kelowna, BC, and became part of the expansion of the heli-skiing and tourism industry. **Dick Everson**, the former general manager, later joined them to form a new helicopter-maintenance and component-overhaul facility under Alpine Helicopters, which quickly became Alpine Aerotech.
- Engineer **Harry Niwranski** started Helicopter Parts International, a supplier of certified civilian and military parts and components; he has recently moved the company from Bellingham, Washington, to a much larger facility in Minden, Nevada.
- **Gordy Brown** and **Tony Ellis**, two engineers, formed Canadian Air Parts, a sales and leasing company, in Delta, BC.
- **Hugh Whitfield** and **Sandy Strukoff** started a mobile helicopter sheet-metal repair facility that expanded from BC into the US. They also invented the "Shortski," a major modification to the S-61.
- Pilot **Bill Yearwood** joined the Transportation Safety Board covering the West Coast of Canada. He has headed up many aircraft accident investigations in Canada and abroad.
- **Peter Barratt** and **Terry Eissfeldt** formed West Coast Helicopters with its head office and main hangar at the Port McNeill, BC municipal airport.
- International pilot **Vic Corrie** formed his own aviation consultancy and became one of the main distributors of fixed-wing aircraft and helicopter services to the Chinese government. Later, returning to his hometown of Nelson, BC, he started a small helicopter company, Orange, to serve the West Kootenay region.
- **Daryl MacIntosh**, an avionics technician, started Maxcraft Avionics to provide major avionics upgrades and engineering design. It was originally at the Langley, BC, airport and is now in a new facility at the Pitt Meadows airport.
- **John Boyko**, who worked in the engineering support division's accessory shop, became disabled after a helicopter crash in 1978 that broke his back. During his time with Okanagan he completed many marathons, winning one in Honolulu and placing fifth in the 1983 world championship wheelchair marathon in Florida,

beating 70 other competitors. He opened his own business in Langley, which is now part of Helicopter Accessory Service with branches in the US.

- When **Alf Stringer** left Okanagan in 1963, he joined Vancouver Island Helicopters (VIH). This company was started by Ted and Lynn Hensen in 1953 with one Bell 47G. (It did not receive approval from the DOT until April 1955.) On the morning of October 17, 1957, Ted took off from Tatlayoko Lake for a five-minute flight to another camp but was never seen again. Lynn kept the company operating with the help of employees and friends and purchased a new Bell 47G-2, CF-KNC. When she went to Vancouver to discuss leasing CF-KNC to Okanagan, she met Alf Stringer. They were married in 1960, and she ran VIH largely by phone from Vancouver until Alf decided to leave Okanagan and join VIH.
- A number of Okanagan people joined VIH. **Didier Moinier** took on marketing and expansion into overseas markets. **Jim Neill** brought a wealth of S-61, IFR and heli-logging experience. **Ross McGowan** became head of maintenance and was instrumental in getting the Russian Kamov Ka-32 integrated into the company's fleet. **Bill Ross** and **Jim Stone** set up the logging operation.
- **Janice Mitchell** worked in the technical records department in King City and Montreal. Upon leaving Okanagan, she moved to the East Coast and started a career in commercial real estate, one of the first women in this field in the early 1980s. She went on to form her own company specializing in leasing office and industrial space. Later she sold a portion of her company to Colliers International, a leading global company and is still a partner.
- The Universal Helicopters Newfoundland team that was formed in 1987 when the company was purchased from Okanagan have had 29 years together, first under **Paul Williams** and now **Geoff Goodyear**. **Norm Noseworthy**, **Greg Baikie**, **Roger Sims**, **Duke Quinlan** and many others from the old days are also on the team.
- **Eric Hicks** who joined Okanagan as a technical store man in 1979 is now the regional sales director for ACRO Aerospace, which offers major support and overhaul for rotor-wing craft worldwide; it had its origins in Okanagan's engineering support division on Viking Way.
- **Harry Chernetz**, who flew for Associated before transferring to Okanagan International, was the base manager for Songkhla's Union Oil operation in Thailand before joining management. He left to start his own helicopter company based in Calgary and became involved with heli-skiing as well as international tourism contracts. In December 1999 his Bell 212 crashed in a rainstorm in the Maldives, killing 10 people including Harry.
- **Luc Pilon** started a one-man helicopter enterprise, Nipissing Helicopters, operating out of North Bay, before founding Helicopter Transport Services, based in Carp, Ontario. With more than 60 helicopters and two fixed-wing support aircraft, it is now a worldwide operation.
- **Robert Ough**, a pilot and manager, became a representative for Hughes Helicopters, McDonnell Douglas, Boeing, Eurocopter and Airbus. He was also the general manager of Canadian Air-Crane Western Canada.

I am sure there are many more good people who came from the "Orange is Really OK" mould and continued to make great contributions to the helicopter industry, and I regret not having information about them to include in this book.

Appendix III
IN MEMORIAM

Pilots killed in helicopter accidents who, at one time, flew for Okanagan:

John Anslie	Sikorsky S-58	Charlie Holmes	Sikorsky S-64
Harry Chernetz	Bell 212	Don Jacques	Sikorsky S-58T
Miro Cmirkar	Eurocopter AS 350	Frank Kearney	Bell 214ST
Roger Cyr	Bell 205	Dennis Light	(unknown)
Greg Czinkawitz	Bell 205	Mike McDonagh	Bell 214ST
Art Druet	Bell 206	Mike Maguire	Eurocopter AS 350
Glenn Fitzgerald	Hiller UH-12E	Don MacKenzie	Bell 214ST
Par Fletcher	Fairchild Hiller FH-1100	Dave Ramscar	Bell 204
Mac Forgie	Sikorsky S-76	Donny Roadhouse	Sikorsky S-58
Gary Fowlow	Bell 214ST	Emile Rogge	Aérospatiale AS 332
Jim Grady	Hiller UH-12E	Vance Schellenburg	Bell 205
John Grey	Bell 206	Vic Schreibler	Bell 206
Marko Grubac	Sikorsky S-61	Peter Steele	Bell 206
Dan Hayes	Bell 205	Ken Steele	(unknown)
Merv Hesse	Bell 205	Bert Warttig	Bell 206
Donald Honeyman	Bell 206		

Engineers: Ray Bolier, Associated, missing and presumed drowned, July 31, 1983.

Appendix IV

EARLY SENIORITY LIST

Pilots

Tom Gurr	November 1, 1951	L. (Bud) Tillotson	March 26, 1956
Tommy Scheer	January 1, 1952	Grant Soutar	January 7, 1957
E. (Bill) Brooks	January 1, 1952	Egan Agar	March 26, 1958
Reg Rivard	December 22, 1954	I.M. Bergh	May 7, 1958
Jack Milburn	January 16, 1956	Don MacKenzie	January 7, 1960
Mike McDonagh	March 26, 1956	Walter Ramsey	May 1, 1961

Engineers

Keith Rutledge	July 15, 1951	Howie Gatin	July 12, 1953
Stu Smeeth	August 1, 1951	Peter Berendt	June 2, 1964
Frank Ranger	May 21, 1951	Rod Fraser	June 2, 1952

Office Staff

Marie Dixon	February 1, 1957	Dorothy Agar	September 1, 1959

Appendix V

OKANAGAN HELICOPTER BASES AND OFFICES, 1982

Western Bases

Banff, AB
Base Manager: Keith Ostertag

Calgary, AB
Manager: Fred Clarke

Campbell River, BC
Base Manager: George Crawshaw
Engineer: Bob Hawthorne

Chetwynd, BC
Base Manager: Jim Peerenboom

Cranbook, BC
Base Manager: Rolfe Ganong

Dawson Creek, BC
Base Manager: Mike Malin

Edson, AB
Base Manager: Fred Nelson
Engineer: Tony Ellis

Fort Nelson, BC
Base Manager: Bob Batchelor

Fort St. John, BC
Base Manager: Maynard Bergh
Engineer: Mark Trainor

Fort Simpson, NWT
Base Manager: Mike Neff

Golden, BC
Base Manager: Don McTighe

Inuvik, NWT
Base Manager: Jim Hodges

Kamloops, BC
Base Manager: Lloyd Siver
Engineer: Sandy Forbes

Nelson, BC
Base Manager: Doug Williams
Pilot/Engineer: Frank Kearney

Norman Wells, NWT
Base Manager: Lee Sexsmith

Penticton, BC
Base Manager: Wayne Grover
Engineer: Ed Brown

Port McNeill, BC
Base Manager: Peter Barratt

Prince George, BC
Base Manager: Bob Coleman
Engineer: Doug Reid

Revelstoke, BC
Base Manager: Brad Wilson

Smithers, BC
Base Manager: Terry Grant
Engineer: John Innes

Terrace, BC
Base Manager: Dave Newman
Engineer: Bill Adams

Whistler, BC
Base Manager: Peter McLennan

Williams Lake, BC
Base Manager: Tom Arduini

Edmonton, AB
Associated Helicopters Ltd.
President: Rex Kaufman
Viva Warden, Tellef Vaasjo, Don Mackinnon, Ross Bradford

Eastern Bases

Bishop's Falls, NL
Universal Helicopters
Base Manager: Frank Beaton

Chibougamau, QC
Lac St. Jean Aviation
Base Manager: Tony Miguel

Dryden, ON
Dominion Pegasus Helicopters
Base Manager: Bob Gibson

Gander, NL
Universal Helicopters
Base Manager: Paul Williams,
Max Oxford & Dave Mclean

Goose Bay, NL
Universal Helicopters
Base Manager: Mike Maguire

Halifax, NS
Okanagan Helicopters
Mobil:
Base Manager: Tony Adams
Shell:
Base Manager: Didier Moinier

Milltown, NL
Base Manager: Gerard Hartery

Montreal, QC
Dorval
Base Manager: Reg Rivard
Engineer: Jim Masse

Ottawa, ON
Dominion Pegasus/
Okanagan Helicopters
Manager: Angela Lancaster

Pasadena, NL
Universal Helicopters
Base Manager: Roger Sims,
Ralph Collier, Liam Venner

St. John's, NL
Universal Helicopters
Base Manager: Gary Fowlow
Engineer: Chuck Taylor

Sept-Îles, Quebec
Sept-Îles Helicopters
Base Manager: Daniel Martin

Sudbury, ON
Dominion Pegasus Helicopters
Base Manager: Gary Gorgichuk

Thunder Bay, ON
Dominion Pegasus Helicopters
Base Manager: Rod Brownless

Endnotes

1. Blatherwick, John. *Canadian Orders, Decorations and Medals*, 5th Edition. Unitrade Press, Toronto. 2003. p. 269.
2. Corley-Smith, Peter, and David N. Parker. *Helicopters: The British Columbia Story*. Sono Nis, Victoria. pp. 14-15.
3. Ibid. p. 15.
4. Ibid. p. 90.
5. Bent, Barney. Unpublished and untitled manuscript. Unnumbered pages.
6. Ibid.
7. Corley-Smith and Parker. pp. 28-29.
8. *Canadian Aviation*. March 1949.
9. *Canadian Surveyor*. July 1949.
10. Swartz, Ken. "Jock Graham, Conversation with a Helicopter Pioneer," *Helicopters Magazine*. Issue 1 (1986): 27.
11. Corley-Smith and Parker. p. 36.
12. Ibid. pp. 37-38.
13. Swartz, Ken. p. 27.
14. Bent, Barney. Unpublished manuscript. Excerpt from chapter entitled: "Operation Helicopter at Reco Copper, 1952." Pages unnumbered.
15. Corley-Smith and Parker. p. 39.
16. Ibid. pp. 40-41.
17. Ibid. pp. 45-47.
18. Askin, Gordon. Personal interview with the author, July 2009.
19. Corley-Smith and Parker. p. 56.
20. Ibid. pp. 55-56.
21. Ibid. pp. 89.
22. Cowden, Eric. Personal interview with the author, April 2009.
23. "The Biggest Egg Beater." *Vancouver Sun*. April 24, 1952.
24. Bent, Barney.
25. Brooks, E.W. *American Helicopter*. August 1953. p. 11.
26. Cowden, Eric. Personal interview with the author, May 2009.
27. Ibid.
28. Ibid.
29. Corley-Smith and Parker. pp. 90-98.
30. Ibid. p. 99.
31. Ibid. p. 98.
32. Cowden, Eric. Personal interview with the author, May 2009.

33. Ibid.
34. Corley-Smith and Parker. p. 98.
35. Ibid. pp. 58–59.
36. Reynolds, Mac. "Air Force Flyers Learn How to Manoeuvre Flying Whales," *Vancouver Sun*. November 1955.
37. "Large Copter Is Ordered by Okanagan," *Sikorsky News*. December 1955.
38. "Okanagan s-58 is Carrying Freight to Radar Sites," *Sikorsky News*. October 16, 1956.
39. McNulty, Mike. Personal recollection by email to the author. May 26, 2016.
40. "Diary of the Sea Lift to the DEW Line: Summer 1958," Okanagan Helicopters Ltd. Internal document.
41. *American Helicopter Society Newsletter*. February 1959, p 6.
42. Delear, Frank J. "Peaks, Platforms and Pioneers," *American Helicopter Society Newsletter*. February 1959, p. 7.
43. McGowan, Ray. "The Way It Was," *RotorTales*, Volume 2, No. 6. December 1981, pp. 2–3.
44. Graham, Jock. *Okanagan Reporter*. May 1960.
45. "s-62 Acquired by Okanagan Helicopter," *Sikorsky News*. January 1961.
46. Corley-Smith and Parker. p. 87.
47. Soutar, Grant. "The Unforgiving Country," *Okanagan Newsletter*. March 1963.
48. Milburn, Jack. "Letter from East Pakistan," *Okanagan Reporter*. January 1965.
49. *Okanagan Reporter*. July 1965.
50. *Okanagan Reporter*. August 17, 1966.
51. Rutledge, Keith. "Atlantic Helicopter," *Aviation News*. June 3, 1965.
52. Gurr, Tom. "Okanagan Teaches Salmon 'Up and Over,' " *Sikorsky News*. May 1966, p. 6.
53. Millburn, Jack. Personal interview. April 2008.
54. Sikorsky, Igor. *Canada Commerce Magazine*. 1984. By permission of Sergei Sikorsky.
55. Eustice, Al. Personal recollection by email to the author. September 9, 2015.
56. Taylor, Chuck. Conversation with the author, 1978.
57. Gosling, Gordon. "We Hunted Down a Man-Killer," *Outdoor Life*. November 1970.
58. Ibid.
59. Eustice, Al. Personal recollection by email to the author. September 16, 2015.
60. Soutar, Grant. "Okanagan Lifts 131 Autos from Storm-Battered Ship," *Rotor Breeze*, Vol. 21, No. 10. May 1972, p. 1.
61. Tarvic, Jean. Interview with Michael Perrier; translation by Denise Dorosz.
62. Shannon, Owen. "Flat Light to White Out." Unpublished recollections.
63. Schabes, H. "Bill." Personal recollection by email to the author. November 17, 2010.
64. Jacques, Don. "Sydney to Songkhla and a New World Record," *Canadian Aviation*. May 1974.
65. Milburn, Jack. "A Disputed Border," *Canadian Aviation*. 1974.
66. Heap, Charlie. Personal correspondence with the author. August 11, 2014.
67. Ibid.
68. Schabes, G. "Bill." Personal correspondence with the author. November 19, 2014.
69. Yearwood, W. "Bill." Personal correspondence. January 12, 2013.
70. Schabes, G. "Bill."
71. Eustice, Al. Email correspondence with the author. September 9, 2015.

72. Simpson, Dale. Personal communication with the author, June 2010.
73. "Rotocraft Support for Sedco H," *Bee Hive*. Spring 1976, pp. 22–28.
74. "Goodbye Tellef," *RotorTales*. June 1986.
75. Vaasjo, Tellef. *Wings, Rotors and Haywire*. Unpublished manuscript on the history of Associated Helicopters. 1990.
76. Taylor, Chuck. Personal communication with the author, 1978.
77. Corley-Smith and Parker. p. 117.
78. Newman, Dave. "A Fish for the Archbishop," *Okanagan Helicopters 32nd Annual Report*. p. 1.
79. Looten, Pierre. Personal correspondence submitted by Anouk and Genevieve Looten.
80. Looten, Pierre. "Another Record Flight," *Okanagan Newsletter*. October–November 1977. p. 1.
81. *Sikorsky News*. May 5, 1979.
82. Shannon, Owen. "Tales of a Base Pilot in BC. 1977–79," Unpublished.
83. Oryschak, Wayne. Conversations based on his *Journey Log, February–May, 1979*.
84. Forbes, A. "Sandy." Personal communication with the author, March 2012.
85. McKay, Dave. Personal communication with the author, October 2012.
86. Castle, Trevor. Personal communication with the author, October 2012.
87. Neill, J. "Jim." Personal communication. Undated.
88. *Okanagan Annual Report*. 1980, p. 2.
89. MacKenzie, Don. "School for Mountain Pilots," *Professional Pilot*, January 1980. p. 28.
90. Steele, Kyle. *RotorTales*. 1980.
91. *RotorTales*. February 1981, p. 2.
92. Bhatnager, Vinay. Personal communication with the author, January 7, 2013.
93. Coalson, Tony. Personal communication with the author. Undated.
94. Shannon, Owen. Personal communication with the author, March 10, 2013.
95. Trann, Doug. *RotorTales*. September 1980, p. 2.
96. Klohn, Randy and Dale Fleming. S-76 C-GMQD. Aircraft Incident Report. September 26, 1981.
97. Klohn, Randy. Email correspondence with author, March 8, 2010.
98. Letter from W.L. Mason. Reprinted in *RotorTales*. April 1982, p. 2.
99. "Avalanche," *RotorTales*. February 1982, p. 5.
100. "International Operations," *RotorTales*. April 1982, p. 4.
101. Riccardo, Rudi. Conversation with the author, June 1982.
102. Melady, John. *Heartbreak and Heroism: Canadian Search & Rescue Stories*. Dundurn Press, 1997. p. 120.
103. Dixon Terry. *RotorTales*. June 1983, p. 7.
104. Melady, John. p. 121.
105. Ibid. p. 122.
106. Ibid. p. 122–3.
107. Ibid.
108. Bernard, Phil. Interview with the author, September 2008.
109. Castle, Trevor. Personal communication with the author, May 2013.
110. Shaw, John. Letter in *RotorTales*. December 1984, p. 6.
111. Long, Ed. "Pilot Training in China," *RotorTales*. March 1984, p. 1.
112. Hessberger, Joe. "Ferry Flight," *RotorTales*. December 1984, p. 8.
113. Corley-Smith and Parker. p. 87.
114. Rivard, Reg. *RotorTales*. May 1985, p. 1.

115. MacKenzie, Don. *RotorTales*. May 1985, p. 1.
116. *RotorTales*. December 1985, p. 2.
117. Shannon, Owen. Personal communication with the author, May 8, 2011.
118. "CHC Helicopter Corporation," *RotorTales*. July 1987, p. 3.
119. Ganong, Rolfe. *RotorTales*. March 1986, p. 7.
120. Aldous, Pat. *RotorTales*. May 1980, p. 7.
121. *RotorTales*. May 1985.
122. Reid, Jim. *RotorTales*. June 1986, p. 2.
123. Stone, Barry. *RotorTales*. March 1980, p. 3.
124. Utting, Aubrey. *RotorTales*. September 1985, p. 2.
125. Vanslyke, Gerry. *RotorTales*. December 1983, p. 3.
126. Yearwood, W. "Bill." Personal communication with the author, January 12, 2013.

Glossary

ADF   automatic direction finder; an airborne navigation aid that works with a ground station and gives direction and station identifier.

ADI   attitude direction indicator, also known as gyro horizon or artificial horizon; it provides pilots with orientation to Earth's horizon and indicates pitch, fore and aft, and bank from side to side. It is the primary instrument for meteorological conditions.

AFC   Air Force Cross; military decoration awarded to personnel of the UK and Commonwealth countries for an act of valour while flying in a non-active operation.

AFCS   automatic flight control system; a system used to control aircraft or marine vehicles allowing crew to focus on other aspects of flight or voyage. AFCS was first developed for aircraft by Sperry Corporation in 1912.

Alcan   Aluminum Company of Canada.

Allison   an American manufacturer of both fixed-wing and helicopter engines.

AME   aircraft-maintenance engineer.

ATB   Air Transportation Board, a Canadian federal government agency.

ATD   anti-torque device; a tail rotor that is mounted vertically on the tail boom and counters the torque effect of the main rotors.

Autorotation   a state in flight in which the main rotor system in a helicopter or auto gyro uses the action of the air rather than engine power to land.

Avionics   aviation electronics; the term covers all aspects of aviation electronics including electrical systems, instruments, communication, navigation, radar, autopilot and inflight entertainment.

B-36   a long-range bomber built by Consolidated Vultee Aircraft Corporation, also known as the Convair B-26 Peacemaker. It was built for USAF from 1949 to 1959. It was the first aircraft capable of delivering nuclear weapons.

BCATP   British Commonwealth Air Training Plan; a training system implemented in Canada to train RAF and Commonwealth aircrew during World War II.

BEA   British European Airways, an airline started in 1946 and amalgamated with British Overseas Airways Corporation (BOAC) to form British Airways.

C-130   a military four-engine turboprop transport aircraft, built by Lockheed; first flown August 23, 1954.

CAA   Civil Aviation Authority; a US government authority that regulates civil aviation.

CAVU   ceiling and visibility unlimited.

CBE   Commander of the British Empire; a Commonwealth award for service.

CHC Canadian Holding Company; CHC took over Okanagan Helicopters in 1987.

CHO Canadian Helicopters Overhaul, a division formed in 1968 by Okanagan to maintain and overhaul helicopter engines and components.

Collective a control usually located on the left side of the pilot's seat that changes the pitch angle of all the main rotor blades all at the same time, increasing or decreasing lift.

Copter Cabs a subsidiary of Okanagan Helicopters set up to provide commuter services for the Greater Vancouver area using a Bell 47J-2.

CPA Canadian Pacific Airlines; it was based in Vancouver and operated from 1942 until 1987.

CW Continuous Wave; a method of transmitting a radio signal, e.g. Morse code.

Cyclic Control a control located in the helicopter between the pilot's legs that changes the pitch angle of the individual rotor blades to control forward, backward, left, right and hover motion.

Dash 7 the de Havilland Canada DHC-7; a four-engine turboprop regional airliner with short takeoff and landing capabilities.

David Clark A US company that made helmets with headphones for Boeing B-17 crews in World War II. Originally an undergarment manufacturer, they became the main suppliers for aerospace protection equipment, space suits and noise-cancelling headsets.

DC-3 Douglas Aircraft Company's DC-3 Dakota is a twin-engine, propeller-driven airliner and transport aircraft, which first flew December 17, 1935. It is estimated that 78 are still flying worldwide.

DEW Distant Early Warning Line; a line of radar stations running from Alaska through the Canadian Arctic to Greenland; it was operational from 1957 to 1985.

DME an airborne navigation aid that measures time and distance from a ground beacon using line of sight (slant angle) with a Morse code identifier. Information is displayed on the DME indicator or primary navigation panel in cockpit.

EFTS Elementary Flying Training School. Under the British Commonwealth Air Training Plan, 36 EFTSs were set up to train pilots from Britain and Commonwealth countries.

ELT emergency location transmitter; a distress beacon fitted to all fixed-wing and helicopters that fly in Canadian airspace. It is activated manually or by G forces.

EPA Eastern Provincial Airways, a St. John's–based airline started in 1949 to provide charters, air ambulances and mail and cargo services, using a combination of fixed-wing craft and helicopters. In 1960 EPA started regular passenger services throughout the Maritimes and Quebec using Boeing 737-200s; it was bought by CPA in 1986.

FAA Federal Aviation Agency; a US federal agency formed in 1958 as the Federal Aviation Administration. The current name was adopted in 1966.

False hemlock looper *Nepytia freemani*, a moth native to North America. The larvae feed on the foliage of hemlock, Douglas fir, balsam, spruce and oak.

FTS Flying Training School; these were part of the BCATP for advanced flying training, which included eight weeks intermediate and six weeks advanced training with bombing and gunnery school.

G-force a measurement of acceleration causing weight. The G-force of a stationary object on the earth's surface is 1G; weightlessness in space or free fall in a vacuum is zero G.

GE General Electric; the developer of turbine engines for US military helicopters in the 1960s; the company later came out with variants for commercial use.

GPS   Global Positioning System; a satellite-based navigation system made up of 24 satellites. GPS receivers lock onto a minimum of three satellites to calculate latitude, longitude, altitude, speed, bearing, distance to destination, etc.

Gyroplane   a type of rotorcraft that uses an unpowered rotor in autorotation to develop lift.

HAA/HAI   Helicopter Association of America. It was started in 1948 as the Professional Helicopter Association of America, changed its name to Helicopter Association of America and then to Helicopter Association International.

HF Radio   High Frequency radio used for long-distance communication, operating in frequency range of three to 30 megahertz. The signals are bounced off the upper ionosphere.

Hot refuelling   a method of refuelling while aircraft engines are running.

HSI   horizontal situation indicator, an aircraft instrument normally mounted below the attitude indicator to give the pilot heading information along with VHF omnidirectional range (VOR) navigation and instrument landing system information (ILS).

HUSS   helicopter underslung spray system.

IFR   instrument flight rules; regulations established by aviation authorities to govern flight conditions when visual reference is unsafe.

ILS   instrument landing system; a radio navigation aid that provides pilots with vertical and horizontal references prior to landing at a fixed point on the runway. The ILS receiver picks up two radio signals, one vertical (glide

IMC   Instrument meteorological conditions; the aviation flight category that describes active weather conditions that require the pilot to fly the primary instruments under IFR. slope) and one horizontal (localizer), which are displayed by two needles. The pilot keeps these two crossed to indicate the aircraft is on the centre of the approach path.

LOREX   Lomonosov Ridge Experiment.

LST   landing ship tank; the naval designation for a vessel created during World War II to support amphibious operations. After the war they were sold to the private sector, and many of them were converted for use in the High Arctic.

McKee Trophy   also known as the Trans-Canada Trophy; it is awarded by the Canadian Aeronautical and Space Institute to citizens who have made an outstanding achievement in aerospace. It was first awarded in 1927; it was awarded to Carl Agar in 1950.

MCL   Mid-Canada Line; a line of 90 unmanned radar stations running across Canada to provide early warning of a Soviet bomber attack. The line stretched from Dawson Creek, BC, to Hopedale, Labrador. It was operated from 1958 until 1965 when new technology made it redundant.

MOT   Ministry of Transport.

NFDF   Newfoundland Department of Fisheries.

NTSB   National Transport Safety Board; an independent agency of the government of Canada, responsible for transport safety. The NTSB investigates accidents and makes recommendations concerning aviation, rail, marine services and pipelines.

OAS   Okanagan Air Services. It was started in 1946 in Penticton and became Okanagan Helicopters Ltd. in 1952.

Omega   first truly global radio navigation system, operated by the US in cooperation with six partners. It enabled ships and aircraft to determine their position by very low frequency signals in the 10–14 kHz range. It was replaced in 1997 by GPS.

P&W Pratt & Whitney, an American aircraft engine manufacturer with a Canadian division in Quebec.

PIA Pakistan International Airlines.

Pitch the pitch axis is perpendicular to the aircraft centre line and lies in the plane of the wings or rotor blades. The pitch motion is up and down, controlled in a helicopter by the cyclic and in fixed-wing aircraft by the elevator.

PT6 a turboshaft engine developed for both fixed-wing and helicopters. It was introduced in 1963 in Beechcraft King Air. In 1968 Bell Helicopters ordered the first turboshaft twin pack and in 1970 installed it in a Bell 212.

PWA Pacific Western Airlines operated scheduled flights in western and northern Canada and international charters from 1950 to 1987. PWA purchased CPA in 1987 and formed Canadian Airlines International Ltd.

QCA Queen Charlotte Airlines; this company flew fixed-wing land and float planes on Canada's West Coast. It was founded in 1946 and bought by PWA in 1955.

QFE Atmospheric Pressure (Q) at Field Elevation (Aviation). The barometric pressure setting causes an altimeter to read zero in reference to an airfield.

QFI qualified flying instructor.

QNSL Quebec North Shore and Labrador Railway; a private, 257-mile-long (414-kilometre) regional railway that was started in 1954; it is now part of the Iron Ore Company of Canada.

Roll rotation about an axis aligned with the direction in which the aircraft is flying; it is known as the longitudinal axis (left or right axis).

Rotor part of a machine that rotates around a central point. A helicopter rotor system is a combination of a number of rotor blades and a central control system that generates aerodynamic lift.

Scintillometer a device used to measure small fluctuations or refractive indices of air caused by variations in temperature, humidity and pressure.

SEBJ Société d'énergie de la Baie James was the company that began building the huge hydroelectric development known as the James Bay Project in 1971. In 1978 it became a wholly owned subsidiary of Hydro-Québec.

Sedco Aquila Sedco Drilling Co., a US oil and gas company with headquarters in Wichita Falls, Texas.

Shp shaft horsepower.

Sikorsky Sikorsky Aircraft Corporation is a US manufacturer based in Stratford, Connecticut. It was established by Igor Sikorsky in 1925 and originally specialized in multi-engine, fixed-wing aircraft, both land and amphibious.

Sud-Nord Sud Aviation was a French aircraft manufacturer that merged with Nord Aviation to form Aérospatiale in 1970, eventually becoming part of the international consortium of British Aerospace and Messerschmitt-Bölkow-Blom known as Airbus Industries.

TAS true airspeed; it indicates airspeed under standard sea-level conditions. TAS is usually calculated by adjusting an indicated air speed according to air temperature, density and pressure.

TCA Trans-Canada Air Lines. Created as a crown corporation in 1937, it was renamed Air Canada in 1964 and privatized in 1989.

Torque a twisting gyroscopic force acting in opposition to an axis of rotation such as a turning rotor or propeller.

Transponder an airborne pulsed transceiver that responds to a ground-based interrogator signal to provide air traffic control with the accurate position and altitude of an aircraft.

Unicom   a VHF radio frequency usually in the 121.0 mHz range that is used in uncontrolled air space.

VFR   visual flight rules; the procedure for conducting flight under visual conditions. Pilots also use it to indicate to air traffic their specific flight plan.

VHF   very high frequency; this is the radio frequency range from 118–137 mHz that is used by air traffic control. The transmitter antenna and receiver must be in a line of sight to operate—the higher the altitude the longer the range.

VOR   VHF omnidirectional radio range; a ground-based navigational aid that works in conjunction with an airborne receiver. The ground station transmits a fixed signal north with a second signal transmitted over 360 degree radials. At one-degree segments the airborne receiver compares the phase differences to provide direction and heading. The signal can also include a Morse code identification or voice transmission; it is normally displayed on a VOR indicator or horizontal situation indicator.

VXU 215   the radio dispatch call sign used at Okanagan Helicopter operations.

Weather Radar   a pulsed radar transceiver that shows pilots the weather conditions ahead. Weather conditions are shown in colour, with red indicating severe weather that should be avoided. Weather radars used in helicopters include a beacon mode that identifies targets such as oil rigs and indicates miles from target.

WX   an abbreviation for weather.

Yaw   one of three axes in flight, which is nose left or nose right in an aircraft. In fixed-wing aircraft it is controlled using the rudder while helicopters use the tail rotor and anti-torque pedals.

Bibliography

Bell, Gordon. *History of Aviation in the BC Forest Service*. Forest Service, British Columbia, August 2011.
Bent, Barney. "The Early Days." Personal notes and taped interview. Donated by Kevin Bent, July 2010.
Blatherwick, F.J. Surgeon Commander. *Canadian Orders, Decorations and Medals*. The Unitrade Press, Toronto, ON, 2003.
Bristow, Alan and Patrick Malone. *Alan Bristow: Helicopter Pioneer*. Pen & Sword Books, Barnsley, South Yorkshire, UK, 2009.
Chartres, John. *Helicopter Rescue*. Ian Allen Printing Ltd., Shepperton, Surrey, UK, 1980.
Corley-Smith, Peter and David N. Parker. *Helicopters: The British Columbia Story*. Sono Nis Press, Victoria, BC, 1998 ed.
———. *Helicopters in the High Country*. Sono Nis Press, Victoria, BC, 1995.
Fredlund, Manley. *Skydancing: High Adventure with Helicopters*. Hancock House Publishers, Surrey, BC, 1990.
Healey, Andrew. *Leading from the Front: Bristow Helicopters, the First 50 years*. Tempus Publishing, Stroud, Gloucestershire, UK, 2003.
Jackson, Robert. *Aviation Factfile: Helicopters: Military, Civilian and Rescue Rotorcraft*. Amber Books, London, UK, 2007.
Melady, John. *Heartbreak and Heroism: Canadian Search and Rescue Stories*. Dundurn Press, Toronto, ON, 1997.
Reynolds, John Lawrence. *One Hell of a Ride*. Douglas & McIntyre, Vancouver, BC, August 2009.
Weir, Charles O. and Leonard Taylor. *Vertical Ascent: Adventures of a Helicopter Pilot*. Hancock House Publishers Ltd., Surrey, BC, 1977.
Vaasjo, Tellef. "Wings, Rotors and Haywire." Unpublished manuscript about Associated Helicopters, 1990.

Journal Articles

Alder, Diane. "Okanagan Helicopters," *Canadian Wings*, Vol. 12, No. 10. October 1970.
Brooks, E.W. "Okanagan's Aerial Elevators Speed Big Alcan Project," Pt. 1, *American Helicopter*, August 1953.
———. "Okanagan Aerial Elevators," Pt. 2, *American Helicopter*, September 1953.

Corley-Smith, Peter. "Okanagan to Canadian," *West Coast Aviator*. November/December 1996.

———. "Jumping off the Cliff," *The Aviator: Aviation in Canada*, May 2001.

Keith, Ronald A. "Okanagan Helicopters," *Esso Air World*, Vol. 32, No. 2. 1980.

McLean, H.E. "Okanagan Helicopters' Copter College," *Vertical World Magazine*, October 1966.

Porter, McKenzie. "How Carl Agar Became the Helicopter King," *McLean's Magazine*, July 23, 1955.

Staples, Don & LeGuilloux, A. "Rotor Review British Columbia," *Western Wings*, vol. 6, No. 5. May 1964.

Thornber, R.C. "Okanagan—A Company Profile," *Rotor & Wings*, October 1967.

Wilkey, M. "Pioneers in Rotary Wing," *British Columbia Aviation Council 60th Anniversary 1938-1998*.

Wilson, Brian. "Archivos," *Newsletter of the Okanagan Archives Trust Society*. Fall 2008.

Wolfe-Milner, Terry. "Interview with John Lecky of Okanagan Helicopters," *Helicopters Canada*. Fall 1982.

NO AUTHORS LISTED:

"The Alcan Project," *Western Construction*, November 1953–March 1954.

"Copters Open a New Bush Flying Era," *Canadian Aviation*, June 1957.

"Fast Access to the Inaccessible," *British Columbia Business Journal*, November–December 1968.

"Helicopter Briefing. Okanagan's FH-1100," *Fairchild Hiller Corporation*, Germantown, Maryland. No. 7. 1967–68.

"Rotors," *Canadian Wings*, Vol. 11, No. 5. May 1969.

Okanagan Reporter and RotorTales: Okanagan Newsletters. 40th Anniversary Issue. Vol. 6. No. 1. April, 1987.

Okanagan Helicopters Annual Reports. 1958–82.

Other Reference Material

Carl Agar's Vertical Flight. CBC documentary, c. 1960s

Okanagan Pioneers & Places, episode #310, "Okanagan Helicopters." CHBC, Kelowna, BC, July 2009.

Personal Interviews

Egan Agar, Sorrento, BC. September 23, 2010
Gordon Askin, Tsawwassen, BC. May 14, 2009
Jean Baine, North Delta, BC. September 25, 2009
Murray Bale, Ailsa Craig, ON. June 8, 2010
Phil Bernard, Victoria, BC. September 4, 2009
Vinay Bhatnagar, London, ON. June 7, 2010
Leslie Birch, Surrey, BC. April 17, 2010
Pierre Bock, Prince George, BC. June 20, 2011
Wally Boyle, Duncan, BC. September 15, 2008
Jim Campbell, South Delta, BC. August 23, 2009
Alec Calder, Elora, ON. June 8, 2010
Trevor Castle, Ladner, BC. March 14, 2009
Eric Cowden, Saanich, BC. September 5, 2009
Sandy Forbes, White Rock, BC. April 3, 2010
Jack Milburn, Prince George, BC. June 20, 2011
Edna MacKenzie, Tsawwassen, BC. April 4, 2009
John McIntyre, Elora, ON. June 8, 2010
Jim Neill, Richmond, BC. October 29, 2010
Reg Rivard, Ladner, BC. March 5, 2009
Jan Rustad, Penticton, BC. September 22, 2010
Owen Shannon, by e-mail, March 10, 2013
Lloyd Siver, Kamloops, BC. September 25, 2010
Anna May Stringer, Egmont, BC. June 12, 2009
Lynn Stringer, Victoria, BC. September 14, 2008
Ray Williamson, Victoria, BC. September 14, 2008
Bill Yearwood, Richmond, BC. November 16, 2010

Acknowledgements

This book came about because of a chat with John Edwards and Bob Farrow over coffee at a small air-side café after I had related (yet again) one of my stories about my days with Okanagan Helicopters. One of them suggested I write this book, but I felt sure it had already been done. When I checked, I found that the only information on the company was in Corley-Smith and Parker's *Helicopters: the British Columbia Story*, which covered the 1950s. That got me started.

When I initially approached the BC Archives at the Royal BC Museum in Victoria, to my surprise they found only a few photographs. On a visit to Ottawa I spoke to the chief librarian at the Canada Aviation and Space Museum to see if they had anything and was told that at the time of the takeover all the archival information had been thrown into a dumpster. After further phone calls to old colleagues, I learned that some ex-Okanagan staff members had gathered up 35 boxes of files and then shipped them to the BC Archives for safekeeping with instructions that they were to be sealed until 2015. When I again contacted the Archives and explained I wanted to document the company's history, they allowed me access to the boxes. As a result, I made several trips to Victoria over a number of months. I'd like to thank the staff at the BC Archives at the Royal BC Museum in Victoria, especially Bob Griffin and Katy Hughes, for their kindness and assistance. I'd also like to thank Tara Hurley at the Okanagan Heritage Museum's Kelowna Archives for access to interview material and for her help with photographs.

Brent Wallace gave me access to the Okanagan Helicopters material in his possession, John Larsen the copies of *RotorTales*, and Gordy Askin photographs and journals. Kevin Bent gave me both his father's notes and a CD of a conversation with his father, Barney, about the early days. Lynn Stringer gave me Alf's logbook which includes the notation about the first landing in Penticton on August 9, 1947, and many other interesting items. Without their help I could not have started.

Special thanks also goes to the many colleagues and their families for their contributions and for allowing me to include their stories: Alec Calder, Anouk and Genevieve Looten, Al Eustice, Anna May Stringer, Bill Foote, Bill Schabes, Bob Heighington of Associated Helicopters, Bruce Hutchinson, Bill Turner, Bill Yearwood, Chuck Roberts, Chuck Taylor, Charlie Heap, Dale Simpson, Dev Anderson, Dick Everson, Dave McKay, Didier Moinier, Eric Cowden, Egan Agar, Edna MacKenzie, Geoff Goodyear, Jean Baine, Jim Neill, Robert Ough, Josie Knight, John McIntyre, Jan Rustad, Kevin Parkin, Lloyd Siver, Leslie Birch, Mark Christie, Murray Bale, Owen Shannon, Reg Rivard, Randy Klohn, Pierre Bock, Phil Love, Phil Bernard, Pucci Basso, Ray Williamson, Sandy Forbes, Walter Ramsey, Wally Boyle, Wayne Grover, Vinay Bhatnagar, Mike McNulty and Vic Corrie.

ACKNOWLEDGEMENTS

Thanks also to authors John Melady and Pat Martin for allowing me to quote from their books and to Jack Schofield for his encouragement. Others deserving mention are photographers Bob Crocker and Graham Cowley and aviation artist Arthur Cox as well as Dave Roberts who provided technical assistance. Thank you also to Linda Cunningham for all her help with the photographs used in this book and to Dave Schwartzenberger and the staff at HNZ Topflight. Not to forget Gerry Corley-Smith and Diane Morris from Sono Nis Press for their assistance with *Helicopters: The British Columbia Story*.

Additional thanks go to Société d'énergie de la Baie James, Sylvie Marten of CHBC News, Don Smith of Panarctic Oils, the University of Saskatchewan's Archives & Special Collections and Sergei Sikorsky and Vinney Devine of Igor I. Sikorsky Historical Archives. Photos obtained from the Royal BC Museum and Archives for this book come from unprocessed records in accession 90-9692, now described as PR-1842.

My special thanks go to Howard White and the staff at Harbour Publishing and to editor Betty Keller for all their work.

Finally, many thanks to my wife, Shannon. She has remained patient with all my changes and has been a great support throughout this big project.

Wherever possible, I have tried to identify the source of the material and give full accreditation. Any omissions are unintentional and I would be pleased to correct any oversight.

If I have missed anyone, I do apologize.

DMG
June 2016.

Index

Numbers in **bold** refer to photos or maps

accidents and crashes, 53-54, 75, 214
    accident investigation, 79
    fatalities, 77, 125, 173-74, 191, 204-5, 234
    Florida crash, 195-96, **xx**
    Kemano project, 42-**43**-45
    Ocean Ranger sinking, 179-80
    spraying demonstration, 20-**21**-**22**
    See also search and rescue operations
Adams, Tony, 223
Aérospatiale, 181
    Alouette, 82
    AS 332 Super Pumas, 165, 217
Agar, Carlyle Clare (Carl, CA), 9, 37, **56**
    aerial spraying, 20-**21**-**22**-23
    as expert, 39-40, 46-**47**-48, 65
    developed training, 34-35
    early years, **12**-14, 15, **16**
    growing the company, 27-28, 29-31, 33
    honoured, 96, 214
    later years, 75, 77, 80, 91, 96
    launching OAS, 17-**19**-**20**
    mountain flying, **24**-27
Agar, Dorothy, 13, 223
Agar, Egan (son of CA), 13, 71, 103, **222**, 224
    Florida crash, 195-96, **xx**
Aguay, Jorge, 195-96
air ambulance. *See under* search and rescue operations
Aitken, Pat, 18, 24
    See also Kemano Project
Aldous, Pat, 146, 179-80, 216, 232
Alpine Helicopters, 225, 232
Aluminum Company of Canada (Alcan), 30-31, 33
Anderson, Dev, 158-59, 160-61, 167, 198

arctic operations, **ii–iii**, **v–vi**, **ix**, **xxi–xxiii**
    DEW Line support, 64, 66-67, 196
    GIUK gap support, **219-20**, **xxiii–xxiv**
    polar bear tagging, 123, 156, **xi**
    Polar Continental Shelf Program, 131, **156-57**-58, 215, **viii**, **xi–xii**
    "Sealift" operation, 69
    surveys, 59-60, 77
    Tuktoyaktuk, 66, 69, **xv**, **xix**
    weather, 207-8
    See also petroleum operations
Askin, Gordon (Gordy), 41, 96
    Kemano Project, 44-**45**, **48**-49
Associated Helicopters, **135**, 173, 183, 191, **vii**
    merged into CHC, 220-21
    history, **131-32**-**33**-34
    survey support, **129-30**

Baikie, Greg, 233
Bale, Murray, 207
Barr, Bert, 213
Barratt, Peter, 232
Battick, Marty, **vi**
Bell Helicopter Corporation, 26-27, 45, 49, 50
    at convention, 73
    Bell 30, **17**
    Bell 412, 165
    J-2, **153**
Bell 47, **48**, **51**, **67**, **105**, **129**, **ii**, **xxiii**
    B-3, 19-**20**, **21**-**22**, **24**-**25**, 34, **43**
    description of, 17, 25
    issues and upgrades, 39, 46
    other models, 27, 50, 67, 69, **130**, **vii–ix**
    replacement, 106

Bell 200 series, **156**, **VI**–**VIII**, **X**–**XIV**
    204B, **90**–91, 106, **107**, **III**, **V**, **VI**
    206 JetRanger, 100, 112, 165
    206A JetRanger, 94, 99, **100**–102
    206L LongRanger, 189
    212, 101, **X**, **XV**, **XXIII**
    214, 158–59, 165, **XXII**
    JetRanger 2, 104–5
Bent, Arnold H. (Barney), 26, 27–28, **I**
    early years, 14–15
    launching OAS, 13, 16, 18
Berendt, Peter, 63–64, 200–201, 224
Bernard, Philip (Phil), **195**, 207
Biggs, Dick, 92–93
Bolier, Ray, 191
Boyko, John, 232
Boyle, Wally, 98, 205
Brinston, Woody, 120–21, 180, **VIII**
British European Airways (BEA) Helicopters, 50, 87–89
Brooks, Bill, **44**, 47, 75
Brown, Gordy, 232
Buckerfield, Ernest (Ernie), 18
Butler, Gordon, 18

Calder, Alec, 155, 210
Cameron, Ev, 72, 83–87, 224
Canadian Helicopters Ltd., 58, 62–**63**, 76, 216
Canadian Helicopters Overhaul, 96, 99
Carlson, Ada, 39
Castle, Trevor, 160, 198
Cessna, 16, 68, 73–74
Chamberlain, George, **44**, 57–60
Charleson, Jack, 58
CHC Helicopter Corporation, 216–18, 220–**21**
Chernetz, Harry, 233
Coalson, Tony, 146, **169**, 171–72, **XIII**
Coggan, F.D., 136, **IX**
Collins, Ted, 224
Copter Cabs, 79, 81
Cornwall, Pete, 41, 49, 50
Corrie, Vic, 148–49
Cowden, Eric, 47, 50–53, 54–55, 210
Cowley, Graham, **171**

Davies, Jim, 152, 189, 199
de Havilland
    Beaver, 54, **135**
    Tiger Moth, 14, **16**
Dewar, Douglas, 18, 28, 31, 33, 67

Dixon, Terry, 160, 161, 189–**91**, 197
Dobbin, Craig Lawrence, 217–18
Dominion Pegasus (DomPeg), 120, 130, 138, 139, 175, 215
    history, 117–18
Douglas, Austin, **VI**
Duncan, Andy, 16, 18, 23, 27–28
Duncan, Ian, 46, 53–54, 62, 210

Eagleston, Dave, 106, 119, 161
Eastern Provincial Airways (EPA), 72, 95, 105
Eilertson, Fred "Tweedy," 47, 49, 61–62, 90
Eissfeldt, Terry, 232
Ellis, Tony, 232
Emerson, Gerry, 25–26, 35–36
Eustice, Al, 97, 106, 122, 160
Everson, Dick, 166, 209, 232

Fairchild Hiller. *See under* Hiller Helicopters
Fairey Aviation Rotodyne, 66, 68, 74, **II**
Foote, Bill, 69–71, 77
Forbes, Sandy, 158–59
forestry operations, 92, 122, 166, **XI**, **XIII**
    firefighting, 67, 80, **135**, 150, 174, 204, 212
    heli-logging, 27, 106, 114, 154, 159–62, 197
    innovations, 78–79, 82, 114, 211, 204
    inventory, 60
    seeding bait, 50
    See also Okanagan Heli-logging
Forgie, Malcolm (Mac), 187, **VIII**
Fortier, Y.O., 59–60
Foster, Jim, 79, 81
Fowlow, Gary, 180, 204
Fraser, Rod, 47, 96

Ganong, Rolfe, 149, 224–25
Godsey, Jack, **67**, 229
Goodyear, Geoff, 183, 233
Grady, Jim, 78–79, 205, 227, 234
Graham, John Fraser (Jock), 37, 47–48, **52**
    fixed s-55 issue, 56–57
    joining OAS, 33–34
    Kemano Project, 41, **44**, 45
Grant, Douglas M., 11, 127, 136–39, 197, 200–201
    international travel, 162–63, 169–70, 177–78
Grey, John, 139, 234

Grover, Wayne, 182, 213, 225
Gurr, Tommy, 47, 91, 106, 120

Hague, Kelly, 147
Haida Helicopters Ltd., 109
Harrison, Tom, 88–89
Hartmire, George, 111–14
Heap, Charlie, 118–20
helicopter industry, 31, 41, 50, 68, 82, 99, 214
    decline of, 180, 188, 196, 203, 211
helicopters, 30, 50, 68, 73–74
    See also Aérospatiale; Bell Helicopter Corporation; Cessna; Hiller Helicopters; Sikorsky Helicopters
Hélicoptères Canadiens, 93, 110, 115, 139
Henderson, Bill, 124–25
Hern, M., 66–67
Heslop, Wilfred, 30–31, 41
Hessberger, Joe, 193, 202–3
Hesse, Merv, 125
Hicks, Eric, 233
Hill, Lois, 206
Hiller Helicopters, 39–40, 68
    Fairchild Hiller FH-1100, 93–**94**, 98–99
    UH-12A, 50
    UH-12E, 73–74, **76**
Hoban, Linda, **94**
Hook, Jack, 132, 183
Hoover, Max, 103, 149, 225
Hubenig, Sig, 36, 55, 58
Hughes (company), 73, 93
Hull, Keith, **VI**

Innes, John, 198–99
International Helicopters, 83, 87
international operations, 162, **168**, **V**–**VII**, **X**, **XIX**
    Australia, 134, 176–77, 194–95, 213
    Canada-Thailand flight, 115–**16**–17
    Central and South America, 120–22, 148, 202–3, **VII**
    China, 173, 201–2, 203, 209–10
    competition, 194–95, 203
    Europe, 87–89, 108, 134, 139–46
    Europe-Canada flight, 146–47
    India, 147, 168–**69**–70, 177–78, 183–87, 208–9
    Norfolk Island crossing, 139, **X**
    Oman, 187–88

international operations (cont.)
    Pakistan, 83-87
    Philippines, 118-20, 122, 172-73, 178, **x**
    Thailand, 115-**116**, 139, **169**, 213, **xiii,
        xv-xvii**
    Vietnamese refugees, **171**-72, 215-16
    See also arctic operations

Jacques, Don, **95**, **116**, 125, 205
James Bay (SEBJ) Project, 109, 114-15, 138-39
Janicke, Bill, **76**, 116-17
Jaworski, Jack, 195-96, **x**
Jeffries, Diane, **94**
Johnson, A.L., 28, 31, 39
Johnson, Kathy, 149
Jones, James C. (J.C.), 217

Kaufman, Rex, 131, 134, 183
Kearney, Frank, 147, 155, 171, 199, 204
Kemano Project, **47**-50, 55, 56
    early days, 41-**42**-44-**45**-46
    preparations, 38-39
Kennedy, Ian, 97, 103, 108
Kennedy, Sean, 206-7
Kenting Aviation, 27, 40, 58
Klohn, Randy, 175-76

Lac St. Jean Aviation, 109, 110, 115
Lannon, Leo, 37-38, 58
Lecky, John, 179, 217
LeGrice, Fred, 92-93, 97
Lennox, Ross, 88-89
Long, Ed, 201-2
Looten, Pierre, 123, 192, 210, 231, **x**
LOREX project, 156-**57**, **viii**
Lunan, Jack, 191
Lyon, Robert, **16**

Macauley, Arnie, 189-91
McDonagh, Mike, 53-54, 82-83, 92-93, 198
    death, 205
McGowan, Ray, 69-71
McGowan, Ross, 233
MacIntosh, Daryl, 232
McIntyre, John, 98, 124, **xxi**
MacKenzie, Don, 78, 98, 103, 174, 205-6
MacKenzie, W.J. (Bill), 29-30
McLean, Davey, 120, 225-26

McLeod, Bill, **47**, 57-58, 61, 64
    Kemano Project, 41-45
    training with Carl Agar, 34-35
McLeod, Joan, 42, 44
McMinn, Ernie, 26
McNulty, John, 63-64
McPherson, Glenn, 46-47, **56**, 61, 77, 97
Madill, Lock (Locky), **44**, 49
manuals and training, 27, 31, 34, 39
    survival training, 173
    See also Mountain Flying School
Marshall, James, 16, 19-20
Marshall, Sherry, 226
Mil Helicopters, **95**, **xix**
Milburn, Jack, **67**, 92, 117, 226
    East Pakistan (Bangladesh), 83-87
Ministry of Transport (MOT), 47, 65, 152,
    193-94
Mitchell, Janice, 233
Moinier, Didier and Maxine, 220, 233
Moore, Fred, 121, 226
Mountain Flying School, 40, 56, 72, 95,
    xiv-xv
    publicity for, 60-61, 92-93, 166-67
    training manual, 229

Neill, Jim, 160-62, 233, **xv, xxi-xxii**
Newman, Dave, 136
Niwranski, Harry, 232
Noseworthy, Norman (Norm), **105**, 233

Okanagan Air Services (OAS), 33-35, 39-40
    aerial spraying, 19-**21**-**22**-25, 27
    becomes Okanagan Helicopters, 46
    formation of, **16**-18
    Fraser River flood, **23**-24
    mining operations, 28-30, 37
    Palisades dam project, 31-33, 37-38
    survey support, 25-27, 29-31, 35-37
    See also Kemano Project; Mountain
        Flying School
Okanagan Helicopters, 9, 46, **50**
    acquisitions, 58, 62, 72, 105, 109
    base and facilities, 92, 165
    becomes CHC Helicopter Corporation,
        216-18
    downsizing, 196, 211
    innovations, 10, 78-79, 95, 99, 114
    internal restructuring, 77, 80, 97
    largest commercial operator, 64-65

    ownership changes, 179, 203
    staff reunion (2004), 220-21
    subsidiaries, 56, 105-6, 117-18
    See also accidents and crashes;
        Associated Helicopters; Canadian
        Helicopters Overhaul; CHC
        Helicopters Corporation;
        Okanagan Air Services
Okanagan Helicopters, operations, 198, 207
    beaver survey, 57
    CN Tower installation, 130-31, **viii**
    commuter service, 74, 76-77, 79, 214
    construction, 167
    crane dismantling, 122-23
    fishing, 136, 154, 174, 211
    heli-skiing, **153**-**4**, 181-82
    Mid-Canada Line, 60, 63, 78, 80, 90
    mining operations, 62, 89, 131, 136, 174
    movie production, 110, 197
    "Operation Skyhook," 68-69
    orca relocation, **128**-30, **viii**
    SEBJ Project (James Bay Project), 109,
        114-15, 138-39
    See also arctic operations; forestry oper-
        ations; international operations;
        Kemano Project; petroleum
        industry; search and rescue
        operations
Okanagan (OK) Heli-Logging, 122, 135-36,
    159-62, 166, 197
    See also forestry operations
O'Neill, Dave, 108, 140-46
Orr, D.K. "Deke," 37, 41, **48**, 49
Oryschak, Wayne, 158, **xii**
Ostrander, Paul, 31-32
Ough, Robert, 233

Pacific Helicopters, 72, 90
Pacific Western Airlines (PWA), 61-62, 64, 96
Page, Ruthanne, 226
Palubiski, Walter, 135-36
Panarctic Oils, 94, 96-97, 183, 200-201, **xxi**
Peare, Henry, 196-97, 226-27
Pearson, Bud, 77
Pearson, Rocky, 98, 205, 227
petroleum industry, 118, **xv-xvi, xxi**
    arctic conditions, 192-94
    arctic operations, 110-14, 133, 212, **v-vi,
        xxii-xxiv**
    drill rig relocation, 167-68

exploration, 57–58, 62, 69–70, 162
operations, 98, 108, **123**–24, 155, 200
See also international operations;
Panarctic Oil; Shell Oil
Pilon, Luc, 138–39, 233
Pinner, Bill, **67**
Pitts, John, 103, 134, 173, 179
Polair DC-3, **XII**
Polar Continental Shelf Program, 131, **156**–57–58, 215, **VIII**, **XI–XII**
Poole, Don, 41, 48, 50–55, 72, 73

Quinlan, Duke, 233

Radovich, J., **44**
Ranger, Frank, 44, **51**, 227
Reid, Doug, 211, 227
Reid, L.G. (Jim), 103, 104, 227–**28**
Reifel, Barney, **VIII**
Resources Service Group (RSG), 179, 188, 217
Riccardo, Rudi, 187–88
Rich, Jack, **48**, 73
Rivard, Reginald (Reg), 161, 205, 228–29
Rochfort, Rocky, 197, **XXII**
Ross, Bill, 161, 207, 233
Rourke, Leslie (née Birch), **94**
Royal BC Museum, 210–11
Rustad, Jan, 229
Rutledge, Keith, 47, 88–89

Schabes, Bill, 115, 120–22, **VI**, **X**
Scheer, Tommy, **48**, 88
Seager, Craig, 189–91
search and rescue operations, 62, 72, 75, 212
air ambulance, 62, **101**, 130, 174–75, 214–15
arctic rescue, 80–82
bear attack, 101–3
Chilliwack rescue, 189–**91**
copper mine avalanche, 89–90
EMPRA Device, 188–89
freighter rescue, **107**–8
Golden Base, 152–53
Kemano medevac flights, 49–50
lost prospectors, 198–99
McNulty & Berendt, 63–64
red button incident, 124–25
salmon rescue, 91, 110
Thunder Bay rescue, 207
train rescues, 91, 102–3

SEBJ Project (James Bay Project), 109, 114–15, 138–39
Sept Îles Helicopters, 113
Shannon, Owen, 111–14, 172, 215–16, **XVII**
Golden Report, 148–54
Shell Oil, 77
geological survey, 57–58, 60
North Sea, 83, 87–89
Tofino, **90**–91, 94, 98
Sikorsky Helicopters, 73
S-48 (later S-51), 50, **I**
S-62, 74–75
VS-300, **40**
Sikorsky, Igor, **40**, 50, **64**–**65**, 88, **I**
about Carl Agar, 96
Sikorsky S-55, 40, **47**–**48**, **52**, **63**, 65, **135**, **III**
manufacturing mistake, 56–57
training school, 55
Sikorsky S-58, 61, 63, 65, 82
innovations for, 67, 68, 73, 78
S-58T, 99, 101, 111, **V–VI**
Sikorsky S-61, 75, 98, **104**, **195**
colour photos, **IX–X**, **XIV**, **XVIII**, **XX**, **XXII**
models, 93, 124, 135
Sikorsky S-76 Spirits, 135, 148, 215, **XIII–XVII**, **XIX**
issues with, 163, 169, 187
Simpson, Dale, 123
Sims, Roger, 233
Siver, Lloyd, 229
Skyways Services, 17, 22–23, 28
Smart Aviation, 58
Smeeth, Stu, 47, 104
Smith, Bill, 41, 44, 49
Snell, Fred, 41, 49, 63, **64**, 77, 88
Arctic Islands survey, 59–60
Kemano accidents, 42, 45
Soutar, Grant, 80–81, **90**, 106–8, 110, 229
SS *Vanlene*, **107**–8, 229
Steele, Ken, 180, 212, 234
Stevenson, Henry, 78–79
Stone, Jim, 233
Stringer, Alf, 9, 10, **56**, 58
early years, **12**, 15
lauching OAS, 16–18
leaving OH, 77, 80, 233
rebuilding helicopter, **22**–23, 25
training, **19–20**
Strukoff, Sandy, 232

Sturges, Ron, 66–67

Tarvic, Jean, 109–10
Taylor, Chuck, 98, 116, 139, 197, **X**
Tillotson, Bud, 62, 72, 73, 92–93, **103**–4
Trann, Doug, 172–73
Tymerick, Ernie, 158, **XII**

United Helicopters, 58, 72
United Helicopters Ltd. (UK), 188, 218
Universal Helicopters, **104**–5–6, 192, 199–200, **IV**
sold, 214, 233
USS *Spadefish*, **219**–20, **XXIII–XXIV**
Utting, Aubrey, 229–30

Vaasjo, Tellef, 132–33, 230
Valpy, Mark, **76**, 104
Vancouver Island Helicopters (VIH), 64, 80, 233
Very, Bert, 230
Vietnamese refugees, 163, **171**–72, **XVII**
Vought-Sikorsky. *See* Sikorsky Helicopters

Warttig, Bert, 166, 173–74
Watson, John, 89–90
Webster, Roy, 94, 107–8, 123, 231, **X**
Westland Aircraft UK Ltd., 50, 74, 209, **XIX**
Whitfield, Hugh, 232
Whyte, Dave, 98, 146, 176–77, 202, 206, 232
Williamson, Ray, 230
Winter, Alan, 231
Wright, Orville, **40**

Yearwood, Bill, 121, 161, 192, 231, 232
Young, Arthur Middleton, 17

Zorenc, Joe, **XXII**

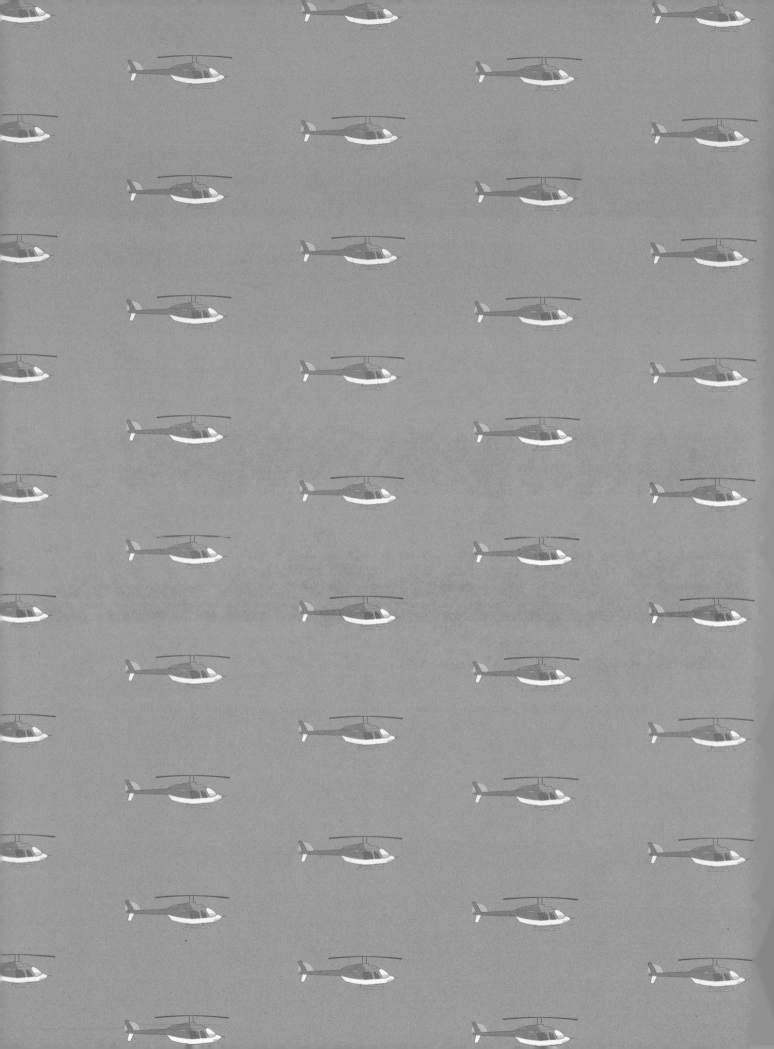